GETTING IT RIGHT IN ITALY

GETTING IT RIGHT IN ITALY

A Manual for the 1990s

WILLIAM WARD

BLOOMSBURY

First published 1990
Copyright © 1990 by William Ward

Bloomsbury Publishing Ltd, 2 Soho Square, London W1V 5DE

A CIP catalogue record for this book is available from the British Library

ISBN 0 7475 0574 8

Printed and bound in Great Britain by
Richard Clay Ltd, Bungay, Suffolk

What should you wear to a business meeting in Milan, or a friend's wedding in Florence? How do you go about renting a flat in Rome, or buying a farmhouse in Umbria? Why are the best discothèques usually gay and the best art galleries usually closed? What's the most effective way of chatting up an Italian girl who's playing hard to get, and the easiest way of getting rid of an Italian boy who just won't go away?

While there are already plenty of books about Italy, most of them represent it as an exotic, puzzling, even slightly dangerous place to go for your holidays; this is the first book to offer genuine insight and practical assistance in understanding the Italians: how they live, what they think, the way they work, and the country runs. It examines Italian attitudes to sex, money, religion, the family and the environment, as well as giving detailed, up-to-date information about politics, the economy, the arts and the media.

Designed for those who want instant, easy access to useful information as well as a fuller background analysis of the facts, the book has two parallel texts laid out in separate columns, thus enabling the user either to consult at speed, or to read at leisure. Whether it is for holidays, for business, or for a longer-term stay, no visitor will be safe on the streets without *Getting it Right in Italy*.

a mia madre

Contents

Acknowledgements

I should like to thank my friends and colleagues, both in Italy and Britain, for their help and encouragement, without which the writing of this book would have been an even more arduous task.

I am also indebted for their constructive suggestions to Marcello Cleri (medicine, education) and Paolo Pepe (history, politics and law), as well as to Alberto Castelvecchi, who read the manuscript, was an invaluable source of research material, and suggested various improvements.

I have been particularly fortunate in having such a sympathetic and rigorous editor as Alison Mansbridge, and in receiving the unstinting editorial support of Liz Calder and Mary Tomlinson.

My especially heartfelt thanks go to Nina Grunfeld and Nicholas Underhill in London, and Francesca Passarelli in Rome for their constant advice, support and hospitality.

Introduction

How *Getting it Right in Italy* works, and what it's about

Ever since I first travelled abroad, I have always noticed how familiar, rather than how different, things seemed there. So when in 1979 I decided to go and live in Italy, I knew I'd feel at home. People in Italy frequently ask me why I chose their country, and whether moving was an incredible cultural upheaval. My answer to these stock questions has always been '*Così*' – 'I just felt like it' – and '*No*', respectively.

I can think of lots of reasons to choose Italy, but none to explain why a citizen of one European country should have any special difficulty in adapting to life in another. The difficulties of travelling or living abroad have been needlessly exaggerated, as has the whole mystique surrounding the Englishman/woman abroad.

However, much as one might like a place, and feel at home in it, there is also a great deal of new information to assimilate, concerning the language, different social and business customs, diet and so on. For myself, I found numerous books about Italy, but none that took it seriously as a country – that told me who and what made it work, and how I could make it work for me. In the end, I decided to write one myself.

One of the problems about books on foreign countries is that they are hard to consult. Chapters tend to be organized as continuous running text, making it impossible for the reader to refer to a specific aspect or area without having to wade through the entire thing. I have worked on the assumption that readers may not necessarily be interested in the entire contents of this book, but will be very interested in certain parts of it. Most books on foreign countries offer a wide-angle, soft-focus overview; I have tried to concentrate my attention on a series of short, sharp-focused entries.

Another difficulty is that while many books offer a comprehensive analysis of a topic, they do not tell you how you can channel your newly found insight to your practical advantage, apart from the general consignment of practical information to a hard-to-consult set of notes at the back. This book is designed to be used both as an insight guide and as an access manual, either separately or simultaneously. So while the main text deals with how Italy and the Italians function, you will find what I call ACCESS notes in the margin showing you how to fit in yourself.

The only series I have ever seen that gives the reader a choice of simultaneous reading levels are the books about Rupert Bear; they were designed to let you read the two-line verses, or the prose text for greater detail, while those with really short attention spans could skip the text entirely and just follow the illustrations. Assuming that adult readers have longer attention spans, I have dispensed with the cartoons, but tried to give you the choice to skim, browse or absorb everything, depending on your needs.

Not everyone who reads this book will necessarily be doing so with a view to going to Italy, while those that do may be going for various different reasons. I have therefore tried to cater equally for the business traveller, the tourist and the short- (or even long-) term settler, working on the assumption that readers would be more inclined to interface with Italy and the Italians if they had a better idea of how to tackle them. The detailed index and cross-references will help you find what you want.

One thing that this is not is a guide book. There is no shortage of excellently written and researched books in print about Italy, centring on specific topics like wine and food, hotels and restaurants, art and architecture, and so on. This book attempts to cover all these areas, in so far as they relate to the present day – from the successful shaping of Italy's national identity over the last decade or so to the regionalism that Italians still cling to; from the workings of the Italian home to the functioning, and non-functioning, of the Italian State.

The Italian State provides a thread that runs through the book, especially with regard to the attitude of Italians towards it.

Chapter IV takes the view that the political parties in Italy occupy the trappings of State as a private fief, whereas Chapter V examines the often troubled relationship Italians have with the concept of legality. It is in these chapters that we have to tread most carefully, because we are dealing with the aspects of Italy (regionalism, corruption, chaos, organized crime) that most easily lend themselves to stereotypes, often at the hands of the Italians themselves, who have fashioned a new cinema genre which subtly glamorizes crisis topics like terrorism, the Mafia, political intrigue, the Resistance, extreme urban poverty and social backwardness in the countryside. This glossy, high-adrenalin vision of Italy poses a new variation on the old E.M. Forster-like theme of the quest for 'the real Italy', beloved of all earnest nostalgics of arcadian myth.

Although there has been a certain shift in emphasis over the last decade, Italy's image abroad continues to be brazenly stereotyped. The old spaghetti/the Pope/Mafia clichés are now being replaced by newer ones based on Armani suits, designer furniture and economic renaissance. The key words used to describe this fantasy Italy have also changed, as has the tone: once foreign commentators were patronizing; now they tend to be acritical. The Vespa, once portrayed as a symbol of poverty (too poor to buy a car) is now a symbol of style. The Italian lifestyle, once dismissed as 'amusing' or 'carefree', and ('Byzantine' or 'Machiavellian') political system is now full of 'flair'; business moghuls and politicians are 'audacious' or 'ruthless'. But these stock shorthand definitions overlook the simple truth that many Italian people are extremely hardworking and capable, and that the success of modern Italy is due largely to them.

Images can be used to show convenient, romantic falsehoods in the same way – like the classic *National Geographic* photos showing an Italian peasant driving a cart past a power station.

Taking Italy seriously as a country does not just entail making complimentary observations, and there are plenty of points in this book where the text may appear to the reader to be sarcastic and negative. This may seem a bit much, coming from a 'foreigner', but most of the criticisms I have made are ones that both ordinary Italians, and the Press in particular, frequently make themselves.

As I wrote, I found a number of expressions cropping up again and again, and decided to put them together here, as a glossary-cum-exposition. The ones in Italian are all in common usage, and describe tendencies the Italians are aware of; the ones in English outline characteristics that I perceive.

● *Abusivismo* embraces the whole gamut of unlawful solutions in response to the state, from not paying taxes to avoiding planning permission on one's house.

● *Campanilismo*: chauvinism on a local level, of a medieval sort; *campanile* is a church bell-tower; *campanilismo* indicates that our village/town/city is better than yours.

● *Casino*: like *'Quel bordel'* in French, *'Che casino'* doesn't mean so much 'brothel' as, 'What a total mess.' Although they profess to be exasperated by it, many Italians are actually quite proud of their country's apparently permanent state of chaos, which they try to believe has a hidden order behind it. This mechanism frequently defies explanation, but occasionally leads one to suspect that there is a puppeteer behind the scenes, pulling the strings. 'It's so complicated' is at times almost synonymous with approval.

● *Crisi*: to judge by what the media and Italians in general tell you, most things and people in Italy are permanently '*in crisi*'. It's not nearly as dramatic as it sounds in English.

● *Dietrologia*: literally, 'behindology' – the conspiracy theory industry from which so many commentators, Italians and foreigners, make such a comfortable living. I personally don't subscribe to the 'Was Pope John Paul I an astronaut?' school of enquiry. So much in Italy that really exists is worth assimilating that I can't waste the time to speculate on what doesn't – or perhaps, just, might.

● *Firmato*: literally, 'signed', meaning Designer Everything. The concept of mass luxury has now been taken further in Italy than anywhere else in the world. As a result, it does not just refer to the lifestyle and tastes of an élite, but to the aspirations of the population at large. Something that is *firmato* or *raffinato* – sophisticated – now says much more about a collective lack of originality than about any statement of individual good taste.

● *Italietta*: 'little Italy' is the ironic name the ever self-critical Italians give their country, to underline their tendency to live in a provincial, folklore dimension, with an implicit rejection of the State: this refers to regionalism, and is in direct opposition to the French myth of *la grandeur de l'état*, which is an important model for the Italians.

● *Mafia*: with a capital 'M', Mafia refers to the Sicilian underworld organization; with a small 'm', *la mafia* refers to organized crime in general, and thus includes the Neapolitan Camorra and the Calabrian 'Ndrangheta. As most Italians will tell you, *la mentalità mafiosa* in a literal sense pervades even most law-abiding Italians to some extent.

● *Mammismo*: the cult of the mother, but only in so far as she does everything for her son. Italians are fully aware of this characteristic, which if anything is growing again after a period of being unfashionable.

● *Protagonismo*: the desire to hog the limelight at the expense of the collective. Fashion blurbs encourage you to be a *protagonista* – to stand out from the crowd; this, however, is what you don't do if you dress up in Italy. For Italians, the term *individualismo* suggests a bloody-mindedness at others' expense, rather than being original in thought and action.

● *Regionalismo*: regional chauvinism; this pervades almost every aspect of Italian national life; Italians consider it not *provinciale* but *autentico*.

● *Il sessantotto*: 1968, not a particularly eventful year in Britain; in Italy, it signalled the most important post-war watershed. Every kind of relationship was taken to pieces, and re-examined. Italy, like France, was never the same again.

● *Xenofilia*: the Italians are generally proud of their unconditional admiration of all that is *straniero* – foreign – although they are aware that their tendency to follow foreign models is often just an exasperated form of provincialism. America has no more faithful world model than Italy, though in the more rarefied atmosphere of culture, it is France which provides the model. There is also a historical key: France provided the cultural and political inspiration for the *Risorgimento*, just as America provides the consumer role model for post-World War II Italy.

● *Biculturalism*: refers to the very Italian phenomenon of maintaining a foot in two socio-cultural camps – the way most Italians instinctively follow traditional social behaviour and yet are equally *au fait* with a more progressive, North European, social culture. This brings with it both the advantages and the disadvantages of bilingualism: being able to switch from one to the other, but getting confused as to one's real identity. With regard to sexual mores, biculturalism becomes more than confusing, to the point of being really critical.

● *Criminal chic*: the intensely aesthetic effect of the murky side of Italian society lends itself to an often brilliant glamorization process by writers and by film and TV directors to create a mystique around the various ills that plague Italian life. It is by no means restricted to Italy; something of the same aura surrounds the Kray Brothers and Arthur Daley.

● *Cultural cloning*: the direct result of *xenofilia*. In an acritical way, Italians tend to adopt wholesale, rather than adapt, habits, ideas, attitudes, ways of dressing and fashions from abroad. This is particularly evident in the field of cinema and TV. Following a tradition invented by Mussolini for reasons of censorship, all TV and cinema products from abroad are dubbed into Italian, which both deprives Italian viewers from ever hearing the real voice of their (mostly American) screen heroes, and, by giving them the impression that they are seeing it in the original version, destroying the sense of distance. In this way, vast tracts of American culture, products etc. are bought up and assimilated by perfectly trained consumers.

● *Hyperchoice*: the extraordinary plethora of alternatives which appear to be offered – four different police forces, twelve main political parties, over a thousand different television stations. Very often, the effective margin of choice is almost nothing.

● *Neo-patriotism*: despite *xenophilia*, there is a widespread new triumphalist mood born of a series of worldwide sporting and business successes, which have done much to improve Italy's overall international reputation, and to boost its morale at home. Although it is an improvement on *regionalismo*, there is nothing very edifying about seeing pop-singers singing rousing songs about 'Italia, Italia' . . .

Notes on style

● Cross-references: the legend at the top of each page includes the numbers of the chapter/subsection and sub-subsections that open and close that page. Cross-references (indicated with an arrow: →) refer to these – e.g. (→ I, 1:i) directs you to chapter I, subsection 1 (*La casa*): sub-subsection i (The family and the individual).

● The use of Italian: useful or significant Italian words found in the text are defined by direct translation – unless their meaning is obvious from the context – on their first appearance. Wherever possible, those words that form natural subject groups have been listed alphabetically as a glossary.

The Italian usage concerning capital letters for the names of official posts and institutions is often quite different from the British. Although the system adopted in this book may not please purists of written Italian, it is clearer to most English readers.

There are six variants in Italian which correspond to the English definite article 'the'. *Il*, *la* and *lo* are for masculine, feminine and words beginning in 'z' or 'st' in the singular, respectively; *i*, *le* and *gli* are for the equivalent plurals. Nouns and adjectives have different gender and singular/plural endings.

Where possible, I have given the standard British translation of book and film titles; where there is none, this may be because the work has not been released abroad, or because it has been, with title unchanged.

● *Sigle* – abbreviations: initials for organizations in Italian are almost always pronounced as words rather than spelt out. The original meaning of some of them, like RAI, has become lost. It is interesting that in so euphonious a language, where all words (except foreign ones, and northern dialectic ones) end in a vowel, such ugly ciphers as IRPEG (a tax) or SNATER (a minor trade union) should be current lexical items.

Plurals are often indicated in Italian by doubling the initials; hence VU stands for un Vigile Urbano city policeman with traffic duties; VVUU stands for Vigili Urbani.

Some commonly used *sigle*

● Public bodies and amenities

RAI – Radiotelevisione Italiana. 'RAI' literally stands for Radio Audizioni Italiane, but few people in Italy are familiar with this pre-TV era name.

SIP – Società Italiana per l'Esercizio delle Telecomunicazioni

ACEA – Azienda Comunale Elettricità e Acqua

ENEL – Ente Nazionale per l'Energia Elettricità

ATAC/ATAM/ATAN – Azienda dei Trasporti Autonoma Comunale (Rome)/Milano/Napoli
ANAS – Azienda Nazionale Autostrade
M or MM – Metropolitana (Rome) or Metropolitana Milanese
● Taxes
IVA – Imposta di valuta aggiuntiva (VAT)
IRPEF – Imposta sul Reddito delle Persone Fisiche (income tax)
ILOR – Imposta Locale sui Redditi (similar to rates)
● Treasury bonds
CCT – Certificato di Credito del Tesoro (3–6 years, floating rate)
BOT – Buono Ordinario del Tesoro (3,6,12 months, fixed rate)
BTP – Buono del Tesoro Pluriennale (3–6 years, fixed rate)
● Companies
IRI – Istituto per la Ricostruzione Industriale
ENI – Ente Nazionale Idrocarboni
BNL – Banco Nazionale del Lavoro
● Trade unions
CGIL – Confederazione Generale Italiana del Lavoro
CISL – Confederazione Italiana Sindacati dei Lavoratori
UIL – Unione Italiana del Lavoro
CISNAL – Confederazione Italiana Sindacati Nazionali Lavoratori
● Political and religious associations
ACLI – Associazione Cattolica dei Lavoratori Italiani
CL – Comunione e Liberazione
FUORI – Fronte Unitario Omosessuale Rivoluzionario Italiano
MP – Movimento Popolare
● Police
PS – Pubblica Sicurezza
VU – Vigili Urbani
SISDE – Servizio Informazioni per la Sicurezza Democratica
SISMI – Servizio Informazioni per la Sicurezza Militare
CESIS – Comitato Esecutivo Servizio di Informazioni e di Sicurezza
● Professional Associations
SIAE – Società Italiana degli Autori ed Editori
ANSA – Agenzia Nazionale Stampa Associata
● Sport and leisure
CONI – Comitato Olimpico Nazionale Italiano
FIGC – Federazione Italiana Giuoco Calcio
ARCI – Associazione di Cultura, Sport e Ricreazione
ENIT – Ente Nazionale Italiano di Turismo
CTS – Centro Turistico Studentesco e Giovanile
CIT – Compagnia Italiana di Turismo
ACI – Automobile Club d'Italia
● 'English' words used in Italian: Many hundreds of English-looking words are now in current use in Italy. Only a handful have maintained their original sense ('*weekend*', '*poster*', '*supermarket*', '*computer*', '*film*', '*detective*'); some have acquired rather glamorized Italian meanings ('*manager*' means 'executive'); others have become somewhat fossilized in a specific usage – '*Topmodel*' is never plain 'model'; some become ugly hybrids – *tivùcolor* = colour TV – or media clichés; some are attached to other words ('*la Oscar-story*' – used to indicate 'the saga of . . .' or 'the day after' – after the post-nuclear horror film); some are simply overused pseudo-technical words – '*lo stress*', '*il marketing*', '*lo share*', '*lo spot*' – TV commercials. There are Euro-classics like *il footing* for jogging, and *lo smoking* for

tuxedo or dinner jacket; there are several dozen false friends in the sartorial/ cosmetics field – *il beauty* = beauty case, *il body* = leotard, *il tight* = morning suit; many foreign generic garments or types of footwear are known almost solely by the leading brand name (*le churches* – brogues; *le clarks* – desert boots; *le timberland* – deck shoes; *il moncler* – padded sleeveless anorak).

• 'Italian' words used in English: the very nature of the Anglo-Saxon world's relationship with Italy means that there are far fewer loan words; those that exist tend to be confined to an élitist or journalistic usage. English-language writers (and even speakers) now use some Italian words and expressions far more than the Italians do. The compulsive media overuse of *al dente* carries the subtext 'I have now learnt how to appreciate *pasta*', while Anglo-Saxon writers who stick '*l'arte dell'arrangiarsi*' – looking after number one, or 'managing' – and *la commedia dell'arte* in every other article about Italian politics are suffering from a simple lack of ideas. Italians cannot understand why English-speaking journalists or copy writers are so obsessed with their purely musical term *con brio* as a means of describing anything Italian. Dining *al fresco* makes Italians laugh – generically meaning 'in the cool', it usually refers to being in prison; they eat '*all'aperto*' – in the open. 'Machiavellian' and 'Byzantine' are routinely used by foreign journalists to describe phenomena they either don't understand themselves, or can't be bothered to explain in pithy form. *Fellini-esque* has become a stock description for anyone, particularly women, or anything that is lurid, overdressed or overweight. Away from its strictly architectural context, 'Italianate' is the ultimate pseudo-intellectual word (usually interchangeable with 'baroque') to suggest anything 'vaguely Italian'. The oddest of all is *braggadocio*, very popular in certain sections of the British and American youth and rock media, who are convinced of knowing the Italian term for chutzpah, or a flash Harry. The Italians have several words of their own to translate this very English word, invented by an ironical Spenser in 1590.

This chapter deals mainly with personal relationships in Italian society. It starts with the family home, the material construction and organization of which is especially significant: it is both a reflection of and an influence on the status quo of Italian family life. The vagaries of the Italian housing market are considered in this context.

Next comes childhood and youth – which to the Italians encompasses everybody under forty. This is followed by a look at sexual relationships and related issues; and then an examination of friendship and social mores. The way in which Italians relate to each other – in the broad, non-intimate context of fellow-citizens – and to foreigners comes in Chapter II. One reason for this division is the totally different way in which outsiders, as opposed to people within the family/social group, are treated. Broadly speaking, the Italians like anyone they feel connected to.

The idea of individuality should be defined before dealing with both chapters: while Anglo-Saxon societies tend to be founded on the twin pillars of the State and the individual, and its success can be seen in terms of the interplay between the micro- and the macro-components, Italian society is still notoriously based on the small group: family or family-style relationships. The individual's response towards the State is essentially one of antagonism – something forty years of democratic rhetoric has never really succeeded in correcting. In subsequent chapters we examine that antagonism; in this chapter the dominating emotion is one of affection.

As in the rest of the book, but particularly in this section, there are constant references to 1968 and post-1968. In Anglo-Saxon countries, nothing special happened in that year, but in Italy, as in France, 1968 signalled an important post-war watershed: every kind of relationship was taken to pieces, and re-examined. Italy, like France, was never the same again.

The treatment of animals, and class distinction are two typically British obsessions, both of which enjoy far less importance in Italy – but fit in this chapter, along with sections on communications: how the post and telephone systems work; and how happy the Italians really are. Those *in crisi* due to their sex lives or economic circumstances provide good media fare, but much less is ever said about the lot of the old, the lonely and the alienated. The boom both of psychoanalysis and telephone helplines in recent years is ample proof that being an Italian is not always such fun as it looks.

1. *La casa:* the family and the home

(i) The family and the individual

Despite all the social upheavals of the last twenty years, Italian life remains firmly based on the family unit. And however much Italian social life seems to take place out of doors (→ 4, below), the family home is its essential forum. While the Anglo-Saxon concept of home is closely linked to the individual, and is often quite independent of family considerations ('the Englishman's home is *his* castle'; 'setting up *a* home of

Forms of address within the family

Relations and terms of address are relatively formal; family members are called very much by their titles. (→ also 6: ACCESS, below) ● Grandparents – *Nonno, Nonna* – are often called by name, to distinguish them, if both sets are alive: Hence Nonna Elena, Nonno Michele.

• Parents – *i genitori*: *il padre*, *la madre* – are known as Papà (Babbo in Tuscany and Emilia-Romagna) and Mamma, abbreviated to Pa and Ma.

• Uncles and aunts, even if in their 20s, are called by their title, but not always by name. Hence Zio, Zia.

• Grandchildren, nieces and nephews: confusingly, there is only one word for both types of relationship – *nipote*; it is usually clear from the context which is meant, especially since the diminutive *i nipotini* tends to designate the grandchildren.

• The average Italian has much more to do with cousins – *cugini* – than does his British counterpart; although terms exist for second cousins – *cugini di secondo grado* – and cousins once/twice removed, the Italians tend to say just *cugini*, rather like the British royal family.

Inside Italian homes

• Social contact tends to take place outside the home: this is truer in some cities, like Rome, than others. Among better off, better educated families there is a more relaxed, Anglo-Saxon concept of casual hospitality, although when the guests are friends of the *figli* – literally children, though they may well be young adults – it is still very common for the parents discreetly to withdraw, in order 'not to get in the way'.

While the hospitality of the *contadini* – peasants – cannot be overstated, their urbanized descendants (even when they enjoy far greater material prosperity) tend not to maintain rural traditions. This has a lot to do with *bella figura* – keeping up appearances: they may feel ashamed that the relatively

one's own'), the whole idea of *la casa* is intimately linked to the idea of family – in fact they reinforce each other as concepts, and as a result tend to be synonymous.

Just as the Englishman aspires to live in a detached house, preferably with garden, so the Italian is happy to live in a *palazzo* – which may mean palace, when applied to an imposing historical building, but generally indicates a simple block of flats. Few Italians dream of *un villino con giardino* – a house and garden; they have other priorities. Very little regard is given by most Italians to such problems as noise and *la privacy* (the latter word being a recent, hence fashionable, imported concept), as though the intensity of the *focolare domestico* – the domestic hearth – were enough to cancel all outside distractions.

Even bricks and mortar conspire to uphold the status quo. Building construction has always been geared around the unit of the family home. Unlike the British Victorian houses of all sizes that since the 1920s have been converted into flats on separate floors with relative ease, the Italian family *appartamento* built as late as the 1970s resists all attempts to break it down into sub-dwellings. Purpose-built bachelor accommodation is still as much a novelty as the concept that spawned it, singlehood. Significantly, there is no convenient word in Italian to express the idea of a non-family-based home, and the meaning of the nearest imported equivalent, the French *la garçonnière*, is rich with sexual undertones. Even the business community is subject to this principle: the businessman's *pied-à-terre* is a room in a *residence*, an exclusive semi-hotel, while most small to medium Italian companies are located in family apartments, complete with kitchen and bathroom.

Despite popular legend, Italian families are no longer as numerous as the Church would desire. Of the 18.5 million families counted in the most recent (1981) census, 46% have two or three members, 31% have four or five, with only 5.5% having six or more. These figures do not include grandparents or other relations living in.

One in three couples have no children, while the remaining two-thirds have 2.7, down from 2.9 twenty years ago. Taken on average, a 28-year-old Italian woman now has only 1.5 children. Twenty years back, only one in eighteen children were born out of wedlock, whereas in 1988, after fifteen years of official recognition of single parents, the figure is one in nine.

One-parent families: Milan, 33%; Perugia, 18%.

Two-thirds of these are run by the mother, 7% by the father; others will be run by grandparents or other relations.

Although the housing shortage, and consequent overcrowding, is considered one of the major social problems, Italians living in close quarters with their family seem to have fewer social and psychological difficulties than the inhabitants of many other Western societies. Although the most extreme examples are to be found in Naples, where huge extended families live in *i bassi* – ground-floor single-room apartments – dining rooms and sitting rooms all over Italy tend to double as multiple occupancy bedrooms for children or other relations. The room occupancy statistics in the large Italian cities are among the highest in Europe (over one person to every room), with an almost world record in Portici, a suburb of Naples, which is second only to Hong Kong in population density per square metre.

Physical proximity to one's family is not always just enforced; it is often elective as well. Even where circumstances permit the purchase of a separate apartment for married children, it is often in the same block of flats, enabling constant contact. Italian TV adverts, with their ominous, though generally realistic, insistence on cutting from the kitchen of the nosy or omniscient mother/aunt/grandmother figure across the landing to that of the daughter/daughter-in-law, especially where domestic cleaning products are concerned, never fail to reassure the viewer how close to each other ideal Italian family members like to live.

For those less fortunate, the problem is not so much a scarcity of accommodation, either for sale or for rent, as the availability of what is suitable in size. It is hard for young couples to set up a home of their own, since there are too few small apartments on offer. Unable to afford an unnecessarily large apartment, most move in with their family or in-laws. This emergency solution often becomes long-term, and although grumbling about 'living with my in-laws' often becomes, after sex, most Italian newly-weds' favourite pastime, the temptation to stay often outweighs the resolve to hunt for something else. Especially towards southern Italy, overcrowding is a lesser evil than under cherishing: living as part of an extended family of eight in a flat ideal for three at least guarantees all the human succour and creature comforts usually expected by Italians. Having one's shirts ironed daily, meals always ready, reliable unpaid baby-sitters, and the free use of the family car and telephone more than makes up for the lack of privacy

cramped conditions or modest furnishings of their homes will let them down (concentrating their spending on their children's or even their own clothes is a more economic strategy for looking smart), or consider that entertaining guests necessarily involves cooking lavish meals, rather than simply offering a cup of tea or a drink. Many Italian families find their social calendar entirely taken up with visiting *parenti* – relations – and thus have literally no time for *estranei* – outsiders. If you do get to visit someone's home, which is inevitably spotless, the woman of the house will equally inevitably be embarrassed and say, *'Scusi per il disordine'* – 'Please don't mind the mess.'

• Among young adults who live away from their parents, the situation is completely different. Perhaps because of the relative novelty value, friends who come round to visit tend to be surprisingly *invadente* – invasive. It is not considered rude to drop in unannounced; on the other hand, to refuse entry to unexpected visitors because you are busy, or simply because you don't want to see people, would be considered churlish. The friendly curiosity of some young Italians towards foreigners is such that you may be a particular target of such visits. On visiting your flat for the first time, many newly acquired Italian friends may subject you to the third degree. Do not be offended if they ask you how you found it, whether your landlord has any other places going, exactly how much you pay; they will also ask, or demand, *'Posso fare un giro?'* – 'Can I have a look round?' – or may simply to do so without asking. It is also fairly common for young Italians with their own flat to allow friends who still live with their parents to use their apartment for sex when they are away, though you won't necessarily be asked this favour as well.

• Except in the North, where parquet or floorboarding is more common, floors tend to be of marble, terracotta or porcelain tiles – ideal for the summer. In winter, oriental-type rugs may be rolled out (Italy imports more Persian and Turkish carpets per capita than any other country in the world); most Italians prefer cold floors to what they perceive as the deeply unhygienic North European/American wall to wall carpeting. Despite this, *moquette* (there is no native Italian word for carpeting) is increasingly used as a cheap floor covering.

• Hot summers, burglars and prying neighbours are all reasons why Italian windows have either *le serrande* – wooden or plastic roller blinds that have to be yanked or rolled down – or *le persiane* – French-style louvre shutters. Consequently, the need for *le tende* – curtains – is greatly reduced. Many homes have none. (→ also V, 2: ACCESS – Protecting your possessions)

• Contrary to what many foreigners fondly imagine, Italian homes are not full of sleek designer furniture: there's probably more in Fulham than in the whole of Florence. Due to the very recent emergence of a large middle class, relatively few families have inherited antiques; those that do tend to have elaborate 19th-century French-style *lo stile impero* pieces; antiques are far dearer than in Britain, although *lo stile inglese* – English style – is much sought after (particularly naval furniture of dubious provenance). Many families tend to have some magnificent, if rather massive, 1930s furniture, generally bedroom stuff, or recent, rather generic things: particularly ubiquitous

of having to sleep in the dining room. It is something Italians are so used to that, while they may moan, they won't feel ashamed about it.

If there are few incentives to move out for the mostly working-class newly wed couples, there are new ones to entice one to move back in for the wealthier middle-class younger singles. This curious anomaly is the result of changing circumstances. Fifteen years ago, young middle-class Italians were, for both ideological and practical reasons, more independent-minded. The post-1968 generation wanted to make a conscious break with their parents' ideas and lifestyle, but they were also obliged to. In order to live with their boy/girlfriends and to dress and behave as they liked, they had actively to avoid their parents. Now, if anything, the roles are reversed. Today's parents of late adolescent/young adult children are sometimes more liberal-minded than their children, having been directly affected by *il sessantotto*, while the latter have grown up in the more conservative late 1980s. So on the one hand parents readily consent to far more sexual liberties (allowing same-bed guests home for the night), while on the other their children tend to be less socially critical or politically rebellious. Having your cake (almost total individual liberties) and eating it (responsibility- and cost-free lifestyle) is a proposition few comfort-minded young Italians can resist. Before 1970 ISTAT figures registered an almost zero figure for under-25s living alone; throughout the following decade, the figures increased considerably, reaching a high point in 1980. Since then, they have receded: in 1988 there were fewer than 50,000 (14%) single Italians under 25 living away from home. Perhaps even more striking is the fact that, over the next decade, 33% are still there, while some 7% remain attached to Mamma's apron strings until they are 44.

The current situation represents a curious inversion of other tendencies too: once it was mostly male offspring of enlightened middle-class children that left home early; now it is above all they who stay. Far more girls now leave home, partly because they still tend to marry earlier, but also, even if they don't, because it is still 'a challenge'. There are now far more middle-class than working-class children living at home, almost as many in the socially advanced North as in the traditionally minded South. A major contributing factor is that nearly all university students frequent their home-town campus – the Anglo-Saxon concept of residential campus life to build adult experience is denied to all but those students whose home town lacks a university. (→ VIII, 5:ii)

While a very high percentage of Italian school-leavers

go on to university, many more seek employment instead. Depending on their parents' line of business, they may do this without so much as passing through the front door. Indeed, it is almost out of the question that a young Italian should opt out of a long, or even recently, established family enterprise, regardless of background. There are veritable dynasties of architects and *trattoria* owners that stretch back five or six generations (→VI, 2), while much of the new Italian economic miracle is based on the kind of loyal, hard-working family firms that work like Indian or Pakistani corner shops, building up through long hours and low pay, no government stamps paid (→V, 1:ii), and sometimes involving the physically less able members of the family, like grandparents and small children. In this way, some Italian families spend their entire waking hours cheek by jowl.

This arrangement, however, is not to everyone's taste, and among the middle classes a remarkable new tendency has developed. Parents are becoming increasingly desperate because they can't get their children to leave. In 1988, RAI TV broadcast a timely series called *'E non se ne vogliono andare'* – 'They just won't go!' – a highly popular social comment soap about a family where the parents end up moving out instead.

The State hardly recognizes the existence of singles as an entity, although according to ISTAT figures there are some 2.5 million of them (4% of the population). The fairly generic English term 'head of the household', which may be applied with dignity also to a single person, is in Italy obliged to become *capo del nucleo familiare* or simply *capofamiglia* – head of the family. Likewise, Italian food and domestic products always bear instructions and messages *per la signora* – for the lady of the house – as though men, single or otherwise, should never clean, cook or shop. (→ 3:iv, below).

It is interesting that the sacredness of 'family' often manifests itself most forcefully among those very people who do break away physically from their parents' home and set up on their own. The typically Anglo-Saxon arrangement of the surrogate family offered by flat-sharing with other young people is viewed with distaste, as are widows who choose not to remarry out of respect for the memory of the deceased husband: a case of accept no substitute. There is also a practical disadvantage to flat-sharing: so many mothers still take an active part in their children's separate homes that the presence of other people's children would complicate things terribly.

Now it is as though the novelty of being *un single* – there is, of course, no adequate Italian term – has

(like British stripped pine) is hygienic-looking white formica in every conceivable room.

Because Italians tend to refurbish whole rooms at a stroke, rather than add or subtract single pieces, they tend to refer to a room and its collective furnishings with the same word. Thus, according to context, *il salotto* (the sitting room), *la sala da pranzo* (the dining room), *la camera da letto* (the bedroom), *la cucina* (the kitchen) and *il bagno* (the bathroom) could equally mean the room or its contents.

- Married couples always sleep in huge double beds – *il letto matrimoniale*; twin beds are very rare.

- Bathrooms always contain a lavatory; only pre-war, low-rent homes have separate ones – usually on the balcony. Thus you would ask if you could *andare al bagno*, never *al gabinetto*. (→ VIII, 3:i) Flushing the lavatory usually entails pressing a wall button like a huge metal nipple. Italy has a wider selection of gimmicky bathroom taps than anywhere in the world: be prepared to get scalded, splashed etc.

- Power points are always the standard continental two-point variety, and have a nasty habit of coming away from the wall when you pull out the plug; they never have switches. They are as dangerous as they look.

- Since people usually live in *palazzi* – shared buildings – which sometimes have several staircases (*scala a destra/a sinistra* – right-/left-hand staircase), or even in groups of *palazzi*, like American apartment complexes, visiting someone for the first time can be more stressful than you would think. Make sure you know what *piano* – floor – they live on. An *attico* may suggest a modest garret conversion, but in fact means a penthouse, usually with ample terraces. At the main entrance there is usually a *citofono* – entryphone – which will usually be deactivated during the day if there is a *portiere* – a concierge. The latter tend to be unfriendly, suspicious people who will invariably demand to know where you are going: *'Dica!'* (literally 'Speak') means, 'Where do you think you're going?' and requires an answer. Be polite – it is unwise to alienate a *portiere*: they have a very good memory for faces – particularly those they don't like. Lifts usually have double doors, and will not work unless both are shut tight. 'T' stands for 'Terra' (ground floor). Some lifts still require 10 or 50 lire pieces, so it's useful to carry some in case. It is customary to greet neighbours or strangers met in the lift (or anywhere inside the building) with a polite *buon giorno* or *buona sera*. To get out again can also be difficult: there is usually an electric door-release in a discreet (sometimes too discreet) position, which may take some locating.

Un appartamento in affitto: renting somewhere

• This is easier than it was a few years ago, since the 1978 *Equo canone* legislation – very pro-tenant fair-rent act similar to the one in force in Britain – has been relaxed in the landlord's favour, thus putting more apartments on the market, albeit at a much higher price. Landlords are generally much more inclined to let to foreigners, since it is assumed that you'll leave sooner. Adverts often specify *solo non residenti* – non-residents only – since *residenza* gives you the legal right not to be *sfrattato* – evicted – at whim. Legally, contracts are for four-year periods, with

worn off. Until a couple of years ago, young people's magazines like *Per Lui* ran quizzes on themes like, 'Would you make a good single?' – the point being that you probably weren't one – posing questions like, 'Does the real single take his washing home to Mum?' and, 'Is it fair to get your girlfriend to cook and clean for you?' (no prizes for guessing the answers – yes and yes). Now the papers publish articles about *la crisi dei single* – the decline of the single – and show how Italy cannot cope with them anyway. This is, of course, true, and the reasons are very interesting. Not only is the Italian housing system not geared for them; neither are the roads (too many under-occupied cars clogging the streets), nor the hotels and restaurants (rooms/tables for one are cost-uneffective), nor the hospitals (more nurses are needed to look after and feed the sick single, who doesn't have a family to do it instead: → VIII, 2:i).

The cohabitation crisis also affects another Italian social group: would-be divorcees. The economic and logistic difficulties of finding alternative accommodation mean that many unhappy marriages are prevented from breaking up. Although existent elsewhere, the phenomenon of *separati in casa* – separated couples obliged to carry on living together – has become typically Italian, with the courts getting very used to working out formulas for which-spouse-gets-use-of-what-room. The problem was highlighted by the comedy film *Separati in casa*, by Riccardo Pazzaglia, who became a popular TV figure in the mid-1980s, thanks to his monologues, based on his own experience, on this very topic – a case of Art imitating Nature.

(ii) Where Italians like to live; buying and renting

Because Italian cities do not have posh suburbs outside the city proper in the way British and American cities do (→ II, 1), prices in the *periferia* – outskirts – are

---

The new tendency to live in *palazzi ristrutturati* – renovated buildings – as opposed to brand-new ones now places Italy right behind Britain, with its traditional dislike of new housing, and well ahead of France in the European table of old versus new homes:

	renovated	*new*
UK	45%	19.5%
Italy	44.5%	27%
France	37.5%	22%

---

invariably much lower than in the centre: only the poor live there. During the 1950s and 1960s, house-buying Italians definitely preferred modern *palazzi*, and were prepared to live a little outside the centre – *il semicentro* – where they were built. This was perfectly convenient in the days when there were fewer cars around, but there is now a great return towards reconstructed older buildings in the *centri storici*. This is dictated partly by taste, partly by smaller families, but more than anything by the increasing difficulty of commuting to centrally located offices, by either private or public transport. As in Paris, the ultimate for the late 1980s Milanese or Roman businessman/woman is to be able to walk to the office.

Although it is not as widespread or as systematic as in Britain, there is a quite a lot of council-owned rented property. *Le case popolari* have been built since the Mussolini era, and some are of architectural note. In the post-war period, plenty of huge *palazzi* were erected by the State or *il comune* – individual city or town councils. Each *comune* also owns a certain amount of property in the *centro storico*. The *comune* of Rome, for example, owns some 26,000 apartments in the suburbs and some 5000 apartments and shops in the centre, worth, according to outdated estimates, 4000 billion lire. Most of the inhabitants either pay *Equo canone* rents or ones set at least thirty years ago. While on the one hand, some 78% of the tenants haven't paid their rents for ten years, on the other, Rome council spends 10 billion lire a year on rented school and office space, as well as paying for the 1700 evicted families who subsist in hotel accommodation at the city's expense. Unfortunately, the *comune di Roma* isn't quite sure what belongs to it and what doesn't, and what it's all worth.

So far as buying a house in Italy goes, prices in most of the country, particularly the big cities, are rising considerably, but they are still reasonable by British or American standards. According to the Italian estate agents' association, the Associazione Consulenti Immobiliari Italiani (AICI), between 1988 and 1989 house prices rose throughout Italy by 25%, with an increase in Rome, Milan and Venice of between 35% and 40%; southern cities like Bari (12.5%) and Naples (7%) were more sluggish. There are few signs of the market slowing down, especially in the largest cities, where international companies looking for office premises and accommodation for personnel in time for 1992 have had an inflationary effect on prices. Renovated buildings in the *centro storico* of Milan and Rome can reach 7–8 million lire per square metre; in cities like Turin, Naples, Bologna, Genoa, Florence and Bari they

several months' rent in advance being negotiable. Even if you don't have a written contract, for the law you have a *de facto* one: that's why it's hard to get in. Your *padrone/padrona di casa* – landlord/lady – will serve you *lo sfratto* – notice to quit – when they want it back. Many Italian *inquilini* – tenants – dig in their heels, which usually leads to lawyers and a court case, but will give you up to two years' grace before *lo sfratto* becomes *esecutivo* – fully enforceable. Besides *l'affitto* – the rent – you will also have to pay *il condominio* – service charges – which usually include *il riscaldamento* – central heating. Unless you are lucky enough to have *riscaldamento autonomo* – your own separate central-heating system – you will have to put up with the temperature and hours laid down at the *riunione di condominio* – tenants' meeting. It is usually worth ingratiating yourself with *l'amministratore del condominio* – the building's managing agent – who may either be another *inquilino*, or a professional outsider.

• While Italian *vicini di casa* – neighbours – are more likely to monitor your activities with irksome regularity, they are less likely to complain about the noise than in most Western countries. This is particularly the case in southern Italy.

• It is as hard, if not harder, to find rented accommodation in Italy as in any other Western country, particularly in the larger cities. Post-*Equo canone* prices put most flats in central locations beyond most young Italians' economic reach, even if *l'affitto* – the rent – works out cheaper in absolute terms than you'd expect to pay in Britain or elsewhere: in proportion to an average Italian income, it works out more expensive. This problem will obviously not arise if you are being paid a British or American salary. *Un appartamento ammobiliato* – a furnished flat – will inevitably cost more than one *da ammobiliare* – unfurnished.

• The size of an apartment is calculated in square metres, which includes wall space – no mean consideration if the *palazzo* is a sturdy, old-fashioned building. Because it is so common to have a *balcone* – balcony – or *terrazza*, a distinction is made between *metri quadri coperti* (literally 'covered square metres') and those outside. While only *un villino* – a detached house – is likely to have *un giardino*, a regular *appartamento* in a recently constructed *palazzo* may well have *un box* or *un garage* for which you will have to pay extra. Otherwise, parking, and the security of your *macchina* – car – Vespa or *motorino* – moped – may well cause you problems. Only the most indulgent *portiere* or *amministratore* will allow you to park your two-wheeled transport in the *ingresso* – entrance hall.

• Rents are always calculated by the calendar month. Unless you are extremely lucky, you will be unlikely to find even a *monolocale con servizi* – one-room flat plus kitchen and bathroom – in any of the larger cities for less than 800,000 lire a month. Because flat-sharing is uncommon in Italy, unless you have access to university noticeboards you will find it hard to rent a single room with shared use of facilities.

Advertisements do not count *i servizi* – kitchen and bathroom – and thus will mention only the number of other rooms. *Tre stanze* could be variously one bedroom plus dining room and sitting room; two bedrooms and sitting room, or three bedrooms – it depends what use

are 3.5–4.5 million lire. Luxury accommodation in some parts of central Milan can fetch as much as 30 million per square metre, one of the highest rates in Europe. AICI find that the greatest demand among most Italian buyers is for high-quality renovated properties, which are now consequently at a shortage. This accounts for the reduced number of completed transactions in 1988 (about half a million) compared to previous years. As usual, Italians want the best. (→ VII, 1:i)

Far better value are the apartments in *palazzi da ristrutturare* – unmodernized buildings. In the last few ungentrified areas of central Rome (near the Stazione Termini, and San Lorenzo) interesting properties at under 1.5 million lire per square metre can still be found, while in smaller cities like Palermo this figure can be as low as 500,000 lire per square metre. Although prices are rising steadily, they have yet to reach those of the 1981 boom (in real terms), making the early 1990s an excellent time to buy property in Italy. Of Italians themselves, ISTAT estimate 59% own their own houses (of which 18.5% have mortgages); 35% rent theirs.

In real terms, house prices have been up and down since the 1960s. Thus, a house in Rome or Milan that cost 25 million lire in 1966 cost 205 million in 1988; one that cost 100 million lire in 1982 cost only 83 million lire in 1986.
(CENSIS)

The situation of country properties is somewhat different: rather like in France, it is only the British, Germans and Scandinavians who can be bothered to buy a ruined *casale* – country property – and do it up. If rich Italians want a second home (it has been estimated that 1.6% of them own one, while 17.9% rent one), it is usually in a prestigious seaside location or ski resort. (→ VII, 2) The prices of so-called villas in Tuscany (generally old farm outhouses tarted up by unscrupulous Italian agents and builders, or, worse still, British ones) are generally outrageously high. 'Chiantishire' was a joke that far too many British holiday-homers now take far too seriously. While much of Tuscany is unquestionably enchanting, so is most of Umbria, le Marche and Piedmont, where prices are much lower.

There are 24 million homes in Italy, of which 5 million have not been declared to the authorities in order to avoid paying tax on them. Some 11 million

home-owners don't even admit on their '740' (the standard tax certificate) to having a home at all.

90% of Italians are never away from home, except when on holiday; this includes 84% of the male working population. Only 15% of Italians are resident outside the region of their birth – *Casa, dolce casa*: home, sweet home...

you choose to make of the available space. Remember that for many Italian families, both *il salotto* and *la sala da pranzo* also double up as bedrooms. In cities like Rome, Milan, Naples, Turin or Florence, you would expect to pay at least 1,200,000 lire per month for a furnished apartment of this size.

Where to look for houses to let

• *Affittasi* – to let – signs outside *palazzi* are now beginning to return, after a long absence caused by the *Equo canone* regime. Check even those outside apparently residential *palazzi* to make quite sure they do not say *uso ufficio* – office space: they will charge exorbitant rents.

• Rental agencies are few and far between, but do exist. Most embassies provide lists of those specializing in lets for foreigners. Subtext: extra high prices.

• Local papers (e.g. Rome's *Il Messagero* on Thursdays and Sundays), though not necessarily every edition, carry pages of *appartamenti da affittare*. Rome's weekly *Trade & Mart*-like *Porta Portese* has a huge selection. Several large cities have an equivalent.

• University or student travel agency (CTS) noticeboards.

• Certain international organizations – like Rome's United Nations Organization agency FAO, Rome's foreign Press association, or large international firms – have a special housing bureau or a noticeboard for employees or members. Cheeky (or desperate) flat-seekers often pose as insiders in their quest for *una casa*.

• If you have the time, energy and linguistic ability, try quizzing the *portiere* of any *palazzo* you like – or even don't like – the look of. Be prepared to pay for any useful information, but only on successful completion of negotiations.

• For ringing up about a flat,
→ 8: ACCESS, below – Phone
manners.

Buying a property

• If you plan to live in Italy,
rather than simply use it as
a second home, it is advisable
to become a resident. Among
other things, *la residenza* (→
V, 4: ACCESS – Getting basic
documents) entitles you to tax
relief (under *la legge Formica* –
the Formica law) if it is your first
home, to a big discount on
property duties payable, and
to various other discounts on
basic charges, such as those
for amenities – water, electricity
and the phone.

• Unlike in Britain, only one
notaio – public notary – is
used, for both parties, although
you can use your own private
one. Certain *avvocati* – lawyers
– also specialize in property
transactions.

• You are strongly advised to
get a good *commercialista* –
accountant – who will skilfully
handle complicated transactions you will never get the grasp
of, and who are legally entitled to
handle property transactions as
well. He/she will advise you on
various property taxes or rates,
such as the Imposte Locali sui
Reditti (ILOR), and in certain
cities *le tasse comunali* – local
taxes – and whether to pay them
or not. Very often you won't have
to. A major headache is to decide
what value to declare for your
new property: the Italian law
works on the assumption that
everybody declares only a third
of their property's real value.
(→ V, 1:ii)

• Italians tend to buy their
property outright, being the
world's greatest savers, and
having a deep dislike of borrowing money. (→ VI, 4) *I mutui* –
mortgages – are comparatively
rare (less than 20% of transactions), but are becoming more

widespread. If you already own
a British property, get a mortgage in Britain: they are still
among the best in the world,
despite current high interest
rates. Italian mortgages, like
so many other financial services, are very inconvenient.
(→ VI, 4: ACCESS) Although the
interest rate is broadly similar to Britain's, it works out
dearer, as you have to pay
an extra couple of per cent
to the bank (building societies
don't exist as such). Mortgages
have to be paid off within ten
years, and are rarely for more
than 50% (occasionally 75%) of
the property value. The main
advantage is tax relief, if you are
an Italian resident. Otherwise,
try and negotiate a mortgage in
another foreign currency. The
latest thing in Italy is to get your
mutuo in European Currency
Units (ECU): there was a 60%
increase in their use in 1988.
If you buy through an *agenzia
immobiliare* – estate agent – you
may find they fix you up with
a better mortgage than your
Italian bank could.

• When you decide on a property, you and the vendor sign a
compromesso – a draft contract
– setting down the conditions of
sale, including exit clauses. You
then pay a *caparra* – deposit –
generally of about 10% of the
total price, before paying the
remaining sum in instalments.
There is a similar plethora of
legal and professional fees to
pay as in the UK.

• Make sure you get the
contracts for domestic utilities
transferred, and that all previous bills have been paid. If you
are *moroso* – in arrears – they
are very swift to cut you off, and
very slow to put you back again
when you've paid.

Where to look for houses to buy

• In the city: as with so many
things, house selling is some-

thing the Italians have not
really organized as well as other
countries. *Agenzie immobiliari*
are comparatively rare, and are
only now beginning to increase;
most Italians still prefer to sell
privately. Also, you are more
likely to be able to bargain
with a home owner than with
an agency. The places to look
are similar to those for seeking
rented property:

Vendesi – for sale – signs outside *palazzi* may give the name/
number of an agency or the
proprietor; the local daily newspaper or weekly buy and sell
paper; *il portiere* of any *palazzo*
you like the look of.

• Country properties: while the
prices of most renovated Tuscan *casali* are wildly inflated
(you should see how much it
cost to start with), buying a
ruin and doing it up yourself
is fraught with difficulty. Many
foreign holiday-home buyers
abandon all the normal cau-
tion they would exercise in
such a transaction at home,
either out of romantic naïvety
('Signor Luigi seems such a
nice man') or because of lack
of time or inclination to do the
ground-work, which in Italy will
generally be more than in most
countries. You may well find a
bargain, but you equally have to
pay dearly for it in other ways.

You may be able to find
a place through an agency,
but you'd be much better off
going to an area you think
you like, and having a good
look round, looking out for the
vendesi signs.

• That British figure, the independent surveyor, doesn't have
an exact equivalent in Italy. You
can get an *architetto* or their
site manager (*il geometra*) to
have a look, but their opinion is
not neutral, since they will then
want to be responsible for the
work. Try bringing your own
with you.

● Make sure the title deeds and right of access are in order, and find out whether any new developments are contemplated in the vicinity. In theory, you should check at the local *comune* – town hall – but they may not know, or may not be bothered to find out for you. Try cross-questioning the locals.

● Even if the person who sells you the property recommends you a builder, don't take their word for it (it may simply be a relation), but get several *preventivi* – estimates – from other building contractors. There are excellent *muratori* – builders – in Italy; you just have to find them.

● Especially if you are planning a swimming pool, go to great lengths to check the water situation. Despite abundant rainfall at other times of year, many rural areas of Italy have a funny habit of drying up completely in summer. Having your own *pozzo* - well – can be more of a mod. con. than a picturesque feature; otherwise you should have a 500-litre *cassone* – reservoir – built in the roof, in order to maintain water pressure.

● Make sure you get all the right *permessi comunali* – planning permission: Italians may prefer to build *abusivamente* – without permits (→ V, 1:v), – but they know the ropes better than you, and occasional official inspections do take place.

2. *I giovani*: childhood and youth

Words for children and youth

Words for children and youth

• Latin languages have a built-in bias towards the male, so except where there are only females present, the masculine term is always used.
Hence, for 'my children', you say *i miei figli* – literally, my sons – or simply *i ragazzi* – the boys – even if you have three girls and only one boy.
• *I ragazzi*, as in *i ragazzi di oggi* – the youth of today – is used interchangeably with *i giovani* to indicate the young in general, along with the more formal and abstract *la gioventù*.
• *Il mio ragazzo, la mia ragazza* indicates boy/girlfriend. To address a young person they don't know, older people usually say *giovane, giovanotto* or *ragazzo*.

So much has been said and written about Italians as children and their relationship with their mothers that it may seem superfluous to add anything else.

The prominent position Italian children play in society is evident from the day of their birth, when a pink or blue rosette is placed for a week or so above the front door of the building where their family live. Restaurants are full of unrestricted small children, who are often fussed over by the owners and other diners in a way that nanny-less Anglo-Saxon parents find entirely enviable. Slightly more irritating can be the custom whereby the smallest of children are entitled to occupy on their own the largest of seats on the most crowded buses and trains. No adult passenger (except, Italians would say, a British one) would dream of asking the parents to gather their *figlioletti* – tiny offspring – on to their laps.

The Italians themselves, as usual, are the first to comment on this national tic, which is called *mammismo* – mummyism – while the spoilt children who acquiesce in this lifestyle are indicated by the term *mammone*. It signifies the all-dominant Mother–Son relationship which pervades everything in society (a man is only really important as a son, never as a father; likewise, a woman only as a mother, never really as a daughter). Italians know this instinctively, and act accordingly. However, there have been significant developments in the recent past which shed new light on the phenomenon.

We have already seen (→ 1:i, above) the mass return to the family nest (4% increase per annum), and the reasons for it: Italian parents do not expect their children to pay for anything while they are at home; and even among those who work, less than 10% offer to pay housekeeping money.

With very few exceptions, the Italian version of the unspoken contractual agreement that sanctions all parent–offspring relationships is almost unilateral, as regards obligations. Parents not only feel bound but also want to sacrifice everything they can for the good of their children. There are several different reasons for this. First is the Catholic ideal of marital duties – i.e. living (and dying, if necessary, in childbirth) for one's children and their betterment. Secondly, the desire for one's children 'to have everything we weren't able to' is a very real factor in a country whose economic growth over thirty years matches that of nations like Britain over a period three times that long. The intense speed of socio-economic change means that parents who grew up barefoot and saw meat at table twice a year compensate anxiously by making their children the best shod and the most protein stuffed in Europe: it is no coincidence that 16- to 22-year-old Italians are now among the tallest of the whole continent. The third reason involves *la bella figura*. Keeping up with the Rossis means spending all available cash on making one's children look better off than those of one's neighbours; how the parents look is almost secondary. The lower-income the family, the more they tend to spend on events like *la prima comunione* and weddings (→ 3:iii, below) often indebting themselves till the grave. The important thing is to look well off. This explains why so many brand new BMWs and Mercedes seen in the streets reveal arrogant-looking 18-year-olds at the wheel, picking up their girlfriends from school. Not quite LA, since the car still belongs to the father; it's just that priority driving rights often belong to the son.

Whenever possible, the son (and, less frequently, daughter) will get his own car bought him. Growing up in modern Italy means milestones measured by purchases: *il motorino* (moped) at 14, *la Vespa* at 16, *la macchina* (car) at 18. Recently, a parliamentary motion to decrease the minimum driving licence age to 16 was defeated because it would have clogged the cities with too many new cars. TV and printed advertising is a clear index of the kiddie car market: every major manufacturer produces whole ranges of 'fun cars' – youth custom variants on the basic model. The combined sales of these make the Fiat Uno and Panda, the Seat Ibiza, the Peugeot 205 and the Renault 5 among Italy's best-selling cars. Interestingly, the artwork for these ads compares with that used by British banks and building societies to lure youthful customers. Italian banks wouldn't dream of bothering; the competition is too strong. In Italy, the favourite young person's bank is called Mamma e Papà.

A fourth reason for this intense spoiling of children involves their current scarcity. After generations of large families, the trend of having one to two children, which represents a rational response to the changes in modern society, is often counterbalanced by the thoroughly irrational desire to protect and spoil them, since, to quote the Milanese Adlerian psychotherapist Federica Mormando: 'now there are so few of them, they are like fragile objects; if they break, they cannot be replaced by anther one'.

The heart of the problem seems to be Italy's dual character – as rational Italy, aware of the benefits, faces the consequences of zero population growth (reached in theory in 1987, when for the first time the number of deaths in the previous twelve months equalled the number of births over the same period), the irrational side gets into a panic search for surrogates or imports. One of the genres of 'human interest stories' dominating the Italian media over the last couple of years is that of adoption and abandoned babies. Exploiting certain loopholes and ambiguities in the Italian law regarding adoption, many childless Italians have imported children from the Far East without official sanction, leading to long drawn out tugs-of-war in court. Both this and the not infrequent cases of *la ragazza madre* – the unmarried mother – who dumps her unwanted new-born child by the dustbins, to be discovered by neighbours, make for very good TV news. Dumping children on the proverbial doorstep has long been a tradition in Naples, as is attested by the frequent occurrence of the surname 'Esposito' (foundling) among Neapolitans.

The gradual decline of the existing child has nicely coincided with the massive projection of the TV advert spawned hyperchild to remind the public of their existence as a concept. Just as the outline of a steam train on road-signs epitomizes more effectively for our post-steam generation the idea of 'train' than a modern diesel locomotive ever can, so collective Italy is now growing accustomed to the idea of the child-as-doll: fragile, precious, to be mollycoddled. If there are fewer children to go round, not only must they be spoilt more, they must also remain children for longer.

Gino Martinoli of CENSIS has devoted over twenty years to this subject, and recently published a report on Italian childhood, where he sums up the problem: 'Italian parents tend to spoil their children so much, and overprotect them for so long, that the latter have great difficulty in growing up at all.' The almost morbid obsession with creating problem-free lives for children creates a 'sickly-sweet infantile environment, out of which only in rare cases do fully formed personalities emerge'.

The Italian State and the Italian language itself are partly to blame. Only in 1988 did Parliament decide not to allow child benefits (in any case, very meagre) to include university students. While the English language is awkward in describing the 16–35 age group (boy or girl is too patronizing, guy is too slang, youth or young person too stiff and formal), Italian has no such qualms: they are all *ragazzi* – boys – and remain so almost until they are 40. An intense but meaningless rhetoric has developed in the field of politics since 1968: *'i giovani'* now exist with a political status of their own, somewhere between VIPs and an underprivileged minority group. They are constantly singled out for special attention by politicians, who want to show sensitivity and concern, at no extra cost. No party manifesto is complete without something about *i problemi dei giovani* (unspecified); any kind of cultural or formal gathering reported by the media always announces how there were *tanti giovani* – lots of young people – present, as though they were major Hollywood celebs. Although they have precious little to say – Italian youth subculture is almost non-existent – their collective name exudes a rhetoric resonance that no sensible public figure would dare contradict.

Returning to childhood, both Italian TV and the fashion business are deeply involved in the exploitation both of children as concrete individuals, and of the idea of childhood in the abstract. In a throwback to the bad old days of child labour (still present in certain forms in Naples and certain areas of the South), children are constantly employed in adverts and programmes to pluck at adults' heartstrings: whether a chorus of 5-year-olds singing the praises of the Aiazzone furniture company, or the 10-year-old co-presenter of the RAI TV variety programme *Domenica In* (1987–8), the intention is the same. Some entire programmes, like *Piccoli Fans* – Little fans – presented by ex-Fellini actress Sandra Milo, are entirely devoted to tiny tots pretending to be adult performers, in front of their adoring parents. Design houses across the price spectrum from Armani to Benetton heavily feature clothes for infants and children, dressing them up as miniature adults, with often decidedly adult prices. There are five or six glossy fashion magazines such as *Vogue Bambino* on the market to encourage mothers to spend even more money on making them look like little dolls.

Not only do TV adverts feature the young; they are now aimed at them as well. Italian R&D group sessions reveal that now it is often they, rather than their parents, who decide on family purchases. Guido Araldi of McCann-Erickson in Milan explains: 'Once the housewife was the vehicle we used to reach the family. Now it is the children who influence the choice of holiday, or new car.'

The question of discipline is interesting: there is nothing to suggest that Italians hit their children less than British parents, though they seem to do so for different reasons. Small children tend to be dressed up at all times, and if they fall and get dirty, they may get a smack; whereas making a noise in public, or disturbing others, will go unchecked. The survival of corporal punishment in some schools leads certain Italians to think of the British as cruel, though it is not so much the punishment as the punisher that causes offence: in Italy, there is no *in loco parentis*. Likewise, the idea of boarding schools represents a threat, rather than a mark of privilege, to most Italians. Except for a few upper-class Italians familiar with foreign boarding-school education, *il collegio* spells economic hardship, or punishment for a naughty child. (→ VIII, 5:i) When a 6-year-old boy was expelled in 1988 from a Palermo primary school for being uncontrollably naughty, there was a national outcry, with the headmaster emerging the culprit: the father merely blamed 'the bad influence of the other children'.

On the other hand, parents are generally very keen for their children to excel in school and play (→ VIII, 5:i), pressurizing them as much as Japanese parents into taking extra lessons in weak subjects, English lessons in private language schools, enrolling them in any number of private sports clubs and building up their bodies with vast intakes of protein. Most adolescents' lack of independence makes them loth to rebel, but those that do often make a more dramatic protest: over 2000 a year run away from home without returning; others fall prey to heroin (5% of Italy's vast junkie population is under 18), while some commit suicide – an alarming tendency on the increase. (→ 7, below) Motives range from the specific (bad marks in school) to the generic, *'Non ce la faccio più'* – the adult-sounding, 'I just can't carry on any more.'

Disturbed by the increasing degree of serious neurosis in children, the Italian Ministero dell'Interno recently published a survey profiling what it called 'this hyperstimulated, hypernourished and hyperprotected' age group. At the same time, Italian parents are, naturally, worried by the consequences of their own behaviour, and are looking for new solutions, one of which seems to be the pre-war Italian tradition of the *colonia estiva* – the summer camp – which in the 1930s produced a very interesting architectural genre. Recently *La Stampa* published an article giving tips to parents on where to send their children, and how to cope without them. It advised parents 'not to telephone the camp *too* often – your children need a holiday from you as well'.

Not everything points to pathological spoiling in Italy: apart from the vast middle ground of fairly balanced upbringing, there is an equally worrying other extreme of specific ill-treatment, which is now being effectively monitored by a child helpline called *il telefono azzurro* – the blue phone. In some eight months they received some 15,000 calls, of which 45% cited physical ill-treatment as the reason for phoning,

20% psychological ill-treatment, 20% neglect, and 15% sexual molestation.

Above all, however, AIPAI, the Italian anti-child-abuse association, estimate that children between the ages of 10 and 14, despite the consumer goods they are showered with, simply feel alone and neglected.

3. Sexuality

(i) Sex and the young

There are two contrasting elements, one positive, one negative, specific to the Italians' cultural and geographic collocation to be considered. On the one hand, there is the Mediterranean naturalness with which sexual experiences are consumed; on the other, the strong degree of repression exercised by traditional Catholic morality, which is now complicated by a third, more recent factor – the intense pressures of the electronic permissive society.

The cases of 9-year-old mothers in southern Italy, which made world headlines in the 1960s, although now more likely to involve 9-year-old junkies, are not just a matter of legend. The Catholic Church in the poorer areas of cities like Palermo and Naples is used to coping with 13-year-old fugitives, who may even set up home together. The Gretna Green-style *fuga d'amore* – elopement – presenting a *fait accompli* to both families, forcing them to consent, is a time-honoured Sicilian custom, which has by no means died out.

There are now lurid variants, reported recently in southern Italy, where the prospective child bride actually moves in with her intended's family, and proceeds to become a sexual prisoner of father and brothers as well, while cases of parents obliging their daughters to prostitute themselves, and of gang rapes of often under-age girls, are frequently reported by the media.

Traditionally, Italian families never instruct their children about sex, and schools do nothing to fill the gap. In recent years, proposals for sex education caused serious public controversy, but current concern over AIDS has done much to neutralize this. (→ VIII, 2:iv) Since such a strong taboo still exists about the discussion of sexual matters between adults (parents or teachers) and children, children inevitably grow up emotionally unprepared, learning about sex from friends and relations of their own age. The kissing cousins syndrome has historical importance in Italy: many Italians have their first experiences with cousins, frequently on the classic joint summer holidays at the beach – group masturbation and fondling each other's bodies.

The pressure now exerted by the modern media means that many just pubescent adolescents now leap straight from innocence to precocious sexual relations, outside the southern cultural context where such practices are implicitly condoned. But while the combination of force-fed sexual maturity with the extreme mental immaturity of the average 13-year-old Italian, and the intense taboos about discussing sex with adults, has caused a major new sexual pathology syndrome, Italian child psychologists are not unduly alarmed about it. A parallel may perhaps be drawn with Nabokov, since, like Lolita, all too many sexually active Italian adolescents seem happy to cope with the psychic strains their anomalous position places upon them.

Apart from the cases where parents now allow their children to bring boy/girlfriends home, there is a whole sexual culture closely linked to the automobile. Except on those occasions when they manage to calculate when the parents are out or away, or when they have friends who have access to another apartment, young Italians generally have sex in cars. Any public park, motorway layby, or unlit lane outside built-up areas at night will have any number of stationary cars with *coppiette* – couples, generally young – having sexual intercourse inside. In the South, where evidently the problem of *guardoni* – peeping toms – is worse, the enterprising partners line their car windows with newspaper to keep prying eyes out. That is why certain Italian streets in outlying urban areas are always littered with newspapers.

The law and young Italians

Until 1988, the age of consent for both hetero- and homosexual activity was 16. Since then, all the political parties, with the exception of the Catholic-inspired Christian Democrats, have been trying to bring it down to 14, unless one of the partners is more than two years older than the other. The additional premise that there should be no more than two people involved is typical of the Italian talent for imaginative legislation.

(ii) Courtship and romance

Exactly as elsewhere in the Western world, the concept of sex before marriage is now insignificant. It would be hard, even in southern Italy, to find a man who was outraged to find his wife was not a virgin. Despite irregular prevention methods (→ 3:vii, below), sexual freedom is very much the norm. Dating couples, however, seem to observe certain old-fashioned niceties. Although it is very common (and increasingly so) so talk about *la mia ragazza*, *il mio ragazzo* – my girl/boyfriend – it is still more common to talk and think in terms of *la fidanzata*, *il fidanzato* – my fiancée/é. The concept of going steady

– *il fidanzamento* – remains deeply embedded in mainstream Italian culture. It is very common for parents
to talk in cloying terms of a friendship between two
children as *fidanzatini* – little fiancés – along the lines
of the French cartoon series *Love is...*, which is very
popular in Italy, along with anything else that presents
a sanitized, sentimental view of 'being engaged'. There
is an extraordinary romance industry in Italy, mostly for
adolescent girls or lonely women, based on *il romanzo
rosa* – the pink novel – by the likes of Barbara Cartland
and her Italian equivalent, the inevitable Liala. For the
younger market exists *il fotoromanzo* – the romantic
photo (as opposed to cartoon) strip magazine.

(iii) Marriage and its alternatives

The institution of marriage in Italy has changed beyond
recognition over the last two decades. In the late 1980s,
almost nobody dared to live together; even those who
got married with civil ceremonies were condemned by
the Church and the reigning public moral code as 'living
in sin'. As late as the early 1960s there were still cases
of 'trial by public outcry' about couples living together.
By 1974, the year when an overwhelming majority of
Italians voted in favour of the divorce laws, only
0.5% of cohabiting couples were unmarried. A 1988
CNR study calculates that 10% of couples now live
together without bothering to marry, of whom 27.5%
are professional people.

Possibly more significant is the radical change of
attitude by the silent majority: a mere quarter-century
after the last 'trial by public outcry' about 'concubinage'
held against an unmarried working-class couple in the
Tuscan city of Prato, a 1988 Computel survey showed
that 70% of Italians consider living together to be
socially acceptable, with over half in favour of the same
legal rights being applied to cohabitation as to regular
marriage; even more surprising, a majority was shown
to be in favour of equal alimony rights for unmarried
ex-partners.

**Right after the First World War, both a seamen's
union contract and a law passed on farm-workers'
illness benefits tacitly approved the same principle
of equal rights for non-married partners.**

While the number of marriages continues to decrease
– the post-war record was 1947, with 440,000 celebrated,
which had decreased by 1970 to 400,000, while in 1986
the number was down to less than 300,000 – there

has been since 1987 a slight increase in the number of people who marry in church, indicating that the Italians haven't completely turned their backs on organized religion. And while divorces continue to rise steadily, broken marriages that end in the Italian courts remain relatively few – 9% compared to 28% in France and 39% in Great Britain. After a record in 1975, immediately after divorce was instituted, with 33,000, there was an initial drop to a third of that figure before its increase to current rates. Legal separations are about 35,000 a year. Also, belief in the institution of marriage doesn't seem to dissolve with divorce: four out of five divorced Italians decide to remarry.

In 1987 there were 15,471 marriages in Rome, an increase from the 15,000 of the previous year. The 1987 figures are in a sense misleading, since they also include some 600 Irish couples who get married at the Vatican on Pope-package tours. There are, in fact, only about 10,000 regular, Concordat-approved (town hall plus church) marriages a year, since many widows who remarry go through only the religious ceremony, so as not to lose their first husband's pension.

In common with other Catholic countries, all Italian weddings have to be celebrated *in comune* – at the town hall – before going on for the religious ceremony in church. As elsewhere, church ceremonies are more social than religious events, particularly since in Italy there is an alarming custom of having hordes of photographers – nowadays video-cameramen – who brazenly interrupt the whole ceremony in order to re-cord the event for posterity. This self-inflicted *paparazzi* ordeal is extremely expensive, but mandatory, for *la bella figura*, for the majority of Italian newly-weds. Despite the expense outlaid for everything, including clothes, it is relatively unusual even for family members to wear a penguin suit, and many of the guests will come without jacket or tie. As in all present-giving situations, Italian wedding presents tend to be very, very expensive, even those from comparative outsiders. In recompense, there is always a big sit-down lunch or dinner of at least six courses, which may indebt the bride's father literally for life. Many prospective brides (or, rather, their mothers) still spend years collecting *il corredo* – the bottom drawer – which will be lavish.

Guests throw rice over the happy couple, and shout, '*Viva gli sposi!*' – 'Long live the bride and groom.' *Confetti* in Italian are the little sugar-coated almonds wrapped in nylon lace bags which are presented to all the guests, and sent to those who couldn't come.

Certain aspects are less formal than British weddings: it is common for friends not to turn up for either of the official ceremonies, and only for the dinner or party – *il rinfresco* – where there are no speeches and no best man as such; two *testimoni* – witnesses – sign the register, but they perform no official function.

• Italian women keep their maiden names throughout their lives on all official documents, adding their husband's name plus *in*. An English woman marrying an Italian would become 'La Signora Smith in Rossi' on most documents, and always for medical records – to visit a married woman in hospital, you must remember her maiden name. You can choose to be known as either for work or financial matters. Since *Signora* generally denotes all adult women, not just married ones (*Signorina* sounds odd applied to someone over, say, 35), there is usually no way of knowing if someone is married from her name. Doorbells with two surnames are therefore statistically less likely to signify a flatshare, or an unmarried couple, than a convenience for the postman.

• There is now a very strong move to introduce elective surnames for the children, so that they can legally choose either parent's name: a revolutionary step in a country where it is impossible to change your name.

(iv) Husband and wife: domestic relations

Compared to the more pragmatic Northern European/-American cultures, the idea that men should collaborate with the housework is still fairly foreign in Italy. Even among the liberal-minded, there is little evidence of men helping their wives. Never, for example, would a politician or other public figure be caught dead in a photo or TV report doing anything more domestic than, say, turning a steak over on the barbecue. Indeed, a man who can cook, iron a shirt, or sew on a button will always meet with a patronizing chorus of *Bravo!* from women. Other men may simply despise him. Although many more women work than ten years ago, only 20% support themselves on their wages. It isn't that they don't wish to; they just don't have the time: 56% of those who don't work cite family responsibilities as the reason for not searching for a job. This is similar to elsewhere in the West, though tests show that husbands think they do much more for the kids than the wife thinks they do. The equal relationship, with evenly divided chores, is the type with the highest percentage of divorces in Italy: this kind of wife can allow herself, economically and emotionally, to divorce.

With an almost identical overall female population (51.3%), Italy has slightly fewer working women than Britain, although the percentage continues steadily to rise. In the North, 33% work; in the South, only 25%. In Britain, 42.6% have work. The British female unemployment rate is 7%; in Italy, 20%. However, Italian women earn more than their British sisters: 84% of male wages, as opposed to 69%.
(EUROSTAT, 1988)

According to the 1987 survey *Men and Women in Europe*, slightly more Italian husbands and boyfriends (51%) prefer their women to have jobs than in Britain (50%).

As merits a Catholic country, the basic idea of sex for anything outside procreation is so closely linked to the idea of sin, and sin to the idea of pleasurable transgression, that it figures that Italians often go for the 'dirtier' side of sex. A certain amorality underlines the basic national sexual philosophy; in theory, do what you want, then go and confess and get it off your chest. Protestant culture, on the other hand, obliges people to reflect on their personal code of conduct by themselves. As in France, the habit of having a mistress, or lover, is considered not just normal but acceptable. Famous people who may recently have died are often commemorated for their sexual prowess, with both wife and mistresses called to comment. A recent RAI TV documentary on the Onassis-like shipping magnate Achille Lauro contained interviews both with his children and with his last surviving lover, who recounted his *grande passione per le donne* – his thing for the ladies – in approving terms. The only crime is being caught, so the important thing is for her not to find out. But such is the degree of 'turning a blind eye' in Italian sexual psychology that many wives, especially in public positions, simply *fare finta di niente* – pretend nothing is happening. In recent years it seems that wives have been getting their own back: an AIED study recorded 32% of men and 52% of women between the ages of 38 and 43 who admitted to being unfaithful to their spouses, but generally in secret.

In the average Italian family, the wife does 36 hours' housework to the man's 5.5 per week, with a gradual increase by the man towards old age. Even when the wife has a full-time job, the husband's average share rises by only half an hour, to 6 hours.
(ISTAT)

The public shame of being *cornuto* – or cuckolded, to give it its rather medieval English rendering – cannot be underestimated, even today. It is typically far worse for men than women: even though they may boast among themselves how often they manage to *fare le corna* – literally put the horns (of the devil) – on their wives, the prospect of their wives doing it back is a fate worse than death. *Cornuto!* remains one of the gravest insults in Italian – motorists who shout it at each other, or make the accompanying hand gesture (the index and little finger in the air, like horns), are liable to end up in serious punch-ups, or even knife fights. National conferences have been dedicated to the psychology of it.

Although the Italians are very fond of pointing a finger at Anglo-Saxon puritanism and moral hypocrisy, it has to be said that until the post-1968 generation, any open support for sexual freedom was very hard to come by. Until the 1970s civil rights crusades, even the anti-clerical PCI (Communist Party) held a holier-than-thou moral position. Throughout the 1950s and 1960s, the main Italian left-wing opposition party upheld a moral code that almost shamed that of the Church. They steadfastly opposed early attempts by minor opposition parties to introduce divorce legislation, climbing on to the civil liberties bandwagon only when they perceived it to be a vote-catching cause. The prime mover in favour of legislation was the Radical Party leader Marco Pannella, although he was aided by the other *partiti laici* and the left as a whole. (→ IV, 2:ii) Divorce was legalized in 1974, and abortion in 1977.

Of course, the 1968 sexual revolution introduced new standards for many liberal types, who theorize about the need for *matrimoni aperti* – open marriages – but whose practice of this principle has caused considerable grief. Whatever the head may think, the Italian heart is extremely jealous. Entire practices of psychoanalysts and lawyers in the larger Italian cities have been sustained by the cases brought their way thanks to *il tradimento consensuale* – mutually agreed adultery.

It is some years since the laws sanctioning *delitti d'onore* – crimes of passion – were rescinded, but in the South cases of murder or maiming for reasons of honour are still quite common.

Being hassled in the street by Italian boys

Remember, they will almost never dare touch you, and would only do so if you gave them the come-on. Their favourite technique is to crowd around you if you are sitting down, and bombard you with stupid questions in often rudimentary English. Sit there and look bored, or scornful. Italian girls are used to doing this all the time, and are hence expert at throwing off unwanted admirers. Never reply to them: that would spell you're interested. In response to their questions, Italian girls dispense a dismissive 'tut' with a shake of the head. If you get up and walk away, you may look as though you are frightened, and are therefore good prey. If they get too pushy, consider the classic slap on the face – that usually works, but may further excite the really persistent. The

(v) Sexual appetite

The old Don Giovanni cliché now needs some serious revising; the way that Italians view and consume sexual experience is changing quite dramatically.

The Caletti Report (1987) estimates that there are 10 million sexual encounters in Italy every day. Excluding the sexually inactive categories of the prepubescent, the old and the professionally celibate (though priests who have lovers of either sex are by no means uncommon), this suggests that every adult Italian has sex once every two days.

The famous Italian obsession with big breasts, as totem of the earth mother and as immortalized by Fellini, is still fairly much in favour, and mediocre actresses still shoot to success as much now as they did in the 1950s, provided they are *maggiorate* – super well-endowed. Good-looking women, especially if blonde or foreign-looking, get almost as constantly hassled in the streets by young working-class Italians as they did a decade ago. However, this is always all bark and no bite: many young Italians are terrified of girls, and do the *pappagallo* bit in the street to impress their friends – out of sheer bravado. If a girl tries to pick them up, they feel immediately *in crisi* – in psychological difficulty. But beyond appearances, and possibly the relatively straightforward passions of the 16–25 age group, there is a whole new phenomenon linked to a serious loss of sexual appetite. Although only 20,000 Italians a year seek the services of sex advisory counsellors, there are estimated to be many millions who are encountering new psychologically based sexual difficulties. In southern Italy, over the last few years, there has been a massive increase in marriages where, after three or four years, sexual activity comes to a halt, with a total loss of desire from both parties. Italian psychologists all agree that this is due to several specific reasons. The media bombardment of soft (and hard) porn has destroyed the ozone layer of sexual mystique that once characterized Italian sexuality: the prospect of the forbidden, or the strictly reserved, rights of the bed. Also, social evolution has brought about the same redefinition of status roles between the sexes as elsewhere in the West, which the Italian has accepted in his/her head, but not at gut level – another case of Italy's bicultural reactions to things, simultaneously atavistic and progressive. Men in particular seem to be unable to cope with the possibility of being prey rather than predator. While most Italian women have spent the last two decades reassessing their position (→ 3:viii, below) most men haven't given theirs a thought, and are now hopelessly out of touch with the new status quo.

best insurance policy is to have a child with you: an Italian, however randy, would never hassle *una mamma*.

Italian men think the sexiest European women are:
  (1) French   (2) Spanish   (3) Dutch.
Italian women think the sexiest European men are:
  (1) French   (2) Spanish   (3) Greek.
(Computel Demoskopea for *Oggi* magazine, 1988)

As a direct consequence of this, the supremacy of regular sexual intercourse is being challenged by the revival of a practice most Italians thought they'd forgotten about: masturbation. The art of making love to the person you love best, to quote Woody Allen, has traditionally been one of the Catholic Church's principal bugbears, with all the warnings of blindness, purgatory and so on. The Church has now significantly shifted its position on the whole issue. Among the various studies recently made, one by the University of Parma has reported a huge increase in masturbation even among married couples:

partly connected to the massive loss in male sexual

desire, and sense of insecurity, often manifested in running away from the female, since sexual penetration can be felt as a form of engulfment by the female. There is also an important component of infantilism involved, recalling one's adolescent experiences.

Roberto Sabatini, in his book *Eros in Italia* (1988), made a detailed survey into masturbation in the country, revealing the existence of numerous 'Jerk-off Parlours' all over northern Italy, where customers pay 100,000 lire to be serviced by a female expert, to whom 50,000 lire is customarily left as a tip. Another recent survey of 1400 Italians revealed that 85% of men considered masturbation normal and were regular practitioners, with only 5% claiming never to have done it; among women, 66% found it both normal and enjoyable, against 20% who considered it abnormal, and an unthinkable activity for a woman.

(vi) Sexual violence

Despite – or perhaps because of – the considerable drop in the collective male libido, there has been a disturbing rise in recent years in cases of rape and sexual violence. One reason for this may be that more women feel able to speak out about it without having to suppress the fact. On the whole, it is mostly in the major cities and in the North that most cases occur, with Rome setting the worst example. The British papers occasionally recount shock horror cases of English girls getting raped, even by police officers, but it would be quite unfair to describe this as a national sport. In 1987 there were 1500 reported rape cases, with another 1000 cases of 'acts of sexual violence'. Over the last five years, during which there has been a steady rise, a clear picture emerges of both victim and aggressor: 33% of victims are girls under 14; 68% are of school age, including 13% of boys; 22% are cases of incest, though experts estimate that only 5%–10% of incest rape cases are reported. Nine out of ten rapists claim their victims were willing, and thus insist on their innocence, and on the provocative nature of the woman, or child, in question. Almost half the rapists are between 18 and 29, and 60% are manual workers, with 13% professional people. Above all, they are normally polite, gentle people who seem miles from the usual stereotype of the violent psychopath, and who almost always know their victim well. In 1988 there was a fierce struggle in Parliament, where the Catholic Christian Democrats wanted to exclude what goes on behind the family walls from the Sexual Violence Bill, to the annoyance of the other parties. The idea that a wife (or, indeed, daughter) might denounce her father for sexual abuse is seen by the Church as against the interests of the family as an institution.

Pill use among European women of fertile age:
Dutch 39%
Swiss 22%
Portuguese 21%
Italian 8% (1984: 5.8%)
(Shering Report, 1987)

(vii) Contraception

Until *Legge* – law – *194*, the liberalization act of 1977, there was a massive back-street abortion industry. While official figures for the early 1980s reveal an average of fifteen per thousand women aborted annually, according to AIED legally performed abortions have since then gone into decline, down from 198,000 to 190,000 in 1987, while back-street abortions remain unvaried at around 120,000 per year, judging by statistics gathered in southern Italy. Some 30% of back-street abortions are on minors, 88% of whom have received legal permission to go ahead with one. The two sums added together indicate that there is an abortion performed every minute in Italy. The Catholic-inspired Movimento per la Vita continues unabashed in its quest to have *Legge 194* repealed, or at least radically reduced: so far with no success.

A 1988 Constitutional Court ruling that only the woman has any rights over whether to abort or not continues to annoy many men, even supporters of *Legge 194*.

Abortion tends to be treated lightly by many Italian women, emerging as one of the most frequently used forms of contraception – over 70% of abortions are practised on married women, who simply can't be bothered to find out about any of the less drastic forms of contraception. The common Italian reflex of 'it can't happen to me' (→ VIII, 3:ii) leads women to chance it. The Italian State health system does little to help: the much discussed family-planning clinics have never been set up, and no organized educational campaign has ever been promoted. Until the anti-AIDS campaigns of the late 1980s, the condom was used infrequently, while the pill is still used less in Italy than in any other Western nation except Greece and Turkey. The coil and the cap have always been more popular, while among practising Catholics the various rhythm methods still have a certain influence.

(viii) Feminism and the position of women

The position of women in society is one of the issues that most reveals Italy's bicultural nature. While at a certain gut level women continue to be patronized, ill-treated or simply ignored, both by institutions and by men in general, on another level Italy's advanced *laico* – lay – culture has repaired its debt towards the female sex as fully as any other Western state. A Catholic Church largely hostile to women's advancement certainly doesn't help diminish a mountain of petty grievances – from certain judges who still tend to insinuate that rape is caused by a woman's provocation, to certain companies who fail to operate equal-pay schemes, to dollybird TV announcers (*'le signorine buona sera'*), all enveloped in traditional *maschilista* – male chauvinist – attitudes.

The early days of feminism were very rough and hostile, to a degree that made many foreign militant feminists blanch. There was a strong emphasis on a totally autonomous existence – no-male-entry communes squatting in priceless Baroque Roman *palazzi*, violent street demonstrations, featuring the cunt sign (joined thumbs and forefingers) instead of the ubiquitous clenched fist, radical lesbian theorizing and so on. All this disappeared as Scandinavian-style legislation was hurried through.

Now the Communist Party has 33% women MPs, including the Speaker of the Lower House; most jobs have female appellatives (no mean linguistic achievement in a Latin culture); there are women police chiefs, important industrialists (Italtel's Marisa Bellisario was, until her recent premature death, the highest ranking non-media executive in the world) and easily as many high-profile arts and intellectual figures as any European country.

The evolution of women's sexuality has arguably been more dramatic than in most countries, with a leap from total repression (in the 1960s a woman's adultery counted as worse than rape) to a dignified self-discovery. Evidence of this change can be seen in the large proportion of Italian women who calmly either have, or would seriously contemplate having, affairs with members of their own sex.

Prostitutes' tariffs

'Vere puttane' – genuine female prostitutes.
Un pompino – a blow job: 25,000–30,000 lire.

(ix) Prostitution

The cliché has it that the Italian male divides women into two basic categories: *sante* – saints – and *puttane* – whores. Obviously, mothers and sisters are of the first category; hopefully, so are wives and girlfriends. Italian men who reason in these terms tend to have a generic underlying attitude to other women, considering them to be mostly *puttane*, ready to surrender to their desires. Thus the figure of the prostitute is paradoxically despised and elevated to mystique status at the same time.

The institution of the brothel – *il casino, or casa di appuntamento*, or *casa di tolleranza* – was outlawed in 1958 by *the Legge Merlin* (laws in Italy tend to be named after their sponsor). Its contents were broadly similar to those proposed by the Woolfenden Report of the Macmillan era in Britain. The custom of receiving *una marchetta* – a token – on entry has, however, remained in the language: *fare le marchette* still means to be on the game.

The effect of the *Legge Merlin* was, inevitably, to put prostitution back on the streets. In Italy, plying one's trade in public has a distinguished history. Particularly in Rome, certain streets are lit up at night by little bonfires which *le puttane* make out of scrap wood, not so much to keep warm as to advertise. This is a tradition that comes down directly from ancient Rome, where the *meretrices* did likewise. This licentious tableau vivant reaches a picturesque historical peak outside the Colosseum in Rome.

Even in the eternal city, there is precious little taboo surrounding prostitution. Italy's main lunch-time TV chat-show for housewives in 1987 (*Pronto, è la RAI?*) featured a regular spot when the main female presenter dresses as a prostitute waiting for customers on the Rome *raccordo anulare* – ring road. In a typically Italian way, it's all very explicit: there's never any mistaking who is on the game: they are out there on the street waiting for you. Stretches of road frequented by *le puttane* are also easily identified by the steady flow of kerb-crawlers. Advertising is limited to certain regional newspapers, and is usually listed under *massaggiatrici* – masseuses. Advertisers usually precede the adverts by a long line of A's in order to assure the reader's immediate attention: *'A.A.A.A.A. offresi'* – is available – has become synonymous with advertised prostitution. There is no equivalent to the British custom of cryptic phone-box advertising, or to the French Minitel computer network.

Prostitution has changed dramatically over the last decade in almost every respect. The number of female prostitutes has increased considerably, as have the reasons for choosing to *andare a battere* – go on the game. Traditional prostitutes are losing ground, as their pitch is getting invaded by more and more young female drug addicts. The 1987 Caletti Report estimated that a good third of the 600,000 prostitutes working in Italy were under 18. While old-fashioned *lucciole* – literally,

Una scopata completa – proper sex: 50,000–60,000 lire.

● Expect to pay 50,000 lire extra for the room; take your own *profilattico* – condom.

● Calculate twice the price for a home-grown *travestito* – transvestite; rather less for a Brazilian *viados*.

Words about love and sex

●Foreigners everywhere seem to know that *ti amo* means I love you in Italian. Actually, they would hardly ever use it; *ti voglio bene* is much more appropriate. It is used not only of the one you love, but also for friends and family; *mi piaci* means I fancy you; while *mi stai simpatico/a* means I like you, or You're a lot of fun. In the third person, talking of someone else, male then female, this works out as: *gli/le voglio bene: lo/la amo: mi piace: mi sta simpatico/a*.

● Anatomical: *cazzo* = cock; *pisello* = willy; *palle* = balls; *culo* = arse; *fica* = cunt; *poppe* = tits; *seni* = breasts.

● Activities: *scopare, chiavare* = to fuck; *fare una pippa* = to wank; *baciare* = to kiss; *venire* = to come; *battere* = to cruise, to be on the game; *rimorchiare* = to pick up; *un pompino* = a blow job; *una sveltina* = a quickie; *una scopata* = a fuck; *una pippa* = a wank; *un bacio* = a kiss.

● Other: *profilattico* = condom; *puttana* = prostitute; *marchettara* = rent boy; *erezione, orgasmo*, needs no translation; *bello/ bella* = good-looking, pretty; *carino/carina* = cute; *bono/ bona* = hunky/tasty.

fireflies – proudly proclaim their good health, many of the young *tossicodipendenti* – junkies – are already HIV-positive. Of their clients, 85% are married men.

The real pavement revolution has been caused by the arrival of the transvestites and the trans-sexuals. There seems to be a basic trait in the psychological make-up of many Italian males that renders the idea of *'un trans'* more attractive than that of a regular prostitute. Perhaps it is that there are two sins to be committed at the same time: not just 'doing it with a tart', but 'doing it with a man dressed up as a tart'. The proof of this argument is invincible – *i trans* charge higher prices.

The whore war does not end just on a female/transvestite front. There are also the foreign invaders, mostly Brazilians, some of whom have 'had the op.', but few of whom have Italian work permits. *I viados*, as the Brazilians are known, infuriate their Italian rivals by their below the belt tactics: not only do they undercut them (and regular female prostitutes) on price in an interesting kind of sexual dumping, sometimes asking less than half the regular fee; they will also offer scare-sex (doing it without a condom), for a slight extra. But above all, they now occupy vast tracts of precious pavement space, where they take the art of flaunting it to an extraordinary new low, by wearing next to nothing – often just a g-string under the lightest of chiffon tops, with a fur stole for winter.

Like the red squirrel in Britain, the native variety of transvestite prostitute now seems in danger of extinction. On occasion, there are pitched pavement battles, when the proverbial fur flies. The mass arrival of *i viados* has provoked the police to smarten up their benign *laissez-faire* attitude. The Rome Questura – police HQ – reckons that 80% of prostitutes working in the capital are now *viados*. There are now frequent round-ups and mass deportations of the hapless (and pimp-less) Brazilians.

Professional female prostitutes have reacted to all this in different ways. In Naples, the streetwalkers displayed signs saying *qui, vere puttane* – get your real whores here; others have formed their own union; others have moved off the pavement (or the motorway sliproads), and gone way up-market. Of these, some have formed their own pimp-free co-operatives, while others work by appointment only.

Parliament has not remained inactive. In September 1989, there were some seven separate *proposte di legge* – bills – each proposing different solutions for emending or abolishing the *Legge Merlin*.

(x) **Transvestitism and trans-sexuality**

The Italian male's penchant for transvestites and trans-sexuals perfectly corresponds with the supply: no other European country has so many. The vulgar caricature of femininity they offer (which Italian women take good-naturedly in their stride, but which may offend more fragile foreign sensibilities) reflects, it has to be admitted, quite accurately the superficial, often fetishistic, concept of *la donna* – womanhood – entertained by all too many Italian heterosexuals. One reason for their large numbers is certainly the immense strain on the psyche imposed by conforming to a strict macho image: although underneath many Italian men may compromise this without damage to themselves, some cannot cope, and have to exteriorize their inability to conform by taking the only other option their instinct tells them is available. Although there is in theory a 1956 law against transvestitism, it is never now applied, and trans-sexualism, after years of official hostility, is not only recognized but 'having the op.' is also now obtainable on the welfare state.

(xi) **Homoeroticism and homosexuality**

The intense physicality of Italian male relationships requires some explanation: all that kissing, hugging and walking arm in arm can look very suggestive. Foreign gay tourists can always be spotted in Italy as they wistfully project their fantasies on to those swarms of muscled, bee-stung-lipped *ragazzi* swaggering their way down the street, locked arm in arm. Actually, there's nothing to get excited about; it's just male bonding, the Latin equivalent of backslapping at the pub.

However, there is a school of thought, exemplified in theory and practice by Pier Paolo Pasolini, that considers almost all Italian males to be latently bisexual. There is much to be said for this, especially in southern Italy, although the cold reality of it does not quite meet the noble savage ideal propagated by Italy's most interesting post-war thinker. The pre-sexual-crisis Italian male defines his virility more in terms of personal phallic potency than of the intensity of his feelings for women. Strictly speaking, he is more of a narcissist than a heterosexual, the conquest of women being more an affirmation of his attractiveness (to himself) than any deep-rooted fascination with the feminine mystique. Hence the incredible immaturity of many Italian men in their relationships with women. Since it is his cock, rather than any invisible mutual bond with the feminine, that is the focus of his sexuality, it is inevitable that, in the long run, he doesn't mind where he puts it, as long as he 'still feels a man'. Centuries

Meeting other men

For those who cannot resist the Latin-lover myth, a good deal of expertise, and some knowledge of Italian, is needed to establish contact with those available-looking but nominally straight men. Most Italian card-carrying gays don't bother to waste their time on *marchettari* – rent boys.

● Even during the day-time, the bars, porno cinemas and public gardens near railway stations and military barracks are an established Mecca of cruising, usually for money. Foreigners can offer a certain curiosity value, but are more likely to be expected to pay for any attentions they may be given.

● Except in Milan and Turin, there are few gay bars and clubs in Italy, and none of the gay restaurants, hotels and shops that can be found abroad. Since the mid-1980s, some newspapers have started listing gay discos in their Leisure sections, often defining them as *un club ambiguo*.

● During the summer, many beaches near big cities have unofficial gay areas, though it's often hard for the untrained eye to tell the difference.

● Just as in every other country in the Western world, most Italian cities have their cruising spots for normal (i.e. non-payment orientated) homosexuals. Since the international gay community seem to have a sixth sense when it comes to identifying them, it is superfluous to give further details here, except to remark that certain cities, like Rome and Naples, have a tradition for cruising on buses. The 64 bus, which goes from Rome's Stazione Termini to the Vatican, is the best known. There also seems to exist a tribal territorial instinct in Italy whereby certain parks and tree-lined boulevards have separate areas where normal and payment-orientated cruising takes place. More detailed information regarding locations can be found in *Babilonia*, the monthly gay magazine, and in their annual bilingual *Italia Gay Guide* (10,000 lire from most news-stands).

● Don't rely on the Italians you meet to be carrying a condom. Although there is more AIDS prevention awareness than a few years ago, some still take the risk. The percentage of homosexuals with AIDS or found to be HIV-positive is, with Spain, the lowest in Europe (less than one in five), but that is obviously no reason not to take precautions. (→ VIII, 2:iv)

● Cruising hours, like other less furtive social events, tend to observe meal-times. As for *lo struscio* (→ II, 6: ACCESS – Street life), cruising areas are very busy between 7 and 8 p.m., but almost totally deserted between 8 and 9.30 p.m. Especially in summer, they can be remarkably busy until well

of the unavailability of women, especially in the South, and the proximity of Arab culture are often cited as contributing factors, but the fact remains that parks, porno cinemas and station lavatories all over Italy are regularly frequented by happily married, or *fidanzati*, men looking for members of their own sex.

All-important is the alibi – 'I was just passing'; the peculiar thrill of transvestite prostitutes is contained in the possibility of pretending not to 'realize'. 'You mean, you're actually a boy?' is the stock phrase used by clients, who get off on their own faked innocence. Money and ambition play a central role. A surprising number of young Italians from poorer central and southern Italian families doing their military service will become rent boys, just to keep themselves in cigarettes, and to pay for their constant long-distance calls home. The former MP and writer Alberto Arbasino, in one of his many homoerotic novels, *Fratelli d'Italia*, estimated that the best way to a young man's body was through his stomach: he recounts how in the 1960s Roman boys would do anything in exchange for food – the important thing was to get them into a restaurant. He now laments how the post-1968 generation, by bringing words like homosexuality to formerly unknowing ears, inhibits the one-time innocent distribution of sexual favours: before, they wouldn't have known what the word meant. This sexual generosity has been written up as avidly by generations of Italian and foreign authors as it has been sighed over by generations of would-be beneficiaries.

The victims of the casting couch are as often men as women in Italy, since the alibi 'I'm doing it to get ahead in my career' constitutes the perfect justification to even normally homophobic men. Whereas in most countries men are either gay or straight, with an increasing tendency to opt for an openly gay lifestyle, in Italy the opposite is true. Few homosexuals come out openly, but far, far more men occupy a shady middle ground. Sexual inclinations, like most other things in Italy, are negotiable.

Italian society has an ambivalent attitude to homosexuality. While at a family level it is considered a serious misfortune (70% of mothers interviewed on the subject defined such a discovery about their son *una disgrazia* – a catastrophe), at other levels a general benign tolerance or indifference is displayed. Apart from such gay-intensive fields as fashion and the media, Italians remain remarkably relaxed about people in high places being *frocio* – gay. Many politicians, among them three recent prime ministers, are well noted for it, with a blind eye being turned even to one former Prime Minister, still a prominent Cabinet Minister, who is extremely blatant in his promiscuity (he sends his chauffeur out cruising for him in his official Cabinet car). In common with heterosexual escapades, gay sex scandals never break into the papers: the public don't want to read about it, and can never understand why the British or Americans do. Even visibly homosexual Italians live with a self-imposed ghetto mentality: they will never tell their parents, who in most cases would throw them out of the house, and thus usually pretend to have girlfriends. Even those old enough to be economically independent still maintain the pretence for the sake of family peace.

The Italian gay rights movement FUORI, founded by Angelo Pezzana in Turin, the city where gay life most resembles that in other countries, has been fairly active since the mid-1970s. FUORI (which as a word means 'outside') have had fairly close links with the civil liberties orientated Radical Party. Their work is not easy, since Italian gays are so attached to the closet mentality, where the whole idea of 'coming out' and 'gay dignity' is missing. Italians have always been very upfront about some things, but very evasive about others. The key concept has to be 'ambiguity', and being mysterious, but not discreet, about it. The idea of ambiguousness, of 'now you see it now you don't', has become the central theme of Italian homosexuality. The newspapers use the term *ambiguo* as a synonym for gay. Although until 1986 or so, gay discos or clubs (which are very thin on the ground anyway, for reasons which should now be clear) weren't even mentioned in newspaper listings, now a gay watering hole is referred to as *un club ambiguo*. Indeed, when you are there, it is rather ambiguous: an innocent abroad could be forgiven for mistaking it for a straight discothèque, with so many *froci* being accompanied by their girlfriends, who provide moral support; also, most Italian gay punters go to considerable lengths in order not to seem the slightest bit interested in anyone outside their group of friends. Contrast this with the explicit stares that even straight Italian men cast each other in the street. The street is a neutral context, allowing glances to be open to interpretation, while an explicit environment like a gay club robs the glance of its essential ambiguity. So fiercely observed is this rule that most boys go home alone from gay discos. There is also a degree of narcissism involved: like all Italian males, they have been convinced since childhood by their mothers that they are *il ragazzo più bello del mondo* – better looking than any one else – and thus don't feel inclined to lower themselves by talking to a stranger, still less by having sex with him.

into the small hours. Although there have been various cases of homophobic violence, and even murder, in recent years, it would be an exaggeration to say that cruising in Italy is physically dangerous. The police make occasional raids, demanding to see identity cards or passports, but rarely do they take the matter further. Usually, they drive around cruising spots for a bit, apparently motivated more by idle curiosity than by a desire to give those present a hard time.

4. Friendship and social relations

(i) *Stare insieme*: hanging out

Unlike the Anglo-Saxon elective view of friendship, for many young Italians there is no question of choosing friends: they feel instinctively part of a *Gestalt* situation. *I Ragazzi del quartiere* – the kids on the block – will form *la comitiva* – the gang – with whom the young Italian will spend most of his or her leisure time outside the home. They don't usually actually do anything, except hang out together – *stare insieme*. In fact, almost the sum total of the Italian concept of friendship is summed up by the phrase *stare insieme*. Especially among the young, whole evenings are passed by a *comitiva* assembling: a car-load passing from house to house (never going in), and waiting outside for the friend to come out. Phone-calls, 'getting ready', arguments with family, may make this a long wait, especially if the group is large. They are not going anywhere, to do anything special; they are just 'hanging out'. The notion of meeting for a specific reason (other, of course, than *stare insieme*) hardly exists. Young Italians don't meet to see a specific film, or go to a specific place; the evening or afternoon just unfolds. Planning often wrecks the atmosphere.

Adults plan a bit more – whether meeting friends for meals out, or going to the cinema (much more of a tradition than in Britain), playing cards at home, or going for an ice-cream (drinking out has almost zero importance, though self-conscious 'pubs' have some appeal). (→ VII 2:i) Older people have *circoli*, like clubs for bowls or similar, though older women usually have no social life at all outside their family, apart from in country or southern areas, where they get to sit out in the street a lot. But few have much spare time, since they live with their families, and in Italy a grandmother's work is never done.

It is unusual among teenagers or young adults to go out in twos; the group is usually obligatory. You would rarely see two girls eating out together; they would either be in a pack, or with their boyfriends. One to one friendships are equally rare, particularly among teenagers. While Anglo-Saxons tend to construct friendships as a family substitute, Italians do not see the family as an institution that can be substituted for. So while it would be normal in Britain or the States to celebrate Christmas with friends (or at least to invite some round to the family home), in Italy this would be unthinkable. '*Natale con i tuoi, Pasqua con chi vuoi*' – 'Christmas with your family, Easter with anyone you like' – is a popular Italian expression.

Dealing with friends

- Italian friendships are the opposite to Anglo-Saxon ones. The latter take a long time to get off the ground, but once they are consolidated will last through thick or thin. Young Italians are socially promiscuous: they seem to make friends with almost everyone they meet, but all that effusiveness is misleading; as with one-night stands, you tend not to see them again. If they do phone you, don't expect it to last. The chances are that if they passed you in the street two days later, they won't remember ever having met you. Out of sight is out of mind. Don't be offended, it doesn't mean they suddenly don't like you; it's just that there are lots of other pebbles on the beach.
- On the other hand, don't be shocked at how straightforward Italians can be about making personal remarks. If they don't like how you are dressed, they will probably tell you, in front of others. They are not being rude just frank.
- Don't feel indignant about being exploited. Literally and metaphorically, fairweather friendships are all part of the game, so no one takes it to heart. It is interesting how many more calls you get from your *amici* in summer, if you have a car (especially a convertible), or you or your parents have a swimming pool, a boat or a nice beach-house. Do the same yourself.

Making social appointments

Whether it is fresh acquaintances or real friends who say it, *ci vediamo/ci sentiamo* – let's see/speak to each other soon – really means a generic 'see

(ii) Breaking the ice

Italians are famous for being born communicators, for talking loudly and at length, and for gesticulating a lot. This is all basically true, though it varies a good deal from place to place, and from person to person. Apart from getting involved in the intricacies of the Italian language (which it is not the aim of this book to do), there is something to say about trying to communicate in the most basic way. Unlike the Americans, the British and the French, who always expect everyone else to speak and understand their language, the Italians have no such pretensions, and are generally perfectly happy to speak/be spoken to in English or French, or whatever they may understand. Communicating with Italians in sign language and grasping at the odd word is not the embarrassing experience it might seem; they will participate, and encourage one wherever possible. It sounds obvious, but there is a certain essentialness in communicating in Italian, which other languages don't allow: English is too quirky and understated. The explicitness of Italian, irritating in other areas, comes in handy for basic communication.

you around', even when it is qualified by a time reference – *stasera, domani, fra qualche giorno* – this evening, tomorrow, in a couple of days. This can be confusing when it refers to an apparently specific appointment (*facciamo qualcosa/ usciamo insieme/ andiamo al cinema/ andiamo a mangiare una pizza* – let's do something/ let's go out together/let's go to the cinema/ let's go out for a pizza) since it signifies only being generally well disposed *at the moment of saying it,* not any real intention to respect the appointment; if you want it to come off, you are expected to *telefonare per una conferma* – phone to confirm it. Standing people up – *dare buca* – or being outrageously late for a meeting is not considered a reason to get annoyed.

Talking to Italians

• As in French and most other languages, there is a basic verbal distinction between the intimate second person *tu* form, and the more formal *lei,* which also means 'she' (Mussolini tried to abolish *lei* because he thought it sounded too effeminate, and to impose the use of the plural *voi,* now common only in the South). *Lei* is even more formal than the French *vous,* and hence the Italians drop it much more quickly. The existence of two 'you' forms, however, constitutes a formidable psychological barrier, which has to be overcome every time, each form imposing a different code of behaviour. Italians get round it often by saying, '*Diamoci del tu*' – 'Let's use *tu*'.

• The degree of intimacy alters the form of greeting you use. On meeting people for the first time in formal and some informal situations, you say *piacere* – pleased to meet you; only in strictly informal situations do you say *ciao*; a common substitute for both situations is to use your name as a simultaneous greeting and identification. To be formal, you use your full name, or just your surname; among friends, just your first name

• On subsequent meetings, you use *buon giorno/buona sera* – good morning/ good afternoon/evening – to say hello, and *arrivederci/arrivederla* (the latter is slightly more polite) to say goodbye. Only if you are on *tu* terms, do you say *ciao*, a slightly more formal version of which is *salve*. If you are under 40 (and thus still *un ragazzo*), older people with whom you are on good terms (e.g. parents of friends) will often say *tu* and *ciao* to you; you are obliged to continue using *lei* and formal greetings to them, unless they specifically tell you not to. You never say *ciao* with the *lei* form, but as a foreigner you will be excused if you forget this basic rule.

• Italians tend to greet strangers far more than Anglo-Saxons do, including people passed in the *palazzo* or the office lift and shop assistants in a family-run shop. Depending on the time of day, you say *buon giorno* or *buona sera* for both hello and goodbye. Use *ciao* only if you are addressing a much younger stranger – say, under 18; otherwise, it sounds rude or patronizing.

Physical greetings

Except between very close friends, it is normal to shake hands, particularly for men and mixed couples. Women very often kiss, as from the farewell of their first meeting. On subsequent meetings, they will usually continue to kiss. In central and southern Italy, it is normal for men to kiss each other as much as they do women. Sometimes this is a touching display of genuine affection; often it is more of a ritual than a spontaneous gesture, as it is between women and mixed couples. The degree of warmth of greeting is also subject to the occasion – it is more likely to take place before/after major absences/departures, or in exciting, eventful or unexpected situations (like at big parties, when it is nice to be able to show that you know someone, or bumping into someone in a different city or abroad). Very often, Italians make a token effort of kissing, touching cheeks (particularly between women, when carefully applied make-up may be at risk), and quite often kiss and shake hands at the same time, as if they aren't sure which gesture is the more appropriate. Italians kiss socially on both cheeks, but never three times, like the French, or on the lips, like Russian politicians. Recently, the rather rhetorical gesture of kissing a lady's hand has made a surprising comeback.

Social etiquette

Every country has its own rules. Italy's are often diametrically opposed to Britain's, even though among most upper-class Italians *la buona educazione all'inglese* – English good manners – is still considered the rule. Sometimes a slight difference in the circumstances (e.g. age group, class background, amount of people present) dictates apparently contradictory behaviour. While they are very tolerant of some things the British find offensive, there are other areas where most Italians find Anglo-Saxon manners overly casual, unfriendly or downright mean.

• *Fare complimenti* – standing on ceremony, or putting yourself out excessively for others – is often the rule. As in certain oriental countries, the more people tell each other not to *fare complimenti*, the more they do. This almost obsessive generosity or hospitality derives from the concept of *bella figura*, and takes various forms.

When you are invited to dinner, it is common practice to take very expensive presents: shop-bought frozen desserts or cakes, an expensive bottle of spirits (e.g. single malt, never blended Scotch – Italians are great whisky snobs), or showy flowers that would look very overstated in Anglo-Saxon countries; among friends, a bottle of reasonable wine will do.

After an evening together, it is also expected that anyone who has a car should offer to drive all the other guests (particularly the female ones) home, even if they could easily afford a cab.

If foreign guests are staying, Italians will often put themselves out to an extraordinary extent to show their guests around, and are frequently upset when on the return visit to London or wherever they don't get the same effusive treatment in return.

• On the other hand, certain habits frowned on in traditional or contemporary British etiquette aren't considered particularly rude, or rude at all. All the following are acceptable:

Smoking without asking permission, even at the table while others are still eating.

Not standing up for women, or making them walk on the outside of the pavement.

Not taking off your shades when talking to people or when indoors.

Being late for appointments, or bringing along uninvited guests to parties (some people even do so to dinner parties); gate-crashing parties of complete strangers; not taking a bottle to an informal party.

Not ringing up or writing to say thank you to your hosts afterwards.

Allowing children to create a disturbance in public.

• Certain things that are considered quite acceptable in Anglo-Saxon countries are considered *brutta figura* – go down badly – in Italy.

Getting drunk and rowdy in any circumstances, especially in restaurants: public school-type food fights are abhorred, as is burping or farting.

For adults (but not necessarily for *i ragazzi*), being shabbily or inappropriately addressed at social functions.

Being socially reserved, i.e. not looking people in the face when you are talking to them, not saying hello or shaking hands with people you have already met in social situations, or not introducing friends of yours who don't know each other.

Meanness, e.g. giving overly modest presents, or none at all, for weddings, birthdays, etc.

---

5. Pets and treatment of animals

Because of the intense relationship the Italians have with children, it goes without saying that they have traditionally had little need for animals as child substitutes. However, there has been a big pet boom in recent years. A lot of it has to do with social status: having a dog fits in with the craving for all that is English-looking, and thus prestige-giving. Dogs' names are more often than not English. The relatively cramped nature of most Italian city dwellings, and the Italian obsession with domestic cleanliness, leads many Italians not to bother, and to discourage children from keeping tortoises, hamsters and so on: Italian education does not stress the practical virtues of animal husbandry as much as the British does.

There is a great vogue among the *nuovi ricchi* for keeping guard dogs like Alsatians and Dobermanns, many of which are badly treated. As in France, there is also a tendency to abandon dogs when going off on holiday, though this seems to be declining as a result of an energetic TV advert campaign over the last few years. The tradition among *contadini* – peasant farmers – of shooting small birds during the hunting season is also highly controversial in Italy. There have been numerous attempts to have it banned. (→ II, 2:i) Apart from these cases, it would be unfair to say that Italians treat all animals cruelly: most Italian cats are wild, but are demonstrably happier that way. Little old ladies feed them *pasta* left-overs the way British ones feed the sparrows with crusts of bread.

6. Snobbery and class distinctions

The class system is now almost non-existent in Italy. A kind of money-based meritocracy is nearer the mark. It is difficult to tell most people's class from their accents, since they are almost always regional only, and people from all classes tend to have the same regional accents. One of the few verbal class indicators is the Roy Jenkins-type soft 'r', for which the members of the Agnelli family are famous, and which is sometimes even affected by others.

Although Italy is a republic, in which aristocratic titles do not officially exist, there is a curious degree of interest in the subject. Even the official phone-directory publishes full titles of its users: they are treated as a rare species, and cherished. Occasionally, exceptional events like the Prince and Princess of Wales's visit in April 1985 spark off incredible storms of royal lust, and all the soi-disant aristocracy barge in for invites.

Even the most apparently left-wing Press frequently run breathlessly acritical social commentaries on high society affairs that make Jennifer's Diary seem anti-establishment; but the tone is very much Hollywood glitterati meeting the Queen. As in France, the doings of Britain's royal family, and to a lesser degree those of other countries too (but above all Monaco), are of constant interest to the burgeoning collection of glossy gossip magazines. The important difference is that, as with the extremely widespread Italian habit of dressing up like an English gent (the David Niven clone), it is all just a game of let's pretend.

On the other hand, commenting negatively on a fellow Italian's social position is one of the most common insults: possibly because there is no really deep-seated sense of superiority involved, it is also often light-hearted. *Cafone, buzzurro, burrino, coatto* have varying nuances of meaning, but all suggest badly behaved plebeians. The class-conscious British could never allow themselves such a luxury.

Work or study titles

While we use only Doctor as a work title, in Italy they use Lawyer/*Avvocato*, Engineer/*Ingegnere*, Architect/ *Architetto* and Accountant/ *Ragioniere*, among others. *Dottore* is an appellative term for anyone with a degree, or who looks as though he's got one; it is used on letters the way 'Esq.' is in English, and is used in formal business situations when introducing people. *Professore* or *Maestro* is used for anyone with a white beard and a suit! The former may apply to a humble school teacher used as an appellative; used with the name, it indicates the same as in English. The latter term is promiscuously applied to anyone over a certain age who is involved in the arts, often quite without merit. Often, leaving a handsome tip in a bar can get you called *Dottore*, or, if distinguished-looking, *Commendatore* or *Cavaliere*. In theory, these last are State-given titles (abbreviated as *Comm.* and *Cav.*) and are similar to the MBE or OBE. *Onorevole* (abbreviated *On.*) indicates an MP.

7. Happiness and alienation

How happy are the Italians? To the more sanguine
Northerners, they seem constantly in good spirits,
though according to surveys they are considerably
less content with their lot than most other peoples,
including the British. Much is connected with a
sense of expectation, linked to economic progress and
development.

Television has had a fundamental role in defining
the artificial reproduction of feelings. Adverts and programmes for young people continue to put across an
almost hysterical degree of joyfulness at all times: this
seems extremely false and contrived to foreign eyes, as
indeed it is. Feeling or looking happy is thus more of a
self-imposed cliché than it is a reality.

On the other hand, the closeness of families, and
the social acceptability of letting off steam in most
situations, tends to cause a long-term stability of
feelings, with a consequently low suicide rate. Italy
has the lowest in Europe, although there has been a
50% increase between 1974 and 1987. 70% of suicides
are male. In 1987 (the most recent available ISTAT figures),
4000 Italians took their own lives, 1500 of them old-age
pensioners – 1071 of them men, 429 women.

One of the inevitable consequences of 'moderniza-
tion' in Italian society is the increasing *emarginazione*
– alienation – of the old. While it is still far more common
to live with one's children than in Britain or America,
more and more elderly Italians are finding themselves
on their own. In their 1989 report on the condition of
the elderly, ISPES discovered that while the majority of
old people were in relatively good health, their ability
to cope with loneliness, especially among elderly men,
was very limited.

People over 65 living alone:
Denmark   **44%**
USA   **40%**
Italy   **19%**
but 25% of Italians over 75 live alone.
(DOXA, 1989)

Isolation is not restricted to the old. In Turin, which
certainly has a more North European lifestyle than
most Italian cities (one in five official residents –
some 169,000 people – live alone), a 1989 survey

conducted by the Centro Studi Pannunzio discovered that some 29% of Turinese of all age-groups admitted to 'being lonely': three-quarters of them saw the TV as their only company, while less than a quarter were members of any club or social group. The Turin helpline for the lonely – *il telefono amico* – calculate that well over a third of the 100–150 daily calls from desperate Turinese are made by 16–30-year-olds.

8. Communicating by letter and by telephone

How to use the post and phone

● The only prompt postal system in Italy is on foreign territory. If you are in Rome, make the effort to get to the Vatican post office in St Peter's Square. Their delivery record for abroad is excellent (three to four days for Europe, overnight for New York); their hours are convenient (they close at 7 p.m., Sats 6 p.m.; PTT closes 2 p.m., 12 p.m. Sats). Prompt delivery.

Otherwise, the only slight remedy is to post your mail from the nearest main train station: this may take a few days off the long wait.

● Confusingly, there are now five quite different kinds of phone in service, including two mutually incompatible types of phone-card, but apart from at airports, motorway service areas and stations, they can hardly ever be found anyway. Newer, more user-friendly phones, which actually take two different kinds of coin, are now replacing those taking the traditional *gettoni* – phone tokens. To use these *gettoni*, you need to ask at a bar or shop: they currently are worth 200 lire and are grooved on both sides. They can be used as regular coinage too.

The short-change shortage (the real emergency finished in the mid-1970s) means that many bars are reluctant to give you *gettoni* unless you use the phone in their bar, so they can fish them out later (quite legal).

Two of the worst institutions in Italy are the SIP telephones and the Poste, Telegrafi e Telefoni (PTT) – the post office: ironic, when one thinks how communication-orientated the Italians are.

Their tariffs are expensive, among the dearest in Europe; their service is the slowest and most unreliable. There are still horror stories about sacks of letters recovered after twenty-five years, or men arrested for evading military service, when their call-up card arrives fifteen years late. Although the service varies according to the season, as a rule of thumb, a local letter will take three days, across the country a week, and abroad (say to Britain) between a week and a fortnight. There is no satisfactory explanation for this, except that the Italian postal system has not been reorganized since the 19th century. Also, there is no evening collection (by far the biggest load). It has been calculated that the average Italian postal worker finishes his work in less than half the time for which he is paid – the system is already vastly overmanned. Express and registered letters take as long as regular post, the only difference being that they are distributed by a different postman (at vast expense to the State). Apart from the irritation caused to private correspondents, for businesses it is crippling. For this reason the Fax machine is opening undreamt of new horizons in Italy, as are the *motorino*-back Pony Express riders.

The phone system is much better in some respects: there are fewer damaged cabins than in Britain and many more of them. Most bars have one, and are obliged by law to let anyone use it, although frequently it has *guasto* – out of order – written on it. Where the phone system is disastrous is in the home: it can take two years to get one, and weeks to get it serviced. Local calls are no longer flat rate, but they are still cheaper than in Britain, though long-distance calls are now the most expensive in Europe.

Italian postal workers should work 1600 hours per annum. On average they do only 730 hours; the telegram man does a mere 295.
(PTT)

Postal efficiency: letters arriving in 24 hours in 1988

Denmark	95%
Germany	77%
France	67%
Austria	55.5%
Italy	0%

(*Harpers Magazine*)

In fifteen years, the PTT workforce has risen by 60% to 240,000; since 1980, productivity has decreased 20%. The average letter takes: Milan to Rome, eight to fifteen days; Milan to Cagliari (Sardinia), twenty days.

(*Il Messagero Survey, 1989*)

Prefix of Direct Dialling, Postal Code and Car Number Plates

	1	2	3
Agrigento	0922	92100	(AG)
Alessandria	0131	15100	(AL)
Ancona	071	60100	(AN)
Aosta	0165	11100	(AO)
Arezzo	0575	52100	(AR)
Ascoli Piceno	0736	63100	(AP)
Asti	0141	14100	(AT)
Avellino	0825	83100	(AV)
Bari	080	70100	(BA)
Belluno	0437	32100	(BL)
Benevento	0824	82100	(BN)
Bergamo	035	24100	(BG)
Bologna	051	40100	(BO)
Bolzano	0471	39100	(BZ)
Brescia	030	25100	(BS)
Brindisi	0831	72100	(BR)
Cagliari	070	09100	(CA)
Caltanissetta	0934	93100	(CL)
Campobasso	0874	86100	(CB)
Caserta	0823	81100	(CE)
Catania	095	95100	(CT)
Catanzaro	0961	88100	(CZ)
Chieti	0871	66100	(CH)
Como	031	22100	(CO)
Cosenza	0984	87100	(CS)
Cremona	0372	26100	(CR)
Cuneo	0171	12100	(CN)
Enna	0935	94100	(EN)

Phone manners

● Business numbers usually reply with their name, or else use the generic social reply '*Pronto?*' Be prepared for the slightly curt '*Sì?*' or even '*Chi è?*' – Who is it?' – from private users. Not uncommon are people *calling* who ask you who you are, though this is rude by most Italian standards too.

● Since the standard after-6 p.m. tariff doesn't come in in Italy until after 10 p.m., it is not considered too rude to call long distance before say, 11 p.m., especially further south, where meal-times and bed-times are generally later.

● Most Italian city networks are truly appalling: expect 10% incidence of wrong connections and crossed lines. Predictably, the Party-Line novelty doesn't seem terribly attractive to Italians.

● In common with the tradition of generous hospitality, should you use an Italian's phone – even if frequently – it is highly unlikely that they will ever take up your offer to pay for your calls.

● Note that Italian area codes indicate geographical position: 1 is North, 9 is South, which is useful for pinpointing where you are calling merely from the number.

Ferrara	0532	44100	(FE)
Firenze	055	50100	(FI)
Foggia	0881	71100	(FG)
Forli	0543	47100	(FO)
Frosinone	0775	03100	(FR)
Genova	010	16100	(GE)
Gorizia	0481	34170	(GO)
Grosseto	0564	58100	(GR)
Imperia	0183	18100	(IM)
Isernia	0865	86170	(IS)
L'Aquila	0862	67100	(AQ)
La Spezia	0187	19100	(SP)
Latina	0773	04100	(LT)
Lecce	0832	73100	(LE)
Livorno	0586	57100	(LI)
Lucca	0583	55100	(LU)
Macerata	0733	62100	(MC)
Mantova	0376	46100	(MN)
Massa	0585	54100	(MS)
Matera	0835	75100	(MT)
Messina	090	98100	(ME)
Milano	02	20100	(MI)
Modena	059	41100	(MO)
Napoli	081	80100	(ND)
Novara	0321	28100	(NO)
Nuoro	0784	08100	(NU)
Oristano	0783	09170	(OR)
Padova	049	35100	(PD)
Palermo	091	90100	(PA)
Parma	0521	43100	(PR)
Pavia	0382	27100	(PV)
Perugia	075	06100	(PG)
Pesaro	0721	61100	(PE)
Pescara	085	65100	(PS)
Piacenza	0523	29100	(PC)
Pisa	050	56100	(PI)
Pistoia	0573	51100	(PT)
Pordenone	0434	33170	(PN)
Potenza	0971	85100	(PE)
Ragusa	0932	97100	(RG)
Ravenna	0544	48100	(RA)
Reggio Calabria	0965	89100	(RC)
Reggio Emilia	0522	42100	(RE)
Rieti	0746	02100	(RI)
Roma	06	00100	(ROMA)
Rovigo	0425	45100	(RO)
Salerno	089	84100	(SA)
Sassari	079	07100	(SS)
Savona	019	17100	(SV)
Siena	0577	53100	(SI)
Siracusa	0931	96100	(SR)

Sondrio	0342	23100	(SO)
Taranto	099	74100	(TA)
Teramo	0861	64100	(TE)
Terni	0744	05100	(TR)
Torino	011	10100	(TO)
Trapani	0923	91100	(TP)
Trento	0461	38100	(TN)
Treviso	0422	31100	(TV)
Trieste	040	34100	(TS)
Udine	0432	33100	(UD)
Varese	0332	21100	(VA)
Venezia	041	30100	(VE)
Vercelli	0161	13100	(VC)
Verona	045	37100	(VR)
Vicenza	0444	36100	(VI)
Viterbo	0761	01100	(VT)

1. **Direct Dialling Code. Low Numbers (1/2) in North, 8/9 in Far South.**

2. **Post Code – *C.A.P.* (Codice D'Avviamento Postale).**

3. **Car No. Plates / '*Sigla*' – Abbreviation for filling in forms (use brackets) (i.e. car nos are two letters – for filling in forms and posting address in full, you must use brackets).**

'Roma' is for cars; (RM) is for forms.

Other car plates: EE – foreign licence
CD – diplomatic corps.

Il paese: the country

Chapter I observed the Italians in the intimacy of their own homes and their close relationships; this chapter focuses on how the Italians relate to the world outside – their fellow citizens, and their physical environment – and on how they organize local government. The previous chapter highlighted the tensions of *biculturalism* in close relationships; Chapters II, III, IV and V consider this dichotomy in terms of Italian national life. The Italian love of emphasis has led too many commentators, both Italian and foreign, to overrate the importance of regionalism, and too many Italians to feel obliged to act this out. Television has its part to play in this.

Naturally, the persistence of regionalism and 'neo-folklore' also has a historical perspective. Rightly or wrongly, many Italians make a great deal of their collective past, and feel that history legitimizes some of their present attitudes.

Macro-relationships in Italy do not have the same degree of warmth as do intimate ones: *campanilismo* – regional chauvinism – is frequently less a question of harmless rivalry than of domestic racism. And if it is true that Italians are great xenophiles (→ Chapter III) when it comes to industrialized nations, in the late 1980s Italy suddenly discovered itself much less tender towards Third World citizens.

This chapter also deals with many aspects of Italian daily life in the street, its natural context. Obviously, more goes on outdoors in warmer climates, but the current obsession in colder countries for street culture generally accords the Italians special honours. The prominence of street culture also derives from a specific historical fact: the city has always, far more than in other countries, been Italy's central unit of administration. Consequently, the urban mentality and traditions of town planning are deeply engrained, even though Italy has yet to experience its first real modern metropolis. Included, too, in this chapter is the section on transport, intimately connected to the life of cities.

The importance of the visual in Italian life is another theme touched on by other chapters, but which gets most treatment here. Visualness is something the Italians have always excelled in, and towards which the rest of the world has only quite recently expressed a greater degree of attention. The two main aspects dealt with here, in relation to the environment, are beauty and upfrontness. Italy is famous for both its natural and its artistic beauty, of which its inhabitants are justly proud (*il bel paese* – the beautiful country – is a frequently used synonym for Italy itself); how they actually treat their country is another matter. Similarly, the visual intensity of Italian daily life, which so overwhelms foreigners on first impact – from the strictly immobile (Baroque architecture) to the way people walk down the street – seems to represent the triumph of the explicit, of style over content. It seems logical that this extreme approach to what you see should have a corollary: the glorification of furtiveness (→ Chapter V). It seems legitimate sometimes to wonder whether all this theatrical upfrontness isn't just a façade – what goes on backstage?

Understanding road-signs and graffiti

- **Road-signs that are irritat-**

1. City outlines

Italy's history and its collective psychology are intimately linked to the history and topography of its ingly difficult to see, because they are too small, or in too obscure a position, are commonly found in many countries. Italian major roads and *autostrade* seem specially designed to confound the visitor: places will be signposted only once, at about 50 metres before the actual turn-off, so calculated that you invariably miss them.

• Street-names are usually large, and engraved on fine marble slabs, but are so placed that you cannot see them from a car: they are second-storey level, and are only on one side of the road.

• *Senso unico*: one-way – go up it if there are no *Vigili Urbani* – traffic cops – around.

• *Passo carrabile anche di notte* (a blue disc with a red diagonal line through it on city drive/gateway access): if you park in front of this sign, you will get your tyres slashed – try it and see.

• *Aperto/chiuso*: open/closed.

• *Guasto*: out of order, generally seen in bars, on public phones or lavatories. This may often just mean that the bar owner doesn't want you to use it.

• *Divieto di/vietato*: forbidden (usually *fumare/ingresso/ sosta* – to smoke/entry/parking): do so at your discretion. Injunctions like this are seen laterally in Italy.

• *Vendesi/affittasi*: for sale/ rent – printed notices in fluorescent colours to be found on walls and windows of *palazzi*, and, occasionally, on car windows. (→ I, 1:ii)

• Shop-signs: spot the disconcerting pseudo–English shop-names, generally literal translations of Italian idioms that mean nothing in English – e.g. a chain of butchers called 'Pork's House'; 'La Casa del Maiale' is fine in Italian though. Shops will announce *no stop* rather than

cities. Phenomena like regionalism and *campanilismo* date back to Roman times and the Middle Ages, when Italian cities were built on hills where possible, and surrounded by fortification almost always, to repel marauding bands and invading armies. Because of the high standard of architecture and the robust quality of construction of pre-industrial Italian cities, *i centri storici* – the old city centres – remain the visible core of the modern Italian city. During the period (17th–19th centuries) in which other European countries were busy modernizing their city layouts, Italy was too poor and disorganized to do so. (→ 2:i, below). And by the time it became capable of doing so, architectural conservation values had been added to those of urban pride to prevent any similar dismemberment, though an honourable exception must be made for Mussolini and his ambitious urban renewal projects. By the same token, the intense building speculation that filled the city centres of so many other European cities with disproportionately tall buildings has always been confined to the *periferia* in Italy. Central Rome, in common with most other Italian cities, has not one building taller than nine storeys – the average is six. Few buildings are much less than this, since the Italian town-planning spirit has always been (like the French, but quite contrary to the British one) intent on creating a certain sustained density. There may be a relative lack of green spaces, but you always have the idea of being in a town, not a pseudo-village. Italian cities have always been allergic to the notion of garden suburbs, though prolonged exposure to the US TV product has stimulated a certain demand for Los Angeles-inspired luxury private estates.

The heart of the Italian city, *il centro storico*, is defined as the area *dentro le mura* – inside the city walls – and is mostly made up of pre-1860s architecture. Depending on political and economic factors, post-*Risorgimento* building – known as *umbertino*, after the reigning monarch – may begin inside or outside *le mura*. *I centri storici* are then divided into boroughs, known variously as *rioni*, *contrade*, or *borghi*, according to city, and are generally identifiable by ancient wall plaques, including the borough's all-important symbol. (→ 3:iv, below).

There are several reasons for the dilapidated look of so many ancient buildings. Partly, it is due to the shortage of cash: as with its ancient monuments, so with its architecture, the Italian State has an enormous heritage to preserve, so much that even more efficient application of conservation funds would do little more than make a dent. Where the buildings are privately owned, the problem is more often a complicated bureaucratic tangle: there are very stringent by-laws governing restoration and maintenance of listed buildings, and it frequently takes years to get co-owners of a listed *palazzo* to agree, and then get the permits from the Belle Arti – the municipal buildings commission. One noticeable exception to this is the city of Rome, where over 70% of the centre's centuries-old 83,000 buildings have *never* been restored. Not surprisingly, some 18,000 of these are considered *interessato di degrado* – a polite way of saying in need of serious repair. In 1987, major legislation was passed (emphatically entitled *Roma Capitale*), providing billions of lire to completely refurbish the entire *centro storico* in time for the 1990 World Cup games, in order to give the city the appearance that visiting Italians and foreigners alike think it should have. At the time of writing, the result is already dramatic; by the time of completion it will completely have transformed the capital. Other Italian cities are naturally irritated about having, indirectly, to foot the bill (→ III, 2:i).

The modern areas – *i quartieri nuovi* – outside the *centri storici* are in three distinct phases: *umbertino*, *fascista*, and post-war, the first of which is invariably based on a post-Haussmann concept of urban layout, in contrast with the cheek-by-jowl construction of the old town centres. The architecture during the Fascist period (→ VII, 5:i), whether of the more Le Corbusier-influenced rationalist variety, or the more bombastic totalitarian sort so artfully lampooned by Osbert Lancaster, is now being reassessed in an ideology-free context. About time, too, since it produced some of the most memorable architecture in Italy, in both public buildings (railway stations, post offices, law courts) and private housing. The post-war building boom led to the construction of vast estates of relatively anonymous *palazzi* in the *periferia*. Much of this building was *abusivo* (→ V, 1:v) – illegal – and resulted in poorly constructed housing with zero social amenities in the neighbourhood. Since these *palazzi* rarely reached over ten storeys, and housed low-income families recently arrived from the country, Italy has not witnessed a socio-architectural debate of the sort that has been raging in Britain over the last decade or so. What remains a generalized complaint is *la mancanza di strutture* (→ IV, 3:iii) – lack of amenities – which is often far worse than in Britain: green space, bus routes, shopping facilities and so on. Whole areas exist around some cities, like Rome, that have no legal existence at all: they are called *le borgate*, and they exemplify all the shortcomings listed above. Pier Paolo

non-stop opening hours.

● Graffiti: Italian motorways are embellished every 10 kilometres, over the entire national network, with the slogan '*Dio c'è*' ('God exists'). Quite evidently the work of one hand, which must have been very busy over the years.

W or *M*: means *Viva*, or the opposite *Abbasso*, something: '*w inter*' is not a commemoration of the invernal solstice but a tribute to Milan's second football team. (→ VIII, 4:ii)

Sede PCI/MSI written on public lavatories/rubbish skips: witty, if overused, political jibe. *Sede* means party headquarters, the initials corresponding to a party, usually the Communists or the neo-Fascists. 'Rosso' and 'Nero' ('Red' and 'Black') refer to the opposite ends of the political colour spectrum, and usually qualify an area; a city might be 'Bologna Rossa' or 'Prati Nero' – the sub-text is, Watch out if you're on the other side.

One is constantly surprised at how well-written much graffiti is, apparently the work of a professional calligrapher. It used to be colour-coded, too, with left-wing groups using only red sprays, right-wing extremists only black. Since the late 1970s there has been a marked decline in standards.

Looking for public lavatories

There are notoriously few in Italy, though recently some of the French-style pay ones (200 lire) have been installed. Usually, one goes into a bar and asks to use theirs. By law, the bar owner is obliged to let you use it, however reluctantly. (See *guasto*.)

Notice that in some places, men use the street itself, while mothers frequently hold their small children over street drain grids.

Pasolini featured them heavily in his work, doing much to sensitize public opinion in a country where there is no serious equivalent to British council housing, or the French HLM (the *case popolari* project has never taken off), but despite much political rhetoric, little has been done.

Until the mid-1970s, property prices were very reasonable (most Italian middle-class families managed to invest in several apartments until the mid-1960s), but since then they have begun steadily to rise. However, they are still considerably lower than those in other comparable European cities. This largely explains why, until recently, *i centri storici* housed a vast quantity of low-rent housing, low-turnover corner shops and artisans' workshops. Only since the mid-1980s has the boom in service industries and mass consumer retailing forced them into *la periferia*, obliging most Italian cities to undergo that crisis of identity that other European cities faced generations ago (→ I, 1:ii). The newspapers are full of earnest debates about whether *i fast food e le jeanserie* (hamburger joints and cheap casual clothing stores) should be allowed to revolutionize the urban fabric. The Rome-based designer Valentino's heavily publicized crusade against the nearby Piazza di Spagna McDonald's branch lasted a year and ended in defeat.

Mussolini's rhetorical views on architecture created the precedent for peripheral mega-developments. West of Rome, towards the coast, is the extraordinary EUR (now pronounced as a word, 'Ay-your', but it once stood for Esposizione Universale di Roma; it was intended as the site of Mussolini's world fair, planned for 1942) development, an unfinished futuristic township that was intended to reach the coast, some 18 kilometres away. He had originally planned to build a heli-port in central Rome, but was deflected by this less destructive plan. *Il comune di Roma* is trying to copy his idea, by building the enormous SDO (Sistema Direzionale Occidentale) project, designed to relocate a major part of the offices currently overcrowding the centre (45% of the capital's jobs are located in central Rome's 2.6% ground space). The plan has been on the drawing board since 1962, since when it has been overtaken by Naple's almost completed, but already rather dated looking, Centro Direzionale, along the lines of Paris's La Défense, and magnate Silvio Berlusconi's Milano 2 and planned Milano 3.

2. The environment

(i) How much Italians care

One of the most disconcerting aspects of modern Italy is the way in which the land itself is treated so appallingly, something that seems all the more peculiar in a country which is so proud of its considerable natural beauty. Surprisingly, the reason for this is largely contained in the initial premise: it is precisely because Italy boasts such incredible natural and artistic beauty that its citizens treat it so badly. Italians tend to think that their country is so beautiful overall that the odd illegal rubbish tip, the occasional eyesore block of flats built without planning permission (→ V, 1:v) won't do too much harm. Unfortunately, too many Italians have reasoned in this way, for too long.

An oft-quoted simile which the ever self-critical Italians use to explain their perverse relationship with nature is that they are like a bunch of spoilt children who inherit a large, beautiful house, and, not knowing how to run it, let it fall to rack and ruin, burning the furniture for firewood, smashing the windows with footballs and so on. This is unfortunately all too apt as a broad description, but it bears breaking down into the various contributing factors.

The first factor is socio-economic, and has its roots in the mid-19th century, when industrial societies like Great Britain and the United States, and, slightly later, France and Germany, were undergoing mass urbanization. This didn't take place at all in Italy until the post-war period, when it coincided with the pan-European reconstruction phase, thus causing a veritable explosion of urban migration and rapid building projects. Despite the extremely severe by-laws that govern all Italian historical city centres, mass construction outside these centres was subject to no such obstacles. In the twenty years following the war, most Italian cities tripled in size, making multi-millionaires out of many *palazzinari* – unscrupulous construction magnates responsible for thousands of ugly blocks of flats – and creating what can only be called a rape-the-land psychosis.

Not to be outdone, millions of individuals followed suit, building smaller but no less aesthetically unacceptable homes, while the State turned a blind eye. This alarming contempt for the land is most evident in southern Italy, with its larger peasant population: the often miserable livelihood to be eked from the land seems almost to guarantee the ill-treatment of the latter by those who perceive themselves as unfortunate, egged on especially by the constant visions of consumer

Italy's most polluted beaches

● Be warned, most Italian beaches are now too polluted to swim at. You may see plenty of people crowding them, but very few will actually be swimming. Those that do avail themselves of the cold showers generally available nearby, no longer to wash off the salt, but the scum.

● Areas never to swim at (don't think of consulting the local tourist authorities: they are naturally loth to tell the whole story, for fear of losing your custom):

80% of the mandatory industrial water-purifying plants that have been installed throughout Italy are calculated not to work, so always avoid industrial or built-up areas.

Almost the whole of the coast of Campania: the once classic bay of Naples is now the uncontested capital of marine pollution, followed by the bay of Salerno, most of the once limpid Calabrian coastline, and northern Sicily.

The resorts near the port of Genoa and most of Liguria.

The Adriatic coast, particularly around Rimini, Riccione and Pescara, which now plays host to vast sheets of algae.

The north Adriatic area between Venice and Trieste, particularly near the ports.

● Areas that are still clean:

Swimming pools along the coastline, as in California.

Deserted stretches of the southern coastline in Calabria, Apulia, Basilicata.

Sardinia – the best place in Italy, but consequently the car ferries are all crowded. Italians book ahead, from February, in order to get a place.

Smaller islands, like Capri,

Ponza or Lampedusa.
Offshore, from a boat or yacht.
Some of the posher resorts
keep the sewage pipes at bay:
Portofino in Liguria, Argentario,
Forte di Marmi and Viareggio
in Tuscany, parts of the Amalfi
coast in Campania.

well-being so prominent in Italy. A large majority of the
forest- and bush-fires that destroy such large tracts of
the Italian countryside – not to mention wildlife – each
summer are the work of disgruntled shepherds and
peasants, greedy for insurance payments or sustaining a
belief that the advantages of burning stubble are greater
than those of destroying trees and wildlife.

Another factor is the residual contempt, common to
many Italians, for central government, and the related
demand for almost total individual liberties. Millions
of Italians perceive it as their inalienable right to litter
the countryside with building detritus (a car journey
through Tuscany may well yield more abandoned white
porcelain lavatories than medieval churches) or to exter-
minate entire species of small birds in – and out of – the
hunting season. The Italian hunting lobby is extremely
powerful (it regularly fields candidates at local elections,
and even wins), but unlike its British counterpart it represents an almost exclusively working-class habit. Apart
from the grotesque incidents of accidental shootings,
the damage it causes the eco-system is considerable.
There have been various, so far quite unsuccessful,
attempts to hold national referendums on the subject,
supported by the quite sizeable portion of Italian public
opinion that is sensitive to ecological issues.

However, ecology and environmentalism have a far
from solid base in Italian society: the Ministero della
Protezione Civile – the Ministry for Public Safety –
and the Ministero dell'Ambiente – the Ministry for the
Environment – are both recent governmental creations,
but are effectively deprived of any real power. Since its
inception in 1981, the latter was mostly run by the very
capable Giuseppe Zamberletti, until 1987, when he lost
his job to a far less able and scrupulous man in a power-
play Cabinet reshuffle, just when he was directing sal-
vage operations after a major landslide disaster. Perhaps
indicative of an evolving public consciousness towards
such matters was the nationwide outcry of indignation
that followed his dismissal.

Unfortunately, *ambientalismo* – environmentalism –
has also become trivialized by high society connotations. If the World Wildlife Fund is associated elsewhere
in the world with earnest schoolboys (and older animal-
lovers) saving their pocket money to help protect endan-
gered species, in Italy the WWF (pronounced Voo Voo
Effay) is of recent constitution, and until recently was
largely the preserve of the jet set. Its social occasions are
among the most sought after in Italy, and few Milanese
grandi signore would think twice about donning their
best furs to go to its annual ball. As ecological issues
became more serious, so did the Italian WWF, who

have now become an influential lobby group: their demands for 100 million lire to save Italy's national parks (including marine ones), which they calculate as a mere 0.01 of GNP, or 1700 lire per head, seem much more likely to be taken seriously than they would have been a few years ago.

Another symbol of Italy's relatively superficial approach to ecology is represented by the RAI 1 programme *Quark* and its presenter Piero Angela. The programme consists almost entirely of British-made (or at least, non-Italian) nature documentaries dubbed into Italian, with Angela's role being merely to introduce them. Yet, curiously, Angela is treated in Italy as some kind of ecological Messiah.

Government environment expenditure (in billion lire)

1986	**340**
1987	**570**
1988	**1830**
1989	**2237**
1990*	**2700**
1991*	**2986**

(La Stampa)
*projected

The principal ecology party (there are currently several), the Greens, were constituted in the mid-1980s as an analogue to the German party of the same name, from whom they imported everything wholesale, from name and logo to ideology and tactics. They were instrumental in sponsoring the highly emotional post-Chernobyl anti-nuclear debate, a bargaining card since used by other, less ecologically minded, parties. Although there is little original thought, and not a little factiousness, among the Italian Green parties, their collective vote if they were to unite would make them the fourth largest party (IV, 2:ii)

There are several other active organizations, such as the *Lega Ambiente* and *Italia Nostra* who have a fairly respectable fighting record. Although *la Lega Ambiente*, with the help of the Italian State railways, recently set up an agit-prop style train which toured the country to propagate their cause, the prevailing cynicism of an economico-political system that pays nominal lip service to ecological values, but then ignores them, makes a tricky sparring partner.

Although Italy boasts of having easily overtaken the British economy (VI, 1), it is far less well equipped to tackle the environmental problem. According to a 1989 report by Turin's *La Stampa*, the turnover of Italian firms involved in this field was only £3 billion a year, against the UK's £4.5 billion and West Germany's £9.5 billion.

In 1989, the Ministro dell'Ambiente, Giorgio Ruffolo, proposed an ecological tax on manufacturing industry, but it remains to be seen whether it will be implemented, particularly since no accurate system of measuring major polluters seems to have been introduced. Similarly, while you can take a catalyser-fitted car to a lead-free petrol pump, you can't make it drink: in April 1989 each of the *regioni* was legally obliged to install a fixed quota of lead-free pumps on their territory; out of the 36,000 service stations in Italy, only a small percentage have bothered. This indifference is largely due to the scandalous foot-dragging of the oil companies, who nonetheless declare themselves in favour. As it is, almost no Italian motorist uses *la benzina senza piombo* – lead-free petrol – considering it an eccentricity for German tourists. There has been no government or media campaign in favour of its widespread use, largely because it doesn't suit the interests of Italy's powerful automobile lobby. The Fiat group, who now account for 64% of national car sales, cannot be accused of not doing their homework on pollution reduction. They have even won a prize in Germany for it, and have low pollution versions of all their models ready for the home market. It's just that these models are not being marketed, or even publicized, in Italy.

Italy's most polluted cities

● **Naples and Palermo: worst noise pollution (Naples average 50–60 decibels, with a maximum of 80 decibels outside Loreto Hospital; maximum permitted limit, 30 decibels; emotional/psychic damage starts at 65 decibels).**
● **Bari and Regio Calabria: highest carbon monoxide rate (maximum permitted, 30 milligrams per cubic metre; Reggio Calabria, 22 January 1988, 41 milligrams per cubic metre). (Lega Ambiente)**
● **Rome: sulphur dioxide, nitrogen dioxide, carbon monoxide, all ten times the maximum limit. (Comune di Roma Health Dept)**

Rubbish recycled 1987: Switzerland, 90%; USA, 70%; Italy, 15%.

The dubious sincerity of big industry and government in fighting pollution in Italy (although Fiat estimate that they invest 1200 billion lire annually on environmental research) is reflected in the attitudes and behaviour of the public at large. While there is widespread sympathy for Greenpeace's activities, and approval for marches and the inevitable *tavole rotonde* (→ IV, 3:ii), the Italian consumer is evidently not ready for German-style practical measures, like paying extra to reduce car exhaust pollution, or accepting less efficient, but less harmful, washing powders: Italian detergents have the highest concentration of chemicals in the world. (→ VIII, 3:i).

(ii) Urban pollution
Urban pollution, especially in cities like Rome and Naples, has long surpassed rates considered unacceptable elsewhere. In the capital, most ancient monuments are now under wraps to prevent them from being eaten away completely. The dangerously high pollution rates have prompted many cyclists to wear Tokyo-style face-masks for practical and rhetorical purposes. In a one-off protest move, the *Vigili Urbani* – traffic police – in Rome and Milan did the same, and received a severe reprimand.

The effects of pollution and severe traffic problems have prompted several of Italy's largest cities to do what they should have done years ago: ban cars from the narrow, overcrowded roads of the city centres. Despite energetic protests by shop-keepers, and widespread attempts at evasion, the move has received general approval. Bologna started with some success in 1986; Milan followed suit in 1987; Rome and Florence in 1988. Working on different timetables, they ban non-service traffic from the *centri storici* during the working day. Exceptions are made for certain privileged citizens (politicians, journalists, doctors), who can obtain a special entry permit; naturally, there is an illicit traffic in these. Naples started a rival experiment in 1983, called *le targhe alterne* – allowing number-plates with alternating odd/even last numbers into the centre – in order to halve traffic. It proved impossible to enforce, partly because most Neapolitan families have more than one car (thus making it more likely that you have both odd and even number-plates), but mostly because so many Neapolitan drivers simply chose to ignore it. However, *le targhe alterne* has been taken up by the authorities of the nearby Amalfi coast with much greater success – there is only one through road to monitor.

(iii) The rivers and the sea
There are a number of contrasting annual or seasonal reports monitoring water pollution; the most ludicrous

is the pre-glasnost Soviet-style one issued annually by the Ministero della Sanità – the Ministry of Health – supposedly based on statistics gathered the previous year. This goes hand in hand with the government decision to put back until after 1992 the EC directive reducing the permitted amount of phosphates in detergents from 2.5% to 1%. Although there theoretically exists legislation to prevent the large-scale dumping of sewage into the sea in the vicinity of bathing resorts, the frequent presence of enormous pipes, with the consequent brown, froth-filled water around them, provides clear, or murky, evidence that few local authorities respect the law.

In the summer of 1989, the tourist season on the Adriatic coast was effectively ruined (numbers were down by 64%) as a result of the mass invasion of vast stretches of it by a slimy mass of algae, the direct result of heavy industrial pollution washed down the River Po from the factories of Lombardy. The government knew about the risk from the beginning of the year, but chose to do nothing, hoping that the algae would simply go away. As a result, Italy's balance of trade figures for the summer months, usually nicely fattened by holidaying German Marks and Austrian Schillings, registered an enormous drop, while the estimated costs of dealing with the mess spiralled as the algae proliferated, John Wyndham style, month by month. Since this crisis, many German and Austrian travel firms have taken to issuing their own independent assessments of Italy's coastline.

Half the world's sea traffic passes through the Mediterranean, with over 2 million tons of crude oil spilled. The River Po contributes some 20,000 tons of phosphates, as well as some 150,000 tons of assorted other metals, oils and fertilizers.

---

3. Regionalism and the sense of tradition

(i) A collective affectation

When Italians want to break the ice, they ask each other where they're from. As with the Indians, much pride and detail goes into the answer: it all matters a great deal. 'I consider myself Roman really, because I grew up here, but my parents say I'm Turinese, because I happened to be born there, but then again I'm really a Southerner, if you think that my mother is from Calabria, and my father's family have lived in Puglia for generations. . .'

Much is made of your accent: people in Italy like to be reassured by being able to place it. And since accents are purely regional, not class-sensitive as in Britain, Italians are actively disappointed, almost suspicious, if your larynx fails to comply with your region of origin – 'You're from Florence, are you? But you don't have the accent!' (→ I, 6) This is a lot like questioning a chap's assertion to have been to Charterhouse because he's not wearing the old school tie at the time.

The Italian sense of humour, especially that of media comedians, depends almost exclusively on regional sensibilities: local behaviour and accent, either as expressed by a 'real' local or as parodied by another. Homogenizing TV culture has succeeded not so much in creating a national sense of humour as in rendering different regional ones accessible to a nationwide audience. Thus Roberto Benigni exists essentially as a Tuscan comedian, Massimo Troisi as a Neapolitan, Renato Pozzetto as a Milanese. Apart from their relative skills as performers, they are liked by Italian audiences because they offer highly recognizable stereotypes: if it's not regional, it's hardly funny. Purely 'Italian' comedians are, as a result, very rare. (→ VII, 4:iv)

Every society seems to have its particular seismic line, as if the burden of totally homogeneous nationhood were too much for its inhabitants to cope with. Splitting into rival camps seems to endow everyone with a sense of identity: the Byzantine Empire tried to keep the punters happy with its Blue, Green and Red parties; Britain notoriously persists with the class system; Latin countries with that exaggerated division into enemy camps of the sexes. By the same token, Italy clings to the outlived notion of regionalism – a

What is still regional in Italy

● **Banking:** lots of even small towns still have their own bank, with no more than one office. Inter-bank transactions are hence complicated. (→ 6, 4: ACCESS Dealing with banks)

● **The Press:** each major city has its own daily newspaper, usually owned by local business interests. As in the USA, there is no tradition of truly national newspapers, although the Milan-based *Corriere della Sera* and the Rome-based *La Repubblica* have gradually built up a more nationwide readership. (→ VII, 7:ii)

● **Television:** by analogy, private stations set up in the 1970s were obliged to have a local constitution; every major city still has dozens of them, which can only be picked up in the immediate vicinity. (→ VII, 6:i)

● **Criminality:** the three main organized criminal associations are still very strongly linked to their respective southern origins; elsewhere, organized crime enjoys far less power and influence. (→ V, 2:iii)

● **Religion:** although Christianity is almost totally synonymous with Catholicism, and despite the proximity of the Vatican, it has flourished along almost autonomous lines in different areas of the country, reflecting local tradition (→ VIII, 9:i)

● **Cuisine:** in a sense, Italian cuisine does not exist; there is only a series of regional cuisines. A Sicilian restaurant in Milan, or a Sardinian *trattoria* in Rome is in a way as 'foreign' as an Italian restaurant in London. However, an Italian abroad, if pressed, would wish to take credit for all 'Italian' cuisine, rather than just that of his/her home region: regional chauvinism is fine when it suits you. (→ VIII, 1:i)

• Accent and dialect: although Tuscan has been considered the most literary version of Italian since the time of Dante and Boccaccio, its purest form, Florentine, didn't become the official tongue until reunification, despite the early 19th-century efforts of writers like Manzoni. (→ VII, 7:i) Despite this, some modern writers still contrive to write in dialect. For all the reasons already stated, most Italians prefer the idea of keeping something of a regional accent, rather than adopting the inflectionless form used by most RAI announcers. (→ III, 2:i) The family use of dialect has, however, steadily declined over the last ten years, with those talking exclusively in dialect diminishing from 51% to less than 40%, and those speaking only Italian at home rising over the same period from 25% to 35%. Outside the family home, those who generally or always speak Italian reaches 46%. (DOXA)

What is truly nationwide in Italy

• The State apparatus: despite the strength of regional politics, the power and influence of central government – what in Italian political jargon is known as *il palazzo* – has been paramount since the *Risorgimento*.

• Transport: the existence of a highly sophisticated motorway network, a serviceable national railway and internal air service has created, despite Italy's geographically inconvenient shape, real accessibility. (→ 7, below)

• The economy: although rationalization has occurred much later than elsewhere, a large degree of Italian commerce increasingly now operates a nationwide distribution

kind of territorial Linus's blanket. It is as though to be simply Italian were too vague a notion for existential comfort.

But while the British basically feel uncomfortable about maintaining their rather anachronistic national demarcation lines, the Italians positively revel in the conceptual and conversational possibilities of theirs. Since a great deal of the historical *raison d'être* of regionalism has vanished, it is not just a neutral, accessible topic of common interest, like the British rambling on about the weather, but more a question of talking oneself into believing something, like a textbook neurotic New Yorker whining on about the state of his psyche. Thus Italians may spend a whole evening discussing the differences, say, between an Emiliano and a Romagnolo – both inhabitants of the same region, Emilia-Romagna. What distinguishes this form of navel contemplation from the classic American form is that it postulates the collective: it is not so much the 'ME generation' as the 'WE generation'. Because the collective affectation of regionalism is so massively adhered to, it occurs to few Italians to question its validity. Even less so to foreigners, who see in it the Romance of the authentic, the 'real Italy'. No one in Italy would seriously think of contradicting a Neapolitan's assertion that their reluctance to pay taxes was directly traceable to centuries of Bourbon misrule; but if an Australian were to justify being drunk and disorderly by virtue of being of English convict descent, he/she would be laughed out of court. Italian logic seems to admit a sort of historical *droit de seigneur* unthinkable anywhere else in the world: no one expects a Norwegian to be partial to rape and pillage just because his presumed ancestors were warfaring Vikings.

Indeed, this argument seems to fall flat on its face at times: despite the extraordinary degree of pride demonstrated by the self-proclaimed heirs of the Seat of Empire (other Italians call it *arroganza*), modern-day Romans have the greatest difficulty in adapting to the type of metropolitan mentality their ancient forebears are widely credited with having invented.

So what are these historical events that have been so convincingly freeze-framed for centuries? A much condensed résumé of Italian conventional wisdom would run more or less as follows. From the downfall of the Roman Empire in 410 until the *Risorgimento* – the process of reunification achieved in 1870 – Italy was divided up into myriad pieces, frequently under the control of invading powers, and generally hostile to each other. However much the presence of these foreign rulers may have infuriated their involuntary subjects, something of their lifestyle always rubbed off. North-eastern Italy (Lombardy and the Veneto) remained strongly influenced by the administrative techniques of the Austro-Hungarian Empire, as did the peoples of southern Italy by those of the originally Spanish Bourbons, who were seen off by Garibaldi only in 1860. Rome represents perhaps the most extreme example, with its clearly demarcated pedigree stretching back past a millennium and a half of papal rule to the foundation of the Roman Empire. This Lamarck-inspired world-view also includes a consciousness of ethnic line-of-descent that would put the Shah of Iran's to shame. Romans are invariably *della settima generazione* – of the seventh generation (never sixth, never eighth – one wonders how they actually know) – just as Umbrians will show you, in all seriousness, their unaltered Etruscan profiles, and just as Southerners have their sexual elasticity, ascribed to the influence of the ancient Greeks, when southern Italy formed part of *Magna Grecia*. It is all rather as though Margaret Thatcher were to claim the legacy of Boadicea. In other words, it is not so much the historical facts that are important as the way the Italians perceive them.

However, there is no doubt that until 1870 Italy was certainly more fragmented than any European country except Germany. One contributing factor was undoubtedly bad communications – ironic for the country that gave the world Roman roads. Hindered either by geography (the Appenines), by lawlessness or by politics (the Papal States in particular thrived on the tenet of 'Divide and Rule'), the circulation of people and ideas in pre-*Risorgimento* Italy was far more limited than in strongly centralized countries like Britain or France. While depriving Italy of the chance of having an all-encompassing capital city, like London, Paris or Vienna, it led to the establishment of culturally autonomous, politically self-sufficient entities which survived, despite their respective varying fortunes, from 410 until 1870. Although the whole of Europe had more of a shared cultural identity up until the 16th century than it does even today, Italians like to see the existence at that time of these independent administrative poles within the geographical borders of Italy as the more salient fact.

The gap between the more centralized nations and fragmented Italy was further compounded in the 19th century, as the various phases of the Industrial Revolution brought Northern Europe rapid transit systems with the railways, and later with metalled road networks. Italy's administrative and industrial backwardness caused it to miss out on these benefits until much

network.

● **Corruption: whether involving political mega-scams, or modest *bustarelle* – bribes – for personal *raccomandazioni* – string-pulling – there is relatively little difference between South and North. (→ V, 1:iv)**

● **Television: the three State-owned RAI channels, and latterly the three privately-owned Fininvest channels, have largely succeeded in completing Garibaldi's work: creating a true Italian culture. The fact that similar age/interest groups all over Italy like the same programmes is ample proof of this. This nationwide homogeneity is tinged with a sort of crypto-regionalism: the Rome-based RAI and the Milan-based Fininvest channels have succeeded in subtly implanting many of the attitudes and sensibilities of their respective cities of origin into their programming. Particularly in the case of the former, the new *romanizzazione* implies an often visible bias: most man-in-the-street interviews or snap polls involve people with audible Roman accents, expressing characteristic Roman cynicism or *disinvoltura* – easy-goingness; media personalities expressing an opinion on football are invariably in favour of *la Roma*; many TV presenters, even non-Romans, use typically Roman turns of phrase. (→ III, 2:i)**

● **Sport: especially with football, the appeal is of the same intensity all over the country, though differing terrain means that cycling may enjoy more support, both as an active and a spectator sport, on the plains of the Po in Emilia-Romagna than in rocky Lucania.**

● **Youth culture: in terms both of consumerism (not only the imported Timberland 'n' Hamburger model, but also the** home-produced variety, from pop music to clothing) and of attitudes (as seen in a CENSIS 1986 comparative survey on the young in Syracuse in Sicily and Trieste in the North), there is a remarkable degree of uniformity.

• Personal attitudes: although a certain number of traditional attitudes and habits (particularly moral ones) remain regionally based, there are many more that are common to all Italians, including 'xenofilia', the often unconditional approval of all that comes from other First World countries; 'perbenismo', moral and consumer keeping up with the Joneses; and 'hygiene mania', the massive attention dedicated to personal and domestic cleanliness – the vast amounts spent on toiletries and cleaning products undergo little regional variation. (→ VIII, 3:i)

more recently, when it caught up with a vengeance. (→ 7, below) Indeed, Italy theoretically has by now almost all the attributes of a functional, centralized modern State, which relegates the significance of regionalism to a question of tradition and of social attitude, strongly encouraged by the media and local politics. (→ 4, below) The strongly regional flavour to some areas of the economy is a result of the widespread habit of family-run businesses, local political patronage (→ 3:ii, below) and an age-old reluctance to rationalize.

(ii) Local government

Parallel to central government in Italy are three articulated tiers of local government. In theory, all three are elected simultaneously for a five-year term of office, though on occasion, unresolvable *crisi* oblige mid-term elections. Although there is evidence of regionalist phenomena and personal feudal power bases at all three levels, local government is surprisingly homogeneous throughout the country, being under the close scrutiny of the Party HQs in Rome.

Population and density

Italy's population is slightly larger than Britain's. On January 1989, there were 57,504,691 Italians, 105,583 more than the previous year.

Italy covers a surface area of 301,000 km2
UK covers a surface area of 244,000 km2

Italy	190 persons per sq. km.
UK	232 persons per sq. km.
EC average	143 persons per sq. km.

The vast amount of corruption in Italian public life often reaches its squalid zenith at these three levels, since the balance between the quantity of government funds available for spending and the degree of effective watchdog controls allows the scales to tip well into the area of unbridled dishonesty.

The three tiers are as follows:

(a) *Il comune* – the town, or local council: like the two higher levels, these generally operate on the same system of coalitions as central government, since the plethora of parties rules out any possibility of an absolute majority for any one party. (→ III, 3:v) Following (not before, as would seem more logical) elections, coalitions are formed, with the post of *sindaco*

– mayor – not always going to the largest local party. *Il sindaco* presides over *la giunta comunale* (like its Spanish homonym *junta*, the word simply means council, far from the 1960s/70s media connotations), assisted by *gli assessori* – the councillors – who have specific responsibilities. There is an overall tendency to follow the same five-party national coalition, but a combination of strictly local issues and personality clashes often makes a nonsense of this. As a rule of thumb, the chance to rule, rather than political coherency, is the main criterion.

Quite often, extraordinary anomalies occur as a result of specific issues, especially in the South, as with the several PCI–MSI (Communist–Neo-Fascist) coalitions in Sicily that were thrown together against Mafia infiltration among the other local parties. Paradoxically, it is in the smaller rather than the larger *comuni* that the national parties are often less keen to impose their will, since an unorthodox but charismatic local party boss is certainly more useful than a loyal but unconvincing one. Also, since it is at local level that the cruder episodes of vote-buying through *raccomandazioni* and *tangenti* – bought favours and rake-offs – take place, they are best left to figures easily shaken off in case of public outcry. The same is not true for the larger cities, where the national parties think nothing of using each and every *municipio* – town hall – as pawns in their overall national strategy. Although their object is to place their man as *sindaco*, party bosses far prefer obvious puppet figures to powerful satraps. (Compare this to Jacques Chirac's Paris power base, or the late Gaston Deferre's feudal empire in Marseilles. Socialist leader Craxi thought nothing of dumping the immensely popular and efficient Carlo Tognoli in favour of his sister's less than impressive, though loyal, husband, Paolo Pilliteri.)

Rome's famous left-wing *giunta* (PCI–PSI plus the *partiti laici*) was replaced by a *pentapartito* – five-party – one in 1985. But if the 1976–85 *giunta di sinistra* was inefficient, the 1985–9 *pentapartito* has been an unmitigated disaster. (The Socialists are unperturbed: their long-term ambition is to place a Socialist in the Campidoglio – Capitol Hill – instead.) But Rome is nothing in comparison with Naples, where it is rare for a *giunta* to last for more than a few months. In the summer of 1989, seven out of the dozen largest cities (Bologna, Turin, Florence, Rome, Naples, Palermo and Catania) were *in crisi*, or governed by *una giunta anomala* – an oddball council.

(b) La provincia – province: the Italian provinces resemble in size the English or American county, but differ from them (with the partial exception of the shire counties) in that they are *il capoluogo* – the local capital

– which gives the territory around it both its name and its *raison d'être*, rather than vice versa. Obviously, *la provincia* is supposed to administer those things that *il comune* doesn't, though in effect they have responsibility only for the roads and transport. Although it sometimes appears to be the least prominent of the tiers, it is often the most evident.

Each of Italy's ninety-four *provincie* has a two-letter *sigla* – sign – which is most noticeable on car numberplates, preceding the numbers (Rome, typically, is an exception, with its whole name shouting at you from the bumper). It is equally evident on post-codes, and official documents like driving licences and identity cards. In this way, all Italians, and especially the police, can tell at a glance where people are from; in the case of the latter, this can take on a rather sinister dimension. (→ V, 3) In administrative terms, *le provincie* are just a good example of bureaucracy existing in order to preserve itself, since almost everything they do is duplicated by the other two tiers of local government; a good deal of their budget goes into sponsoring often costly cultural and other prestige projects, which are thought to further their good reputation. They are another example of hyperchoice, especially when they are headed by a *giunta* of a different political colour to that of the *comune* of the *capo luogo*. Proposals to trim their powers are, of course, indignantly rejected.

(c) *La regione* – the region: this is the largest administrative unit, and Italy is divided into twenty of them. Broadly speaking, they correspond to the dimensions of the historical states from which they take their name, and thus have resisted English-style rationalization. Tuscany is made up of some ten *provincie*, while neighbouring Umbria boasts a mere two. While most (fifteen) belong squarely to the mainstream of Italian history (this is evident from the familiarity of their names: Piedmont and Lombardy in the north, to Calabria and Apulia in the south), five of them are officially titled *regioni a statuto speciale*, indicating a semi-autonomous status justified by geographical or ethnic reasons. (→ 3:iii, below) Hence the regional assemblies of Sicily and Sardinia in the south, Trentino–Alto Adige and Friuli–Venezia–Giulia in the north-east and Valle d'Aosta in the north-west are more like parliaments, with wider ranging economic and administrative powers, though these may vary: Sicily, for example, has control of education, unlike the others.

A further decentralization of central government was brought about by a major reform in 1970 (though not fully ratified till the late 1970s), when such ideas were internationally in political vogue, and regional assemblies were set up for the remaining fifteen. The powers of *le regioni* have been subsequently modified; in theory, they have power over tourism, the promotion of industry, roads and transport, but above all health – most notably the highly controversial 1980 reform of the USL, the hospital and health-care system. (→ VIII, 2:i)

Like *le provincie, le regioni* are almost entirely funded by central government, which is convenient for the poorer southern regions, but less so for the richer northern ones, which end up footing the bill.

In 1989, major new legislation paved the way for the creation of five 'metropolitan areas' out of the *comuni* and *provincie* of the five major cities (Rome, Milan, Naples, Turin and Genoa), much along the lines of the Greater London reforms: this created several horizontal, borough-like, *municipalità*, instead of the previous two vertical tiers, giving far greater powers over local spending and restoring the power, removed in the 1970s, to raise taxes. The legislation is also designed to make it far harder to overturn the ruling *giunta* by creating unnecessary and problem-exacerbating *crisi locali*, as happened in Naples. The *provincie* in general were given greater powers, and many municipal departments were privatized. New *provincie* were created around cities that could claim 200,000 inhabitants in the vicinity.

(iii) Ethnic minorities and autonomy movements

(a) Trentino–Alto Adige has a significant portion of German-speakers, as a result of its annexation after World War I from the remains of the Austro-Hungarian Empire. The province of Italian-speaking Trento was liberated; that of Alto Adige was summarily annexed. In many ways, the latter province recalls Northern Ireland. Despite an active neo-colonial policy to populate it with ethnic Italians, the pro-Austrian lobby remains significant: the Sudtirol Volkspartei (SVP) is by far the largest party (34% in 1985 regional elections), backed up by a private militia in folk attire, the notorious Schützen (sharp-shooters), who are intent on putting the lead back into *lederhosen* (in their more pacific moments, they opt for spectacular pathos: they recently marched through the streets of Vienna carrying a gigantic crown of thorns on their shoulders, to the vast irritation of Rome), and by an undercover terrorist group who plant bombs, so far aimed only at the property of Italian-speakers.(→ V, 2:v–vii)

(b) Friuli–Venezia–Giulia has an even more complicated ethnic and political past, having been occupied by

the Austrians until the end of World War I, and subsequently taken over by the Italians, who to their immense chagrin lost the eastern flank to Yugoslavia after World War II. The city of Trieste was the object of a long territorial dispute with Tito's Yugoslavia, resolved only in 1954 after an interminable Allied military occupation. Although ethnically overwhelmingly Italian, Trieste conserves a Slovene minority which is also politically active. The *assemblea regionale* contains several ethnic parties (13.5% at 1985 regional elections), including l'Unione Slovena (1.2%), la Lista per Trieste (5.7%) and il Movimento per Friuli (4.3%). Italians generally admire the *friulani* for their steadfast courage and initiative in overcoming the disastrous earthquake of 1976, in contrast to the debâcle that followed the Naples tremor of 1980.

(c) Valle d'Aosta is a single-province region (with, incidentally, the highest pro capita income in Italy, which possibly explains why the francophone Unione Valdôtaine, which took, with its regionalist allies, 42.5% of the vote in 1985, advocates peaceful methods of flexing their muscles).

(d) Although Sardinia has always been part of Italy, the Sardinians, who in many ways resemble the British, advocate a semi-separatist movement, expressed in both the regional and national parliaments by il Partito d'Azione Sarda – the Sardinian Action Party (16% in 1985).

(e) Regional chauvinism is politically expressed in the northern regions by small political parties, which are increasingly successful in local elections: la Lega Veneta, la Lega Lombarda and la Lega Piemontese, with their various splinter factions, exploit indigenous northern resentfulness towards both immigrants from *il Mezzogiorno* and what they perceive as the big, corrupt government down in Rome.

(iv) The importance of being urban

In Italian history, the city-states have traditionally played the predominant role, with their vassal territories, however vast, always taking their name. The example of Rome should suffice to demonstrate the peculiarity of this tradition. (→ III, 2:i) While the Romans left most of Europe with a considerable urban heritage, it was Italy's rapid economic development, and more intense political and military struggles (→ 1, above) during the Middle Ages and Renaissance, that left it with a far denser network of sizeable towns, and a consequently much stronger concept of urban identity, than anywhere else on the continent.

In contrast to the tedious heartiness of *campanilismo*,

the deeply felt sense of identification Italians have for their city or town cannot but be admired. This feeling is underscored by the emphatic nature of the Italian language, which comfortably defines the inhabitant of any Italian town as a *cittadino* – citizen is too pale a translation; rate-payer, with all its 19th-century self-righteous, class-conscious connotations, is nearer the mark.

The Italian delight in endless observations about people *qua* inhabitants of a certain place is rendered possible by the existence of an apposite adjective for every city. This process would be almost impossible in English, hampered as we are with long circumlocutions like 'the inhabitants of Bradford' and 'people who live in Brighton'. Although most American cities offer their inhabitants a label (New Yorkers, Dallasites, Los Angelenos etc.), only in a few cases in Britain can we show the same urban sense of belonging (though, significantly, British public schools do).

This tendency is equally noticeable at official level, on municipal posters, which tend to announce things like, *'Il sindaco invita i romani '* or *'I napoletani salutano il papa.'* Of course, this process is not just verbal, but visual, too: each *comune* has its own insignia, a crest usually surmounted by a crown of bricks, symbolizing the all-important city status, and a flag. Every Italian city is thus full of visual reminders of its uniqueness – a corporate identity exercise designed to inspire the envy of the most aggressive American multinational. Everything, from street furnishings (the Queen, on her last state visit, was surprised to note that Rome still, after 2000 years, embosses its drainpipes and poster hoardings with the SPQR logo) to municipal buses and public buildings, is emblazoned with the medieval equivalent of modern-day designer labels stitched on the outside of garments.

Each city also has its *gonfalone* – banner – which is carried around after the mayor. In a nice mixture of periods and rhetorical styles, the official *gonfaloni*, recalling ancient Roman legionaries, are frequently to be seen accompanying the mayors of certain left-wing governed cities on occasions like anti-nuclear marches, a visual touch that cannot but compare favourably with the calculated boorishness of the 'Greenwich is a nuclear-free zone' genre of street-signs.

The mayors themselves have a curious, slightly frou–frou, badge of office, in marked contrast to the spurious Victorian–medieval mayoral chains of their British counterparts. They can be seen on the most solemn of occasions sporting a huge satin ribbon in the colours of the national flag tied in a big bow round their waists, worn over a regular business suit. The effect, especially on fatter mayors, is of an outsize mobile Easter Egg.

It is ironic that the country which so embodies the concept of urban consciousness should be devoid of any real metropolitan spirit. Although there are eleven *provincie* with over a million inhabitants (both Rome and Milan have over 4 million apiece), the feeling remains that of a much smaller grouping. Despite Milan's dynamic efficiency, it has the character of a provincial town, while Rome today is far nearer its Renaissance character (60,000 pop.) than its imperial one (2 million pop.), to judge by the lifestyle of its inhabitants, many of whom have arrived from the country since the 1950s. Despite its disastrous, run-down, state, it is Naples that has the most metropolitan atmos phere; Neapolitans would ascribe this to Naples having been a capital (of the Kingdom of the Two Sicilies) until 1860. There is something strongly reminiscent of the slightly paranoid, high-adrenalin New York lifestyle there.

(v) *Campanilismo*

The mania for regional differences does not end as a fight simply between Italy's twenty regions; in really competitive areas like Tuscany, it fragments down further, past provinces, towns, villages to borough level. Tuscany thus embodies the most extreme case of *campanilismo* – deriving from *campanile*, bell-tower, as in ours is taller than yours. This medieval form of urban chauvinism, which set individual towns at loggerheads with each other, remains an important concept for Italians. Certain cities hate each other on principal: Florentines are traditionally loathed by all other Tuscans, and especially the Sienese. Romans and Milanese have a deep-rooted sense of rivalry, meaning resentment by the Milanese towards Rome for being undeservedly the capItal, and for its lazy, happy-go-lucky, under-industrialized nature, and disparagement by the Romans for Milanese petty-minded, provincial officiousness.

(vi) Domestic prejudice and *il Mezzogiorno*

If *campanilismo* generally concerns rival adjacent towns or provinces, there is a form of real racial prejudice, between North and South, which seriously affects the country. The antagonism is theoretically mutual, with the Southerners calling their rivals *polentoni*, from polenta, the typically northern Italian, rather porridge-like, savoury dish, and the Northerners returning the compliment with the epithet *terroni*, from *terra* – earth – suggesting peasant. However, in substance, it is the considerably poorer, less socially and industrially advanced *Mezzogiorno* (the South) that gets all the stick. Taunts are of the 'Saudi Calabria' and 'Tunis, capital of

Sicily' variety, with a tradition of hostility stretching back many generations. Apart from the rather obvious Mafia digs, northern city walls all too often display crude hate graffiti: *'morte ai terroni'* and the slightly subtler, but more menacing, 'Forza Etna' (as in Mount Etna 1, Sicily 0). One interesting prejudice of the 1950s was that *terroni* who moved north didn't wash, but grew parsley in the bath tub, similar to the English middle-class suspicion of the 1930s that the working-class didn't wash either, and kept coal in theirs.

The *Palio di Siena* (2 July and 16 August) is an example of an ancient tradition that not only does not depend on the outside world for its survival, but actually tries to keep it out. Although Mussolini was instrumental in bringing this costume-drama horserace to the notice of the world, more recent would-be sponsors have failed miserably. Both Silvio Berlusconi and Luciano Benetton made offers they felt the Sienese could not refuse, but the *campanilista* Tuscans wanted none of it. In order to film the *Palio*, the RAI has to pay out a million lire to each of the town's seventeen *contrade* – boroughs – but they are not made to feel very welcome. No one could accuse the Sienese of being Mediterranean Morris Dancers – the genuine roots and authentic ferocity of the event preclude that – but they are not averse to exploiting its financial potential; touts sell grandstand tickets for up to £150 each, and street–traders offer the various *contrada* flags at inflated prices. The real winners of the *Palio* are the manufacturers of the rock-hard Sienese cake *panforte*, once an obscure local speciality, now marketed all over the country.

The problem has grown steadily worse since after the war, when there was the first truly massive wave of internal migration from the impoverished *Mezzogiorno* to the North, with massive cheap housing developments springing up around industrialized cities like Turin and Milan – *la periferia* literally means the suburbs, but in Italy indicates proletarian deprivation, not bourgeois respectability. (→ 1, above)

Turin's population in 1951 was 721,000; in 1961 it was 1,025,000, and in 1971 it was 1.2 million; in twenty years, 400,000 immigrants arrived, of whom 140,000 were from the South and Centre of Italy; the

others were from the province of Turin, the rest from other northern provinces.

Films like Luchino Visconti's classic *Rocco e i suoi fratelli* (1960) – *Rocco and his Brothers* – were set in the *periferie*, and ably recounted the urban alienation experienced by *terroni* who found themselves surrounded by *polentoni*. Southerners inevitably did all the jobs Northerners didn't want to do – exactly like the new Commonwealth immigrants in Britain, or North Africans in France. There are now whole generations of Southerners who have been born in the North, and yet who still often find themselves rejected by their home environment, and unable to relate to their ancestral one, when they return to visit. Then there are many older people, who attempt to resettle in their home town in the South after a lifetime's work in the northern factories. Over 100,000 have attempted this in the five years between 1983 and 1988, 35,000 alone from Turin. On returning to the South, they find themselves totally alienated from the people and environment in which they grew up, partly from being unable to readapt to local customs, and partly because of the resentful attitude of those who never left.

From time to time the media seize on spectacular cases, like the 1988 example of the twinned primary school classes between villages near Bergamo in Lombardy and near Agrigento in Sicily. After several exchanges of letters, a school visit from Bergamo to Agrigento was set up, but at the last minute was cancelled, because of the northern parents' protests. The rather plaintive letter written by the children to their Sicilian pen pals telling them the news became the most over-media-exposed piece of paper since the Hitler diaries; after several weeks of retractions, counter-accusations, and parallel inquests into the state of racism around the nation, the touching climax came on a RAI 3 News programme, with a ceremonial meeting in the studios between the two reluctant enemy classes, involving much hugging and kissing for the viewers at home.

How poor the South actually is

In a 1988 Bank of Italy report on the relative wealth of the 160 European Community regions, based on 100 as the average GNP pro capita income, Calabria came 155th:

Groningen, Holland	**237%**	**1st**
Hamburg, Germany	**195.5%**	**2nd**

Ile de France, France	159.5%	3rd
Greater London, UK	155%	4th
Val d'Aosta (top Italian region)	137%	10th
Lombardy, Italy	119%	20th
Calabria (poorest Italian region)	50%	155th

From 1950 till 1987 the South was aided by a special government development fund known as *La Cassa del Mezzogiorno*; it was then wound up, to be replaced by smaller, more specialized aid bodies. It has pumped trillions of lire into the *Mezzogiorno*, creating all the necessary infrastructures, such as roads, drainage and electricity networks and airports, and giving vast grants to industries of all size. Much of the money has been used for blatantly political patronage, and has finished in private hands. Not only corruption, but inefficiency and lack of an overall investment policy, has led to most of this enormous sum being wasted. The Catholic-inspired Christian Democrats have always opposed real industrialization in the South, for fear that this would create a more left-wing, urbanized, working class out of the traditionally devout, conservative, *contadini* – peasants.

After several years of a gradual reduction of the economic differences between North and South, SVIMEZ (l'Associazione per lo Sviluppo dell'Industria nel Mezzogiorno) – the government-funded agency to aid southern industry – calculate that the gap is widening again, largely because of the effect of the EC. Southern Italy feels left out. After 1992, even SVIMEZ's role will be abolished, and the South will depend entirely on the Community's Regional Development Fund for help. The Ministero per gli Affari Regionali – the Ministry for Regional Affairs – is worried that the *malavita* – organized crime – will increasingly monopolize daily life in the *Mezzogiorno*.

In 1988, GNP rose in the North by 4.2%, and in the South by only 3.2%. The productivity of a worker in the *Mezzogiorno* is only 74% (industry), 63% (agriculture) of the national average.

Il Mezzogiorno comprises 36% of the total Italian population but contains/produces:

Unemployed	52%
Employed	27%
Legal exports	7%
Tourism	17%
Bank accounts	21%
Telephone lines	26%

(SVIMEZ)

(vii) How Italians treat each other

By North European/American standards, Italians can appear startlingly selfish and anti-social towards others, since the premise on which Italian society is based stipulates mutual friendship and solidarity with people with whom you have intimate regular contact (the family model), but not with society at large, with whom, by definition, you can't. The North European concept means being civil to all in a disinterested way, irrespective of bonds of family or friendship. It is reasonable to observe that this tribal approach is intimately linked to the Mafia phenomenon. (→ V, 2:iii)

How Italians feel about others depends on the context: two *romani* who meet in a context that exalts their common *romanità* will immediately treat each other like old friends, hurdling all the intermediate stages of acquaintancehood necessary to, say, a Briton. But should one of them scratch the other's parked car, or find their wallet in the street, there is no natural impulse to do what we might call 'the right thing'. This reaction can be justified by the commonplace observation, 'They'd do exactly the same', which is indeed true. Although there are regional variants on this rule, it must be observed that Italian society as a whole does not work on mutual trust.

North about South: gradual improvement

	1976	1988
negative opinion	52%	39%
positive opinion	8%	10%
'Southerners are less educated'	6.6%	0.8%
'Southerners are backward'	57%	41%
'Southerners are generous'	31%	41%
'Southerners are intelligent'	27%	31%

South about North: generally lower opinion

	1976	1988
positive opinion	54%	47%
negative opinion	7%	13%
'Northerners are hardworking'	47%	54%
'Northerners are socially evolved'	52%	52%
'Northerners are practically-minded'	50%	39%
'Northerners exercise self-control'	42%	44%

4. Neo-folklore

The weakest point in Italy's otherwise fully justified claim to dignified modern nationhood is its morbid obsession with folklore. This is perhaps hardly surprising, seeing how the rhetoric of regionalism is still so dominant in Italian life. In other countries, traditional rituals have been obliged to adapt to the times in order to survive; the way in which the British royal family and its related pageantry have evolved to cater for television without losing their moral essence is a good example. Most industrialized countries, however, have left their folk traditions behind, to the point where people can no longer remember them. Britain's were lovingly recorded by earnest anthropologists before they disappeared completely, but although Morris Dancing may still occasionally be practised by consenting adults (usually bank clerks), it is done so more or less in private, because no one would seriously think of featuring it on television.

The same cannot be said for Italy, where the economic and social changes that other nations assimilated gradually over a century or so have been experienced as though on fast-forward in less than half that time. This has inevitably caused the strands of its peasant past to get caught up in the wheels of the television age. A whole series of rites and customs in their natural death throes have therefore been given an artificial lease of life – a fate that might have befallen Britain had Cecil Sharp been armed with a video camera rather than a note-book.

Folklore has become effectively nationalized, as well-known events like the liquefaction of S. Gennaro's blood in Naples Cathedral and *la Carnevale di Venezia* are no longer confined to a dwindling local cast but are now beamed to millions of armchair participants up and down the peninsula.

The presence of television cameras means that everyone in Italy can indeed be a star for fifteen minutes: all they need do is resuscitate a dying local ritual. The exacerbated *campanilismo* that comes across on screen is, like *Dallas*, very telegenic; the knowledge that other Italians are watching with interest means that the inhabitants of the town in question discover a renewed enthusiasm for the *rioni* or *contrade* in which they live, or for the folklore ritual being televised. The favour is returned, since the *idea* of authenticity provided by such visual events invests the artificial medium of television with a legitimacy which it gratefully accepts. Television's hunt for authenticity is a universal reflex shared by advertising. In Italy, this mania reaches

Folklore manifestations

Most of these folklore manifestations fall into three main categories, though they may not be what they seem. Fans of the authentic might wish to check out the details before making a pilgrimage anywhere.

● **Religious:** invariably dedicated to the Madonna or the local patron saint – *la festa della madonna/del santo patrono.* These often involve carrying effigies, sometimes in organized races. In southern Italy, these manifestations are often Catholic in name alone – the pagan element is overwhelming.

● **Historical:** commemorating some particular event of local significance. Like their British counterparts, they have usually been thought up in recent years, but are cloaked in spurious historical trappings for the tourist trade. Italy, with its vast architectural heritage, inevitably offers a tempting pretext for such initiatives.

● **Gastronomic:** *le sagre* are seasonal gastronomic feasts celebrating the harvest, or preparation of one particular kind of produce. They usually take place in small towns or villages with a specialist agricultural tradition. Some of them date back centuries, others have been thought up recently by a crafty local *ente del turismo* – tourist board. The extraordinary gourmandise of the Romans bears special mention: anything from the famous *fragoline di bosco* – wild strawberries – grown at Nemi to Italy's finest *carciofi* – artichokes – from Ladispoli warrant *una sagra*, where Lucullian feasts take place, to be recalled in great detail by the participants at subsequent celebrations.

extraordinary peaks with television commercials, particularly those for mass-produced food products such as biscuits, cheeses and wines, which are sold on an exclusively folklore pitch. The Ridley Scott/Hovis genre of nostalgia advert is given a sinister new twist, with an underlying suggestion, made without the slightest hint of irony, that these zombie-like peasants, their clothes and their customs still exist on some nearby time-warp plane.

These campaigns cunningly play on the *nostalgie de la boue* of many Italians, who have direct memories of a peasant upbringing, but have forgotten the poverty and oppression. Author Dacia Maraini, interviewed about her Sicilian childhood in Rome's *Il Messagero* in 1988, was critical of neo-folklore:

> Carnival had some sense when I was a child, when the peasant lifestyle was hidebound by rules and prohibitions, so that once a year it was necessary to let off steam, otherwise the rigid hierarchical social system would have collapsed. Now that we live in a society which parties non-stop all the year round, why bother with carnival? Now it's just commercial exploitation of folklore, or a contrived resuscitation of ancient values quite devoid of meaning.

5. Racism and *xenofilia*

The Italians have always passed as being very tolerant racially, and think of themselves as more friendly than the French or the British to foreigners from Third World countries. This slightly complacent attitude has recently been rudely shaken by a number of simultaneous events, sparked off by the furore generated by Le Pen in the 1988 French presidential elections. Le Pen's formal links with Italy's neo-Fascist (MSI) movement led to initial knee-jerk denials of racist policy by the latter ('contrary to Italian traditions'), followed by a general rethink: we try to emulate France in everything political – let's be racist!

A number of incidents of racial intolerance occurring in different parts of the country led *il razzismo* to become the media buzzword of 1988, and the subject of numerous inquests, surveys and pronouncements by the *grilli parlanti* – talking crickets (i.e. media pundits). It became apparent that if Italians were not intolerant of Third World immigrants, it was above all because in the past they hadn't even registered their presence. Making the most of the collective distraction of Italian authorities and the lack of restrictive immigration legislation, immigrants from the Third World have been arriving in ever larger numbers over the last few years. (→V, 1:vii) In 1988, according to an ISPES survey, there are 1.1 million immigrants in Italy, which makes it odd that so many Italians say they 'just don't notice them'.

However, as in other countries, treatment varies depending on the race. Far East Asians, quick to absorb both language and customs, are treated well. The massive increase of Chinese restaurants over the last few years (Rome had three in 1980; in 1988 there were over 100) and the vast number of Filipinos in domestic service attest to their successful integration.

There is a sizeable African community who make their living selling trinkets on the beaches and on the streets, who now generically get called *Vu comprà* ('psst! wanna buy this?'), a post-war Neapolitan nick-name for street vendors. Some immigrants, especially those from the Maghreb who settle in southern Italy, get regular jobs as manual workers, but are usually paid way beneath official rates, and have no insurance contributions paid for them. This seems to be more a question of exploitation than of prejudice.

Even the fairly sizeable Yugoslavian gypsy community, with their highly unfriendly street attitude, are viewed with considerable indulgence by both the police and the public in general. (→ 6:iv, ACCESS – Stressful street scenarios) Sporadic anti-gypsy demonstrations by residents' associations are roundly condemned by the Press as 'racist'. The fairly substantial presence of other European or North American residents generates mostly positive reactions, even if many of the better-off ones have a distinctly colonial attitude towards the host nation. Unfortunately, quite a few Italians (above all in the scenic southern locations that attract this curiously anachronistic breed) allow themselves to be patronized, especially if they feel there is another way (generally economic) in which they can exploit the other party.

The Italian attitude to the mass influx of tourists varies, of course, depending on how hit their town is, and on what they may make out of it. Non-tourist service industry Florentines and Venetians (the two worst-hit cities) bemoan the days of élite tourism, when they felt proud to have the odd handful of the culturally minded consulting Baedeckers and appreciating everything. Now the massed hordes of intercontinental package tourism offend their sensibilities, and, more important, make it hard for them to walk their own streets. There has been a very strong Anglo-Florentine link for over a century, with Germans and French opting for Rome. Figures like Sir Harold Acton, Dame Freya Stark or even Gore Vidal are the objects of a certain local pride.

6. The visual

(i) Visual immediacy

If the sense of official identity is strong in Italian towns
(→ 3:ii, above), at a personal level it is even more so. What
tends to overwhelm foreigners on arriving in Italy is not
so much how different things look as their sheer intensity. Everybody and everything seems to be making an
emphatic statement, the whole time. Visually speaking,
compared with the more discreet tradition of Northern
Europe, Italy seems so very explicit. The message seems
to be: Why talk quietly when you can shout? And why
just pump up the volume, when you can use your hands
as visual aids as well?

The only catch is that sometimes non-Italians may
not correctly decode this visual language, however
loudly it is transmitted: extra insight is often required.

(ii) Baroque around the clock

People raised in a non-Catholic culture frequently
have a knee-jerk reaction to Baroque architecture.
They say: This is too overwhelming for me, too
elaborate; give me a Renaissance or Gothic building
any time. The formal simplicity of Renaissance architecture is beyond question, but Gothic isn't: it's often
more ornate than Baroque is. The difference is that
Protestant Northern Europeans read Gothic instinctively, even if they are non-believers. Gothic seems to
say: This is a monument to spirituality, which suggests suffering, perseverance and contemplation. It is
coolly symmetrical and straightforward.

Baroque presents a problem, because it is over-
ornate, asymmetrical, full of optical tricks and, as
far as churches are concerned, apparently devoid
of spirituality. Baroque exploded on the world at
the time of the Counter-Reformation and Copernican
revolution. The Roman Catholic Church was no longer
the centre of Christendom; Earth was no longer the
centre of the Universe; and contemporary architecture
indirectly reflected offended pride and existential panic
by underlining what was left. Churches became symbols
of the most massive corporate empire of its day; *palazzi*
now described the power and caprice, rather than just
the learning, of their owners. Eminently Baroque cities
like Rome and Naples are full of massive churches,
towering aggressively above tiny streets, that were specifically designed for people to crane their necks up at
in awe. Contrast this with the 'human scale' architecture
of the preceding Renaissance period. Baroque buildings
were thus the New York skyscrapers of their time. Don't

Visual taboos

In Italy, you can make as much
noise as you like, but not look as
you like. This tendency reaches
an absurd pitch in the South,
where no one would ever
think of revving motorbikes
at 2 a.m. or mobile salesmen
with megadecibel loudspeakers
on their vans at 7 a.m., as a
public disturbance; sunbathing
topless on a roof-terrace where
the neighbours could see you
only by climbing a ladder, on the
other hand, they would. Visual
taboos are a very nice point,
with infinite subtleties, some
according to region and current notions of fashion. (→ 6:iv,
below) This may all seem paradoxical, considering that mut-
ton dressed as lamb and most
sexually provocative clothes are,
socially speaking, fine.

The key concept you need
to know is that of *la bella
figura* – of looking your best at
all times, however exaggerated
this may seem.

How not to dress in Italy

• Italian fashion is so conventional, and so widely observed,
that foreigners cannot help
but get it wrong most of the
time. Particularly unfortunate
are those tourists, anxious not
to look like lumpy, unstylish
foreigners, who come to Italy
with a painstakingly 'Italian-
made' wardrobe, thinking that
they will fit in. They shouldn't
have bothered: Italians still
think they look like lumpy,
unstylish foreigners.
• On the other hand, peo-
ple whose personal dress
code does not derive from,
or particularly refer to, the
standard-issue Italian look,
may be the object of respect-

ful curiosity or admiration. Whether they shop in the stuffier stretches of Jermyn Street or the groovier areas of Soho, their sartorial style looks distinctive in the midst of the wide centre-ground of regular Italian fashion.

Areas of bared male flesh fashionable at different times

● Shorts worn as streetwear. Only since summer 1989, with the tardy arrival of knee-length acid-house vintage beach jams or cycle shorts, have groovier young Italian males taken to the streets with their legs uncovered. Even the valiant attempts of Giorgio Armani over the years to launch shorts with suits have floundered. The collective notion of *bella figura* still sees shorts as unflattering to the male physique, at least out of a sporting context.

● Open-neck shirts (John Travolta) – fifteen years out, now seen only on immigrants from the Maghreb.

● Summer jackets with rolled-up sleeves, *Miami Vice*-style – five years out.

● Short socks on men – hence bared calves – considered to be the disqualifying sartorial trademark of the British and the Germans.

● No socks on men – still in fashion, especially on tanned legs.

● Bare chests, football fan-style – never.

Nudity on the beach

A surprising number of Italian beaches permit nudity of some sort. If in doubt, just check out what everyone else, or at least some other people, are doing; there is a lot of mixed nude and clothed sunbathing, in a pleasingly ecumenical manner. Most beaches permit women to

expect them to hint at a contemplative spirituality. They just yell corporate power.

(iii) People

People in the street are equally upfront. Especially in central and southern Italy, people stare at what intrigues them. It is not intended to be offensive, though foreigners who are not used to it take umbrage. Checking people out in the street observes certain rules: it is look, but don't touch, even though people look as though they are going to. (→ I, 3:v and I, 3:xi)

The same is true of how people present themselves: through what they are wearing, and how they walk. Although the world is now more familiar with Italian dress codes than it was a decade ago, the blatantness of it all still tends to make non-Italians loosen their metaphorical tie. Hence the raunchily sexual display common to the young, and the *nuovo ricco* come-on typical of the middle-aged. Very often, it is the not so young who wear the most provocative outfits, and the not so rich who dress as though they were (Italian supermarkets are as full of furs as La Scala premières) – Italian street style is not so much 'If you've got it flaunt it' as, If you haven't, why not pretend you have?

The all-the-year-round tan is a case in point. Although aided both by nature (Mediterranean skin tans in minutes) and by geography (there are lots of conveniently located ski resorts in Italy), many Italians resort to the tricks of science (jokingly referring to the solarium as though it were a tropical island: Los Lampados – from *lampada*, sun-lamp). However fake the tan looks, it doesn't matter. As a result, the new anti-sunbathing lobby is a Californian import the Italians are finding difficult to assimilate.

(iv) Keeping up appearances

Unlike the British, who have traditionally tended to dress socially down-scale, the Italians always want to look posher than they actually are. This simple notion may reasonably be deemed responsible for one of the most important socio-economic trends to have swept the planet over the last decade: designer label fever. However international a phenomenon it has become, its Italian roots are still visible. It took Italian genius to realize that in a rapidly expanding mass fashion market it was illogical to expect *le masse incolte* – the unrefined masses – to identify the subtle notions of cut, style and volume. People wanted to feel elegant without having to do their homework. The answer was simple: stitch the label on the outside. The fact that the quality of Italian fashion garments is now falling fast is closely connected with the way many Italians now just look at *la firma* – the label – not the product itself. This explains the massive diversification strategy undertaken by Italian designers in other fields: Italian consumers will now buy anything (Versace kitchen tiles, Missoni-upholstered cars, Armani telephones, Valentino plates), so long as it has a visible designer label on the outside. (→ VI, 3:iv)

Conscious of the terrible poverty they endured until the economic boom bore fruit, older Italians are anxious to compensate as much as possible. (→ I, 2) Recent memories of only hand-me-downs mean that they never wear clothes that suggest the idea of poverty. This goes not just for themselves, but for their children, who must never wear anything either faintly dirty or in need of slight repair: that is why every Anglo/American youth clothing style of the last twenty-five years has had great difficulty in laying down Italian roots, despite all the theoretical enthusiasm displayed by the pundits. The pattern is by now familiar: each new imported look takes between a year and eighteen months longer to catch on than, say, in Britain, and then it is in a sanitized, watered-down, form. Although the revived mini-skirt, unlike in America, has had no trouble in being accepted, the idea of men in shorts away from the beach is definitely out. Italians of all ages are deeply irritated to see young German tourists wandering around in running shorts and nothing else. In 1989, the Comune di Roma brought in tough new by-laws, to be introduced in other cities as well, allowing Vigili Urbani to fine on the spot, or even arrest, those seen as being underdressed in public places. Notices have been posted in major squares and streets, like those outside churches, warning passers-by (but essentially tourists) of their sartorial obligations. This is not a moralistic move; it is an aesthetic one. There was a controversy in 1987, when a magistrate in southern Italy decided to allow bare-breasted women on the beach, 'as long as they were attractive, and had breasts worth displaying'. Although many Italians said they were shocked, there was a general tendency, even among liberals, to agree with the judge. The French expression *la physique du rôle* is widely used in Italy, especially to indicate who's got 'it' and who hasn't.

remove their bras. Total nudity is permitted, or at least tolerated, in specific areas, to be found near most major resorts or in rocky coves away from the madding crowd. Try not to start a trend though: there are also places (mostly small seaside family resorts, especially in the South) where this could still get you into trouble.

Street life

● Young Italians hanging out in the street tend to stand rather than sit down; if they do sit, it's usually not for long. The more of them there are, the more comfortable they feel. (→ I, 4:i) Italian hanging out is not so much about relaxing in public as about being on display. Older people, too, do not have the notion of relaxing in public; they like to be mobile (hence *lo struscio*, below). That's partly why street benches are rare in Italy: they are largely unnecessary. In the South, if older people want to sit out, they do so outside their front door, since the road in front counts as home. One of the most crucial US imports is that of cruising endlessly around the block in cars with the stereo at full volume. The effect of films like *American Graffiti* on Italian youth cannot be overemphasized. Driving may involve sitting down, but the important thing is that cars move.

● Bars follow the same principle: during the daytime, you will see foreigners sitting down only in or outside bars – Italians always stand, whether they are in a hurry or not. In the evening, things change, especially in fashionable bars. People may then spend a whole evening seated, nursing one drink. If the bar is very fashionable, then lots of people may have to stand anyway, as though they were at a party: all the better for people watching.

● *Lo struscio* – strutting your stuff: in all provincial towns, especially in the South, there is an extraordinary time each day before dinner, between about 7p.m., and 8.30 p.m. – *lo struscio*. At this moment, the streets suddenly fill up with people taking their evening stroll. It is not the same as a constitutional, because *lo struscio* is all about wealth, not health. The idea is to strut up and down three or four times, until everyone has thoroughly checked out everyone else. It is neither classist nor ageist – everyone is invited, wheelchairs and prams included. Staring, turning round and nudging are all permitted, but being late isn't. At a given moment, the streets are deserted, as everyone goes home for dinner. It is not done to hang around a moment longer: the mad dogs and Englishmen line is nowhere more appropriate.

● Dealing with people: be like the Italians – pushy but relaxed. Italians may raise their voices in street situations, but they are rarely angry: and if they are, it's over in a matter of seconds. It generally just underlines a mood. The Italian manner is to express your feelings as you go along. Non-Latins tend to try to look calm but get bottled up inside and then explode, which the Italians don't like.

● Not speaking Italian obviously reduces your effective range of communication with strangers, whether in a service capacity (places like shops, banks, hotels, bars or restaurants) or with simple fellow *cittadini* encountered anywhere, but at times it can be transformed into an advantage. By capitalizing on the Italians' proverbial fascination with foreigners, you can usually get them to help you. They will try and speak English or French, or listen to your faltering attempts in phrase-book Italian, with much less reluctance than any native English or French speaker ever would. Never be afraid to attempt the latter, however pathetic the outcome – Italians are always pleased when people try to speak their language. (→ I, 4) This insight can easily transform those necessary daily contacts from the embarrassing to the pleasurable. Being obviously identifiable as a foreigner also exonerates you from that apparently rather ruthless treatment that is the basis of Italian civic behaviour.

Stressful street scenarios

● Junkies – Italy's vast army of heroin addicts are among its most prominent street habitués. Many of them even like to jack up in public. Apart from the presumed AIDS risk if you are barefoot, there is nothing to worry about if you find yourself in an area where discarded syringes outnumber cigarette butts. Italy unquestionably has more needle parks (river walkways, alleyways etc.) than public parks, so this is not an improbable occurrence. It may appear macabre to the unseasoned eye, but Italians don't notice any more.

● Being hustled for spare change – Italians are generally very generous with hustlers (mostly junkies), who have hiked their demands as a consequence. 100 lire is no longer enough; now they ask for 1000 lire; since anything less than that can earn you a robust *vaffanculo* – fuck off! – some don't bother.

Being hustled for cigarettes – a sociably acceptable pastime: generous to a fault, Italians will offer you more than one; try it and see.

● Gypsies – the only really serious danger you will face in large Italian cities is being mugged by marauding bands of pint-sized, often Yugoslavian, *zingari* – gypsies – looking like extras who've wandered off the set of the psychedelic *Oliver Twist* remake (check out their dress code while they're checking out your credit rating). Often no more than five or six years old, their usual technique is to thrust a piece of cardboard with something written on it in your direction, which you are supposed to read, while they work your pockets. If they catch you unawares, it is already too late – your wallet, passport, or purse will be halfway down the street before you even realize it. If you see them coming, take sensible precautions, like entering the nearest shop, or brush them aside with an arrogant 'tut' (Italian for 'no thanks', even to friends). Whatever you do, don't run: they can spot panic at fifty yards, and you may unexpectedly find yourself involved in an action replay of the final sequence of *Suddenly Last Summer* with you, reluctantly, in the role of Sebastian. Apart from the occasional clean-up (few of them have residency permits), the police are conspicuously inert in dealing with them.

● *Venditori ambulanti* – street-traders hardly seems the term for the people who assault your car at the traffic lights. Once these unauthorized hustlers were Italian; now they are predominantly foreign. You will still be offered the morning paper by an Italian, but most of the rest has been taken over by illegal immigrants: roses by a Senegalese;

cigarette lighters and Kleenex by a Moroccan; a windscreen sunshield by a Tamil. The real kings of the road are the Poles, who tend to specialize in cleaning your windscreen before the lights change; most of them are graduates. 200 lire is a minimum; generous Italians give 1000 lire. Sometimes you have a hard time insisting that you don't want your windscreen cleaned, and you may have to cope with their hostile reaction. On the beaches and in large piazzas, there is now a large number of West African *vu comprà*, although their wares have now changed. Their extensive marketing research has shown that Italian holiday punters prefer imitation Raybans to genuine hand-carved elephants.

• Petrol pumps at night – after the regular attendants go home, the pumps are manned by *abusivi* – often junkies, but now increasingly respectable Poles, who wish to be paid for serving you petrol. 200–500 lire is expected. If you really object, they won't stop you doing it yourself.

• *Pazzi* – ever since mental hospitals were closed down, and the inmates invited to 'return into the community', Italian streets have been ennobled by the presence of a sizeable contingent of ex-mental patients, most of whom have inevitably become bag people. Overall, this ambitious approach has worked: *i pazzi* are largely accepted in their capacity as roving ambassadors for the theories of David Cooper, even though you may find yourself getting shouted at when you least expect it. (→ VIII, 7)

• *Scippatori* – Italy's supposed army of Vespa-mounted muggers, never more than an arm's distance from the nearest string of pearls, is something of a modern urban myth, like the Italians thinking London is always foggy. This custom has some currency in Naples, but is relatively rare elsewhere. Italian muggers have the reputation for being non-violent: if they can't snatch it off you, they let go and vanish.

• *Tifosi* – young Italian football supporters get extremely high-spirited after successful games, tending to paralyse the city centre traffic in their cars; they have been known to damage monuments. Since they run on adrenalin, not alcohol, all of this is done without the slightest damage to other people. Even gangs of young Italians wandering the streets late at night are absolutely not to be feared: you would have to insult someone's sister to get hit.

7. Transport

(i) Public transport

Italy has more buses than any other European country, though by no means the most efficient service. This is partly due to inefficient management in certain cities, but also because the buses often have physical difficulty in moving: it is calculated that for every bus on the bus-only routes in Rome, there are seven 'stray' cars.

The Italian railways – FS (Ferrovie dello Stato) – unlike the French, have been on the political back-burner since the war, when the Christian Democrats got busy building the *autostrada* network. (→ 7:ii, below) However, there has never been anything resembling a Beeching plan in Italy. The overall network is extemely inefficient and antiquated, but at least it is still there.

Since 1988, there has been an attempt to upgrade services to meet European levels, with new intercity lines destined to furnish a regular, on-the-hour service, and largely renewed rolling stock. A rationalization programme is planned for the 1990s: expect prices to reach European levels. Time and motion studies reveal the FS to be far less efficient than either SNCF or even British Rail. Revenue covers a mere 17% of expenses, with the remaining 83% coming in State subsidies; British, German and French railways pay their way to the tune of 68%, 58% and 53%, respectively, with between 28% and 30% in government subsidies.

In 1985, the FS were made into a semi-autonomous *ente* – public body – which is theoretically freer from government control. The management was so corrupt and inefficient that the government recently placed an emergency commissar, the successful business executive Mario Schimberni, at the head of the State railways. His attempts at rationalizing are being largely defeated by negative union reactions to his proposals on manning levels: the FS have over double the workforce of British Railways, with less than half the productivity rate. Although the FS has a similar number of kilometres of track as British Rail, much of it is single–track. Schimberni has caused another major controversy by cancelling all existing plans to link Italy to the new European high-velocity rail network. There is an excellent train already in service on the Rome–Milan line, the ETR 450, known as *il pendolino* – the pendulum – which challenges the French HGV or the German ICE, but it seems unlikely that Milan or Turin will be connected to the rest of Europe on a new HGV circuit.

Buses, trams and coaches

● Buses and trams are now nearly all orange, though a few of the older ones are still hospital green, out-of-town coaches are usually bright blue.

● Ticket prices are generally cheap in Italy, but pricing systems and variety of tickets vary from city to city. The basic types you will find are the single ride *corso semplice*, costing between 700 and 800 lire (Rome, Naples); a *biglietto orario*, which is either a half-day ticket (i.e. mornings or afternoons only) around 1000 lire (Rome); or a fixed-time period ticket – usually 60 or 75 minutes, when you can either take as many rides as you want, or do so as long as you don't go back the same way, for 700–900 lire (Florence, Milan); season tickets – *abbonamenti* – vary in length and price: a monthly season ticket for the *intera rete* – i.e. bus, tram and subway – costs between 20,000 and 25,000 lire.

● Long-distance journeys by coach are cheap, but not always that comfortable. They often follow a regular hourly timetable, unlike the trains, their direct rival; they usually have their *capolinea* – terminus – near the central train station.

● Tickets can never be bought on board buses; you have to get them from tobacconists where the black 'T' sign is displayed, from certain newsstands, or at the ticket cabins near the *capolinea*.

● Riding buses can be stressful at times, since there is no limit to the number of passengers who can squeeze on and may thus provide an ideal terrain for pickpockets and gropers. If you are stuck in the middle and need to get off in a

(ii) Private transport

As with other matters in Italy, negotiating the streets follows the Italian rule of *forte con i deboli, debole con i forti* – tough with the timid, timid with the tough. The highway code idea of respecting less protected road-users, like pedestrians and cyclists, does not apply: it's the law of the jungle, but you can adapt and live with this – the Italians have, and survive in large numbers. They are fleet of foot, and hypersensitive to dangerous situations; they think much faster than most British drivers do; they are expecting trouble. Also, however dangerous Italian drivers may look, they have extremely quick reflexes, and as a result avoid accidents that would ensnare other drivers. The bumps that seem to cover most Italian cars are more the result of the excessively crowded driving conditions in the *centri storici*, and the fact that few drivers are honest enough to leave a note with a phone-number if they dent someone. Italians have an extremely pragmatic idea of driving, and of its theoretical restraints. Red lights are considered optional, especially at night or when there is little traffic about. (Indeed, the State acknowledges this, by leaving most traffic lights on the blink after midnight: they blink amber, leaving the initiative to the driver: to take the risk, or not? This is an interesting example of Italian mental flexibility, a considerable gift often not appreciated abroad.) Short stretches of one-way streets are also to be considered negotiable. British drivers may be unnerved by the habit of crowding in lanes where they would leave ample space on either side. For the Italians, if there is space in the road, why not use it? Likewise, barging in front, or squeezing past other drivers: it's cheeky, but not considered unreasonable. When Italian drivers get angry with each other, it is only for a matter of seconds: it passes immediately.

Only 30% of Vigili Urbani actually work on the street; the rest are doing bureaucratic administration work.

In 1945, there were only 150,000 cars on the roads; in 1989 there were 25 million.

In 1988, there were seventy-five vehicles per kilometre of Italian road.

Two-wheel traffic is even less governed by rules, especially the number-plateless 50cc Vespa model and the *motorino*, which have the tacit consent of the Vigili Urbani to do as they please: driving up one-way streets, or in pedestrian zones.

Italy's *autostrada* system is one of its greatest post-war

hurry, yell *'Un momento!'* start elbowing your way hard towards the central door (the only one you can get out of).

Travelling by train

This requires extra planning and patience. You should consider the following:

● Try getting your ticket from an authorized travel agency like Transalpino, which in Italy caters for all ages, not just the young; the queues at station ticket windows are endless. If you must get your ticket at the station, leave yourself at least 30 minutes before departure for a larger station (more during holiday periods). Although all the myriad system of reduced rates for different categories has now, thankfully, been abolished, the queues are still held up by poor computer training among ticket window staff and the constant shortage of change for large notes (VISA is the only credit-card accepted, and not everywhere). Another way to avoid the queue is to pay on the train, which costs 5000 lire extra, although if the inspector thinks you are fare-dodging, there is a fine.

● The unusual shape of Italy makes for some extremely long journeys, made more wearing in the summer months, when whole families migrate south for the holidays from the industrial North. The *Doctor Zhivago*-style overcrowding leads to many arguments over even pre-booked seats (see below) and a mass invasion of first-class seats.

● Make sure you consult an up-to-date timetable: they change every six months. You can buy one at the newsagent, but you may have trouble deciphering it. Notice that the train service is sparse and at odd times, never on the hour.

• There is a bewildering choice of different categories of train in Italy – hyperchoice again:

TEE, EUROCITY, RAPIDI and INTERCITY: fast, air-conditioned and, by Italian standards, expensive (in descending price order). They may require obligatory booking – *prenotazione obbligatoria* – several hours in advance, and may be first-class only. The TEE/EUROCITY has its own new Rome–Milan line, which takes only 4 instead of the ESPRESSO's 8 hours. It costs only slightly less than the plane, but is like one inside, complete with hostesses.

ESPRESSO: fairly fast, reasonably priced but generally totally overcrowded – you risk standing all the way. However, since so many Italians realize this, the luxury trains listed above are sometimes crowded and the ESPRESSO less so.

LOCALE and DIRETTO: avoid at all times, unless you are thinking of researching for some whimsical travel book about painfully slow train journeys. They stop at every tiny village station, of the sort Lord Beeching axed in the 1960s, and not just at stations.

• Stations can be stressful places to wait in; an immense quantity of people use them as doss-houses, cruising places, sales or pickpocketing pitches.

Aeroplanes

Because of the inordinate distances between major cities, the practical difficulties of rail travel and the high cost of driving, Italians often prefer to fly. Although nowhere near American levels, the average Italian takes far more internal flights than the average Briton. Alitalia and its offshoots Alisarda and ATI serve all the major cities on the mainland and islands. All the airports have cheap buses to

monuments: built by Christian Democrat politicians with the same zeal as the French gave to their railway system, it often veers out of area to go near a party potentate's feudal domain(→ IV, 4:i, V, 1); in Calabria, it is toll-free, to remind the Calabrians to be grateful and carry on voting DC. These are motorways constructed with real art – exceptional bridges and tunnels, feats of aesthetic engineering, highly imaginative motorway service areas straddling the road like giant crabs. There is now a major project to increase the number of lanes. The Italian network is still vastly superior to the UK's, largely because you have to pay to use it.

the city centres, though taxis or limos are always there too.

Taxis

Official taxis are bright yellow, though there are the inevitable *abusivi* waiting for you outside major stations. They are the only ones to offer their services; the authorized ones wouldn't dream of it. They are now dearer than London black cabs per mile, especially as there is a series of pile-on surcharges that often make one feel ripped off: big luggage, night journeys and holidays; as in London, many will not take you to out of the way locations. A sullen bunch at the best of times, and generally despised as a social group, they will rarely exchange friendly words or tell you much of interest.

Driving

● Bringing your own: driving in Italy is fraught with hazard, but has its own rewards. The ENIT (Ente Nazionale Italiano di Turismo) – the Italian Tourist Authority – issues petrol coupons (very useful, with Italy charging the second most in Europe) and motorway toll discounts to foreigners. When you park, you should never leave anything visible in your car, especially car radio/stereo. All Italian cars have had detachable stereos (replaced the male handbag fifteen years ago as socially downscale fashion accessory) and alarms for years. Driving in major cities, especially Rome and Naples, is stressful but exhilarating so long as you don't mind the odd scratch to the paintwork: notice that few Italian cars are unscathed.

● Hiring a car: although all the familiar Italian car-hire firms are there, you will get a shock looking at the price list; it is very expensive compared to other countries. It may be worth it if you are in a group for visiting outlying manuments or out of the way towns, especially at the weekend, when there are good reductions.

● Buying a car: to buy a car with Italian plates you need to be an Italian resident. Like estate agents, used–car dealers are thin on the ground. Most people advertise in *Porta Portese*, Italy's answer to *Trade & Mart*; in the daily papers; or simply put a *vendesi* – for sale – sign on the inside of the window stating phone-number and details. Having bought the car, your problems start:

Bureaucracy: you need to pay the *passaggio di proprietà* fees – ownership transfer – which costs about 200,000 lire; it then takes an average of two years for your *libretto di circolazione* – log book – to come back from the *agenzia* where you did the transaction. ACI (Automobile Club d'Italia) – the equivalent to the AA – will also do it, but will be no quicker. Since there is this irritating two-year wait, you are supposed to carry a *foglio sostitutivo* – provisional documents – which must be renewed every three months. The police can get nasty if they stop you without it.

Insurance: rather dearer than in other countries, and it covers the car, not the driver: tailor-made for indulgent fathers. It is almost always third-party only, though fully comprehensive (Kasko) can be negotiated. Italian insurance companies are even slower and less generous in honouring claims than British ones. Consequently, the number of minor accidents that Italians do not bother to report is high. Older cars need a *revisione* (MOT) after ten years, but the police rarely check.

● Passing your driving test: the EC-approved test has now been introduced, superseding Italy's rather eccentric notions of learning to drive. These involved learning hundreds of questions and answers by rote about mechanics and road safety, but having to show very little actual driving ability. You need 'P' plates (like 'L' plates) in order to go through with the exam, which can be done either through a *scuola guida* or as a *privatista* – privately – which means making visits to the local *ufficio di motorizzazione* – transport office – for very complicated paperwork.

● Always have paper and pen handy to take down details of someone who damages your car: even if you cannot be bothered to go through the complicated bureaucratic business of trying to claim, at least you have gained a certain moral satisfaction. Bearing in mind that few Italians would leave you a note if they damaged your car in your absence, reflect twice before doing so to them.

How to park

Because of the concentration of cars in Italian cities, parking is a special problem: the inconsistent efforts of the Vigili Urbani to curb *il parcheggio abusivo* mean that, generally, you can get away with parking on the pavement, or in places not permitted by the highway code. It is possible to get away with illegal parking in the same spot for months, only to get a *multa* – fine – two days running. There is no evident logic to their behaviour.

The *autostrada*

As in France, most of Italy's motorways cost you. Add this to the high price of petrol, and driving becomes an expensive activity. The *pedaggi* – toll stations – do not accept credit-cards; you should have cash ready; some will accept foreign cash, albeit at an exorbitant exchange rate.

Observing the speed limit

There has been so much controversy in recent years about the various speed limits that it is hard to keep track. In theory, it is 130 k.p.h. (110 k.p.h. during the summer months) on *le autostrade* – motorways, 90 k.p.h. on *le strade statali* – high roads – and 50 k.p.h. in built-up areas. Rarely do the Vigili stop you for speeding inside built-up areas; since 1988, the police have become much more vigilant on the motorways. (→ VIII, 3:ii for legislation and practice regarding seatbelts, drinking and driving, crash helmets etc.)

Being a pedestrian

Because of the traffic-crowded streets, many Italians simply prefer to *andare a piedi* – go by foot. However, walking in the narrow, pavement-less *centro storico* streets seems tricky because of the fast-moving traffic, which tears past. Italians have a very developed sense of pitch and distance, and can tell how near the approaching vehicle is, and step aside accordingly. Foreigners tend to panic, and freeze, rabbit-in-headlights style, almost getting run down. Learn the subtle art of stepping aside. Rule one: stay calm.
• Crossing the road in larger cities, like Rome or Naples seems a serious problem, especially at pedestrian crossings, which drivers never observe, and which are frequently rubbed out and not repainted. Facing the oncoming traffic, walk calmly into the road, looking the drivers directly in the face. If necessary, hold out your hand in a 'stop' signal. Never run: you may trip, especially on the cobbled streets of most *centri storici*. With ordinary traffic, this works every time. In the case of buses, lorries and motorbikes, who might have trouble stopping anyway, it's best to let them pass. If you are still in doubt, just watch how Italians do it.

Lo stato: the state

The last chapter was mostly about how the Italians have shaped, and been shaped by, their immediate physical environment; this chapter examines the relationship between the Italians and Italy as a political and administrative unit. Chapter II also looked at some of the historical factors responsible for this 'fragmented Italy', all of which date back to before the 19th century. The historical period covered in this chapter has three parts: the first is from c. 1815 until 1870, and covers the *Risorgimento*; the second features the development of the proto-democratic State, leading up to its exhaustion and the rise to power of Mussolini in 1922; the third phase looks at the Fascist era until its collapse towards the end of the war. History is used to give some perspective to the official Italian attitude towards territorial expansion and aggressive colonialism, as well as to the feelings of the Italians themselves concerning the subject.

The present phase of modern Italy starts in 1947 with the declaration of the republican Constitution, along with the founding, and in some cases consolidation, of the parliamentary institutions that still govern it. This chapter deals with the theoretical form of the modern Italian State, and with its models; the next chapter concentrates more on how it all really works.

Despite their pervasive sense of regional identity, it is in an international context that Italians, both individually and collectively, begin to stand up to be counted. After some difficulty in defining its position in the fields of international affairs and defence, the Italian State has now, since the beginning of the 1980s, begun to enjoy a rekindling of patriotic fervour of a sort that might be thought rather jingoistic in any other country. On the other hand, the lack of any militaristic pretensions and the presence of an apparently boundless, though in reality pragmatically limited, *xenofilia* means that there exists no greater advocate for a united Europe than the average Italian.

1. Historical factors

(i) *Il Risorgimento*

The birth of a unified Italy was particularly difficult, especially if compared to that of the other main political puerperant of 19th-century Europe. While Italy had its Prussia and its Bismarck (Piedmont and Count Camillo Cavour, respectively), it notably lacked several of the other factors that made the birth of modern Germany a rather less painful affair. One reason was geographical: Italy's extremely distended shape made for awkward communications and disastrous strategic organization, while her weak, under-industrialized economy simply couldn't cope with the expense that unification entailed. Indeed, Italy was spending beyond its means even before it was born.

Maintaining the status of even a major nation is an expensive business: in Italy's case, it entailed all the costs of a vastly expanded conscript army, and a major naval refitting which had to be financed by heavy taxation and a massive foreign debt. There was also the prestige/practical question of the capital. Since unification took place in stages, it had to move three times: it was situated in Turin until 1865; then it moved south to Florence for six years; and finally, in 1871, it came to roost in Rome. Rather as nowadays, the almost terminal confusion and vastly increased expenditure caused by this early case of bussing made many wonder whether the token gesture was actually worth it. (→ 2:i, below)

But what really exhausted Italy's resources was being on a permanent war footing. The Piedmontese had never imagined that they'd have so much armed opposition, since the prospect of unification was universally so popular. However, its opponents fought back – the whole of the South, the ex-Kingdom of the Two Sicilies, was in a state of civil war, being largely overrun by marauding bands, encouraged from exile by the deposed Bourbon King Francesco II, while a total of four wars had to be fought against Austria to win occupied territory in the North.

Italian unity's first serious advocate was actually a foreigner – Napoleon. During the short period in which he occupied Italy (1796–1814), he set up the bases of an efficient modern State, regulated by the *Code Napoléon* and governed by an enlightened, meritocratic, civil service. Compared with the heavy-handed rule of the Austrians in the North (Lombardy and Venetia), the feudal Papal States of central Italy (Umbria, Latium, the Marches, Emilia-Romagna) and the corrupt inefficiency of the Bourbon rulers of the South (the Kingdom of the Two Sicilies), French domination was an interesting novelty. (→ 3:i, below)

Il Risorgimento began as an autonomous, liberal and idealistic movement, but it became increasingly dependent on foreign help and unprincipled bargaining in order to reach its goal, in a way that accurately prefigures the modern post-war period.

Street-names (indicated •) commemorating the heroes of the Italian Risorgimento

• **Giuseppe Mazzini (1805–72) was the main ideologue: he was fiercely republican, democratic and anti-papal, and was active in the political secret society of the *Carbonari* – the 'coalmen' – before founding his own movement, *Giovine Italia* (1834) – Young Italy – which played a crucial role in inspiring** the 1848 popular uprisings in most major cities. The Palermo revolt resulted in a new liberal constitution being granted, first in Sicily, then for all the South, its example being copied later by Tuscany, Rome and Piedmont. Leading the republican revolt from Rome, Mazzini even managed to make Pius IX flee for a short while, until French troops reinstated him. Following this defeat, popular enthusiasm reverted to the Piedmont monarchist option; further evidence of his decline in influence was that in 1864 the First International in London, where he was in exile from 1837 to 1848, rejected his projected constitution in favour of Marx's.

- Giuseppe Garibaldi (1807–82) arrived back in 1848 from fighting in Uruguay (hence his epithet, 'Hero of the Two Worlds'), along with his famous red-shirted Italian Legion, famous for its skill in guerrilla warfare. Of republican sympathies, he immediately joined Mazzini, defending the Roman Republic against four armies. When Mazzini's influence declined, Garibaldi switched to Cavour's Piedmontese monarchist group. Despite his immense popularity, both in Italy and round the world, he was given a pretty hard time by Cavour. In 1860 he conquered the entire South for Vittorio Emanuele II; he invaded Sicily with a 1000-strong band, • '*I mille*', which he led victoriously up to Naples, overturning the Bourbon monarchy. Cavour and the Piedmontese King rushed down to Naples to steal his thunder. Famous for his laconic turn of phrase, Garibaldi handed over southern Italy to the Piedmontese King with the words, '*Maestà, l'Italia*' – 'Your Majesty, kindly accept Italy'. On being recalled from the invasion of Trento, he sent the King the shortest (and most reluctant) telegram in Italian history: '*Ubbedisco*' – 'I obey.'

- Count Camillo Cavour (1810–61) was an able politician; Prime Minister of Piedmont (1852–9) he was constitutionalist, monarchist, and a great admirer of the UK system. He had wanted Britain's military and political sponsorship for the *Risorgimento*, but Palmerston would give it no more than his moral support. A consummate master of realpolitik, he turned to the capricious, somewhat perfidious Napoleon III, with whom he cynically planned a series of diplomatic and military coups which eventually worked where Mazzini's idealist republicanism hadn't. Their Plombières pact (1858) planned to carve up northern Italy, handing over Savoy and Nice to France, which was to help Piedmont defeat Austria. Through military action, and diplomacy, backed up by popular referendums, between 1859 and 1860 he annexed to the Piedmontese Kingdom most of northern and central Italy, to which, thanks to Garibaldi's efforts, he added the South. His jigsaw puzzle was completed after his death by the addition of Veneto (the region around Venice, secured for Italy by Bismarck in 1866) and Latium (the region around Rome, abandoned by the French in 1870);

• XX Settembre – 20 September – was the day in 1870 when Italian troops led the breach on Porta Pia, entering into Rome.

• **Vittorio Emanuele II (1820–78)**: the Piedmontese King who became, on Cavour's death in 1861, the sole benefactor of the efforts of the previous three names. He was nominally responsible for losing battles like Novara and Custozza, as well as for winning in 1859 those of • **Magenta** and • **Solferino** against the Austrians.

• **Massimo D'Azeglio (1798–1866)**, artist and writer, backed the Piedmontese cause, as the only political/military force capable of defeating the Austrians; he was Prime Minister of Piedmont from 1849 to 1852.

• **Daniele Manin (1804–57)** was the leader of the brief-lived Venetian republic (1848), who heroically stuck it out against the Austrians.

• **Abbé Vincenzo Gioberti (1801–52)**: Piedmontese leader in favour of a federation of Italian states under the leadership of the Pope, which seemed quite a possibility in the 1850s.

(ii) Colonialism and *irredentismo*

Following reunification, Italy, busy developing a rudimentary national network of communications and administration, and crippled by massive foreign debts, was in no position to have any ideas about overseas expansion. But Italy wanted an Empire, and fast. Immensely irritated by France's snatching of Tunisia from under its nose in the early 1880s, and envious of the rest of Europe, which was busy gobbling up Africa, Italy started on the Horn of Africa in 1885 with Eritrea, and went on to take Somalia, though its claims to form a protectorate over Abyssinia were indignantly fought off by the Abyssinians themselves.

At the same time, in order to sustain its colonial drive, Italy embarked on an extraordinary series of diplomatic intrigues, making a mockery of the whole 19th-century pact system. In 1887 it adhered to the Triple Alliance, linking up with its traditional enemy Austria and Germany in a pact against France, with which it made a separate secret pact in 1902, two years after making another one with Russia aimed against Austria. Despite being bound to Turkey, subsequent to the latter's own adherence to the Triple Alliance, in 1911, Italy wasted no time in exploiting the weaknesses of the rapidly declining Ottoman Empire by seizing Libya, Rhodes and the Dodecanese archipelago, while the Young Turks fumed from the touchline.

Despite the imminence of World War I, Italy remained a nominal member of the Triple Alliance until 1915, when it switched horses and allied itself to the Triple Entente at the secret Treaty of London. Its reasons were unashamedly opportunist: on the shopping list were a series of objectives – for starters, the recovery of the Trentino and the conquest of the South Tyrol/Alto Adige, Istria and Trieste, with Adriatic Dalmatia and a slice of Turkey (Adalia) and the rest of Libya and Somalia for negotiable seconds. Italy considered the areas north-east of its borders rightfully Italian, on account of the largely Italian-speaking populations. According to the rhetoric of the times, they were '*territori irredenti*' – the unredeemed territories. *Irredentismo* became the buzzword of the era.

By 1917, the Italian people were showing considerable reluctance about the war, since it had brought them no visible advantages. Influenced by Russia, left-wing workers were mostly pacifist, and organized serious industrial unrest, which was matched by widespread desertion and fraternization by similar-minded troops. On the other hand, many reactionary clericalists were often pro-Austria. The massive defeat at Caporetto (now Kobarid, Yugoslavia) in 1917, when 600,000 were lost, made the nation sit up with a start. There was a renewed effort, culminating in victory at the battle of Vittorio Veneto (another street-name) in 1918, the importance of which subsequent Fascist propaganda enormously exaggerated.

The immediate post-war period was extremely confused. The country, rocked by strikes and a breakdown of law and order, was further demoralized by not having received full territorial satisfaction. By 1919, with a populace terrified on the one hand by the serious prospect of a communist revolution, and obsessed on the other with the unredeemed territories, public opinion was at fever pitch. With a brilliant sense of timing, one of Italy's best-known literary figures, Gabriele D'Annunzio, equally famous as a military fetishist, decided to exploit the situation by invading Fiume (now Rijeka, Yugoslavia), part of the Adriatic territories not awarded to Italy. Backed up by a squadron of like-minded uniform queens, and armed with the slogan 'Fiume or death', he then staged a spectacular air raid on the unsuspecting Adriatic city, whose non-Italian-speaking citizens immediately surrendered before this vision of massed leather boots, cloaks and dagger- and feather-daubed flying caps. He then set up a sort of *opera buffa* régime – short-lived, since Prime Minister Orlando was then obliged by the Allies to play the spoilsport and hand Fiume back to Yugoslavia. Although logistically it was a totally useless gain, Mussolini felt obliged to regain Fiume after he came to power, in order to save face. For his pains, D'Annunzio was awarded the appropriate title of 'Principe del Monte Nevoso' – 'Prince of the Snowy Mountain' – while Fiume itself is commemorated in numerous Italian street-names.

What the Allies did decide to offer Italy at the Versailles conference, as a sop, was Georgia, then an independent State. Before they could make up their minds, Georgia was absorbed into the Soviet Union, If they had said yes fast, Stalin would have ended up with an Italian passport.

Gabriele D'Annunzio was famous above all for his sexual and sartorial eccentricities. With a motto like 'Frivolity and Excess', it comes as no surprise to discover that he amassed the largest wardrobe in Italy. His specially made shoes with erect penises in red bas-relief were a mere trifle compared to the Ultimate Narcissist's operation he underwent: the apocryphal tale recounts how he had his bottom rib removed so that he could give himself a blow job whenever he felt like it. Il Vittoriale, his estate on Lake Garda, a sort of delirious futuristic Bateman's is still open to the public, and features a battleship in the grounds, *à la* Fitzcarraldo.

It took former socialist journalist Benito Mussolini less than three years to exploit widespread anti-communist fears by combining them with an openly fetishistic use of Imperial Roman symbolism, in order to conquer the whole country. Strong Soviet-inspired unrest in the northern factories had put the frighteners on the rich and the middle-classes to an extent that in the 1921 elections the Fascists entered Parliament with thirty-five seats. By late October, a *crisi di governo* (→ IV, 1:i) threw the institutions into turmoil, and Mussolini decided to repeat d'Annunzio's gesture. He then organized the famous March on Rome by mobilizing some

30,000 black-shirted supporters, who converged on an intimidated capital, where they besieged Parliament. Parliament and the King were impressed: some 400 non-Fascist MPs decided to vote Mussolini a one-year all-out dictatorship, renewable, while Vittorio Emanuele III obliged by inviting him to form a government. It was to last twenty-one years, the longest one-man show since the Fall of the Roman Empire.

The invasion of Abyssinia in 1935 led to the constitution of the Italian East African Empire, with Marshal Badoglio as its Viceroy. Mussolini openly compared his régime with ancient Rome (among other things, he always referred to the Mediterranean in Latin, *Mare Nostrum* – our sea), and since the former hardly passed muster in territorial terms, it had to compensate with an elaborate use of recycled military iconography. There were several other quite convenient uses for the founding of this Empire. It took 325,000 off the employment list, allowed tens of thousands of political and social undesirables to be forcibly exiled, and gave a sop to the otherwise disgruntled public. Overnight, Mussolini's success rating soared.

Fashion Fascists

Getting the look right had as much importance in Mussolini's political ascendance as any other single factor. But, like collarless Beatle jackets, the Fascist Corporate Look hadn't yet developed when the product was launched. In 1921, after several years of militancy, he had the idea of taking a leaf out of Garibaldi's book: colour-coded supporters. (→ III, 1) First he copied the scarf, and then the shirt. The right-wing Nationalist Party had already copied Garibaldi's idea, with scarves and shirts in blue, but that no longer mattered, as they had been forcibly merged into the Fascist Party shortly afterwards. Dreaming up such a sexy outfit was a very sly way of imposing his will on the nation. Enticing the uniform-mad Italians to dress up helped them swallow the nasty ideological bit.

The rich Roman/Napoleonic symbolism usurped by Fascism had a major legitimizing role to play in Italy's colonial exploits. The conquest of the Empire looked like an action replay to the historically-minded Italians, and all those Roman salutes, Roman banners and pompous Roman military titles contributed to the general impression. With the aid of pet régime architect Marcello Piacentini, Mussolini evolved an architectural language out of

the current Le Corbusier-ish *razionalismo*, creating perfectly the illusions of grandeur Fascism tried to express. Fortunately, it is his Futurist–Roman Empire genre buildings that have become Fascism's most enduring legacy, if you don't count the Emporio Armani's sinister eagle logo. (→ II, 1; VII, 5:i) But it wasn't always a question of recycling the heroic past: Mussolini shared that perennial Italian fascination for hi-tech., which meant that Marinetti's Futurism and the whole industrial design Modernism movement became fused with the Fascist credo.

(iii) Fascism: the acceptable face of Nazism?

The exact pros and cons of Fascist rule in Italy are currently being re-examined after a forty-year knee-jerk taboo period, though there is no doubt that it was considerably less harsh than Hitler's régime. It may sound trite, but the Italians could never be that nasty, for that long, on behalf of an institution.

Fascism's own roots confuse the issue. It was an improbable hybrid of extreme socialism and right-wing nationalism. Although they were gradually all purged, many of his early supporters were genuine socialists, whose *irredentista* sentiments led them into the Fascist camp. Furthermore, after seizing power, Mussolini showed a surprising respect for democratic institutions. His script said nothing about heavy-duty totalitarianism for at least the first three years.

If Italian constitutional rule had tended to mean weak, ineffectual institutions, the corporativist Fascist State offered the very opposite. Industrial troubles, which had greatly weakened the State prior to 1922, vanished with the official Fascist trade unions and employers' federations in one interlocking, strike-free, unit. A strongly centralized, authoritarian government led to some generalized improvements in living conditions – though at the total expense of individual liberties. Like Napoleonic rule, Fascism imposed on Italy a certain administrative efficiency which undoubtedly straightened out much of the confusion that had unsettled the country since the *Risorgimento*. This is evidenced by the immense legacy of Fascist administration and ritual that was inherited and even preserved by the post-war democracy, and that included many of the worst sides of the judicial system. (→ V, 5:i)

The aspect of the régime that worked best was undoubtedly the propaganda unit: for every 'triumph', like the draining of the Pontine Marshes, or the trains running on time, there were dozens of dismal industrial or agricultural failures that no one ever got to hear about. Mussolini also pulled off a couple of quite useful coups which consolidated his international reputation – principally the 1929 Lateran Pact, which finally established a reasonable working relationship between Church and State. (→ VIII, 9:ii)

There is no doubt that Fascism responded to something in the Italian psyche; the continued existence of the MSI as the fourth party makes this clear. (→ IV, 2:ii) On the other hand, many Fascists themselves during *il ventennio* – the twenty-year régime – took quite a lot of Mussolini's rhetoric with a pinch of salt. Most of Nazism's cruellest principles were avoided, the treatment of the Jews being the most important case. Although squadrons of *le camicie nere* – blackshirts – gave the public a pretty hard time, they were hardly like the SS. And when the régime collapsed in 1943, many were quite happy to forget it. Following the fall of Rome in 1943, the deposition of Mussolini by King Vittorio Emanuele III, and the declaration of a provisional government led by Marshal Badoglio, the Fascist die-hards regrouped around Il Duce, newly escaped from imprisonment, and formed the Republic of Salò (of the eponymous Pasolini film) in north-east Italy, which survived until 1945, when Mussolini was recaptured and shot before being strung by his feet, with his faithful lover Claretta Petacci, in Milan's busy Piazza Loreto. The famous *Times* editorial of the period, which stated, ironically, that post-war Italy contained 90 million inhabitants – 45 million Fascists and 45 million anti-Fascists – is still fondly quoted by Italians.

2. The capital and the micro-states

(i) Rome: not such a capital idea

The decision, in 1870, to site the capital of newly united Italy in Rome seems, for historic and geographic reasons, obvious enough. There were, however, other factors; and although Italy's unhelpful geographical shape, and the need to reassure the South that it wasn't merely being occupied by the North, were not to be ignored, it would have been far more practical to site the capital in any of the northern cities.

Unlike Naples or Turin (in continuous use as capitals for centuries), or Milan or Florence (major regional administrative cities), Rome was totally unprepared to become a capital city. Several centuries before, its population had gone down to a mere 4000, and although it housed the Vatican, it had nothing else. The apparatus of the papal administration was so closely guarded and so antiquated that it was scarcely in a position to serve as a working model for the modern secular State.

Armed only with rhetorical considerations, the new Piedmontese régime went about constructing a capital from scratch. (→ II, 1) The time and immense expense that went towards this late 19th-century political prestige operation was ruinous to the nascent Italian State.

Mussolini simply redoubled the efforts of his predecessors with massive building projects designed to enhance Rome's 'imperial' stature at the expense of every other Italian city, a process analogous to that undertaken in Paris, Berlin or London. With projects like EUR as a start, he planned to extend Rome to the sea at Ostia, some 15 miles away. All this grandiose town planning could have worked (as it has elsewhere), had its imperially minded proponents managed to create a capital-mentality among the inhabitants.

As countless, mostly post-war, books and films amply demonstrate, this never happened. Rome is now the largest city in Italy, with over 4 million inhabitants, but in spirit it resembles a village. As the Milanese in particular, but other Italians in general, never cease to point out, the present-day Romans have succeeded in holding the nation hostage, so hopelessly inefficient are they in administering the entire State apparatus.

The problem is compounded by the very nature of the modern Italian State, founded as it is on *lottizzazione* and *sottogoverno*. It is the lax, tolerant Rome atmosphere that has allowed the Christian Democrats to administer this system so effectively over the last forty years, under the not-so-invisible protection of their sponsors *oltre il tevere* – across the Tiber.

the Vatican. A majority of Rome's inhabitants have arrived over the last couple of generations from the economically backward, Catholic-minded South to find work in government service, following a demographic pattern now more familiar to the Third World. In the doubtlessly well-intentioned process of providing work for hundreds of thousands without other immediate job prospects, the Italian State effectively mortgaged its future.

The chronic (however good-natured) inefficiency of the present-day Romans has ensured that the economic capital of Italy remains Milan, and that those Italians who can afford to avoid coming to Rome at all, whatever its climatic and cultural attractions. The whole rise of the Craxi-led PSI is intimately linked with this derisive rejection of Rome, while the process of socio-economic international developments of the 1980s, with their heightened significance in Italy, and Craxi's clever exploitation, have made Milan as fashionable a city as Rome is unacceptable. The fact that Craxi ostentatiously continues to live in Milan, and commutes to Rome only when he has to (like chairing the odd cabinet meeting if he happens to be PM), is symbolic of his decision to de-Romanize Italy as much as possible. He likes to talk of moving the RAI to Milan, while many new-breed Socialists boast of transferring the whole capital there.

This will, of course, never happen – quite the contrary. Laws like *Roma Capitale*, outlaying trillions of lire of public money to beautify Roman buildings in time for the World Cup in 1990, 'so that the place at least looks like a capital', have predictably provoked massive outcries up and down *la penisola*.

In fact, the process of *romanizzazione* continues inexorably, but in a less immediately obvious way. Since its establishment in 1954, RAI TV has gradually and inevitably created an identikit TV-Italian who is essentially a Roman. While this is a natural process in the case of long-united countries dominated by an all-embracing capital, in culturally autonomous, regionalized Italy it has been far more momentous. When *Le Monde* in July 1989 printed a front-page article describing Rome as 'culturally dead', there was an outcry among the Roman chattering classes – but in general, reluctantly, they had to agree. Federico Zeri, a prominent art critic, speaks of *la definitiva meridionalizzazione* – the terminal southern Italianization process – which Rome is undergoing,

Italians have had to swallow seeing '*romano*' become synonymous with '*italiano*' in all those marginal ways that the mass media impose: the Roman accent, slang terms and cultural usages are employed by everyone (originally Roman or not) on television, whether professional media folk or simply people featured in on-the-spot street interviews.

This is true not only for the people, but also for the physical surroundings – of which the Italians are more aware than most. (→II, 6) Thanks above all to news programmes, Italians from all over the peninsula are now more aware of Rome's physical appearance – its shops, *palazzi*, streets, urban layout – than of that of their own neighbouring city. This process started before the war with the establishment of the Rome-based national film industry at Cinecittà, when the majority of films were set in the most convenient location possible – the city itself.

In this way, Rome has accurately mirrored the example of Los Angeles, by printing itself on the nation's subconscious as the archetypal environment, via the large, and subsequently the small, screen.

(ii) Micro-states

Italy contains three internal sovereign states within its territory: San Marino, located between Le Marche and Emilia-Romagna; the Vatican City, in central Rome; and the Knights of Malta, which has several minuscule locations in central Rome.

Each of these has its own government and statutes, and heads of state. San Marino has Western Europe's only communist head of state: since the Middle Ages, it has been governed by two elected Captains. The current *giunta* is a DC/PCI coalition.

Italy's other two independent states are both ruled by foreigners: one Polish, the other Scottish. The 78th Grand Master of the Order of the Knights of Malta is Sir Andrew Bertie, a cousin of the Queen Mother, elected in 1988. This Catholic order was founded in 1048 in Jerusalem, and, after many different homes, finally settled in Rome in 1834. It has 10,000 subjects, issues a passport, and, like the Vatican, has diplomatic relations with most of the world, excluding the two superpowers, but including Cuba.

All three mini-states have their own car licence-plates and emit currency and postage stamps.

Rome is a truly international city, if one considers it is possible to visit four different states in half an hour (if one includes the UN Food and Agriculture Organization (FAO)). One's small change may well be composed of coinage from all four. Smart Romans try and get admitted to their various duty-free facilities, which, particularly in the case of the Vatican, are splendid.

3. Parliament and the Constitution

(i) The Constitution

Although Mussolini was officially deposed in 1943, it wasn't really until 1948 that Italy acquired its definitive post-war shape. The Allies entered Rome in 1944, with King Vittorio Emanuele III and a grand coalition of all the political parties called the Committee of National Liberation. However, the war was not over for another year, since the Fascist Republic of Salò, which Mussolini had set up in the North, survived until mid-1945. The provisional government that was running Italy was largely hostile to the royal house of Savoy for its accommodating relations with Fascism. In May 1946, Vittorio Emanuele took the hint and abdicated in favour of his son, Umberto II, a Tin-tinesque figure known in Italy as *il re di maggio* – the May King. This sobriquet derives from his embarrassingly short innings: on 2 June there was a national referendum held on the monarchy, which was bowled out. Although there were suspicions of fraud, the final vote was 12.7 million for the Republic, 10.7 million for the monarchy. On the same day there were elections for the Constituent Assembly which was to draw up the Constitution. It took the Constituent Assembly a year and a half to decide what kind of constitution to give Italy. The parties that participated in drawing it up are still known as *l'arco costituzionale* – the constitutional range – which excludes the neo-Fascists.

In April 1948, there were the first republican parliamentary elections, won by the Christian Democrats, who have never since lost them. These elections signalled the end of the Communists' experience as a government party, and the beginning of a long period out in the cold. Although the PCI has since had its slice of the national *sottogoverno* pie (→IV, 4:i), never again has it had the power and influence it enjoyed in the 1944-8 period, when although a Christian Democrat, Alcide De Gasperi, was Prime Minister, the left-wing parties were in the moral ascendancy, on account of their valiant partisan record. This was not unique to Italy: both in France and Belgium, Communists were part of the immediate post-war coalitions.

Far from their present cuddly left come-on, both Pietro Nenni's Socialists and Palmiro Togliatti's Communists were rabidly unreconstructed Stalinists. In fact, *il baffone* – ol' big moustache – was the great unspoken presence in Italian politics until his death in 1953, which was marked by extraordinary scenes of working-class mourning: little candle-lit shrines bearing his image dotted the streets of northern industrial cities.

The force of the Marxist rhetoric of that era is nowhere better preserved than in the Constitution's first article, which states: 'Italy is a democratic republic based on work. Sovereignty belongs to the people ...' The symbol chosen to represent the State underlines this impression. (→II, 3:iv)

Like most Eastern European constitutions, the Italian republican one is a model of democratic precision; unlike the former ones, it has been much more closely adhered to. However, thanks to the Italian addiction to fine words and noble ideas, it promises an awful lot, but very often fails to specify how its good intentions will be carried out; ever since 1948, for example, women have theoretically been granted total equality in all fields (article 3); but the sexual equalities legislation to back it up started materializing only in the mid-1970s, inspired by the prevalent international mood. (→ I, 3:viii)

In fact, the Constitution's wording is so abstract that a special judiciary branch – the Constitutional Court – had to be set up in 1956 to interpret what it actually means, an initiative obstructed for decades by the DC, who enjoyed manipulating it to their own ends too much to allow a neutral view or interpretation of it.

The French Revolution initially inspired a series of copy-cat constitutions in various regions of pre-*Risorgimento* Italy, with notably short life-spans. Among others:
- **1796–7: Cisalpine Republic**
- **1812–15: Sicilian Parliament with British-inspired House of Lords and Commons**
- **1820: Naples (lasted six months)**
- **1848: all regions had one, stopped in 1849, except Piedmont, which became the basis of the later constitution known as *lo statuto albertino*, which was successively adapted into that of united Italy. Unlike the post-war Constitution, it could be altered by further decree.**

(ii) The Presidency

The State hierarchy is headed by the President of the Republic, who is also Commander-in-Chief of the armed forces, Chairman of the Defence Council and President of the Superior Council of the Judiciary. Next comes the President of the Senate, who is followed by the President of the Chamber of Deputies.

The Presidential powers and prerogatives have never

been precisely laid down, and have sometimes caused serious constitutional confusion, but they are generally similar to those of a British monarch. These powers include: to dissolve or refuse to dissolve Parliament; to choose the Prime Minister (non-DC Pertini broke all precedent by selecting non-DC ones); to appoint one third of Constitutional Court members; to convoke extraordinary sessions in Parliament; and to sign or refuse all new laws and decrees.

The official residence of the President of the Republic is il Palazzo del Quirinale, in the former papal and royal residence. There is a summer estate at Castel Porziano by the coast near Rome, formerly the royal hunting reserve. The Presidential Guard, *I Granatieri*, have to be over 1.9 metres tall.

Presidents

Enrico De Nicola	**(DC:1946–8)**
Luigi Einaudi	**(DC:1948–55)**
Giovanni Gronchi	**(DC:1955–62)**
Antonio Segni	**(DC:1962–4)**
Giuseppe Saragat	**(PSDI:1964–71)**
Giovanni Leone	**(DC:1971–8)**
Sandro Pertini	**(PSI:1978–85)**
Francesco Cossiga	**(DC:1985–)**

● **The best-loved: Sandro Pertini.**
● **The most corrupt: Giovanni Leone (he resigned over the Lockheed scandal).**
● **The most intellectual: Luigi Einaudi.**
● **The most self-assertive: Giovanni Gronchi.**
● **The touchiest: Enrico De Nicola.**
● **The most discreet: Francesco Cossiga.**

The trio of presidents, Saragat, Leone and Pertini, were popularly known by the Romans as *Bacco, becco e becchino* – Bacchus, the beak, and the undertaker – referring to their reputations: namely, that Saragat drank, Leone's wife, Donna Vittoria, betrayed him (with the chauffeur), and that Pertini did little but attend State funerals of terrorist victims. The first and last are true, the second apocryphal.

(iii) Parliament

Like those of the Constitution, the mechanisms of the parliamentary apparatus are really too finely tuned to be used outside a dust-free environment, which Italian politics notoriously is not. The system of perfect bicameralism is a case in point. The Camera dei Deputati and the Senato have identical powers and privileges, even for finance bills, with no formal precedence of either house. There exist no fixed procedures against the inevitable and all too frequent conflicts.

La Camera dei Deputati is situated in Palazzo Montecitorio, in a vast turn-of-the-century chamber. The 630 deputies are seated in an ascending crescent formation, on the French model. They sit facing the straight benches of the government, which are dominated by a high top row occupied by the speaker – il Presidente della Camera – who is assisted by ushers dressed like posh waiters in bow ties. Plenary parliamentary debates are flanked by the activities of its fourteen permanent all-party parliamentary commissions, each comprising between thirty-six and forty MPs, the leaderships of which are keenly fought over. There are ten parliamentary groups represented in the current (1987) Parliament.

Il Senato is situated in Palazzo Madama, in a separate part of the city, just by Piazza Navona. Although its layout is almost identical, there are far fewer members. The number fluctuates, but in the current legislature there are 324 elected *senatori*, plus a small number of *senatori a vita* – life senators, as in the House of Lords. All ex-presidents are automatically members, while each serving president can nominate up to four national heroes or cultural luminaries as life senators, although some constitutionalists insist that there can be a total of only four life senators (excepting ex-presidents). The argument remains unresolved. As at Montecitorio, there are ten *gruppi parlamentari*, though the tenth is the *gruppo misto* – mixed group – which contains those national or regional parties too small to reach the quorum that Senate procedure requires.

There are thirteen permanent all-party commissions, each with twenty-five members, flanked by various occasional committees or commissions set up to examine specific issues.

Italian parliamentarians are much less rowdy than their British counterparts: ample seating and the vast lecture-hall disposition of the two chambers create a rational sense of distance compatible with more dignified proceedings. Despite this general rule, the odd scuffle occasionally breaks out, especially between ex-black-shirted Fascists sitting on the MSI benches and some of those older members who fought against them during the war: these have involved exchanges of books, hand-slaps and the odd volley of saliva.

Both houses have been televised for some years, but make fairly soporific viewing. All three RAI TV channels have on-site premises, pandering to the insatiable thirst of Italian politicians for constant screen appearances. These two factors constitute towards an extremely professional visual style.

Despite tough outside security, the Press have unrestricted access to most areas of both houses. Most interviews or briefings take place in *Il Transatlantico* – 'the ocean liner', a vast, hall-like corridor – and *la buvette* – the adjacent bar – where the deputies of all parties hang out between sessions. However fierce and uncompromising Italian political rhetoric may sound, few national parliaments have such good-natured personal relations between deputies of rival parties.

Since the parties exercise their power outside (*sotto-governo*) rather than inside Parliament, it follows that parliamentary discipline is slack: absenteeism is very high, since there is no whip system. The American-style lobby system is only now coming into practice, with pressure groups doing the rounds of the parties.

Whips are superfluous regarding voting, which is by secret electronic ballot, the results of which are flashed on to a screen for all to see. The passage of important legislation creates considerable nervousness on the government benches, since the secret ballot system has allowed the chronic development of voting against one's own party. The actions of *i franchi tiratori* (literally 'sharpshooters') mean that the government is consistently defeated by its own deputies secretly voting with the opposition, often for the obscurest of reasons. This singular phenomenon causes the legislative procedure of both houses of Parliament untold delay.

For the election of important State functionaries, joint sessions are held, sometimes, as on election of the President of the Republic, augmented by members of the regional assemblies.

One third of the members of the Corte Costituzionale – the Constitutional Court – and the Consiglio Superiore della Magistratura – the Higher Council of the Magistrature – are elected by the two houses in joint session.

(iv) The role of the Constitutional Court

The Constitutional Court, envisaged in the 1948 Constitution but set up only in 1956, thanks to deliberate footdragging by the Christian Democrats, is supposed to have three functions: to judge the legitimacy of all legislation; to decide on cases of conflict between State organs, the State and the regions, or between regions; and, lastly, to impeach, if necessary, the President, the PM or members of government. Its fifteen members serve for nine-year terms. Despite the obvious need to be above politics, its members are blatantly party-orientated: one third are elected by Parliament, one third by the President, one third from the various supreme judicial organs. Under its current President, Francesco Saja, it is finally flexing its muscles, ordering Parliament to take note of its judgements. Above all, Saja has managed to reduce the delay in reaching constitutional judgements from ten years to a matter of weeks. (→V, 5)

(v) Elections and voting

Like the Constitution, the Italian electoral system expresses the most finely tuned democratic representation system in the world. More the pity that its votes mean so little.

Italy is divided into thirty-two electoral colleges, more or less corresponding to the *regioni* (→II, 3:ii), each with a number of seats allotted it in proportion to population. There is one *deputato* for every 80,000 voters. In order for a party to gain parliamentary representation, it must poll a total of 300,000 votes nationwide.

Voting is simultaneous for both houses, and is very often hitched on to regional, provincial and local/city elections as well. If Euro-elections were being held simultaneously for any reason, that would make a total of six national elections to vote in on the same day.

The obvious disadvantage of proportional representation on this scale is that voters are unlikely to know anything about most of the candidates, while those elected have no responsibilities towards their electors. Polling day in Italy means scanning lots of names: unlike the British system, with three or four names on the ballot paper, Italian voters have to face up to twenty-five separate party lists with up to fifty candidates per list. More hyperchoice.

Since only major party figures are going to be familiar to voters, it is usually they who get elected first, while lesser known candidates who have been canvassing hard will get passed over. This politician-as-celebrity routine is so effective that well-known party figures frequently stand in more than one *collegio elettorale* – mega-constituency – in order to attract more votes from other parties, and then stand down to allow a lesser-known candidate to get in on their votes. There is no law against this, and it works.

Over the last few years, the Italian political glamour system has gone a stage further, with the enlisting of real stars – or, at least, public figures – as party candidates. Most of them get in, turning Montecitorio into something like a backstage party. The most famous example is porno star Ilona Staller, or 'Cicciolina', but there are also a small army of well-known writers, a couple of singers, a disc-jockey, and an ex-footballer.

In contrast to other countries, where voting for smaller parties seems almost pointless, in Italy it is just the reverse. First the two-tier seat-awarding system means that candidates who do not get a straight 80,000 in one electoral college can pick up stray votes from all the other constituencies to put together a quorum of 300,000 votes. Smaller parties thrive on this. Second, one is more inclined to vote for a small non-governmental party, because you have more idea of where your vote will end up: supporting the policies you have voted for. (→ 3:vi, below)

In the first-past-the-post system, most votes are by definition 'wasted votes'. In Italy, there are almost no losers in politics – there is always something for everyone. In the 1983 elections, only 700,000 voters were left unrepresented – those supporting some twenty-one regional/whacky parties.

The gradual enlargement of the franchise: electoral reform

- **1861: Cavour – 150,000 out of 20 million.**
- **1870: Mazzini complains 'less than 2% of Italians have the vote'.**
- **1882: De Pretis expands electoral roll to 2 1/2 million.**
- **1912: Giolitti: from 3 to 8 million on electoral list.**
- **1924: vote at 30 for men.**
- **1928: Fascist system introduced: 400-man party list voted '*en bloc*' – 'not men but ideas'.**
- **1947: women finally enfranchised; votes at 18 for Camera dei Deputati, at 25 for the Senato.**

Italians are extremely conscientious about voting. There is usually an 88% average turn-out, slightly higher in the North than in the South. Italian electoral law does not allow a postal vote for Italian voters abroad, but the State subsidizes their return journey. This measure was designed for all the hundreds of thousands of Italian emigrants working in other European countries.

Despite such a wide array of parties to choose from, the phenomenon of the protest vote is growing fast: between *schede nulle* – spoiled votes – and *schede bianche* – blank votes – some 12% of Italians give the parties the thumbs down. Italian political pundits note that protest voters hypothetically form the fourth largest party.

(vi) The electoral platform

In stark contrast to the highly developed political interest and voting conscientiousness of the Italians is their tendency to have little or no idea what the party they vote for will do with their vote. While all Italian governments are formed by coalitions, and these coalitions must hammer out a *programma di governo*, none of this is arranged in advance or presented to the voter as a concrete option. The Italians vote for vague notions, not electoral platforms, and in doing so they allow the parties to use their votes as mere blank cheques. *Trasformismo* – the effortless altering of party policy to suit circumstances – is so strong that voters have no guarantee that their party will not jettison a much paraded policy in some political plea-bargaining session.

(vii) Parliamentary reforms

The current parliamentary system is so obviously unworkable that, finally, the parties are committed to serious reforms:

(a) The secret parliamentary voting system is to be abolished. This may be in two phases, with financial laws first being subject to open voting, followed by other legislation later. Every year *la Finanziaria*, the equivalent of the Budget, is ambushed constantly by *franchi tiratori*, and can take a whole year to get through.

(b) The roles of la Camera and il Senato are to be reviewed. All parties agree on reducing numbers (almost 1000 parliamentarians): the PCI and MSI want to abolish the Senate; the other parties want merely to reduce its powers.

(c) There will be closer definition of the powers of the Presidente del Consiglio and the Cabinet, tending to bring them closer to their equivalents in other countries.

(d) Regional devolution will, finally, give the regional, provincial and local assemblies powers to raise funds without asking Parliament.

Both the Socialists and the Neo-Fascists are very vocal in their support for a 'Repubblica Presidenziale' – Presidential Republic, presumably on the French or American model. Neither party, however, has done their homework on the complicated constitutional changes this would involve.

(viii) Symbolic reforms: logo no-no

In 1987, the then PM, Craxi, decided to abolish the post-war national symbol and replace it with a more 'modern' one in time for the fortieth anniversary of the Republic in 1988. A national competition was proclaimed, like the one that produced the winning design in 1947. The old one, which still graces every Italian public building, printed document and police car, as well as all cigarette packets and matchboxes sold in Italy, actually looks fine, the subtext for 'out of date' being 'too communist': Craxi evidently thought that a cog wheel, with a five-pointed star, surrounded by a wreath of olive and oak leaves, with a ribbon reading '*Repubblica Italiana*', could easily be mistaken for most of the East European state logos.

A committee of Italy's most fashionable intellectuals (even Umberto Eco) was formed to judge the entries, but the results were so poor that Craxi's visual de-Stalinization of Italy had to be abandoned – though not before Giorgio Giugiaro had taken a shot at redesigning the national flag. Italy's best-known industrial designer shuffled with the proportions of the existing flag by converting the three vertical bands into triangles, so that the central white band appeared to be a road disappearing into the future. It did not meet with much approval, and was promptly forgotten.

4. Foreign policy: all dressed up and nowhere to go

The Ministero degli Esteri – the Italian Foreign Office – is, like its French equivalent, Le Quai d'Orsay, known by the name of its location: La Farnesina. The Italian diplomatic service contains many of the country's best administrators, and, coincidentally, is largely the reserve of Italy's officially non-existent aristocracy. Unfortunately for them, one of Italy's traditionally least convincing cards played at the international table is foreign policy, which means that their talents are largely wasted. Italy doesn't really have a foreign policy, nor has there been one since the war. Generically, Italy both seeks and maintains good relations with the entire international community, as though perennially anxious to live down twenty years of Mussolini madness. Two other reasons for this lacuna are, first, the tendency to treat the Ministero degli Esteri as just another bargaining card in domestic politics, often resulting in unskilled, uninterested foreign ministers (hence Kissinger's well-known remark about being unwilling to talk international affairs with an unnamed Italian foreign minister, in case it bored him); secondly, the rapid turnover of governments makes it difficult to maintain a regular profile at international forums, both in terms of faces and of policies. All of which is a source of constant mortification to La Farnesina's permanent diplomatic staff, currently run by Bruno Bottai, the ex-UK ambassador, who find themselves hamstrung by the immobility and ignorance of many of their political masters.

(i) Maintaining an international profile: *chi ce lo fa fare*?

If there is no exact policy, there is at least a distinct house style: entertaining fawning relations with the United States (→ 4:ii, below) while simultaneously flirting with Gaddafi, or backing both Britain and Argentina during the Falklands crisis, is vintage Italian elasticity. It is fair to say that, over the last forty years, Italian diplomacy has followed a pragmatic, opportunistic line of agreeing with the last person it spoke with, waiting for others to move first, and then running with the pack.

This is at least realistic, since that way Italy neither over-stretches her resources, nor indulges in the prima donna histrionics of her allies. Episodes like Suez, the Falklands or Grenada are unthinkable in Italy. The armed forces simply aren't equipped to cope, nor would public opinion accept such events. (→ 5, below) Thus, while Italy is a vocal supporter of all the right international organizations – NATO, the UN and its spin-offs, the EC (→ 4:iii, below) etc. – it neither demonstrates, nor is invited to demonstrate, any real interest in taking a role in international affairs – even less, in fact, than its two former Axis allies, which is curious, since Italy became reabsorbed far more quickly into the international forum than either of them.

Despite the firm all-party commitment to NATO, in 1948 over half of them were against membership, favouring neutralism, and the American Secretary of State, Dean Acheson, had to persuade a reluctant Italy to join in. This flattering attention, which was certainly not extended to Germany at the time, was due to American fears of what the PCI might do if Italy were left in a neutralist vacuum – like be tempted to veer Eastwards.

Unlike Britain, Italy has a generally strong all-party consensus for most foreign policy agreements. Even the PCI has moved light years from its anti-everything stance of the early 1950s, except for the odd *de rigueur* anti-US defence statement. This idyllic arrangement is certainly aided by both the relative insignificance of Italy's international commitments, and the tradition of *trasformismo*.

Italy's slightly ambivalent attitude towards international events is a bit like a dog pissing on a lamp-post: the token gesture is sufficient. Italy craves world recognition of its right to be there, but doesn't have anything to say or do when this right is accorded. In 1984 Italy initially clamoured to join the UN task force in Lebanon, where its forces performed their task in a friendly manner but with great effectiveness and were highly valued by the various Lebanese factions. Not so at home: the government eventually succumbed to strong domestic opposition to having a military (albeit peacekeeping) presence there (→ 5, below). Similarly, the Italian naval contribution to the Allied Fleet monitoring the 1987–8 Persian Gulf crisis was initially welcomed, but before long the national mood changed. The reflex reaction of both government and public opinion is always '*Chi ce lo fa fare?* – 'Why should we bother anyway?'

The total predominance of often trivial domestic politics over major international events, and the subsequent lack of interest by the public in the latter, is amply illustrated by the degree and quality of media coverage. Only recently do most international papers have more than one page of foreign news, while the TV news usually relegates foreign coverage to under a quarter. The parties have their time quotas on the news to fill.

(→ IV, 4:i) Most educated Italians are very well informed about the nuances of domestic party politics, but would be hard pressed to identify the capital of Nigeria. More than facts, their knowledge is made up of generalized notions about international affairs, mostly of the classic 1970s parlour pink variety.

(ii) The USA: a very special relationship indeed

Among the least enviable epithets used about Italy is 'the Bulgaria of the West'. The truth hurts. Since the war, there has been an outrageous degree of interference by America into Italian political affairs, of the sort that one generally expects in Central America. The idea is to 'stem the communist menace', a somewhat specious argument, seeing that the PCI has been solidly to the right of the British Labour Party on most issues for the last decade. That the Americans are guilty of poor political analysis in Italy is manifest – most of Washington's post-war ambassadors to Rome are of the sort who found Ronald Reagan intellectually intimidating; but it would appear that they continue to humiliate Italy because the latter just keeps on taking it. Not that Italian statesmen enjoy rough treatment; it's just that they get paid for it. Washington is endearingly candid about it all: non-PCI politicians are summoned for pep talks about containing the Red threat, following which major contributions are made to fund those parties and trade unions perceived as combating communist expansion. Washington was directly responsible after the war for setting up two out of the three main trade unions, as well as the Social Democrat Party. (→ IV, 2:ii; VI, 5:i) Sometimes the Italians just take the money and ignore the advice, as Moro did in launching *il compromesso storico* – the historical compromise between the DC and the PCI. Apart from the cash-flow side, there is also the psychological pressure: Italian politicians, like the rest of the country, live in a symbiotic Stockholm Syndrome-type relationship with the States.

Washington is often irritated by half-hearted support for, or even downright criticism of, certain American foreign policy decisions that Italy sees as expansionist or neo-colonialist (Libyan bombing, Lebanese peace-keeping force, Gulf task force), while tending to overlook the really important detail. Italians, more than any other Western country, want to be colonized, to be expanded in, by America. If many educated Italians affect to despise American culture, and choose to ignore American political traditions and sensibilities, it is because they know that '*Quando piove in America, in Italia si aprono gli ombrelli*' – 'When it rains in the States, in Italy they put up their umbrellas.' (→ II: 5)

(iii) Commitment to the EC: *L'importante è crederci*

The usual dichotomy applies: Italy is the fiercest proponent of EC membership, and by far the worst observer of its directives. Unlike Britain, which obstinately refuses to go along with majority Community opinions, but implements them when obliged to, Italy enthusiastically approves everything, but then fails to do anything about them. Despite initial hostility, followed by a phase of purely opportunist interest, Italy is now the country with by far the most favourable popular sentiment towards the EC. Parliament, the Press and public opinion press for political union now. The memory of Altiero Spinelli, Italy's nearest equivalent to Spaak or Monnet, is revered in religious terms. The breathless, idealistic rhetoric that characterized the 19th-century *Risorgimento* has been dusted off, and is being heavily recycled for Europe. The signature tune of the news bulletins of Italy's Radio 3 is now a tackily 1960s Walter Carlos-style electronic rendition of the 'Ode to Joy' from Beethoven's Ninth, and the broadcast is called 'Radio news *for Europe*'. It is neither *about* Europe (it features the usual mixture of party news and comment), nor *in* other European languages – it is simply an abstract gesture. Like the signature-bearing petitions that get drawn up calling for the immediate constitution of a strong federal European parliament with executive powers, *l'importante è crederci* – it's the thought that counts.

This is largely because Italy knows that, alone, it will never have a real say in international affairs, and that there is strength in numbers; but it is also because its own feeble governmental structures have everything to gain from the imagined invigorating breeze of North European efficiency. To which, the reasonable corollary is: how much of Italy's *malgoverno*, *lottizzazione* and *partitocrazia* – inefficient government and official corruption – is likely to rub off on the rest of Europe, via an expanded Strasbourg Parliament? (→ VI, 1:ii–iii)

Relations with individual EC members

● **France: close, but on France's terms. Italy's inferiority complex towards the country it most closely models itself on is perfectly reciprocated by a distinctly patronizing France, which applauds Italy's well-disposed attitude, but shuns any Italian attempts to insinuate itself into the Franco-German axis.**
● **Germany: ambivalent attitude – politically and**

economically full of enthusiasm and admiration, especially for the SPD and its leaders, which increasingly serves as a role model for the Italian Communist Party. Plus a certain sense of identification due to strong parallels in their history. However, this contrasts with quite a strong antipathy to the Germans as people.

• Great Britain: gone are the days when Lord Curzon, the British Foreign Secretary, made his Italian opposite number hang around for eight days at Claridge's before he would deign to receive him; and when Mussolini subsequently defined the United Kingdom as 'a little old lady who will die off soon, leaving us a huge legacy'. Relations could be much warmer, considering that an unofficial alliance between the two would do much to redress the imbalance caused by the Franco-German *entente*, but London isn't interested. Relations are thus polite but cool: there is very little understanding of each other's motives and methods, especially since 1979. Italian politicians express a grudging admiration for the Thatcher order of things, but cannot imagine why anyone would destroy a tame rule-by-consensus régime, such as works so well in Italy. Britain's 'realistic' policy of refusing further binding economic/political integration agreements is something that Italy, even more than most other states, sees as gratuitous boorishness. Despite this, bilateral trade is booming (imports to UK: £405 million for January 1988 from £325 million for January 1987). There is also a strong and sincere admiration of British political and social culture, particularly evident with Anglophile President Francesco Cossiga.

• Spain: Despite a certain rhetoric about fellow Mediterranean status and ex-President Pertini's highly publicized friendship with King Juan Carlos, bilateral relations remain limited, as with both Greece and Portugal. This indifference seems all the odder in view of Italy's selfless (in terms of economic competition) role in campaigning for the admission of all three to the Community.

• Other: for geographical and cultural reasons, both Greece and Portugal feel close to the Italians. Although Mussolini invaded Greece during the war, individual Italian soldiers showed great kindness to the Greeks, who to this day show their gratitude to the startled Italians by mechanically repeating the phrase, '*Stessa faccia, stessa razza*' – 'We've got the same face, we're from the same race.' Portugal is where Italy's last king, Umberto II, lived out his days, while Belgium is where the largest European community of Italian *Gastarbeiter* (mostly coalminers) will be living out theirs. As a result, Belgium gets RAI 1. Holland and Denmark send football players, Ireland pilgrims.

(iv) Non-EC Western European states

The most commonly seen foreign number-plates in northern Italy are those of the Italian-speaking cantons of Switzerland, whose inhabitants come in their droves to shop in cheaper (by now, only just), more stylish, Italy. However, the Swiss have a collective horror of Italy's 'dirty, noisy and dangerous streets'; Italians working in *Svizzera* resent the somewhat racist nature of Swiss residency laws. Apart from the enormous trade figures between the Alpine neighbours, it is across Switzerland that a vast amount of Italy's imports arrive.

Despite occasional tension over the Alto Adige issue (→ 1:ii, above) with Italian-born *Schützen* demonstrating on the streets of Vienna in favour of reincorporation into Austria, relations are excellent. Since 1988, stringent border controls have been abolished for an experimental period. Like Germany, Austria ia a source of tourists, who flock across the Brenner Pass.

During the 1960s, pert Scandinavian blondes were a collective male obsession, the subject of many Italian *Carry On*-style films. Now Scandinavia is more famous for football trainers, marauding multi-nationals and the Nobel Prize.

(v) Eastern Europe

Italy is undoubtedly the NATO country most qualified to deal with the Communist countries, with which it is in some ways very close. The links engendered by the West's largest Communist party were once considerable, and although now much reduced, they have left Italian politicians with a strong working knowledge of the system, while Italian newspapers, even more than West German ones, have the strongest tradition in Western Europe of specializing in Eastern European affairs: many of their best commentators are in fact Eastern bloc émigrés. Yugoslavia and Albania are direct neighbours, and Budapest is nearer Rome than Palermo is Milan, while the Romanian language is close enough to Italian for the two to be mutually comprehensible: the Romanians love the Italians as much as the Greeks do. Both in Yugoslavia and in Albania, Italian is still widely spoken and understood; communities of Slovene-speakers (around Trieste) and Albania-speakers (in Apulia) reinforce the link.

Economically, Agnelli has been a tireless bridge-builder, with the result that Fiat is now practically *the* East European car. Gardini, Berlusconi and IRI are also highly active in the Soviet Union (→ IV, 4:iii; VI, 2:iii–iv): Berlusconi part-owns Yugoslavia's Capodistria TV channel, which broadcasts all over Italy (→ VII, 6:i), while Poland has recently bought the rights to rebroadcast RAI 1 live.

Finally, it is hard to overestimate the impact of a Polish Pope on Eastern European affairs, especially during such an era of thawing relations. Thanks to the input received from the ever-expanding network of papal envoys and local Church hierarchy, the Vatican now has an unrivalled intelligence service monitoring grassroots (and Central Committee) level developments in Eastern Europe.

(vi) The Middle East

Italy has cultivated a strong Mediterranean connection over the last forty years, which reached a feverish level of intensity during the 1973 oil crisis. With the obvious exception of Libya, the Arabs don't feel patronized by the Italians as they do by ex-colonial powers like Britain and France. By exploiting this fact, and playing their 'cultural/geographical common heritage' suit very hard, the Italians have made considerable headway in their scheme that the Arabs should choose them as their natural privileged partner in Europe. Apart from some considerable achievements in the economic field, Italy in some ways has been a victim of its own success: Middle Eastern terrorists now regularly use Italy (particularly Rome) for target practice, while there is a vast influx of illegal immigrants from the Maghreb. At an EC and NATO level, Andreotti's ambiguous, not-so-honest broker stance with Gheddafi, and Craxi's more straightforward but belligerent endorsement of Arafat, have not gained Italy the prestige they'd perhaps hoped for. Only in Iran has Italy played a really constructive role; Andreotti maintained good working relations with the Khomenei régime from its inception, and particularly with Foreign Minister Velayati. After Japan, Italy is Iran's leading foreign trade partner. It did a lively business in armaments during the Iran–Iraq conflict, and is now hoping to pick up the largest portion of contracts for the reconstruction era.

(vii) Asia and the Pacific

Asia is an almost closed book to Italian diplomacy, despite sharing its glamour-based, dynastic approach to politics. Italy's attempts to do business in India on a large scale (Fiat once looked poised to follow the crypto-Austin Hindustani Ambassador as the sub-continent's leading car) have substantially failed; the Japanese got in there instead. Only Italian professional hippies still keep the flag flying, as they once did in Afghanistan too.

When Goria, then PM, visited the ASEAN states in 1987, it was the first time an Italian leader had ever set foot in any of them. Italian business is now trying to follow the Japanese example there, with particularly energetic business deals in China. Trade figures with Japan remain fairly healthy, thanks partly to the almost total embargo on Japanese cars into Italy, and partly to the enormous influx of Japanese tourists – and also to the huge exports of Italian fashion.

Trade links with Burma, Laos and Thailand are lively but strictly unofficial: the Golden Triangle is responsible for most of the raw materials imported by the Sicilian heroin refineries. (→ V, 2:iii)

Australia boasts a large Italian community (particularly in Melbourne), but bilateral relations, as with New Zealand, are distinctly limited.

(viii) Africa

Apart, obviously, from its ex-colonies – propping up the Siad Barre régime in Somalia, attempting valiantly to soften the spikier aspects of the Mengistu one in Ethiopia – Italy keeps a fairly low profile on the Dark Continent. The only exceptions are Nigeria, where Italian industry likes to dump its toxic wastes, and Mozambique, which has benefited from large amounts of Italian aid (cash and know-how) in recent years.

(ix) South and Central America

The Latin connection helps a lot: both ethnically (50% of Argentinians are of Italian descent), and politically (Italy currently chairs the Christian Democrat International, most of whose members are from Catholic South and Central America). Argentina once had much closer contacts with Italy, but it is now viewed mostly as a source of world-class, if occasionally quixotic, football players. Both Uruguay and Brazil fulfil the same useful function, although the latter country has become, over the last decade, the object of an extraordinary lifestyle fixation among many young Italians – for Khatmandu and *kif*, read Rio and rumba – while among the literate, most South American authors are currently enjoying a vogue out of all proportion to their real worth.

5. Defence and warfare

Identifying Italian servicemen

At certain times of day, some parts of Italian cities, especially around stations and main post offices (phoning home), are so crowded with servicemen that you may suspect you've stumbled on to a film-set. No, they are real, and they are doing their military service, and if you are young and female, they will waste no time in telling you about it. Many will be in civvies (you can always tell by the haircuts), but some of those that aren't have well-known uniforms.

• *I Bersaglieri*: the most popular. A crack regiment, who wear broad-brimmed hats covered with black feathers, and who run instead of walk or march – *at all times*. Mussolini was one. They get the most concentrated applause at official parades; they pass faster.

• *Gli Alpini*: the best troops. Distinguishable by a funny little grey pointed peasant's cap with a feather in it. Lousy at marching: more used to clambering up the Alps.

• *La Folgore*: the most macho; also excellent troops. A parachute regiment with a strong, though largely anachronistic, reputation for being Fascists. This is not surprising: they have an inimitable swagger, take pride in tattoos, and wear a skull, lightning flash and parachute badge.

• *Le accademie militari di Modena, Livorno e Pozzuoli*: if you see pairs of soldiers who look as though they've just popped off a 'Quality Street' box in fuchsia and navy uniforms, with silver buttons and dainty little swords, this is who they are. The State spends a total of 111 billion lire on its crack

One of the best-known negative stereotypes about Italy concerns its fighting capacity: Helmut Schmidt's inopportune joke about the Italian tank having only reverse gears, like the more recent *Times* article which appeared to mock Italy's crack regiment, the *Bersaglieri*, for 'wearing dyed chicken feathers', upset a lot of people.

Regarding their past battle record, Italians explain that they have been regularly immersed in wars none of them really believed in: 'defence of the Triple Entente' rhetoric was needed to justify Italian entry into World War I, while the hysterical Fascist propaganda did the trick for World War II. In a worthwhile cause, like the *Risorgimento*, or the partisan groups of World War II who took on the Nazis, Italians have performed many acts of considerable heroism, which foreign commentators conveniently ignore. Likewise, the present-day Italian armed forces contain many professional units full of world-class combatants. Having a soft spot for *la mamma* doesn't mean you can't be a *vero uomo* – a tough guy.

Whatever their collective weakness for fancy uniforms, few Italians entertain any such fantasies about their potential as a military world power. So, while keen to be seen 'in there with the big boys' doing their bit on various recent peacekeeping exercises, neither the Italian government nor the Italian people really take their presence on such occasions all that seriously. This is a form of official realism that other governments, including the British one, would do well to take into account. In a 1989 Gallup International poll for the *Daily Telegraph*, it was revealed that the percentage of Italians (32%) who would not be prepared to defend their country was lower than that of either Belgium (43%) or West Germany (33%), and not much higher than Britain's (28%).

(i) The armed forces

If Italy has little foreign policy, there is no defence policy at all. The role of the armed forces appears confused and obsolete, due partly to a historical sense of mortification at Mussolini's expansionism, and partly to hopeless government organization. The country's top brass generally make valiant attempts to conceal their sense of frustration at having to be Cinderellas in uniform. In the corridors of Italy's Stato Maggiore della Difesa – the Combined Chiefs of Staff – they are fond of pointing out that Italy's current annual military expenditure of 22,500 billion lire (2.04% of GNP) is exactly half the sum spent in Britain (4.8% of GNP).

Despite an enormous contingent of conscripts (283,000 in 1989), only a much smaller proportion (140,000) of the Italian armed forces are professionals. The presence of a vast majority of reluctant national servicemen probably eliminates, through sheer inefficiency, what it contributes in manpower terms. For a country with such non-bellicose traditions, it may seem paradoxical that there should be military service, but according to conventional post-war wisdom, it is there as a bulwark to resist any sabre-rattling or *coup d'état* attempts by Fascist-inclined colonels (a conspicuous number of MSI deputies are former army officers: (→ IV, 2:ii), but also as a melting pot for the different social and regional elements. There is much to be said for the second reason, but the first is hopelessly outdated.

The strategic thinking behind the division of troops and resources is somewhat obsolete too: *L'Esercito* – the large Land Army – soaks up 43% of expenditure, on the grounds that Italy is more likely to be invaded than bombed. *La Marina* – the Navy – with 21.6%, is probably the most up to date and well equipped force, with the best trained personnel. *L'Aeronautica* – the Air Force – with 35.4%, began in 1988 a ten-year rearmament programme estimated at 32,000 billion lire, much of which will be devoted to the Eurofighter Tornado, which the Italian aeronautical business has participated in. The Air Force are the lucky ones, as the Army are condemned to use hardware (tanks, missiles, rifles) that the Stato Maggiore della Difesa doesn't hesitate to define as obsolete. Only regular, skilful maintenance keeps much of their armoury serviceable.

military academies, of which Modena (Army) and Livorno (Navy) are of ancient constitution. Together with Pozzuoli (Air Force), they are the source not only of your classic Italian 'officer and gentleman', but also the background for syrupy films and TV adverts for *pasta* (→ 6:iii, below).

● *La Ronda*: if you see a soldier, a sailor and an air-man walking down the street together towards dusk, they are not impersonating prune-stones, but performing a slightly obsolete Italian military task – looking out for deserters or soldiers who are badly dressed or behaved.

Professional armies in Europe

Great Britain	**320,000**
West Germany	**260,000**
France	**220,000**
Italy	**140,000**
(NATO)	

Defence spending as % of GNP

Great Britain	**4.8%**
France	**4.0%**
West Germany	**3.0%**
Italy	**2.0%**

The higher echelons of power are complicated by having a non-executive President as chairman of the Consiglio Supremo della Difesa – National Defence Council – which also includes executive officers like the Prime Minister, the Defence and Foreign ministers and the various Chiefs of Staff. Furthermore, coalition politics means that the Defence and Foreign Ministers are rarely, if ever, of the same party, and hence may have radically different ideas on policy. The only thing that gets agreed to by the politicians, but not by the Stato Maggiore della Difesa is the regular defence cuts, which in 1990 will total 1600 billion lire.

Since 1987, there has been an attempt to enlist professional soldiers, using an advertising strategy intent on overcoming the largely sentimental, antiquated, 'our brave boys' notion the Italians have of their armed forces. The concept of heroic defenders of the nation has just been replaced by the concept of what the forces can do for you, evidently borrowed from HM or US armed forces adverts. Just like those definite-article-less adverts for 'Army', 'Navy' and 'Air Force' common to the British Press for well over a decade, '*Esercito*', '*Marina*' and '*Carabinieri*', accompanied by 'Me generation' blandishments about 'personal fulfilment' and footed by terse, neo-butch graphics, now help press-gang young male Italians into *le forze armate*.

Young females need not apply, however. Those that do are turned down, although the new Army Chief of Staff, General Domenico Corcione, estimates that the effects of the baby boom will soon leave Italy with a seriously depleted professional sector, unless women are admitted into the services. Almost two-thirds of the 18,000 vacant places in the Army's professional corps remain unfilled.

Numbers of military: 1988–9

Esercito (Army)	**283,000**
Carabinieri (Police)	**85,000**
Aeronautica (Air Force)	**70,000**
Marina (Navy)	**40,000**

(ii) Military service – *la naia*

La naia, as military service is known in army slang, is usually a bit of a shock for its victims, most of whom have never been away from their families before for so much as a weekend. The steadily rising number of barracks suicides has recently caused the government to make a few cosmetic improvements, but there has never been a concerted attempt, even by the anti-militarist Radical Party, to call for its abolition. Only in 1989 did the PCI call for *La naia* to be reduced to six months. The military have responded that this would not be cost-effective.

This character-building exercise lasts twelve months (eighteen months for officers), and is ameliorated by a daily pay of about 4000 lire a day, which not a few of the poorer, southern, *militari di leva* – military servicemen – contrive to supplement in other ways. (→ I, 3:xi) The government are trying to find ways of increasing conscripts' pay, and to stem the cases of mental and physical cruelty that go on in the *caserme* – the barracks. Apart from the enormous figure of accidental deaths among *naioni* – conscripts – the number of suicides is rising constantly. The strict pecking order allows *i nonni* – literally 'grandfathers', but in this case conscripts in their final months – to treat *le reclute* – the new recruits – much as they like. Senior officers traditionally turn a blind eye to *gavettoni* – hearty, often quite unpleasant, practical jokes – even though they sometimes develop into a form of systematic persecution.

It is not surprising that most young Italians who receive their draft card try and get out of obeying it. There are countless techniques for avoiding *il servizio militare*: enrolling for university puts off the fatal day until graduation, when, as a mature adult surrounded by 18-year-olds, the whole experience could be much worse. All official jobs require young Italian males to produce a certificate to say they are *milite-esente* – that they have done, or have been excused from doing, their military service. Making the best of a bad job, many families rely on *raccomandazione* – string-pulling – to ensure that their son gets to stay in his home town, or at least somewhere reasonable. The army now proudly states that 70% of conscripts serve within 350 kilometres of home. If you're being woken up by some fun-loving *nonni* at 3 a.m. to scrub out the lavatory with a toothbrush this may not be much of a consolation.

The armed forces have a form of trade union – Cocer – which is now actively trying to promote improved living conditions for their members. They want 10,000 lire a day, a more impartial application of certain military regulations and the liberalization of others. Despite the spartan conditions, the poor quality catering and endemic cruelty, Cocer consider that boredom is the main enemy facing the 283,000 conscripts; as a result, they estimate that 50% of *militari di leva* smoke hashish or marijuana regularly, while a smaller, but still surprising, number of conscripts are regular heroin users. As a result, there are

125 'psychological support centres' spread throughout Italy's barracks.

Conscientious objectors have a hard time too; in 1989 there were 532 'total' conscientious objectors (i.e. those refusing to do even the substitute *servizio civile*) languishing in Italian military prisons for up to four years, of whom 90% were Jehovah's Witnesses. (→ VIII, 9:iii) There are some 5000 'partial' objectors who work for a series of welfare organizations, from the Red Cross and the Catholic Caritas, to the Communist-run Arci.

6. *Xenofilia* and neo-patriotism

No industrialized country has quite such a self-deprecating view of itself as Italy, articulated as a lucid insight into how badly things work. The natural reflex is to emphasize how well they work abroad. If 'Northern' countries are somewhat despised for their cold, rigid approach to life, they are above all extolled for being honest, efficient and 'progressive'. Objective factors largely corroborate this view, but there is an important psychological element as well, which is worth underlining. Italians *qua* Italians have a basic lack of self-confidence which makes them ill disposed to find qualities even in each other – regionalism again; hence they look abroad for a role model. A historic anxiety to be accepted with dignity at the international forum leads to an exaggerated tendency to accommodate one's prospective peers. The other main reason for loving everything foreign is the natural Italian talent for shameless cultural and consumer assimilation, rather like the stereotype Texan millionaire shouting 'I'll buy that!' Other countries might think twice before lifting wholesale enormous chunks of a foreign culture, but not in Italy. Anything can be repackaged and sold in Italy, provided it is American – sports, clothing, foodstuffs, social mores, office equipment.

(i) Italians abroad: emigration

One of the most persistent causes of Italy's inferiority complex has been the humiliating role which emigrants have had to endure since the early 19th century. The intense poverty which forced so many Italians to emigrate was often matched by even worse conditions in the host country, causing many to come back to Italy. Others naturally came home for the opposite reason: having made their fortunes, they came home to enjoy them. (→ II, 3:vi) The Italians' tendency as emigrants to maintain highly introspective cultural traditions and community ties explains their high-profile image as an immigrant entity: they brought southern Italy with them. 'Brooklynese' is the name they give to the Anglo-Italian patois spoken in New York. As bad as the poverty they had to endure was the reputation for being so near the bottom of the ethnic pile. Hence the extraordinary pride felt in Italy for 'the sons of Italy' who do well abroad. Even though the families of people like Lord Charles Forte, Mario Cuomo and Madonna (there was recently a strong move to erect a statue to her in her grandparents' native village in the Abruzzi) may have emigrated generations ago, they remain fundamentally

'Italians'. Only in the last few years has Italy's new cliché image as the ultimate designer nation started to overshadow that of the terminally poverty-stricken peasant factory. (→ VI, 3)

(ii) Italians abroad: socialites

The new economic boom and the subsequent new self-confidence means that it is now terribly chic to be an Italian abroad. Naturally, the people concerned have taken full advantage of this new-found admiration, whether they have much to offer at a personal level or not. Like the Eurotrash set in New York and LA, International Professional Italians have become a highly recognizable species in their own right in the party fauna habitat the world over. They don't have to say or do anything special, just look Italian. This new voguishness may be exploited for personal gain – particularly true among Italian foreign Press correspondents, who strike ridiculous poses they'd never dare try on in Italy – but it has also been profitably used for acquiring serious professional prestige. This involves Italian business-backed exhibitions, both temporary and permanent, like the new Accademia Italiana delle Arti e delle Arti Applicate at 25 Princes Gate in London, Olivetti's 'Glasses of the Caesars' at the Royal Academy, or the Pirelli Garden at the Victoria & Albert Museum. Sometimes this ambitious new form of *presenzialismo* – 'being there' – goes too far: in 1988, Alitalia's boss, Umberto Nordio, was sacked for not having bought a 'prestige location' skyscraper in New York in which to install the Italian airline's international offices.

(iii) Patriotism: the new mood

Italians have always had an awkward relationship with the idea of national pride. The immense fervour generated by the process of the *Risorgimento* soon dissipated into disillusionment, while Mussolini's 'triumphs' obviously caused a sense of guilty embarrassment after his downfall. The fact of losing the last war, and, more, of being beaten *by both sides*; a sense of disgust at the ill-functioning national institutions; the regional rather than national sense of pride; the rebound effect of the old foreign view of Italy; and, perhaps above all, the ideological opposition to patriotism instilled by the 1968 and 1977 student movements and the *anni di piombo* – the terrorist era that followed it up – all helped to reduce Italy's national morale by the end of the 1970s to zero. Despite the immense optimism caused by the '*boom economico*' of the 1950s and 1960s, the Italians were aware that this was more than anything a case of catching up, of making up for lost time.

However, the beginning of the 1980s witnessed a dramatic reversal in Italy's fortunes, and, before long, of this attitude too: Italians rediscovered *amor proprio*, and national self-respect.

The first sign of this was a moral one: the discovery that the little old man elected as a compromise choice to the presidency was in fact a beacon of righteousness, and a really good guy into the bargain. In his mid-80s, Sandro Pertini became Italy's first ever loved politician: the Italians discovered that *il Palazzo* could also produce honest, upright men. He had the same effect as the Queen Mother has in Britain: dignified, but with the best common touch ever dreamed of by a campaign organizer.

This was reinforced by an important sporting victory: Italy's spectacular World Cup win at Madrid in 1982 had a galvanizing effect on the nation that is hard to convey in words. (→ VIII, 4:ii) It was as if they had just won a major war. Pertini's decidedly un-protocol-minded celebration of the victory from the box of honour, next to King Juan Carlos, which was broadcast round the world, represented a deeply significant moment in Italian history. This was the first time the Italians had seen a Head of State (or any important political figure) as someone who was truly interpreting their feelings in that moment. For the first time they felt: *He's one of us!* Suddenly, affection for this kindly old man ('*Viva Pertini!*') became associated with the previously unconvincing '*Viva L'Italia!*'. From that moment onwards, Pertini became the personification of the State, and both were loved, in a way that had hitherto seemed inconceivable. '*Viva Pertini!*' '*Viva L'Italia!*' The President's occasional, highly ill-advised, political outburst and fairly bloodstained record as wartime partisan leader were completely blotted from view: he was celebrated in pop songs, toasted at informal parties.

No longer do a vast majority of Italians think that *il prato del vicino è sempre più verde*; nearly half of them think that Italy's grass is greener after all. Attribute this to vastly improved living conditions, increased sense of national pride, and the widespread publication in Italy of the various international polls that always place Italy among the best three countries on earth to live in.

% of Italians who think the best country in the world to live is:

- **Italy 47.6%**
- **France 15.9%**
- **USA 15.9%**
- **Germany 9.3%**
- **Japan 6.8%**
- **Other countries 5.1%**
- **Britain is conspicuous by its absence.**

'The Spirit of Madrid' soon spilled over into other sporting events, turning them into 'victories' regardless of the outcome. Shortly afterwards, the Italian long-boat *Azzurra* was to smash through the English-speaking nations' monopoly of the America's Cup, and managed to reach the quarter-finals before being eliminated. To judge by the collective euphoria unleashed by this honourable defeat, one could have been forgiven for thinking that Italy had come first. (At least semantically speaking, this can be justified, since the verb *vincere* – to win, to beat – can be stretched in Italian to mean to do very well.)

Subsequently, Italy's first division, with its billions of lire spent on world-class football players (Platini, Maradona, Gullitt, Rush), convinced Italians that theirs was the finest championship in the world. Media commentators couldn't speak or write an article without saying it at least twice – '*il campionato più bello del mondo*'.

Ever since then, the amount of exuberance and exaltation displayed at sporting 'victories' has quadrupled. The Italians, more than most, are media whores. They know when a television camera is focusing on them, and they know what to do, instinctively. The world now recognizes Italian Sports Rhetoric (certainly preferring it to the British version), and so the fans rise to the occasion, like Pavlovian quadrupeds.

Lo spettacolo – showbiz – came next. San Remo, the annual song festival, which had had its moment of glory in the 1950s, but which had dragged on frumpishly ever since, had a massive shot of adrenalin pumped into its veins by the New Mood of national rhetoric. Fifty years after its birth, Mussolini's precious concept of *italianità* ridiculed and reviled ever since, was re-evaluated. The winning song (it actually came second, but, as we have learnt, this is often a minor detail in Italy) was a stirring patriotic dirge called '*Un italiano vero*' – 'A true Italian' – that faintly recalled a US Marines Vietnam battle song in slow motion. This dreadful song by Toto Cotugno, which actually mentioned all of the above trophies by name, was to become *the* song of summer 1983 – not just in Italy, but right across the Mediterranean: *Mare Nostrum* indeed.

The most important vehicle for launching the New Mood was, naturally, television. It was television that was to complete Garibaldi and Cavour's work in unifying the peninsula, in giving Italy a linguistic and cultural identity previously missing. Of course, a single unifying, charismatic figure was necessary, a national figure capable of commanding respect and *simpatia* from Sicily to the Alps. Pippo Baudo was very much the right man in the right place at the right time. Tall, handsome and thoroughly un-regional (very un-Sicilian for some-one from Catania), Baudo achieved a rare stranglehold on the nation's viewing public in the early 1980s by presenting all three of Italy's major variety shows on the main State channel RAI 1 – Friday evening, Saturday evening, Sunday afternoon. After years of shoddy, back-ward, monopolistic programming, and then prodded by the challenge of the newly established private channels, the State TV broadcasting authority RAI had finally come into its own. (→ VII, 6:i)

Baudo became Pertini's co-star, in this epic drama of how the Italian nation discovered its true identity, with a cast of 57 million. His lowbrow Messianic rhetoric, coupled with his unquestionably professional TV man-ner and underlined by his extraordinary domination of air-time, made him an incisive candidate for the job of interpreting the nation's new-found self-confidence. More Dan Rather than Terry Wogan, he exalted the spirit of *italianità*, and mocked Italy's enemies and putters-down. He was Italy's Malcolm X, and he knew it. He once declared in public that if there were presidential elections in Italy, and he were to stand, he would win hands down. The Press called him 'il Pippo nazionale'.

Contemporaneous to all this was the enormous inter-national success culled by leading fashion designers like Armani, Versace and Valentino, and, with a slightly lower profile, design and industrial products. The key phrase was 'Made in Italy'. What was once a neat description of Italian industrial output became an all-embracing, acritical, cliché. Like the use of the word 'designer whatever' in English, 'Made in Italy' has become an automatic synonym for 'classy product' to the Italians themselves. From being embarrassed at all things Italian, they now believe more in this hype than do the foreigners for whom it was originally intended. (→ VI, 3)

In 1986, the generalized expression 'Made in Italy' was joined by a more specifically triumphant term, '*il sorpasso*'. This usually refers to one car overtaking another. Here, though, the two cars were the UK and Italy. The idea that the Italian GNP now outdistances the British one has embedded itself in the national psyche. Italian papers now regularly refer to Italy, not only as *la penisola* or *il bel paese*, but also as *il quinto potere economico mondiale* – the fifth world economic power – after the USA, Japan, Germany and France. Frequently there is talk of overtaking France too. Heady stuff. (→ VI, 1:i)

Advertising has taken like a duck to water to this growing new national mood of self-congratulation. Products and services of every kind are now advertised almost exclusively in terms of their Italianness. Mussolini, who had to impose the doctrine of *autarchia* – economic self-sufficiency – in the 1930s, would have loved it. Advertising agencies vie with each other for the most jingoistic headline or story. A make of *pasta*, Barilla, probably wins on points, with its pompous '*Chariots of Fire*' sound-alike theme music (not difficult, since it also was written by Vangelis) and a series of syrupy storylines featuring 'typically Italian' events that until the late 1970s would have been judged ideologically inadmissible: 'Quality Street'-like soldier boys from the Modena Military Academy (→ 5:i, ACCESS) welcomed into private homes; ancient, calm-looking hospital corridors filled with efficient nuns – and so on. In Britain, lots of adverts like this are made, but they are always set in the past: the keyword is nostalgia. In Italy, they are resolutely present-day, and the keyword is jingoism. All the positive-image 'officer and gentleman' genre TV adverts in Italy over the last few years have had a knock-on effect in real life, and public attendance at military parades, after years of indifference, has soared. The Italian Armed Forces: as advertised on TV.

Pertini's period of office and Baudo's period of glory are over now, and recently both export figures and international sporting successes have been checked somewhat, but that doesn't really matter. They've done their job – convinced the public that the old slogan '*Italiani – brava gente!*' – they're a really good bunch, the Italians – was true after all.

The international reputation enjoyed by the Italian political system seems confined to tired notions about revolving door governments and Byzantine intrigues, which is particularly misleading in view of the fact that what Italy suffers from is not political instability but quite the opposite: a dogged refusal to change. Italian politics are in fact much simpler than they may appear, and Italy has actually had fewer general elections than Britain since the war; it just has more government reshuffles.

The plethora of Italian political parties provides another source of confusion, since they all have a great deal in common, and exist largely because of the system that accommodates them, while at the same time helping to make that system yet more complex: the electoral laws of Italy's political structure are those of an almost perfect democracy; but its parliamentary procedures are those of a totally constipated one. And whatever the conscious inspirations (mostly French) of the Italian political parties, it is ironic – especially for a country where American pressure keeps the Communist Party out of the button room – that the greatest unconscious influence on party style, right across the political spectrum, should be that of the Soviet Union – pre-*perestroika*, at that.

Italian politics are also characterized by a keen sense of showbiz – long before this caught on elsewhere – and a marked discrepancy between the relatively dirty daily business and the high-falutin' idealism that provide much of its stimulation (this priority of words over deeds comes up again in Chapter VIII). Most ordinary Italians are inured to the blandishments of *il bel discorso* – fine words – but that doesn't alter anything. Rhetoric is the heroin that pumps through the veins of Italian politics, and naturally there exists a rich lexicon of political terms for its adherents to draw upon.

Whatever the modern foreign influences the parties may draw on, the matrix from which Italian political science takes its shape lies much nearer home, and is much more ancient, often giving rise to a Machiavellian use of power for short-term benefit. This chapter deals with the way the political parties perceive themselves as part of the State apparatus itself, and with how they divide and administer it to their own advantage; for the degeneration of this process into something more sinister, see Chapter V.

A larger part of industry is State-run in Italy than in any other Western country, but it is at least run with some success; the same cannot be said for their Welfare State, such as it is. In an era when the cutting back of the protective role of government has become a central issue, most Italians want to know how their government can reduce its commitment to something that was hardly there in the first place.

---

1. The government

(i) *Crisi di governo*: forming a government

Although Italy has constant *crisi di governo*, politically it is really very stable. These government 'crises' are no more than government reshuffles, where the Presidente del Consiglio is reshuffled too. If daily parliamentary business grinds to a halt during a *crisi*, it is because it hardly moves anyway. The real business of politics is decided at the various party headquarters so it makes little difference if there is a formal government or not. Even if there is no smooth-running civil service along French or British lines to administer the country while it is elected-leader-less, the party commissars responsible for the *sottogoverno* see to everything.

Traditionally, the role of Prime Minister has been weak, which accounts for the title, Presidente del Consiglio di Ministri – President of the Council of Ministers – a term used in other European countries too.

Il Presidente del Consiglio at least gets very impressive premises – Palazzo Chigi, located next to Palazzo Montecitorio, the Chamber of Deputies, and nearly as big. Only rarely have party leaders – *segretari di partito* – contrived to be Presidente del Consiglio as well, thus wielding far more power. Just as the Presidente del Consiglio exercises little of the customary executive authority in running the government, so he has little say in choosing who his ministers will be.

To paraphrase Mark Twain, forming a government in Italy is easy: they do it so often.

(a) Following elections or a *crisi di governo*, the President of the Republic holds talks with the leaders of all the parties (this takes some time – there are between ten and twelve to consult), who all air their views.

(b) On the basis of these talks, and with many party 'recommendations', the President invites some party notable to form a government. This person is not necessarily the party leader. Until recently the choice was automatically made from the Democrazia Cristiana (DC) – Christian Democrats – now it may be from one of the other government coalition parties.

(c) Very often the person charged with forming a government is unable to: his coalition colleagues may favour someone else. Since there is no official opposition in Italy, the failure of the DC-orientated coalition to deliver the goods never leads to the Partito Comunista Italiano (PCI) – Italian Communist Party – as second largest party, being invited to have a shot instead. With some justice, the Communists protest at being the Cinderella of Italian politics: they are never invited to the ball.

(d) The President will finally find another coalition figure whom the other *correnti* – faction – leaders find acceptable. How long this takes depends on how much the *correnti* are prepared to wrangle over increasing their strategic position in the government.

(e) Il Presidente del Consiglio *incaricato* – charged with forming a government – will then sit down with his copy of the *manuale Cencelli* and get to work. Cencelli was a 1950s Christian Democrat who had the brilliant idea of writing a pseudo-scientific treatise regarding the specific political value of each government post, calculated on a points system. Every new government is formed with scrupulous attention to the *manuale*, with every post, from that of the most powerful minister to that of the humblest under-secretary of parliamentary commission leader, being awarded in relation to it. The balancing act requires considerable finesse, and takes weeks to work out perfectly. Should a minister resign or die in office he must be replaced by someone from the same *corrente* in order to maintain perfect symmetry. Italy has the largest cabinets in the democratic world: they can reach 100 members between ministers, under-secretaries (up to four per ministry) and other minor officials. It is on this brilliantly accurate bible that the whole nationwide system of *lottizzazione* is based. (→ 4:i, below)

(f) At this point, a *programma di governo* – government programme – may be discussed, but never in detail. The politics that get officially adopted have a purely token value, generally representing a palliative to the parties that may have espoused their cause. Hence the Partito Socialista Italiano (PSI) – Italian Socialist Party – first caused, then fought the 1987 general elections on an anti-nuclear platform of purely strategic, not ideological, value. The succeeding government was then obliged to adopt an anti-nuclear stance, in order to symbolize an increased PSI vote.

(g) The new government goes before the two houses for a vote of confidence, which it generally receives. If it fails, it is back to stage one.

(ii) Regular elections and irregular governments

The fast turnover of Italian cabinets says little about the real state of politics, but makes interesting reading. There have been a total of forty-nine cabinet formations from 1945 to mid-1989, with an average length of ten months. The longest lasted almost three years (1058 days: Bettino Craxi, 1983–6), with five lasting under two weeks (the shortest, Andreotti's first, lasted all of nine days in February 1972). Frequently, prime ministers succeed themselves, and so their governments are

---

The pre-Fascist era was characterized by even shorter governments. In the first fifteen years after reunification (1871–86), there were eighteen cabinets, while in the whole period up to Mussolini's march on Rome (1871–1922), there were sixty-seven *crisi di governo*.

---

numbered like Kings. De Gasperi had eight on the trot; Fanfani reached Fanfani VI; the current Presidente del Consiglio is jokingly named Giulio VI, making him sound like a pope.

A more reliable barometer of the Italian political system is the number of general elections. The eleventh legislature since the 1948 Constitution began in 1987 (two fewer than the UK in the same period). However, since the fifth legislature in 1968, Parliament has always been dissolved before the end of the five-year period, usually after four years.

Votes: the spoils (1987 elections)

(1) Democrazia Cristiana (DC)	13,253,000
(2) Partito Comunista Italiano (PCI)	10,285,000
(3) Partito Socialista Italiano (PSI)	5,511,000
(4) Movimento Sociale Italiano (MSI)	2,280,000
(5) Partito Repubblicano Italiano (PRI)	1,431,000
(6) Partito Socialdemocratico Italiano (PSDI)	1,142,000
(7) Partito Radicale (PR)	990,000
(8) Verdi	972,000
(9) Partito Liberale (PLI)	812,000
(10) Democrazia Proletaria (DP)	643,000

Total: 37 million votes

Percentages

	1987 elections	1989 Euro-elections	1984 Euro-elections
DC	34.3	32.9	33.0
PCI	26.6	27.6	33.3
PSI	14.3	14.8	11.2
MSI	5.9	5.5	6.5
PRI	3.7	4.4	6.1
PLI	2.1		
PSDI	2.9	2.7	3.5
Verdi	2.5	3.8	
Arcobaleno		2.4	
DP	1.7	1.3	1.4

The Euro-elections, 1989

Italy, like Britain, France and West Germany, has eighty-one seats at Strasbourg, but unlike Britain they allot them on a strictly PR basis. Seats are as follows:

DC	27	PSDI	2
PCI	22	Verdi Arcobaleno	2
PSI	12	Lega Lombarda	2
MSI	4	Partito Sardo d'Azione	1
PRI/PLI	4	DP	1
Verdi	3	Lega Antiprotezionista	1

(The Lega Antiprotezionista is the lobby for legalizing drugs. For profiles of the other parties, → 2, below.)

2. The parties: who's who and what's what

(i) What they have in common

As is the case in most countries, Italian parties have much more in common with each other than with their namesakes or ideological bedfellows abroad. Hence the Liberals are nothing like the British Liberals, the Social Democrats thankfully have no equivalent elsewhere, while the Communists have more in common with the rump of the British SDP than they do with the Communist Party of Great Britain.

They have in common a heritage of strong ideological positions, involving much time-consuming expostulation of political theories and 'grand designs', rarely sketched in detail. Taking one's ideas extremely seriously is *de rigueur*. Paradoxically, this results in a tendency towards pragmatic compromise on anything – *trasformismo* – in a show of incoherence that a British politician would find embarrassing. They also share a morbid devotion to their past leaders, who are honoured with constant conferences and round tables, while speeches are larded with copious references to them. Party HQs or local branch offices – *sezioni* – always display their sepia-tint photos, like dusty ancestors or political pin-ups. Generally speaking, the fiercer the proclaimed attachment, the less faithful the adherence to his/her principles.

The Italian parties manage to get paid fabulous sums of money from the State coffers. These are linked to their most recent electoral performance. In 1988, they voted themselves an 80% increase, at the same time decreasing their own taxes. They now divide 150 billion lire between themselves, with no obligation to declare where their other finances came from, although the PCI, with their Honest Joe policy, do in fact come out and do this.

As elsewhere, all parties have been affected by the radical decline in ideology since the hot mid-1970s: since much of the rhetoric, if not the concrete changes, brought on by the 1968 movement has now been absorbed by Italy as a whole, at least in a superficial way, the gradual embourgeoisiement of the Left has brought the whole country much closer together. Political differences are almost minimal. More than ever, Italian politics are about a feudal power struggle between well-placed individuals.

Each party has fragmented into *correnti* – factions –

which vie with each other for control of the party, and hence the party's control of State power or assets. These factions are fluid, representing no more than feudal interests (party leaders with strong local, personal or lobby-based power), and tend to unite, coalesce and battle according to purely strategic, rather than ideological, reasons. Every successful political leader has a *corrente* behind him.

Every party has its HQ in a Rome *palazzo*, which in the case of the biggest parties is synonymous in political parlance with the name of the party.

(ii) Who they are

Democrazia Cristiana (DC) [HQ: Piazza del Gesù].The Christian Democrat formula is common to nearly all Catholic democracies. Despite its logically close adherence to the Vatican, it is a populist rather than a right-wing party. It has stronger populist roots than does its German equivalent, with a political span from tough right-wing to left of centre, like early Gaullism. What holds it together at an ideological level is its professed Catholicism, in contrast to the *partiti laici* (→ 3:iii, below). However diverse its views may be on economic or international affairs, on social matters the DC is obviously very 'old-fashioned': anti-divorce, anti-abortion etc. A tough line on these issues contrasts with a soft line on pardoning terrorists, deriving from the Catholic rhetoric of forgiveness.

By far the most divided into *correnti*, it is itself more a coalition of different factions, which often have more acrimonious relations with each other than they do with other parties.

Although its relations with the Vatican are sometimes quite distant, it has managed to install itself as the natural party of government in a big way: it hasn't been out of power since 1945. Simultaneously loved and hated by the Italians – loved as the party responsible for social stability and economic progress, but hated for the total moral stagnation it has induced. Its closest relations in world politics in corruption, generic populism and power-hogging are the Indian Congress Party and Mexico's ruling Institutional Revolutionary Party.

Pin-ups: founded in 1948 by **Alcide De Gasperi**, Italy's Adenauer, who presided over its first eight governments, and currently the object of a serious canonization campaign, it drew its basic inspiration from **Don Luigi Sturzo**'s pre-war Catholic party, Partito Popolare. It has a martyr in Apulian **Aldo Moro**, a brilliant but totally hermetic politician slaughtered in 1978 by the Red Brigades.

Major figures (no. of governments they have formed as Presidente del Consiglio in brackets):

Giulio Andreotti (6). This slyly witty Roman is undoubtedly the most consummate politician in Italy, with probably the finest political mind in Europe, bar Gorbachev. He is also the most compromised, with a total of twenty-seven Watergate-style parliamentary investigations for corruption to his name. Although a man of refined manners, he habitually surrounds himself with the most questionable associates: considered in some circles to be the leader of P2, thanks to his friendship with Licio Gelli, he has also been photographed in the company of almost every right-wing subversive, Mafia-connected business moghul and international gun-runner in Italy. Rather than disqualifying him, these relationships seem only to enhance his domestic reputation. His talents are warmly appreciated everywhere, from the Vatican to Communist Party HQ. In fact, his tireless activity as Foreign Minister led his talents to be warmly appreciated everywhere in the world, from Washington to Moscow, from Teheran to Baghdad to Jerusalem. Since his chances of becoming President of the Republic seem limited by his chequered record (although former incumbent Pertini recommended him for the post), it has been suggested that he is aiming at becoming the next Secretary-General of the UN. In July 1989, he succeeded his arch-rival, De Mita (see below), in becoming Presidente del Consiglio, and returned the DC to its old, 'pre-glasnost', style. Interestingly, for a man who understands better than anyone else how power works in Italy, he has never wanted to be party secretary. (→V, 2:vi)

Amintore Fanfani (6). This wily, midget-sized Tuscan is responsible for having transformed the DC into an efficient party of permanent power. He is over 80 and, although still active, unlikely to become President, as he would like (though his wife Maria Pia Fanfani already pretends to be Italy's First Lady: →3:i, below).

Ciriaco De Mita (2). Despite his recent humiliations (in the space of twelve months, in 1988–9, he was stripped of both his posts, as Segretario del Partito – party leader – and Presidente del Consiglio), and his much mocked Southern accent, De Mita has proved a brilliant political strategist, responsible for the substantial revamping of the DC, making it less automatically influenced by the Vatican, carrying out a major moral clean-up and encouraging a more gentlemanly attitude towards the PCI. His declared blueprint was to create a DC–PCI two-party alternative. The antithesis of Andreotti, both in personal style and in political goals, he is now stepping back from his attempt at a reformed DC, at least for the present. His enmity with Craxi is legendary, and uncharacteristic in the world of chummy hostility in Italian politics.

Arnaldo Forlani (1). This ageing Tintin lookalike strongly favours a close pact with the PSI, and is thus Craxi's closest ally in the DC, used as a willing lever against de Mita. He is currently Party Secretary, and middleman in the devil's pact between Andreotti and Craxi.

Giovanni Goria (2). This good-looking, bearded Piedmontese in his mid-40s was the classic example of the powerless Prime Minister. Despite a relatively good job record, he lacked both a *corrente* and any experience of party intrigue, which led him, while in office, to be manipulated mercilessly by other party bosses. Despite a record share (536,000) of preferential votes in the 1989 Euro-elections, beating even his chief tormentor Andreotti (531,000), he is currently out in the political wilderness.

***Partito Comunista Italiano* (PCI)** [HQ: Via delle Botteghe Oscure].The Communist Party is the mirror image of its principal opponent, the Christian Democrats, in that it is a 'church' inspired by an ideology. Like its eternal antagonist, the PCI was for years very prudish, allowing the centre parties to take the lead on all the major social issues. Recently, the PCI has redressed the balance, and now presents itself as the Italian 'rainbow coalition' party. But for all its desperately post-modern poster graphics, gay activist candidates, 30% women MPs and sponsored rock concerts, it remains essentially a dreary political dinosaur: harmless but anachronistic.

Although, as in all other parties, hard-nosed pragmatism always takes precedence over theory, the PCI has, more than almost any other party, maintained a relatively corruption-free existence (although there are many who would argue that it is simply much better at hiding its corruption). In any event, it is also the only party with no real *correnti*, though Italians see this party unity more as an expression of sinister 'centralism' than of laudable political discipline. Despite its refreshingly honest appearance, its message has disagreed with too many voters for it to taste real power: the maximum that it has ever reached at the polls was 36% in 1976, which has now been eroded to around 27%. This would, in any case, be difficult, since Washington formally forbids them to enter government (→ III, 4:ii). The only way they could gain power would be to enter a stable coalition with the Socialists, a solution occasionally put forward in theory – *l'alternativa di sinistra* – but never in practice since their 'natural allies' have always been keener on allying with the DC and the *partiti laici*.

Thanks to Craxi's manoeuvring, and its own lack of good leaders with a broad national appeal, the PCI now seems destined to serious, permanent decline. The party is currently like a rabbit trapped in a car's headlights: paralysed by indecision: over whether to opt for a tough, uncompromising attitude, in the hope that the political climate returns in its favour, or to change tack completely. Many PCI high-ups now feel that only a decisive break with Marxism itself will do, achieved by changing its name and symbols, and by identifying even more closely with other European socialist and social democratic parties.

As of 1989, the active leadership of Achille Occhetto is doing much to underline this second strategy: the PCI no longer sits with the Communist group at the Strasbourg parliament; and while professing admiration for Gorbachev, Occhetto has declared that the international Communist movement 'simply doesn't exist'. Indeed, they are shedding their traditional Marxist ideology so fast now that Giulio Andreotti remarked in 1989, 'Soon, it will be up to us in the DC to stick up for Togliatti.' In 1989, Occhetto finally formed a *governo ombra* – shadow cabinet – a significant event in a country with no formal opposition, although his rivals dub it a publicity stunt to gain more TV coverage. Occhetto has also completely overhauled the party hierarchy, replacing the venerable old guard with *la generazione dei quarantenni* – the generation of 40-year-olds.

During the golden era, from the early 1970s to the early 1980s, over 50% of Italians lived in Communist-run municipalities, including every major city except Palermo. Voters trusted them to run cities, but not the country. Their erstwhile coalition partners in local politics (though never on a national scale), the Socialists, then dumped them for *il pentapartito* – the five-party centre-right coalition. Their vote remains solidly urban-working-class (they never managed to entice the more conservative rural working-class vote away from the DC), though their support among intellectuals remains important.

Pin-ups: founded in 1921 from a split with the Socialists at the Livorno conference, the PCI was until the war a Moscow-based élitist party. During the latter war years, it was instrumental in organizing partisan opposition to the Nazis, leading to its refounding in the post-war years as a mass party. Its membership even reached 2.25 million, making it by far the largest Communist party outside the Soviet bloc. It was led briefly in the 1920s by the brilliant political philosopher **Antonio Gramsci**, whom Mussolini imprisoned almost as soon as he came to power and whose writings later became the party's alternative bible. Its great post-war leader was **Palmiro Togliatti**, whose political stature was comparable to the DC's de Gasperi. He is currently being debunked for his over-zealous Stalinist attitude, having been Stalin's deputy in the Third International. Even though he never reached power, he is surely Europe's only recent politician to have a major city named after him: Togliattigrad (USSR).

His successor, Luigi Longo, provided continuity before the PCI's very own saint **Enrico Berlinguer** became Party Secretary in 1972. This aristocratic Sardinian completed the party's conversion to the Western camp, enthusiastically embracing the EC and NATO, and denying first Moscow's supremacy and later even its relevance. He genuinely epitomized the PCI's clean-living, anti-corruption stance, and was widely respected by all Italians. Four days after his death in 1984, the PCI, riding on a sympathy vote, managed to overtake (*'il sorpasso'*) the DC in the Euro-elections of that year ($\rightarrow$2:i, above), the first and only time a Western Communist party has ever held a majority, albeit a relative one.

Major figures:

Nilde Jotti. The only Communist to hold high public office, as President (Speaker) of the Chamber of Deputies since 1976, she is number three in the State hierarchy. This distinctly regal, though slightly school-ma'amish, woman, who was Togliatti's companion from 1945 until his death in 1964, is highly respected across the Italian political spectrum for her scrupulously coherent administration of parliamentary affairs. Her non-partisan, institutional style would make her an ideal Head of State, but unfortunately her party's declining fortunes outweigh her personal abilities.

Achille Occhetto. In 1988, this 50-year-old, owl-like, uncharismatic figure was elected to preside over the PCI's decline in what initially seemed a tactical gift to all its enemies. Something of an intellectual lightweight, he has provided a leadership that resembles in several ways that of Kinnock over Britain's Labour Party. His highly pragmatic policy statements, the move towards the centre and his decision to surround himself with technocrats rather than ideologists have to a remarkable extent helped the PCI to recover prestige and the popular vote.

Giorgio Napolitano. Napolitano is one of the few older survivors; he is currently shadow Foreign Secretary, leading exponent of the party's *migliorista* right-wing element and is responsible for the close contacts with other European socialist parties.

Armando Cossutta. This good old-fashioned Stalinist commands a mere 5% at Party HQ, but a solid 25%

of grassroots support, rendering him an undumpable embarrassment.

Walter Veltroni. One of the most promising leaders of the 'new-look' PCI, with a sharp eye for strategy.

Partito Socialista Italiano (**PSI**) [HQ: Via del Corso]. The Socialist Party has totally shed all its left-wing associations over the last decade to become, in the most astonishing political make-over in history, the personal vehicle for the powerful personality of its leader, Bettino Craxi: Stalin to Thatcher in three decades. Craxi has been successful in projecting the PSI as a modern, post-ideological package, in grasping an inordinate amount of *sottogoverno* power, in staying Prime Minister for three years, and in adding some 5% of votes – but not in destroying the party's terrible reputation for corruption.

Realizing that a streamlined centre party could attract disillusioned votes from the big two, and could equally use its position for playing them off against each other, Craxi embarked on an ambitious campaign, entering into agreements with both sides in order to obtain an extortionate number of *poltrone* – literally armchairs, or places in power. The PSI now holds Italy to ransom like a spoilt child, causing governments to fall at whim, and insisting on having its candidates accepted in every available para-statal post: with only 14% of the national vote, they hold over 30% of the plum administration jobs. Many Communist voters are beginning to think, If you can't beat 'em, join 'em, making the PCI's electoral eclipse by the PSI look increasingly likely.

What holds this event back is the party's shocking corruption record, too much for even the most cynical Italian voter to stomach. Scarcely a week passes without some highly placed Socialist ending up in court on serious embezzlement or fraud charges. Thanks to the political indulgence of Italian justice, they rarely go to prison.

Apart from this, Craxi has been singularly canny in constructing the right image for his new-look PSI. Hitching the Socialist bandwagon to the whole Milan-based economic boom, he has enlisted the support of powerful or prestigious business figures from media magnate Silvio Berlusconi to most of the fashion designer community, and, after an aggressive campaign in RAI and the Press, maintains an extremely high media profile. He has been efficacious in creating a good relationship with Washington, and respect elsewhere, while trying particularly to associate his name with those of Mitterand and Gonzalez on the Euro-Socialist efficiency train:

Pin-ups: founded in 1896, the PSI underwent a split in 1921 (→PCI, above) with the Communists, whom, thanks to **Pietro Nenni**, their leader from 1930 for four decades, they continued to resemble, not least in their slavish devotion to Stalin. Despite his enormous intellectual and leadership qualities, Nenni also presided over their disastrous splits and haemorrhaging of votes. From their ranks also came much-loved President **Sandro Pertini**, who despite party loyalties has never thought too highly of the current party leadership.

Major figures:

Bettino Craxi. A Milanese, and more than any other party leader almost synonymous with his party, his biggest enemy is vanity: he sees himself as a de Gaulle-cum-Gorbachev figure. Like them, he aims to transform Italy into a presidential republic. He is constantly in a state of fury over word-plays on his first name and Mussolini's and over the work of Italy's most influential political cartoonist, *La Repubblica*'s Forattini, who always portrays him as il Duce. Unfortunately, Craxi's ruthless methods have been adopted by his side-kicks, who are all waiting in the wings.

Claudio Martelli. Deputy leader: his naughty choirboy features front one of the most ruthless minds in Italian politics. He long refused cabinet experience, in order to manipulate better from the sidelines, but Craxi, fearing for his own future, made the reluctant Martelli become deputy PM in 1989.

Gianni De Michelis. This plump, bird-faced Venetian disco-goer has proved that in Italian politics, it's all down to which party you go to, not which one you belong to. He is currently Foreign Secretary. Considered by some to be bright, he has gone to great pains over the years to get to know every foreign leader possible. He considers himself 'well liked' in Washington. If he is right, his *presenzialista* strategy will pay off in due course.

Movimento Sociale Italiano/Destra Nazionale (**MSI–DN**). Although open Fascism is banned by the Constitution, the neo-Fascist MSI was founded without much difficulty just after the war. Its fortunes have been steadily declining through the 1980s (in 1989 it stood at 5.5%), but it remains the fourth largest force in Italian politics. In the late 1970s, it merged with the monarchist rump of Destra Nazionale, giving it a certain hybrid character. Although the central body of the party is a fairly tame mixture of former Fascists, monarchist nostalgics (many of their southern supporters, particularly in parts of Sicily, where they are often the second party, have more sympathy with the deposed

Bourbon dynasty than with Mussolini's) and frustrated DC supporters, who would fit comfortably into Britain's Tory party, on the fringes of the party there are various groups of rabid hotheads out for a punch-up. The party hierarchy likes to play down, or even deny, its links with sinister, extremist youth movements like Fronte della Gioventù or terrorist units like Terza Posizione and NAR (Nucleo Armato Rivoluzionario), but young *picchiatori* – fist-happy militants – usually act as stewards at party meetings.

Despite this alarming element, the MSI–DN have always been somewhat unfairly kept outside the mainstream of Italian politics: they are not within *l'arco costituzionale* – the range of democratic parties – and are thus rarely consulted on most issues of national importance; more important, they get few of the *poltrone* that are up for grabs. This situation is beginning to change, with the evolving post-ideological binge of Italian politics. This often startling trend is most evident among MSI supporters, who now show an increasing sympathy for Craxi (35% of them would like an MSI–PSI coalition), while 20% view themselves as 'left-wingers'.

At the Euro Parliament, they share a group with the Ulster Unionists, but no longer sit with Le Pen's National Front or the new German Republikaner. They have a substantial difference of style from, not to mention disagreement with, the latter party over the Alto Adige issue. (→ II, 3:iii)

Pin-ups: Even though Fascism is illegal in Italy, nostalgia for Il Duce, **Benito Mussolini**, is widely tolerated. Their recently deceased (1987) leader **Giorgio Almirante**, who closely resembled Enoch Powell in many ways (looks, academic erudition and old-fashioned good manners), was responsible for the party's increased respectability. The party has been *in crisi* since his death.

Major figures:

GianFranco Fini. Almirante's *delfino* – dauphin – is a slightly uncertain new leader in his 40s. He remains undecided over whether to climb on to Le Pen's racist bandwagon, remain attached to nostalgia-issues, or attempt closer alignment with Craxi.

Pino Rauti. This leader of the internal opposition, vintage example of the good old-fashioned, unrestructured *picchiatore*, openly labels Fini a wimp.

Partito Repubblicano Italiano (PRI). The Italian Republicans are a lot like their American namesakes regarding economic issues, and are the most pro-US party, although traditionally very progressive on social issues. They are the most important *partito laico*, founded by Mazzini in the 19th century (but suppressed under Mussolini, along with all other parties). Most of the major post-war party figures have been extremely well educated – internationalist in outlook, well suited to ruling, and from patrician families. Their institutional influence is considerable, their electorate impact not so: they have averaged a meagre 2.5% since the war, though that is now growing slightly.

Apart from the PCI, they are the only party to specialize in the *questione morale*: they are largely uncorrupt, though they can afford to be, since most of them are very rich anyway. They are supported by nearly all the major capitalist dynasties, like Agnelli (whose sister is a Republican junior minister) and De Benedetti. Despite this support, though, the PRI risks disappearing altogether.

Pin-ups: **Giuseppe Mazzini** (→ III, 1:i) and **Ugo La Malfa**, a highly competent post-war leader, whose economic policies remain an important reference point.

Major figures:

Giovanni Spadolini (2). Generally considered a pompous old windbag, in 1981 this Florentine academic became Italy's first post-war non-DC Prime Minister, as a result of the shock waves following the P2 scandal. Very similar to Edward Heath in many respects, he did a fairly good job, forming two administrations, until ousted by Craxi's intrigues. He is currently Presidente del Senato, the second position in the State hierarchy, and hopes to succeed Cossiga to the Presidency.

Giorgio La Malfa. The son of the influential Ugo, Giorgio is the less charismatic current party leader, attempting to steer the PRI away from the PSI towards DC positions, in order to pick up their disillusioned votes. His recent attempts to form a *federazione laica* – a federation of 'lay parties' – with the Liberals, and, unbelievably, with Pannella's nutty Radicals, proved disastrous.

Partito Socialdemocratico Italiano (**PSDI**). The least edifying of all parties, the PSDI was cobbled together out of American bribe money in 1947, causing a split inside the PSI, at the time pro-Stalinist. Their last three leaders, Tanassi, Longo and Nicolazzi, have all been involved in serious embezzlement and corruption cases, though they continue to command support at the polls, thanks to a cleverly calculated policy of backing specific interest groups (hospital workers and pensioners, whose votes they effectively buy): 3% is an acceptable figure in Italy. They are politically dead, but refuse to lie down: since the PSI has now moved so far to the right they have no reason to exist – a fact tacitly acknowledged by hundreds of PSDI councillors and party members, who are joining the PSI in floods.

Pin-ups: **Giacomo Matteotti** was an influential left-wing figure who in 1926 was gunned down by the Fascists on the Aventine hill in Rome. His death signalled the final crack-down of the Fascists. Although totally extraneous to the PSDI, he has been hijacked by them, since he makes such a good hero figure. **Giuseppe Saragat** – a former Italian President and the founder of PSDI, who died in 1988, is remembered for his deathbed political testament, 'Let me die a Social Democrat,' which has been interpreted in a number of ways, few of them flattering to the current leadership.

Major figures:

Antonio Cariglia. The present leader, presiding over the rump of the party.

Vincenza Bono Parrino. The Minister for the Arts took office in 1987 in an area of which she admitted to knowing nothing in a country with the world's largest single cultural heritage. From her initial promise to 'lock myself away in my office for fifteen days to mug up on the whole subject' (fifteen days? the Italian cultural heritage?) to the scandalous awarding of contracts for historic buildings restoration (still under investigation), her period of tenure arguably marks the nadir of *lottizzazione* in Italian politics.

Partito Radicale (**PR**). Founded by ex-Liberal Marco Pannella in the 1950s as a kind of pressure group, the PR has remained closely identified with this maverick figure ever since, even though he has long since abandoned the secretaryship. This is the thought-provoking funny left of Italian politics, and despite their derisory support (maximum 6%, currently 2.3%) they have had an enormous effect in Italy, especially during the 1970s, when their colourful, almost dadaist tactics provided a perfect handle for the Press. They were responsible, almost single-handedly, for the successful passage through Parliament of the divorce and abortion laws, to the official opposition of the DC, and even, at one stage, of the Communists. (→ I, 3: iv,vii,viii)

Their impact has been muted throughout the 1980s, though their policy of proposing controversial, generally non-political, figures as parliamentary election candidates has provoked much world-wide attention: from the imprisoned – like terrorist leader ex-university-professor Toni Negri (to become MP in Italy automatically gets you out of jail) and Enzo Tortora, well-loved TV presenter, jailed for allegedly dealing in cocaine – to the outrageous, like the porno-star Ilona Staller, alias Cicciolina. They understood earlier, and better than anyone else in Italy, how to manipulate the media by sensationalizing political events to their best advantage. The party retain a high media profile, with a lively publication (*Notizie Radicali*), a private radio with a regular following (Radio Radicale) and a TV station (Canale 66).

After constantly threatening to dissolve in recent years, they have recently decided to proclaim themselves a *partito trasnazionale* – a 'trans-national party' – exchanging their rose-in-fist logo for a rather presumptuous one using Gandhi (Mahatma rather than Indira), holding their first international conference in Budapest; international party recruits have, however, yet to materialize in droves. They have decided not to run for further elections in Italy under the Radical banner, and the ramaining elected deputies call themselves *federalisti europei* – European federalists.

Major figures:

Marco Pannella. One of the most interesting and original figures in Italian politics, like the party he founded, he is also one of the most logorrhoeic: his recorded daily talkathons on Rome's Canale 66 last up to six hours. Since the mid-1980s he has left the secretaryship to lesser figures, like **Francesco Rutelli** (now in the Verdi-Arcobaleno), **Gianni Negri** (at 27, the youngest party leader in Europe to be elected), and, latterly, **Sergio Stanziani**. His decision to allow Cicciolina to stand almost split the party.

Partito Liberale Italiano (**PLI**). Like the Republicans, the PLI were founded in the 19th century, and in the pre-Mussolini era were one of the main parties. They are slightly more to the right than the Republicans, though you'd need a magnifying glass to tell. The difference is entirely one of 'tradition'. (→ III, 3:iii) Their vote is now a mere 2.1% nationally, and if the talk of a 5% minimum hurdle for parliamentary entry becomes reality, their merging with the Republicans is a certainty.

Pin-ups: **Camillo Cavour** is one major historical figure (→ III, 1:i) adopted by the PLI, while the important pre-Fascist–era philosopher **Benedetto Croce** became their first post-war party president. **Giovanni Malagodi**, currently party-President and leading elder statesman, is their most important post-war leader.

Major figures:

Renato Altissimo. The current party leader is trying to arrest the PLI's inevitable decline through aggressive, Craxi-like, gestures. Most notably, he caused President Cossiga's 1987 UK State visit to be cancelled, simply in order to demonstrate that the PLI could do so.

Francesco De Lorenzo. The attractive personal style and efficient policies of this hyperactive new Health

Minister could help stave off the PLI's death sentence.

***Democrazia Proletaria* (DP)**. Along with the Radicals, the DP represent the historical remnant of the *sessantotto* movement in Parliament. Their *raison d'être* was always to be a real Communist opposition, in place of the too bourgeois and conservative PCI. Since the reabsorption of the rival ultra-left grouping PdUP (Partito dell'Unità Proletaria) back into the PCI (where their charismatic leader Luci Magri is again in the central committee), they are the only extreme left-wing group in Parliament, but are likely to precede the PSDI and the PLI into extinction, since most left-wingers now identify with the Verdi.
Major figures:
Mario Capanna. This great, bear-like intellectual was the founding father of the DP, but retired to become a media celebrity, appearing on husband-and-wife chat-shows and writing a nostalgic best-seller about the 1968 revolts. He has now completely abandoned the DP for the Verdi, and is fiercely critical of his successor.
Giovanni Russo Spenna. With his permanent Palestinian keffiyeh round his shoulders, and vetero-Communist slogans on his lips, he keeps the ghost of old-fashioned student extremism alive.

I Verdi. After two consecutive electoral successes (1987 general elections, 1989 Euro-elections), the Greens are currently flavour of the month. With Italy's constant stream of ecological disasters (→ II, 2) to bring their message home, they are destined to grow and grow. They still maintain a substantially apolitical position, seeing themselves as more of a movement, although the pressures of political success are beginning to change this, and the decision whether to amalgamate with the Verdi-Arcobaleno group will influence their choice. Currently, **Gianni Mattioli**, **Rosa Filippini**, and trouble-shooting left-wing magistrate **Luigi Amendola** are the best known of this essentially leaderless group.

Verdi-Arcobaleno. The 'rainbow greens' were formed in time for the 1989 Euro-elections, where they scored handsomely (2.4%). While agreeing substantially with the mainstream Verdi on most ecological issues, their more classic left-wing origins (major figures include ex-party secretaries **Francesco Rutelli** and **Mario Capanna**) preclude any sort of electoral pact of the sort the other grouping would contemplate with the centre-left *pentapartito* government coalition. If the two parties do unite, they will become Italy's fourth largest.

The regional parties. The **Sudtirolvolkspartei** (SVP) (South Tyrol People's party), the **Union Val d'Otaine** (**UVA**) (Val d'Aosta Union) and the **Partito Sardo d'Azione** (PSdAZ) (Sardinian Action party) all have significant weight in their respective regional assemblies and in local government, and are also represented in the national Parliament. The more recent **Lega Lombarda** (Lombard League) has two seats at Strasbourg, but none as yet at Montecitorio, while nationalist movements for the Veneto (**La Lega Veneta**), Piedmont and Sicily have no national standing so far. At a national level, their accumulated votes are no more than 3%.

The single-issue parties. Although there are a few Italian equivalents of the Raving Loony Party variety, most of the single-issue parties are in deadly earnest. Favoured by Italy's PR system, they tend to do well at local elections. The Marco Pannella-controlled **Lega Anti-Proibizionista** (legalize drugs now party) won a seat at Strasbourg in 1989. The various rival parties set up by angry pensioners, anti-legislation hunters (→ II, 2:i) and other alienated interest groups usually cull a few seats at *comune* level.

3. Political characteristics: fun and word-games

(i) Politics as showbiz: the life and soul of the party

The meeting of two of Italy's most significant examples of hyperchoice – politics and the media – has created another interesting syndrome. Having a dozen major parties and several hundred TV stations makes the one indispensable to the other for purely political reasons, but there is another, completely different, side to it too. Italy's intensive-development glamour industry's insatiable appetite for personalities (called in Italian *vips*, pronounced as a single word) is capable of turning almost anybody into a star. Politicians fit the bill perfectly: they love to show 'their human side', and work hard at becoming TV chat-show, or glossy gossip magazine, stars in their own right. The Italian public is familiar with the personality, wit and family vicissitudes of dozens of these consummate media whores. Seeming to be everywhere, at the right function, at the right moment, is called *presenzialismo*. Italian politicians are the ultimate *presenzialisti* – their light parliamentary duties make that easy enough.

Christian Democrat mandarin Giulio Andreotti is famous for his wry but lethal sense of humour; Communist Party leader Achille Occhetto has himself photographed smooching passionately with his wife; Socialist Foreign Secretary Gianni De Michelis is celebrated for his hip social life – he is always in the *vip* box at every major rock concert, and has recently written a book about discothèques. While this kind of publicity hype is quite common now in other countries, what makes it so much bigger in Italy is that no one expects public figures to set a moral example: they can say and do what they like.

In promoting party men so assiduously, the Italian media are following a tradition well established in the higher echelons of Italian social life. In the drawing rooms of the nation's society hostesses there are so many more politicians, who each wield correspondingly so much more power, than in other countries, that they are deemed more fascinating and are certainly statistically more available for such affairs than anywhere else in the world. In Italy, political glamour knows no party boundaries, and suffers no fears of seeming too bourgeois: some of the most notable lounge lizards are Communist leaders, while the most *presenzialista* party of all is the PSI, where the distinction between socialist and socialite has long been blurred.

The most extraordinary female figure in Italian political high society is Maria Pia Fanfani, the second wife of DC veteran Amintore Fanfani. No important party, official reception, fashion show, gallery opening, *tavola rotonda* is complete without her pushy presence in the front row. While the wives of presidents Pertini and Cossiga have deliberately remained in the background, Maria Pia Fanfani likes to project herself as unofficial First Lady of Italy, particularly in front of foreign potentates.

She is worthy of praise in becoming the first woman in Italian public life to elbow her way to the limelight, a daunting task. Apart from her husband's position, she has been able to exploit her own position as head of the Italian Red Cross, and deputy head of the International Red Cross, to take the Ladies-that-Lunch ethos into a higher stratosphere.

(ii) *Il bel discorso*: abstraction and rhetoric

The real substance of Italian politics, as in the Gospel of St John, is *logos* – the Word. Nobody expects Italian politicians to do anything, just talk. This is partly the fault of the Italian language, which lends itself to elegant but meaningless abstraction, and encourages long-windedness. The *linguaggio* – the pitch – is *celebrativo* – commemorative, pompous, rhetorical. Italians talk about *il bel discorso* – fancy words. It is therefore no coincidence that Italy has no tradition of sharp or witty parliamentary debate – politicians don't want to be interrupted, or popped, like a balloon. Their *forte* is speeches. In fact, since parliamentary absenteeism is acceptable, and MPs have no constituency responsibilities ($\rightarrow$ III, 3), the principal activity of some Italian politicians is to appear at *tavole rotonde* and *convegni* – round table conferences – to make interminable speeches full of abstract concepts about very abstruse topics, which are rarely connected to anything you might consider as the mainstream of political action. Well, in so far as making speeches is the mainstream of Italian politics, this is all fully justified. These conferences are then tirelessly reported, Soviet-style, by the TV news on all three RAI channels. Every day, there are dozens of round tables up and down the peninsula, and conventional wisdom says: be there or be square.

What is actually discussed at these festivals of the Word is not an appropriate question. Not so much what, as how? The organization of these events pays lavish attention to visuals: fancy designed pamphlets, folders and posters are prepared, luxurious conference facilities are laid on (every self-respecting Italian hotel has at least one conference suite). The chosen topic may range from the seemingly instructive ('*Sistemi di trasporto e di telecommunicazioni nella metropoli degli anni '80: l'esperienza giapponese'* – 'Metropolitan transport and communications in the 1980s: learning from Japan') to the ostentatiously hermetic ('*Verso una nuova analisi del ruolo del pensiero gramsciano nella politica contro il degrado socio-ambientale degli hinterland post-industriale'* – 'Towards a re-evaluation of Gramsci in the light of social and environmental decay in post-industrial zones'). But however concrete-looking the conference theme may appear, the speeches (for there is no real debate) never get to the nitty gritty; that is not the point. It is not *sostanza* – substance – but *rappresentanza* – corporate image – that counts, and at that level, it all works. In fact, at first glance, these *convegni*, with their always carefully co-ordinated graphics, look very impressive – the sheer austere chic of the title in Italian! Designer Thought! Forget Milan fashion and industrial design – this is the real 'Made in Italy'! The Word as a successfully marketed Product!

Italy has made a veritable cult of the inscrutable. One of the most memorably meaningless phrases was Aldo Moro's, in his much vaunted theory concerning '*le convergenze parallele*' – parallel convergences. The subtext of these sublimely elegant weasel words was, however, quite straightforward: 'I wish to justify the unjustifiable, and create a political pact with our enemies, the Communists' – *il compromesso storico.*

Essentially a post-modern product, too: for although political ideology, as elsewhere, has completely collapsed in Italy, the pre-eminent role of the Idea (and its handmaiden the Word) remains. This is technically an exciting era for the Italians to live in – one in which the Idea can develop freely, far from the shackles of ideology. The hegemony of the Idea is copied from France, and explains the importance of intellectuals in political, as well as cultural, life. (→ VIII, 6)

While irony is quite justified, in reviewing the generally meagre results, it is only fair to see politics from the Italian perspective. Which is – who says politics are just about nitty-gritty details? Why not exalt our mental capacities instead? In fact, at its best, this phenomenon contributes a depth and variety altogether lacking in the petty world, made up of bread-and-butter issues, of Anglo-Saxon politics. It can make a pleasant change to hear highbrow political debates by card-carrying philosophers, instead of all those rhetorically grim grassroots interviews imposed by the conventional wisdom of British or American politics. Another fact not to be overlooked is that this is what the voters want: although there are sporadic complaints against 'il Palazzo', they, too, are substantially interested in the Word and the Idea.

In 1988, relations between the two main left-wing parties, the PSI and the PCI, were strained not so much by policy differences, as by a divergence of opinion over Togliatti's role in the implementation of Stalinism. Public commotion. At the same time, the PCI had voted in favour of a potentially explosive government bill limiting the right to strike of public servants. Not a squeak from the public, despite wide media coverage. During July 1988, *Terza pagina*, a RAI Radio 3 phone-in show, was flooded with calls, as never before: 90% of them regarded *il caso Togliatti* as something that had happened over thirty years ago; of the remaining 10% of calls, a mere handful were about Italy's major left-wing party stabbing the working masses in the back. Words, not deeds.

It is the Italian public's respect for the Idea, their innate conservatism, that permits the dead wood in the political class to survive. In the political logic of most countries, the tiny Liberal (1.2%) and Republican (3.5%) parties would be destined to die – or, at the very least, amalgamate, seeing as they now hold identical views on almost everything. But this is not the point: apart from the massive electoral funds they receive, they have something to conserve: their *patrimonio politico* – political heritage! Clutching Cavour and Giolitti on the one hand, and Mazzini on the other to their respective political breasts, these bite-sized dinosaurs survive, and flourish in decline! They are the Italian equivalent of the House of Lords: vigorously anachronistic, in a parliamentary climate where the political ideas of the 1870s often count for more than the political realities of the 1980s.

It follows that political disputes about ideas, even historical ones, are as much the cause of *crisi di governo* – government collapses – as are disputes about daily policy.

The all-round devotion to the Idea tends to make electoral clarity very difficult. Voters are motivated by strong ideological or rhetorical convictions, but, since coalitions are necessary to make any form of government, have no idea whom their vote will end up supporting. The absence of any such thing as a pre-electoral pact in Italy (that comes later, with the wheeler-dealing) accounts for the contrast between the very strong political consciousness of 'ideas' (Italy has a regular 88% polls turn-out: → III, 3:vi) and the incredibly low level of information about what actually happens in the mechanics of forming or running governments.

- **In 1988 14.8% of Italians thought they lived in a presidential republic, while 60.4% thought the President was also elected by the government.**
- **67.3% of Italians didn't know how many countries there were in the EC; 73.3% were, however, favourable to more member states joining. 24% were convinced that Switzerland was a member; 6.5% that Turkey was; 4.5% that Hungary was too.**
- **90% of Italians could correctly name the US President; 23% were convinced he was a Democrat. 9% said they would approve of a US intervention to overthrow a communist government in Western Europe.**

(ISPES)

Traditional political analysis elsewhere tends to be fact-based, and thus condemns governments that promise things but don't come up with the goods. Although Italians always complain about *il governo ladro* – crooked government – they are basically quite happy with this system. The difficulties that arise with access to information (→ V, 4) occur because Italians don't think in terms of facts (unless talking about money) but of notions. Where this system goes horribly wrong is in an international context, like the EC, where two different political criteria, the concrete and the abstract, meet in head-on collision.

(iii) Political buzzwords

Some of these have been in use for over a century; a few are falling into disuse; while others are quite recent. All of them help to shed some light on the Italian political mentality.

Alternativa di sinistra: the hypothesis of a general left-wing coalition government (PCI–PSI, or possibly including other, smaller, parties) as an alternative to eternally DC-dominated ones.

Amnistia: amnesties are a common political instrument in Italy, offered to, or debated about being offered to, terrorist (cf.* *pentitismo*) and those responsible for *reati minori* – petty crimes. They help clear the overcrowded jails and are usually associated with the election of a new president.

Assistenzialismo: what in Britain is called the Welfare

State mentality, or what Thatcher calls scrounging. Italy
has so few comprehensive welfare arrangements (→ 4:
iv, below) that the attempts of the poor and 'lazy' seem
all the more desperate. The term *scroccone* – scrounger
– is a political taboo word in this tolerant, indulgent
country.

Base, la: 'the grassroots', or electoral base of a party,
particularly left-wing ones.

Cattolico: used interchangeably with *cristiano*, which
seems logical in an overwhelmingly Catholic country
but is none the less disconcerting for *protestanti* or
ortodossi; the latter are merely members of *sette* – sects
– while *il cattolicesimo* is a *religione*. Used in a political
context around election time to remind the baptized
that they should be voting DC.

Compromesso storico: the 'historic compromise' is the
corollary of the *alternativa di sinistra*, and for two years
in the late 1970s meant that the Communists were
practically part of the government. Dreamt up by Aldo
Moro (DC) and Enrico Berlinguer (PCI), *il compromesso
storico* didn't survive them, and is now, political fashions having changed so much, a serious embarrassment
to both parties. De Mita's recent unsuccessful attempts
to polarize Italian politics between the two large parties
at the expense of the PSI and the *partiti*laici* was a sort
of variant on a theme.

Comunismo: in a country where il Partito Comunista
makes the Kinnock Labour Party look like a bunch of
extreme left-wingers, *comunista* has none of the hard
edge, or mystique, that it does in England. Confusingly,
many of the extreme left-wing terrorist groups of the
1970s and early 1980s called themselves *comunisti* –
hence Kissinger's theory that cuddly Italian *comunismo*
was morally responsible for **terrorismo*.

Condono: in use since ancient Roman times, and much
more widely applied than **amnistia*, this usually refers
to tax dodgers (*evasori fiscali*), in the form *condono
fiscale*; or to those responsible for illegal buildings,
condono edilizio. (→ V, 1:v)

Crisi: literally 'crisis', though usually not nearly as
dramatic as the English translation would imply. For
a party or individual to be *in crisi* simply means they
don't know what to do next. Usually, in the context
of *crisi di governo*, or Government crisis, it is used
simply for a cabinet reshuffle in which the Presidente
del Consiglio gets shuffled too. Some last a few days,
several have lasted months, when the President has not
found anyone capable of forming, and holding together,
a majority coalition. (→ 1: i, above)

Democratico: a late 1960s and 1970s buzzword, used
as a synonym for 'left-wing', apparently excluding even

moderate right-wing groups or people from political credibility. *Un giudice democratico* or *un generale democratico* would describe a judge or a general who wasn't **Fascista*.

Emarginato: socially alienated. A much-used term for any social group, real or imaginary, whom the speaker wishes to champion. It is generally employed in direct inverse proportion to anything the speaker's party actually does for the *emarginati* in question (see ** giovani*, below).

Fascista: the natural complement of **democratico*, as well as a distinct historic designation for Mussolini and his supporters. The present-day MSI neo-Fascist party never quite dare take off the 'neo'.

Giovani, i: the young, seen in knee-jerk rhetorical terms as social Cinderellas not invited to the ball. (→ I, 2) Fully interchangeable with *le donne* – women – *la terza età* – senior citizens – and several other groups of presumed unfortunates.

Impegnato: derives from *engagé* in French – to be 'involved', or, as the Americans say, committed. Fitting in with the rhetoric of 'living in the realm of ideas', to be *impegnato* means not so much to do something as to think something 'politically useful'.

Integralismo: fundamentalism, used disparagingly and now usually reserved for the ideologically minded, particularly the theocratically minded groups allied to the DC (see *I *movimenti* and cf. **Kabulista*).

Kabulista: unrestructured Stalinists; few remain on the *comitato centrale* – the central committee – of the PCI (→ 2:ii, above), but all too many among *la *base*.

Laico: literally 'lay', hence the opposite of **cattolico*: anything which is specifically non-religious. *I partiti laici* are those political parties (PRI, PLI, PR) with a specifically anti-clerical tradition, and which do not profess a 'religious' creed like the Democrazia Cristiana, and, interestingly, the Partito Comunista.

Mezzogiorno: not just midday, but the term used for the south of Italy, faithful companion to political rhetoric for almost half a century. *Il mezzogiorno* is synonymous with the idea of deprivation, hard times, organized crime.

Migliorista: literally 'betterist', a jargon term to describe the right wing of the PCI, characterized by the belief that communism can be improved from within, without jettisoning the original model, but by 'constructive dialogue with capitalism'.

Movimenti, i: used, occasionally disparagingly, to describe those rather evangelical unofficial one-issue pressure groups across party lines, or fundamentalist groups close to specific parties. The DC has Comunione e Liberazione *and* Azione Cattolica to cope with; other parties, like the PSI, lobbies in favour of certain referendums, fraternization with certain other parties etc.

Palazzo, il: literally 'the palace, or building' but meaning the secretive and arbitrary monopolization of power by the parties – thus rather different from the fairly neutral concept implicit in 'corridors of power'. This usage was coined by Pier Paolo Pasolini in the famous editorial he wrote for the *Corriere della Sera* in August 1975.

Partitocrazia: 'partyocracy' was a convenient word coined after the war to describe multi-party democracy, but it is now generally used in a more sinister context, in which it was placed by Marco Pannella, who used *partitocrazia* to describe the Soviet-like stranglehold 'the parties' have on all State machinery. (→ 4:i, above)

Pentapartito: the five-party coalition government, composed of DC/PSI/PRI/PSDI/PLI. This formula, with a few interruptions, has ruled Italy for over a decade. *Governo di coalizione* is too vague for most Italians.

Pentitismo: being a supergrass, the phenomenon that followed *il *terrorismo*. When most terrorists, and latterly *mafiosi*, were locked up, many of them started having serious doubts about the validity of their past actions, especially since 'repenting' – grassing on still wanted ex-comrades – led to generous use of the **amnistia*. The nominally centre-right DC, with its Catholic traditions, is much more in favour of parlaying with, and pardoning, *i pentiti* than, say, *i partiti *laici*.

Questione morale, la: 'the moral question' is rather immorally used by the relatively more honest, self-righteous parties (PCI, PRI) when trying to score points off the dirty ones (PSI, PSDI, DC), or by the DC's De Mita when duelling with the much mud-covered Andreotti.

Riflusso: now fallen into relative disuse, this useful term ('the ebb flow') signifies the period after the heady days of *il *sessantotto*, when all that white-hot political activism dissolved into apathy and bourgeois values. Now people prefer the French post-Revolutionary term, *la restaurazione*.

Sorpasso, il: literally 'overtaking', but practically applied in two contexts: (a) when Italy's GNP overtook Britain's, making it, according to Italians, the world's fifth instead of sixth Western economic power (→VI, 1:i); (b) it is also used for election results, as when the PCI overtook the DC, or now for when the PSI overtakes the PCI.

Strutture, le: literally structures, or administrative or governmental organizations that provide essential services. Since so few work, or even exist, the term is used almost exclusively in the context of lacking public services – *mancanza di strutture* – generally by people passing the buck instead of accepting any personal responsibility for their actions.

Sessantotto, il: for Italians, this date has all the gravity of 1066. Despite the **riflusso* and the following period, the events of 1968 remain of the utmost importance in Italian intellectual folklore. It is the most definitive watershed of the post-war years. It has a sequel in *il Settantasette*: 1977 was a sort of action replay of 1968, which branched off into **terrorismo*.

Terrorismo: one of the few negative socio-political phenomena to have been almost completely eradicated, largely because so many *terroristi* became *pentiti* instead.

Trasformismo: undiluted opportunism; being prepared to sell your party's dearest principles, or closest allies, in exchange for power. The way in which no Italian party even closely resembles what its name signifies is the clearest example of this. The constant alliance-changing in Orwell's *1984* is vintage *trasformismo*.

4. What the parties control

(i) The leading role of the parties: *lottizzazione* and *sottogoverno*

Although Italy would like to think of France as its political model, in practice it is the Soviet Union that best fits this description.

There is an astonishing number of parallels, if one makes the initial adjustment from 'the Party' (as in the USSR) to 'the parties', between the effective political system of post-war Italy and that of Soviet Russia. Being firmly in the Western camp, Italy is technically a pluralist democracy – given the number of parties, a hyperpluralist one. But thanks to the unconscionable degree of collusion between them, it is almost as though there were only one. In Italy, 'the parties' form a state within the State. Since there is no established principle or precedent regarding the alternation of executive power, 'the parties' administer it in tandem, permanently. Some parties get more than their fair share of power; others less.

Not only the political institutions, but also the civil service is controlled in this way. In Italy there is no concept of a civil service technocracy, broadly above political currents, as exists in other Western democracies. Anyone who holds any office in government administration, from a director to a janitor, has obtained his or her post through political patronage, which for higher jobs means being a party member. Not only is this true in government administration, but it is also true in any of the other areas of employment directly or indirectly controlled by the State. Every field of commerce, industry, banking and culture is dominated by State participation. (→ 4:ii–iv, below) Translated into simple terms, this means, we give you the government's money in exchange for political control of your company.

In this way the Italian State has created (a) the largest network of State control of public life in the West; and (b) total control of all appointments, the criterion for which is political, not professional.

Since 'the parties' are a plural entity, this power is divided up into segments roughly respecting the voting power of each party, in a way analogous to the formation of governments with the *manuale Cencelli*. (→ 1:i, above) Thanks to this *lottizzazione* of para-State power, the parties can go about running this major segment of the country without any form of reference to the public: this is called *sottogoverno* – submerged government. Thus vast areas of Italian life have been transformed into a purely feudal system. *Sottogoverno* is obviously

The semiotics of party rule

An important feature of Italian political life is the ceremonial rhetoric and symbolism, which is almost entirely communist in inspiration. Although founded on post-war Stalinist values, it received a further impetus in the Left-dominated events of 1968. To first-time foreign observers, the PCI's manifestations look impressively hard-line, but it's all dressing up.

• Party symbols: in many countries, the party name and colour is enough, but Italy goes much further. The symbolic resonance of the PCI's hammer and sickle in the post-war democratic era obliged all the other parties, long before the existence of the 1980s' corporate image merchants, to have a symbol too. So powerful is the hammer and the sickle, though, that in the late 1970s there were ten different Marxist parties all featuring it on their logos. The PSI have, significantly, dropped it off theirs recently, after previously shedding the book (*Das Kapital*), leaving them with a red carnation. The red rose, fancied by British and French socialists alike, was the symbol of the whacky Radicals before they changed it (along with their name) in 1988 to a mug-shot of Gandhi. The DC have a crusader's red-cross shield, the PRI a green ivy leaf (nicely relevant to their American preppy aspirations), the MSI a flaming torch (not unlike that of the Tories), and so on.

• Terms of address: left-wing parties – PCI, DP, PSI and PSDI – all use the term of address *compagno* – literally 'companion', but the equivalent of 'comrade'. In the case of the decidedly post-ideological PSI, this is distinctly anomalous. The neo-Fascist MSI use *camarata* – 'comrade', but uniquely Fascist in tone. The DC felt the need for a term of address, and thus adopted the slightly oily, oriental *amico* – 'friend'. The *partiti laici* (PRI, PLI) avoid such nonsense altogether.

• Gatherings: the Communists have *la Festa dell'Unità* – a huge gymkhana/ fête/ ceilidh popular gathering in a public park or open space. Every local party organization sets one up each summer, while the national party organizes one mega-*festa* in a different location each year. Italians of all parties then enjoy going of a summer's evening – free entry, cheap food and drink, films and concerts (British bands positively swoon at the idea of playing them: desperately right-on thing to do), political debates (yawn), bookstalls, and exhibitions by foreign CPs and Third World groups. The only thing it lacks is a jumble sale.

The DC had to follow suit with *La Festa dell'Amicizia*, a bowdlerized carbon copy with far less popular support.

The PRI have *la Festa dell'-Edera* (the Ivy League Fête), which is, as their party line suggests, rather more sober and conservative.

•Newspapers: Italy has lots of little *Pravda*s, which are lavishly financed by the State, like the parties that produce them. *L'Unità* (PCI) is the only really important one, with sales comparable to those of a regular national daily. Once interminably dreary, it now dutifully reflects the PCI's slightly dire attempt to get hip: much snappier, less doctrinaire reporting, stock market reports, and a biting satirical weekly supplement, *Tango*, which is as merciless with PCI party leaders as with their rivals.

a self-perpetuating system: favours are exchanged for other favours, and thus create an important power base for party potentates.

One of the most immediately detrimental side-effects of *sottogoverno* is the impact it has on the quality of personnel. When appointments are made with political criteria uppermost, specific professional values naturally suffer. On the whole, most State participation business entities are not that badly run, because competent executives can usually be found in most parties. Where it really shows, though, is in the Arts. Since every branch of cultural production in Italy is subsidized by the State, it follows that every appointee or entity – conductor, musician, museum director, drama company, arts festival director – has a party's initials tattooed on their arm. The disastrous effect party control has had on the Italian arts cannot be overstressed. Artists are powerless to complain, because they are unlikely to find work if they do. It is much easier to follow the tide and shut up. To fall foul of a local party boss means becoming a cultural *refusnik* of the first order, however talented one is. (→ VIII, 6)

The *lottizzazione* of the media is even more blatant, since not just prestige but propaganda can be generated. The three RAI channels, each 'belonging' to a different major party (RAI 1, DC; RAI 2, PSI; RAI 3, PCI), broadcast what their respective party patrons order them to, which generally means more air time to 'their' men than anyone else's. This system is slightly complicated by the fact that each of the main parties has a slice of interest in the other channels, as do the minor parties. It requires an experienced eye to notice the nuances, but the signs are all there. Since the parties control almost every aspect of public life, there is never a problem in finding party members, or people who owe their positions to a party (known in Italian political parlance as *vicino* – 'near' – such and such a party), to interview or profile.

Thus the *telegiornale* – the TV news – on, say, RAI 2 (PSI-controlled) will open with a long feature on a speech by Craxi (PSI); an EC feature will be commentated on by a PSI cabinet minister, a feature on Africa by a PSI Third World expert (yes, charity is *lottizzato* too), a new opera production by a PSI-supported director, a new heart-transplant method will be praised by the PSI-sponsored head doctor of the hospital where it was pioneered, who will take care to thank the PSI-dominated *regione* (→ II, 3:ii) for being so efficient and generous. And the newsreaders? No prizes. If these news stories are important, they will also be carried by the other two channels, but in such a way as to reduce their pro-PSI impact.

The intention of the PSI-controlled bosses of RAI 2 is that it should be possible for a RAI 2 viewer to see a PSI-only Italy, where the other parties have been all but airbrushed out of the picture. Naturally, the bosses of RAI 1 (DC) and RAI 3 (PCI) do the same thing. But after a while, the distinctions blur, and one is aware only of the propaganda subtext to everything. Un-(rather than de-)regulated technology does its bit: living in a hyperpluralist régime with over 250 TV stations means non-stop propaganda from all the different parties simultaneously.

In view of the immense power offered by the *sottogoverno* system, it is hardly surprising that the Party Secretary (we would say leader, but the Italians copy the Russians in this too) is rarely Prime Minister as well. They have too much to do controlling their party's share of *il sottogoverno* to worry about anything as trifling as *il governo*. Only recently has this precedent been broken, with Spadolini, Craxi and De Mita occupying both posts simultaneously, to the great chagrin of their relatively power-starved colleagues. For the same reason, lesser party high-ups prefer to stay out of the cabinet: they can amass much more power and influence administering their party's feudal interests in State and para-State organizations than they ever could simply expediting the functions of some government ministry.

The State also accords an almost oriental degree of practical and ceremonial privileges to important party functionaries. One of the most apparent can be noted in the streets of Rome, which at certain moments resemble those of Moscow. Although they tend to be Lancias rather than Zils, a similar number of large dark blue cars (*macchina blù* in Italian is synonymous with 'official limo') containing party notables flanked by bodyguards roar up and down the major thoroughfares of the capital. Since the Italian capital's streets are too narrow to permit an extra 'party' lane like that in the Russian's, other transport is made to stop and pull over by special police on motorbikes.

Radical Party leader Marco Pannella recently took the unusual step of criticizing these privileges in Parliament. One of the main platforms of the Radicals has always been to denounce the *partitocrazia* as being incompatible with democracy. He is, of course, right, but the cynical reaction of his parliamentary colleagues was to attribute his outburst to sour grapes. His party has never been offered much share in the spoils.

Gorbachev's declared aim of separating the Russian

Il Popolo (DC), like *L'Avanti* (PSI) – once edited by Mussolini – is read only by party faithful.

L'Umanità (PSDI), *La Voce Repubblicana* (PRI) and *Notizie Radicali* (PR) are no more than broadsheets, with a smaller readership than the scuzziest fanzines. However, they continue because (*a*) party bosses still love writing the propaganda contents; (*b*) they are a symbol of political machismo: '*habeamus iournalus; ergo sumus*'.

Communist Party more from the State is naturally viewed without much enthusiasm in certain circles in Italy – it would certainly set an uncomfortable precedent for restructuring this deeply conservative political system.

(ii) The ministries and public administration

Considering the ineffectualness of the parliamentary institutions, all could be well if the State could be run in the meantime by a strong, professional and non-partisan civil service along the lines of the post-war French ENA-trained one. Unfortunately, this is not the case. Thanks to early leaders of the unified Italy like De Pretis and Giolitti, the tradition of an inefficient, politically partisan civil service took root. Shaken up at least superficially under Mussolini, it returned to its deep 19th-century slumber in 1945. Deriving its inspiration from the mid-19th-century French civil service, all ministerial administration in Italy is vertically organized, allowing inter-ministerial contact only at senior level, thus causing immense bottlenecks and communications breakdowns. One of the problems inherent in this system is that ministers are unable to spend their budgets in time – it takes too long for the expenditure request to filter through. If the country continues to run, it is thanks to Italy's energetic business community.

Government offices are so hidebound by intricately legalistic procedural rules that they devote more than half their working time to simply following them. The Italian civil service has always been the receptacle for the tens of thousands of fine legal minds that southern Italy traditionally produces: although the Italian mind is generally elastic by nature, it also has an unbending theoretical side, seen at its worst in the higher echelons of the civil service, where the solution of pressing logistical problems on a national scale is perceived as secondary to purely bureaucratic exigencies.

The exasperating slowness of the Italian bureaucracy is compounded by another fact: civil servants are highly union-protected, and cannot be sacked. Although the job is not brilliantly paid, it is secure, offers good holidays and provides an adequate pension. To make it a sinecure therefore encourages an attitude of indifference and irresponsibility among the employees, and since their working day is from 8 a.m. to 2 p.m., some 80% of them have a second, many even a third, job – obviously undeclared – giving them the best of all worlds: job security, variety of work, and a decent income.

Non-Romans, particularly Northerners, despise Romans for their straightforward attitude to these cushy jobs. Rome news-stands sell a broadsheet called *Il Posto* – 'the cushy number' – listing all ministerial posts going. Unlike in other countries, where white-collar jobs appear dreary, in Italy there is a scramble to get such work, and the papers are constantly full of stories of how hordes apply for every single post: a recent advert for 659 posts at il Ministero del Lavoro – the Ministry of Labour – occasioned 140,000 applicants.

The problem is not even that *la pubblica amministrazione* is over-bloated: considering the vast areas of State-run activity, its 4.4 million workers are hardly too many, while the figure, seen in relation to the population, corresponds closely to numbers in France, Great Britain and West Germany. (CENSIS estimates that there are six civil servants for every 100 inhabitants, and that one in five of all Italian job-holders are State employees.) Among the 2.3 million workers employed by Central Administration (therefore excluding State-owned and run concerns), there is a 24% incidence of undermanning.

Italian State employees in 1987

Schools and universities	**875,000**
Health service	**700,000**
Public sector industries	**700,000**
Regional civil service	**650,000**
Communications (post, telephone, railways)	**475,000**
Public agencies (Alitalia, RAI etc.)	**400,000**
Armed forces and police	**330,000**
Ministries	**250,000**
	Total: 4,380,000

This is a ministerial claim, of course, and would find little credence among the public at large. Especially in certain sectors like *le poste*, Southerners accept jobs in undermanned northern towns (where other workers prefer better paid industrial or tertiary jobs), and after a brief period apply for *trasferimento per motivi di famiglia* – job transfer for family reasons – back to the South. Hence in the North, post offices are undermanned, while in Sicily they are exploding at the seams with surplus personnel. This solution is certainly the lesser of two evils: since the State has no adequate unemployment benefit system, and those without work in the South are strongly tempted towards crime or contraband, regional overmanning 'keeps them off the streets'.

(iii) IRI: Europe's largest corporation

Characteristic of Italy's post-war quasi-communist profile is the mammoth State holding company IRI – Istituto per la Ricostruzione Industriale – which is Europe's largest single company, excluding oil companies. Set up in 1933 under Mussolini, it survived the war. It is based on a highly successful, flexible formula of joint holding, with some companies entirely belonging to

---

Expenditure of *la pubblica amministrazione* 1985 (as % of GDP)

	Capital account expenditure	Direct investments
USA	1.2%	1.4% (1983)
Japan	6.0% (1984)	4.4%
EC average	3.7%	2.7%
Germany	3.8%	2.3%
France	3.0%	3.0%
UK	2.1%	1.9%
Italy	5.5%	3.8%

---

the State, others with a State holding of 51% and others again with a lower percentage. IRI has permitted Italian industry since the war to develop by exploiting the best of both worlds: the finest entrepreneurial talents directing major business ventures underwritten or financed by the State. Despite near total *lottizzazione*, most of its 45,000 *enti* – component agencies – function efficiently. The Italian State has another three such holding companies, including ENI – Ente Nazionale per Idrocarboni – the State fuel-producing agency, which, though smaller than IRI, is more profitable. According to *Fortune* (1987) magazine, it is the world's ninth largest company in terms of sales. The Italian State also owns two huge financial agencies, EFIM and GEPI, as well as

---

While personal *raccomandazione* for the lesser posts and political *lottizzazione* for the higher ones always decides who gets what job, some 35% of ministerial jobs are awarded by exams. This extraordinary procedure, which CENSIS calculates on average costs 10 million lire per candidate, and takes four years from start to finish, applies at every level, from management down to janitors.

having almost complete control of the nation's banking system: Italy's thirty-one lending banks and eighty-nine savings banks, as well as various other major credit organizations, like IMI – Istituto Mobiliare Italiano. The entire banking and finance sector is thus organized as autonomously managed individual public corporations. (→ VI, 4)

(iv) The Italian Welfare State

In terms of organization, the Italian Welfare State is administered not by the government, but by autonomous corporations of a somewhat fascist corporative inspiration. These are being gradually merged under the umbrella of the notorious Istituto Nazionale di Previdenza Sociale (INPS) – National Insurance and Pensions fund – which has funds that total well over a quarter of the country's GNP.

There is also a vast number of officially public, but in all aspects privately administered, welfare and charity concerns, often dedicated to quite fictitious or anachronistic purposes. Although the State is trying to cut away the dead wood – some 9000 have been closed down – there are still at least 40,000 of these Mickey Mouse charity outfits up and down the country.

Despite the shady character of the second category, the first group of organizations should be capable of providing a satisfactory welfare service, but most Italians are hard-pressed to know how to access to it. There are certain areas where progressive legislation, mostly enacted in the 1970s, has proved successful, but on the whole State care is disastrously inadequate. Italians are obliged to fall back on their stand-by: the family.

Especially in the case of national emergencies, like the 1980 Naples earthquake, or the 1986 Stava dam disaster, the public's reaction of outrage is justified. Non-existent or cynically ignored safety precautions, lack of sufficient ministerial controls, and then tardy relief measures (→ II, 2:ii–iii; VIII, 3:ii) ensure that Italians will never be able to rely on the State as a guarantor against natural or man-made disasters. One of the most common phrases heard on Italian lips is, '*Mancano le strutture*' – 'There aren't the facilities.' Italians are painfully aware of what *strutture* there are in other countries, from reliable pension and medical schemes, to amenities like free or subsidized sports facilities, public libraries and meals on wheels, or employment retraining schemes, and strongly resent their own government's reluctance to do anything along the same lines. Their own complicity in the *sottogoverno* and *lottizzazione* systems makes it easier for civil servants to allocate government money to their own pockets than to some community project, a

Welfare facilities

For non-Italians who are citizens of the EC, and for non-EC citizens with regular work permits, all of these facilities are theoretically available. Apart from health and schooling, it is highly unlikely that you would want to use them, since the coverage they offer is so meagre. If you have a regular job with an Italian firm, you will be paying INPS contributions in any case. For EC countries, there exists, at least on paper, a reciprocal points system. There are those in Italy, despite the massive public-spending cuts planned for the early 1990s, who are trying to expand *lo stato assistenziale* – the Italian Welfare State – if not exactly 'from the cradle to the grave', at least somewhat.

●USL (Le Unità Sanitarie Locali): the notorious Italian health system has, despite several phases of reorganization over the last decade, with more on the way, steadily deteriorated. It may seem odd to a non-Italian that something as politically neutral as basic health assistance could be *lottizzato*, but that's the way the bitter pill crumbles. (→ VIII, 2:i)

● *Maternità/paternità* – maternity/ paternity benefits: eight weeks' pre-natal and thirteen weeks' post-natal at 80% of earning, plus 30% of earnings for a further six months, if wished; the additional six months may be split up into blocks, but these must be within the child's first year.

● *La scuola*: schooling is of a generally high academic standard all round, even though it is fairly chaotic from an administrative point of view. There are serious financing problems, which often mean unsatisfactory technical facilities, staffing levels and class sizes. Universities are a particular anomaly, lacking a ceiling limit on student numbers. Tertiary education is dominated by *lottizzazione*. (→ VIII, 5:ii)

• *La casa* – housing: the *case popolari* – council-house system – begun by Mussolini with considerable success, has been continued ever since, but with more limited results. There are many Italian cities where overcrowding due to a chronic housing shortage reaches Third World levels, but where the State seems unable to act. The well-meaning but unsuccessful fair-rent act, *l'Equo canone*, is now being repealed. (→ I, 1:ii)

• INPS (Istituto Nazionale di Previdenza Sociale): the National Insurance and Pensions fund is thoroughly arcane. Founded under Mussolini, when it worked much better, INPS effectively dominates the whole pension system, although there also exist several pension funds linked to certain State industries (water, gas, the railways etc.), as well as private pension plans, which are now growing rapidly. For employees, the retirement age for women is 55, and 60 for men, while for the self-employed it is 60 and 56 respectively. Apart from the old-age pension – *pensione di vecchiaia* – the *pensione sociale* – supplementary benefit – for those not eligible for a retired worker's pension, but with no other means of support, and the *pensione di invalidità* – an invalid pension (widely abused in southern Italy by able-bodied people getting their doctor to certify them as *invalidi*) – there is also something called *la pensione di anzianità* – a long-service pension, after thirty-five years of work. There has recently been an attempt to abolish a scandalous variant on this system, awarding pensions to certain State employees, such as teach-

fact that often (though not always) passes unobserved. Where people are aware of the relationship between honesty and poor social services is in tax-paying. Humble employees invariably pay more income. (→ V, 1:ii; vi) Thus the lower paid get all the more infuriated when they see how poorly the health and pensions system works, and how little they are getting back for their money, while the better off invest in private schemes anyway. It is at this point that the Italians' tendency to be lulled by *il bel discorso* comes to a grinding halt. The angry cry then goes up: '*Dov'è lo stato?*' – 'Where the hell is the State when we need it?'

ers, after only ten years' service (allowing 30-year-olds to 'retire' and get another job on the quiet), but it was not successful, thanks to the efforts of certain areas of the DC and the PSDI, the parties that gain the most votes through it. Pensions for employees are calculated at 80% of earnings in the three most favourable years out of the last five served; in 1987, the *pensione di vecchiaia* had an upper limit of 36,800,000 lire per annum; calculated at a monthly rate, the minimum is 400,000 lire. On the other hand, old-age pensioners have got militant, forming a series of political parties to fight their case, particularly grievous when a promised pension is then summarily abolished. (→ IV, 2: ii)

• *Sussidio di disoccupazione*: unemployment benefit is obtainable for previously employed workers from the Ufficio di Collocamento – a highly bureaucratic version of the unemployment exchange – but it amounts to a mere 800 lire (45p) a day. For industrial and building-sector workers, this sum fortunately rises to 30,000 a day, to a maximum of 925,000 a month. In both cases, there are also discretionary *assegni familiari* – family allowances – which include children up to the age of 26, if still in full-time education.

• *Cassa integrazione*: a special fund for workers temporarily laid off from large industries, like Fiat. Although the payment for the initial period is quite good (80%, descending in gradual phases after six months and a year), most workers strenuously oppose it, since it usually leads to a permanent state of unemployment.

Written about any other country, this chapter would add up to rather less; but then, Italy's relationship with law and order is rather different to that of most other countries. We have already seen why most Italians care little for the State as such; here, we see the manifestations of this indifference, or even hostility. Many Italians point an accusing finger at the inadequacies of the State as an excuse when apprehended for their wrongdoings.

Abusivismo is a blanket term which can be stretched to cover, quite literally, a whole host of sins, from selfish social behaviour to organized fraud. If it is almost always true that you can get away with *abusivo* behaviour, then crime in Italy definitely pays. In some ways, Italy is a more dangerous country than most; in others, less so. The world has the same prurient interest in the criminality, in all its various forms, of Italians as it does in their sex lives. From petty crime – the bag-snatching *scippatore* on a Vespa – via organized crime – the sleazy drug-running *mafioso* – to political crime – the balaclava'ed *terrorista* – there exist well-delineated stereotypes in the international media's image bank, which in themselves help glamorize the figures portrayed. The Italian news media and entertainment industry have been particularly instrumental in launching criminal chic; in their different ways they also cater for the Italians' apparently inexhaustible appetite for elaborate conspiracy theories.

If Italian criminality seems imposingly complex, the opposition is just as formidable. Although less immediately noticeable than they were a decade ago, the police are hard to ignore, partly because there are so many different, almost parallel, forces. The judicial system, into which they feed their prisoners, is currently undergoing a major reform. At present, it is emblematic of the currents that underscore Italian public life, from the most draconian legislation, and nakedly political judgements in some areas, to some of most indulgent sentencing imaginable in others.

The last two chapters showed how the current political structure of Italy is post-war, with an unintentional left–wing slant; this chapter shows how the bureaucratic and judicial systems are distinctly pre-war, based on almost wholly unrestructured Fascist principles. Most Italians have learnt how to deal with a Kafka-like bureaucracy; foreigners usually require some help. The hostility of the individual towards the Italian State becomes more comprehensible in the light of such an otiose bureaucratic system, which seems designed at every turn to obstruct the citizen's access to information and justice. Ironically, it is that very same well-meaning liberal idealism so typical of Italian public life that permits the sinister reality of the entire bureaucratic machine to continue, by assuming that it can be just wished away, by fine words.

---

1. *Abusivismo* and asocial behaviour

(i) *Disonesto ma simpatico*

Few countries can boast such an all-encompassing alternative régime to the State as the Italian phenomenon of *abusivismo*. The adjective *abusivo* means not so much 'criminal' as just 'illegal', and often simply 'unauthorized'. *Abusivismo* derives from several mixed

An *abusivo* word-list

● *Abusivismo*: the cult of the illegal or unauthorized; everything that is done without correct permission, from the construction or altering of houses, to setting up businesses without going through the red-tape procedures.

● *Amnistia*: (→ IV, 3:iii)

● *Arrangiarsi*: to set oneself up nicely – the implication is, 'despite unfavourable circumstances' (see *sistemare*);*L'arte dell'arrangiarsi* is every foreign journalist's favourite Italian cliché.

● *Assistenzialismo*: (→ IV, 3:iii)

● *Autorità, le*: fat cats, VIPs, who get to sit in the best seats (free, naturally) at concerts, football matches etc. and are cordoned off with ropes and/or sub-machine guns. Not to be confused with *Un authority*', in the English bureaucratic usage (viz. IBA, ILEA), which Italian leaders are always wishing Italy could have too. No sign of any yet.

● *Bolla*: literally 'bull', as in the medieval 'papal bull'. Now used mostly in '*carta bollata*' – paper with a government duty stamp incised on it, as opposed to '*carta semplice*' – normal paper. (→ 4, below)

● *Bustarella*: literally, 'a little packet' – a bribe.

● *Carcere*: prison; *i carcerati* are those in prison (the slang term is *al fresco* – cf. 'in the cooler'); *scarcerato* is someone who gets let out.

● *Concussione*: embezzlement.

● *Condono*: (→ IV, 3:iii)

● *Denunciare*: literally 'to denounce', but very often simply 'to declare' some fact to the authorities. *Un film da denuncia* is a film that makes a blistering attack on some form of injustice.

● *Dietrologia*: literally 'behind-ology', or the science of conspiracy theories. Many Italian journalists make their living out of this – *dietrologhi* – while for others it is an amusing after-dinner sport.

● *Emarginazione*: social alienation, as an excuse for criminal

factors, some of which we have come across in earlier chapters. First, a deep-felt sense of alienation towards the State and all that it stands for. Secondly, a cult of selfishness, of looking after number one. Thirdly, a certain streetwise business acumen. Certain attitudes condone its existence, from the traditional Catholic indulgence towards wrongdoers, to the proverbial Italian capacity for self-congratulation: for many Italians, to be agin the system is *simpatico*. This attitude is even evident from TV adverts. The deodorant 'Impulse' is marketed across Europe with a standard romantic formula: girl (wearing 'Impulse') walks down street; captivates nostrils of handsome stranger; handsome stranger buys 'Impulse' girl bunch of flowers. In the Italian version, the boy *steals* his flowers: the slogan even underlines this fact verbally. Ştealing, if 'justified', can be *simpatico*.

In 1988, in a study which *La Stampa* christened 'L'Italia disubbidiente e fracassona' – disobedient and rowdy Italy – CENSIS coined the interesting neologism 'alegal', rather than 'illegal', to describe the mentality of a people for whom the concept of civic conscience is a vast no-go area. Their findings are significant, because they represent an unemotional survey of all the issues raised by the *abusivismo* question, usually an area highly charged by partisan considerations. According to CENSIS, the root factor lies with the modern Italian State's almost total inability to impose itself on the country. This is equally true of all three main power areas – the legislative, the executive and the judiciary. The State's actions are weak, contradictory, and too compromised by partisan political and personal interests to set an acceptable example for the country to follow.

Where the State's presence may be felt through legislation, it is either so inaccessible or so outdated as to be unworkable. The inefficiency and partiality of the State is such that only a masochist can flourish by observing all the rules. The only way to survive is to bend them; the only way to prosper is brazenly to flout them.

The feeling that you can never trust the State or 'the community', but must rely on your own wits, has many positive, as well as the more obvious negative, aspects to it. One is the average Italian's mental alertness and personal resourcefulness, the result of having to make a snap decision every five minutes: they consider other nationalities incredibly boring, because they always 'go by the book'. Apart from their unquestioning adherence to the *bella figura* principle, Italians never conform, charming foreigners with their 'spontaneity' and 'unpredictability' (even though, in many respects, most northern Italians have more in common in this sense with the rest of Europe than with those from the Centre and the South).

(ii) *E io non pago*

The 'I'm not paying' syndrome has always been of cult proportions in Italy, and includes practically every Italian in some way or other. Seeing how generous they are to each other, it seems odd what they will do to save a few bob at times. The gamut runs from the harmless to the indictable:

(a) Shameless invasion of official or private events where there is food and drink to be had free. Gatecrashers are known as *portoghesi* – after a memorable party at the Portuguese Embassy in Renaissance times, when hundreds of Romans passed themselves off as *portoghesi* in order to get in. The posher the party, the more brazen they are.

(b) Hustling free theatre tickets. In Rome there is even a saying, '*Gli unici che pagano per andare al teatro sono gli scemi e gli stranieri*' – 'The only people who pay to go to the theatre are fools and foreigners.' The fact that a policy of all-paper houses eventually results in lower standards seems to occur to no one. (→VII, 4 : ii)

(c) Hustling free entrance into discothèques and night-clubs. Young people will spend hours waiting to get in free, not just to save money, but in order to feel important – the 'Let me through, I'm a star' syndrome.

(d) Jumping bus fares. 30% of Italians are estimated to be free-riders. They too are known indulgently by the Press as *portoghesi*. In Milan in 1987 alone, some 80,000 free-riders were apprehended by inspectors.

(e) Not paying TV licences. Out of Italy's 20 million TV homes, only 65% are *in regola*. The State TV RAI desperately tries to entice the other 35% to pay up, by offering fabulous prizes in the new lottery attached to the list of subscribers' names.

(f) Shoplifting and stealing, or 'liberating', things was especially popular with the student Left of the 1970s. They call it *esproprio proletario* – proletarian expropriation. The whole Italian 'Can't pay, won't pay' rhetoric played well with London alternative theatre-goers, but it is now as dated as Dario Fo.

(g) *L'evasione fiscale* – tax dodging – is of such mammoth proportions in Italy that at the Ministero delle Finanze – the Finance Ministry – they estimate that three-quarters of Italy's massive national debt ($750 billion – over a trillion lire) could be paid off at a stroke if everyone came up with the back taxes they owe. Only the trade unions – whose members have their taxes deducted at source – keep the pressure up. The culprits are businesses of all sizes and the self-employed. In trying

activities. (→ IV, 3:iii)

● *Faccendiere*: the ubiquitous, omnipotent, but usually invisible Mr Fixit figures who glide through the upper echelons of political power striking illicit deals.

● *fregare*: to steal, rip off, get the better of someone. The supremely arrogant '*Me ne frego!*' – 'I don't give a damn!' ('Give 'em hell!') – was one of Mussolini's top political slogans; *menefreghismo* corresponds to the French '*s'enfoutisme*' – not giving a shit about the world, and elevating this attitude to a personal philosophy.

● *Furbo*: no exact translation, rendering the implied sense of approval, exists for this key adjective: smart, sly, clever, streetwise are the nearest you get in English.

● *Furto*: theft.

● *Incendio doloso*: arson.

● *Intrallazzo*: an intrigue, deal, scam.

● *Kafkaiano*: Kafkaesque, as in the Italian State bureaucracy.

● *Killer*: a Mafia hitman.

● *Ladro*: thief. 'Stop thief!' is '*Al ladro!*'

● *Mafioso*: used figuratively as well as literally; note the difference between the Sicilian Mafia, the Neapolitan Camorra and the Calabrian 'Ndrangheta. (→2:iii, below)

● *Malavita, la* (often simply *la mala*): describes the underworld as a whole.

● *Oltraggio*: an outrageous act, as in *oltraggio ad un pubblico ufficiale* – answering back a policeman, or even a post-office worker.

● *Omertà*: the Mafia concept of loyal silence.

● *Paraculo*: a smart arse – invariably used positively; *paravento* is a politer variant; the more vulgar *faccia di culo* suggests chutzpah.

● *Pentitismo*: (→IV, 3:iii)

● *Politicante*: the pejorative term

derived from *politico*, referring to a minor league, wheeler-dealer politician: not as serious as **faccendiere*.

● *Portoghese*: freeloader, gate-crasher. (→ 1:ii, above)

● PS: Pubblica Sicurezza – the forces of law and order.

● *Raccomandazione*: 'recom-mendation' – the national cult of nepotism or string-pulling, which remains the principal way of getting where you want: into a plum job, out of mili-tary service, a good seat at the opera. *Un raccomandato* is someone who gets a job thanks to their personal or political connections – the subtext is often that they are inept as well. (→ IV, 3:iii)

● *Rapina*: a hold-up, or bank robbery.

● *Rapimento*: kidnapping.

● *Reato*: a crime, of which you can be *innocente* or *colpevole*. When a lawsuit (usually a murder case) gets wide media coverage and excites public debate, peo-ple tend to become *innocentisti* or *colpevolisti*, depending on their personal theory.

● *Rubare*: to steal; 'Mi hanno derubato!' – 'I've been robbed!'

● *Scippare*: to bagsnatch, Ital-ian *scippatori* tend not to use, or threaten, violence; hence 'mugger' is inappropriate. (→ II, 6, ACCESS, Stressful street scenarios)

● *Tossicodipendente*: drug ad-dict; *eroinomane* is specific to heroin users.

● *Scroccare*: to scrounge; a *scroccone* is a scrounger.

● *Sistemato*: depends on the context; 'Ho sistemato mio figlio' – 'I've found a nice job for my son/I've set him up nicely'–while 'Ho sistemato quel lo stronzo' means, 'I gave that arsehole a bunch of fives.'

● *Spaccio di droga*: drug dealing.

● *Stronzo*: a shit, or arsehole; 'Non fare lo stronzo' – 'Don't be such an arsehole.' Used by many

to recoup undeclared IVA (VAT) payments, the Ministero delle Finanze has now decided to change strategy, since the major offenders – big businesses – have found that by taking the matter to court, even if they are found guilty, they can gain a delay of at least ten years: that

---

The tax inspectors' organization, SECIT – il Servizio Centrale degli Ispettori Tributari – estimates that the average annual income declared by 83% of all self-employed categories was 8.6 million lire – less than £4000. Many of them declare even less. The tax authorities reckon that 95% of shopkeepers fiddle their '740' – income tax form – and that in 1986, they managed to collect only 80,000 billion lire of a total 330,000 billion lire, leaving some 250,000 billion lire owed in income tax, or £115 billion. The Inland Revenue's 1988 estimates of some £5 billion in evaded taxes in the UK appears insig-nificant by comparison. The Milan-based financial daily *Il Sole–24 Ore* calculates that for the five-year period 1983-87, for VAT declarations alone, the self-employed have cheated the State out of some 200,000 billion lire.

---

is how long it takes for the sentence to be handed down against them. The Ministry is now going after the small fry – individual professionals and shop-keepers – who cannot sustain the costs of a lengthy court case, and will generally pay up if they are found out. The fiscal police – La Guardia di Finanza (→ 3:v, below) – aren't entirely inactive; in the first seven months of 1989, they carried out some 15,000 tax raids, resulting in 2,500 ascertained cases of serious tax fraud, worth 610 billion lire. There are about 250,000 more general checks a year, in the majority of which some element of fraud is detected. In 1986, 868 out of the 987 reaudited corporations that declared an operative running loss were discovered to have cooked the books. The courts find themselves overwhelmed with tax fraud cases. Even in relatively law-abiding Milan, the offices of the Procura della Repubblica – the legal authorities – reckon that well over two-thirds of cases pending regard tax fiddles committed in the city.

In order to defeat tax evasion, the Finance Ministry has worked out a rule-of-thumb calculation system to complement the existing code, whereby an individual must pay taxes in relation to what he/she possesses. Since in Italy, the more speed-boats, country villas and racehorses a person possesses, the less they declare on their tax, this seemingly arbitrary system makes very good sense. Thus, a more accurate idea of the real earnings of a company director will be calculated by the fact that he owns a racehorse, rather than the sum he declares to *il fisco* – the taxman.

Top tax evaders by category

percentage of their income not declared
Economists; statisticians 73.5%
Furriers 65.5%
Accountants 42.7%
Stockbrokers 37.8%
Tobacconists 34.4%
Hospital specialists 33.4%
Writers/journalists 27.8%
Engineers, architects 27.4%
Pharmacists 27.0%
Stationers 26.4%
Artists, actors, film directors 20.7%
Doctors 20.5%

(*Il Sole – 24 Ore*)

Italians with a social conscience to chide their friends without one.
● *Strutture, le*: (→IV, 3:iii)
● *Stupifacenti*: drugs, in the collective sense, as when the police make a big haul of them.
● *Stupro*: rape; also called *violenza carnale*.
● *Tangente*: a rake-off; an illegal percentage off an *appalto* – tender to contract.

(iii) *Io faccio come mi pare*

The 'I'll do as I please' syndrome would seem hard to justify. The reaction of Italians to anti-social behaviour is interesting: from passive tolerance to short-lived anger. The concept (and the words to say it) of self-righteous indignation doesn't exist in Italian. Never do they say, – 'Hey – you can't do that, it's not allowed!': the answer would be, 'Who sez?'

The systematic lack of respect for others paradoxically becomes a form of civil liberty: the right to 'do your own thing', however destructive or pointless, is tacitly accepted as greater than the duty to observe by-laws. Hence reactions to the following scenarios:

(a) Dropping litter in public: 'It's up to them – I'm not a street-cleaner.'

(b) Making a noise at the cinema: 'They're having a good time, I mustn't be a spoilsport.' If the noise becomes intolerable, then they will yell an exasperated but rancour-free, *'Zitti!'* – 'Shut up!': never a falsely courteous, clenched teeth, 'Do you mind keeping the noise down?'

(c) Not stopping at red lights, driving the wrong way up one-way streets: 'Why not? There are no *vigili* (traffic cops) about.'

(d) Vandalism is less noticeable in Italy than in other more alcohol-orientated countries, but it still takes its toll: CENSIS calculated that one in ten plastic rubbish skips in Venice are burnt out each year, while the national phone company SIP say that in 1984, 56,500 of their public booths were damaged 67,000 times.

(iv) *Forte con i deboli, debole con i forti*

'Hard-nosed with the weak, weak with the hard-nosed': The ultimate consequence of (iii) – classic bullying and exploiting of one's position of power, while toadying to one's own superiors. Italians are no respecters of authority, but often pander to the powerful, trampling on the less strong. This goes from the banal, in the form of driving manners, to the corridors of power:

(a) Not stopping for people waiting at pedestrian crossings: 'Why should I? They wouldn't if they were driving.'

(b) Never slowing down at puddles so as not to splash passers-by.

(c) Parking: even if there is space for a second car, they will plonk theirs in the middle.

(d) The *ante camera* system: always making other people wait for you, not vice versa. Not returning business calls, or replying to business letters, if you detect no immediate profit from it, is the obvious example.

(e) Exploitation of personal position by encouraging bribes and favours: *raccomandazioni, bustarelle, tangenti*. This is most pronounced among politicians, who always get off: Italy's most *furbo* (→ ACCESS: an *abusivo* word-list) politician, Giulio Andreotti, has been involved in twenty-seven full-scale Watergate-type inquiries during his long career; never has he been even minimally impugned as a result. Research by Franco Cazzola in 1988 showed that abusing one's political position of power pays: since 1976, politicians have received some 33,000 billion lire in corruption pay-off money, while there have been over a quarter of a million *reported* cases of political corruption since 1880.

(v) Taking the law into your own hands

This varies from justified personal initiative in the face of official inefficiency or delays to the sneaky muscling in on the rightful pitch of others:

(a) Construction without building permits – *abusivismo edilizio* – is perhaps the largest and most complex aspect of all: on the one hand, there is the unjustifiable, from single-property owners carrying out unauthorized restructuring of listed buildings, to whole rows of jerry-built tower blocks on green-belt land by Mafia corporate interests; on the other, there is a justifiable impatience with the local *comune*. Few local councils have any clear, updated *piano regolatore* – town-planning survey; going by the book means waiting up to fifteen years for an official reply. Il Catasto – the Land Registrar's office – has no record of some 8 million houses and

The most *abusivo* town in Italy

**Having struggled for decades against the phenom-
enon of illegal building, the government's *condono
edilizio* was designed to encourage people to make
a clean breast of things. In 1988, millions followed
up the suggestion, including the village of Mazzano
Romano, a few miles from the capital, where 3667
requests were made, out of a population of 2000
souls. That makes two *case abusive* for each inhabitant. Despite the mayor's protest, the State's *Gazzetta
ufficiale* insists that this is true.**

14 million apartments built (mostly legally) over the
last fifty years, for which the Guardia di Finanza could
have picked up 20,000 billion lire in back taxes. The
1987 *condono edilizio* – illegal construction amnesty –
encouraged some 2.3 million illegal home-owners out of
the woodwork, while an estimated 600,000 continue to
lie doggo despite the knowledge that the State, fighting a
losing battle, has declared, 'Come home, all is forgiven.'
(b) Not getting permits to start a business: from un-
licensed street hawkers and self-appointed parking
attendants to major companies with multi-billion lire
turnovers, the temptation (or necessity) of not being
in regola affects over 2 million Italians. The papers
are always uncovering fraudulent doctors and dentists, who've been practising *abusivamente*, undetected,
for years.

(vi) *L'economia nera*: sloth and fraud
Self-employed Italians work extremely hard; Italians
working for the State tend to work as little as possible:
(a) *Il secondo/terzo lavoro* – second/third jobs: several
million Italians actually fit into both categories, working
8 a.m.–2 p.m. in a government office before slouching
off to their own second or third job. (→ IV, 4:ii) This is
anti-social since, according to conventional economic
wisdom, they are preventing the unemployed from
working at all. Italy's blossoming black economy (estimated at 15%–20% of official GNP) is tangible proof,
that this is probably not true.
(b) Skiving off: less justifiable is widespread *assenteismo*
– absenteeism – when many of the above don't actually
go to work at all, just call in sick and come in at the end
of the month (the 27th) to pick up their pay cheque.
In 1986, Rome judge Elio Cappelli ordered all hospital
managements to investigate all cases of sick leave, especially immediately following holiday periods. The police

make frequent raids on post offices, hospitals, railway stations and other State concerns, with sweeping arrests for absentees. The trade union movement hotly defends the rights of its members to frequent, even continuous, *permessi* – permits to stay home. A 1988 report by the Corte dei Conti showed that ministry workers got official *permessi* for an average of twenty-three days a year, with employees at the Ministero della Sanità – Health Ministry – taking thirty-five days. This wasn't counting days not worked without the relevant *permesso*.

(c) The sweet smell of success: an estimated 10% of State clerical staff carry out second jobs from their desks: free phone-calls and indifferent office managers allow RAI TV office staff to run private theatrical agencies in office time, while ministerial business is heavily slowed down by secretaries hawking knitwear, beachwear and designer brand perfume between dictation sessions. They call it *arrotondare lo stipendio* – topping up your salary – but they often manage to double it.

(d) Contrabrand: mostly cigarettes, and in the South. Alcohol is too cheap anyway. The Naples Guardia di Finanza rarely intervenes, since smuggling Marlboro and Camel from the US provides work for tens of thousands of Neapolitans, and is worth 750 billion lire.

(e) Counterfeiting: based mostly in Naples, this thrives on its low-risk element (maximum fine 800,000 lire; two-year sentence), and plays on the Italians' mammoth label snobbery. It gives work to an estimated 60,000 people, and it has a turnover of 3,600 billion lire. It represents an interesting form of backhanded flattery to major designers, although they fight back: Louis Vuitton sued 374 times in 1988, while Milan designer Trussardi has sued 200 times in the period 1983–8. Krizia's founder, Mariuccia Mandelli, has helped co-ordinate a scientific research project, funded by all the major Italian labels, into finding a foolproof detection system, as for banknotes: knock-off copies of couture clothes are now so perfect that the designers themselves often can't tell them apart.

Naples: a special case

Naples is the capital of *abusivismo* in Italy, and provides the rest of the country with endless amusement, thanks to the extent and variety of its non-stop scams. Some examples reported in the Press:

• The municipal services were so badly run, they had to be privatized in 1988. As the dirtiest city in Europe, with over 1.5 kilos of rubbish per day per person, you'd have thought it needed all of its 7000 garbage collectors for survival. However, over half of them were officially in admin. posts. Furthermore, there were 1005 drivers assigned to drive 455 trash carts, of which fewer than a quarter work, despite full-time maintenance from 1045 mechanics. A hammer blow to a wing mirror was judged sufficient to take a cart out of service. As if this wasn't enough, most of those with non-existent jobs don't turn up. The Carabinieri recently arrested twenty-five out of 125 dustworkers in one depot.

● *Assenteismo* in hospitals is so bad that when the Polizia recently raided one Naples hospital and handcuffed dozens of orderlies in the wards, the patients sat up from their sickbeds to give a hearty round of applause.

● Hospital staff in Naples also make a bit on the side by selling corpses back to their families, for several million lire a shot. Superstitious Neapolitans prefer elaborate family wakes to antiseptic morgues, and are prepared to pay up. In 1988, the Naples police made a concerted attempt to crack down on the recycled stiff trade.

● Dead people are even brought back to life for electoral purposes: some 4500 voters were resuscitated for the 1987 general elections, and are currently under enquiry. (→ VIII, 10)

1988 case of fraud in Cagliari hospital of Santissima Trinità: 214 artificial penises were ordered at 7 million lire each; the 1.5 billion lire purchase was initially approved by the Sardinian USL health authorities, before the ruse was stopped.

(vii) Illegal immigration

Until ten years ago, there were only a handful of African immigrants in Italy, generally from the ex-colonies of Somalia, Eritrea, Ethiopia and Libya – and it was common to meet Italians in walks of life who admitted to never having seen, or spoken, to a black person. This extraordinary degree of ethnic isolation was due mainly to the very strict immigration laws of the period. Since the laws themselves have been liberalized, and vigilance in maintaining them even more so, this situation has completely changed, and over the last decade there has been such a massive influx of illegal immigrants into Italy that it is hard to say how many there now are – estimates vary from 750,000 to 2.5 million. Almost half a million of these are now *in regola* – have their papers in order – mostly those who live in cities like Rome, Naples and Milan.

Most Western countries, such as Britain or France, have gradually tightened their entry laws in the face of considerable social problems. Italy has gone the other way. Even the most tentative suggestions over limiting the influx are politically taboo, and since the Customs officials take their cue from the politicians, there is no need for boat-people-style incursions on the coastline.

But if the official line remains humanitarian and *terzomondista* – pro-Third World – to a remark-able degree, encouraging ever-increasing numbers of *immigrati illegali*, there is mounting evidence that the living conditions of the new arrivals are another matter. On the one hand, there is economic exploita-tion of Dickensian proportions (unregistered foreigners working for wages and in conditions far inferior to the legal minimum standards); on the other, a frightening increase in the number of cases of ethnic intolerance, ranging from petty insults and racist graffiti to violence and even Ku-Klux-Klan-style killings.

A curious law of the jungle seems to have sprung up, whereby different sectors of the *economia sommersa* – the 'submerged' (i.e. illegal) economy – are now domi-nated by different ethnic groups, partly dictated by the degree of social acceptability each group elicits from the Italians. According to this cruel anthropological logic, whites and Christians certainly do better than blacks or Muslims. This whole phenomenon is much more marked in the South than the North, in larger rather than smaller cities.

Rome has by far the largest community of illegal foreign immigrants, and is the city preferred by most of the East European ones (the reassuring presence of the Pope?), while Naples is the city most favoured by Africans. Most of the Hong Kong Chinese community is in a class of its own, having arrived with both money and entry permits, which they wasted no time in converting to regular work permits. As a result, the number of Chinese restaurants in Italy has expanded at an incredible rate since the late 1970s. The capital is also host to between 70,000 and 100,000 Filipinos (according to different estimates), who are employed as domestics in wealthy homes, although many of them are not registered as such.

The latest thing in Rome is to get a well-educated Pole as a cleaner, while Capo Verdeans are much prized in Naples as nannies, and Egyptians and Tunisians are beginning to replace Italians as kitchen staff in restau-rants in Rome, Naples and the South. Up to half of the underpaid seasonal jobs in the agricultural sector in the

South – particularly Sicily – are now done by North Africans; Brazilians are gradually taking over the lucrative cut-price prostitution sector; Russian Jews, with their battered suitcases full of Soviet handicrafts and lo-tech. products, are a familiar sight in every flea-market where once the Neapolitans reigned supreme.

As each of the new communities takes root and expands, so does the number of self-help facilities. Twenty years ago, a restaurant specializing in the cuisine of a different Italian *regione* was considered foreign; now ethnic restaurants are mushrooming in low rent *quartieri*, along with food-shops, market stalls, newsletters, graffiti and informal social action groups. The African *vu comprà'* (→II, 5) have even formed their own trade union.

Exploited by rich home-owners, restaurant owners and farmers, generally tolerated by the police and the majority of ordinary citizens, Italy's new crypto-slave class (it is tempting to draw a historical comparison with the later years of the Roman Empire, when as much as a third of the capital's population was from the overseas imperial provinces) is fortunately not entirely without real friends. The Catholic Church, both nationally through charity organizations like Caritas and in individual parishes (some rather more than others), does a great deal at a primary level for the new arrivals and the destitute (emergency accommodation, clothing, food kitchens), while the Italian Trades Union Confederation are conducting an impressive campaign – unusually of deeds, rather than just words – on behalf of those who already have jobs, whether on or off the books.

Another organization, 'Italia-Razzismo' – similar in scope to the French 'SOS Racisme' – is, with active support from various political parties, currently concentrating its attention on the plight of those *immigrati illegali* languishing in Italy's already overcrowded jails. The results of their recent survey (1989), based on figures released by the Ministero di Grazia e Giustizia – Ministry of Justice – leave one in no doubt about the gravity of the situation. At any one time in 1989, there were more than 3000 foreigners in Italian jails; during the whole of 1988, a total of 10,000 passed through them. Of the 1989 figure, well over half (1800) were from African or Arab countries. Yugoslavians (almost all gypsies) accounted for almost 400, with South Americans not far behind. Almost half of all those detained in Italian juvenile remand centres (over half in Rome) are foreigners. Italia Razzismo is concerned that language and logistical problems mean that they are inevitably discriminated against. Most of them cannot make phone-calls (which by law must be in Italian), nor can they be under house arrest, or be released on bail, lacking the effective guarantee of both fixed abode and income.

Whether they come to Italy with the intention of committing crimes, or get forced into crime by penury is hard to assess. What is quite clear is that the overwhelming majority of foreigners in Italian prisons were arrested for drug pushing and theft. Although in 1988 illegal immigrants constituted only 6% of all arrests, they were responsible for 41% of all heroin and 55% of all cocaine busts. That this figure should be so high is evidence not so much of a Third World immigrant domination of drug running as of their lack of any effective protection back-up, which saves most Mafia drug smugglers from ever being caught. Some, like those Tamils committed to their liberation movement, do it for a cause (smuggling heroin to buy weapons); others are used as carriers for international drug cartels.

There is, however, a far more worrying prospect facing Italy at present, which neither the police nor the judiciary quite know what to do about: the proliferation of activity by Mafia gangs linked to the South American drug cartels. At present, the Italian police know little about their organizational structure – whether they have formal or informal links with the Italian *malavita*, or whether they are remote-controlled from Medellín.

2. Crime and its rewards

(i) Crime and security

In relation to crime, the Italians display an odd mixture of almost oriental resignation, carelessness and paranoia. It is hard to reconcile the various strands. Like almost every other Western country over the last two decades, Italy has witnessed a dramatic rise in crime, especially theft and offences against property. In fact, until the mid-1950s, Italy had one of the lowest crime rates anywhere; rapid industrialization, especially in northern cities, changed all that.

More specific to Italy is the fact that some 70% of all crime is now drug-related, while crimes against the person are now on the decline. On the one hand, the naturally boisterous, alcohol-free groups of *giovani* are far less violent than their equivalents abroad (the word 'hooligans' is a recent import, along with the concept of gratuitous, mass violence), but on the other, few countries in the West could match the organized crime death rate in hot spots like Calabria and Naples, or the coldly calculated cruelty of the kidnapping industry. (→2:iii, below) The decline of terrorism, which had led to empty streets after 10 p.m. in the 1970s, now means they are full again, often until the early hours. Some verbal harassment of foreign women, and handbag and jewellery snatching by young *tossicodipendenti* may still occur, but urban mugging with threatened violence, especially after dark, is far less common than in most Western metropoli. Despite their high-profile macho image, Italian men are by no means more responsible for sexual violence than elsewhere. (→I, 3:vi) The odd exceptions all gain intense media coverage, several mid-1980s Roman 'masked rapist' figures – Joe Codino (pigtail), Johnny lo Zingaro (the gypsy) and Arancia Meccanica (Clockwork Orange) – going on to become household names. Nor is the carrying of weapons among 'ordinary' criminals such a big thing: less than 2% of Italians have firearms, and those are mostly registered hunting rifles, while *le armi bianche* – 'white arms' (i.e. blades) – tend not to play the role that foreign myth assumes (it's the American, not the Italian, Mafia that idly clean their nails with flickknives).

While Mafia and drug-related criminality continues to escalate, and to claim ever more victims, it seems that economic well-being has largely neutralized the latent social threat everyone was predicting fifteen years ago. During the 1970s, the police paranoically assumed that all gangs of youngsters were potential rioters; in the more relaxed consumer boom 1980s, they know

Protecting your possessions

● **Cars are all fitted with noisy burglar alarms, which often go off if you brush past them; at night you can hear them wailing, like a distant nightingale. If you take a car to Italy, a fixed stereo is unlikely to last you a week. If you have a portable stereo fitted, don't leave it under the seat – that's the first place thieves look. Never leave anything of any conceivable value in your car if you park it for any length of time, especially in large cities. Many drug addicts will break into a car on spec.: don't tempt them. Many Italians simply leave their car doors unlocked, but with no valuables inside, to save the expense of having the windows repaired.**

● **Apartments have complex triple locks to match New York's (→ I, 1:ii), as well as window grilles on lower floors. Not to do so seems to be courting temptation. ISTAT figures for 1988 show that 96% of burglaries were unsolved. However, in many parts of the countryside, people still leave their houses unlocked, even when they are out.**

● **The contents of a house or apartment or a car are rarely insured, premiums being extremely expensive (two or three times as high as UK or US ones), and companies being so reluctant, and slow, to pay out. (→ VI, 4:iii) For example, to insure a Persian carpet worth 3 million lire in Milan would cost you 30,000 lire a year. According to the insurance agencies association, the most dangerous cities to live in are, in order: Milan, Turin, Bari, Catania and Messina. Some smaller** provincial cities have dropped their premiums by 30%, due to declining risk.

all those shopping bags are full of new clothes, not Molotov cocktails or propaganda leaflets. Consequently, *le forze dell'ordine* – the forces of law and order – are far less trigger-happy, contributing to a substantially lower death rate. Of the twenty-eight specialized private police agencies that opened during the late-1970s period of fear and loathing, half are now inoperative.

The Italians have always been bemused by the sheer volume and the style of Anglo-Saxon violent crime, especially the psychotic mass-murderer variety. Britain's violent crime industry – from established classics like Jack lo Squartatore (the Ripper) to neo-American novelties like il Rambo di Hungerford (Michael Ryan) – remind them of vintage Hitchcock or Agatha Christie. The regular American output of campus killers, or mass child rapists, is put down to 'too much TV violence', as well as the reasonable observation that if the Anglo-Saxons let off more steam more often, they wouldn't need to spill the blood of others when they finally do.

The rise and fall of crime
• **Crime in general has gone up, from 1978 (1.9 million) to 1988 (2.1 million).**

	1971	1986
Robbery	750,000	1,195,000
Bouncing cheques	132,000	318,000
Physical violence	184,000	125,000

• **There has been an increase in cases of fraud between 1984 and 1986 of 87%.**
(ISTAT)
• **In 1988, 96% of Italian robberies went undetected. Prime crime time: 11 p.m. – 2 a.m.**

As the statistics show, all forms of violent crime against the person (excluding organized crime) are in decline in Italy. Therefore, when an interesting case, particularly where sex is involved, does appear, it gets exhaustive attention from the media as well as the police. There may have been some justification for the exhaustive publicity for il Mostro di Firenze – the

14% of all homes were burgled over the ten-year period 1978–88; 17% have had special locks fitted, 14% have armour-plated doors, 12% have guard dogs (Alsatians, Dobermann Pinschers).
(DOXA)

Florence Ripper – during the early and mid-1980s (many young couples were brutally murdered, and the real assassin is still at large), but the coverage accorded to the 1989 case of la Mantide di Cremona – the Praying

---

The most crime-ridden regions of Italy (crimes per 100,000 inhabitants) are Lazio (6645); Puglia (4325); Liguraia (4099); Lombardia (3878); Piemonte (3712); Campania (3345); Sicily (3342); Sardinia (2867); and Calabria (1674). The national average is 3555. Calabria's low figure suggests two rather sinister things: that people are afraid to report crime; and that the 'Ndrangheta does a better job at law enforcement than the police.
(ISTAT, 1987)

Mantis of Cremona, where an attractive woman was convicted of murdering her lover – was quite excessive. If Italy does have its own interesting genre of murders, it is those with a family flavour. The cases where heroin addicts kill both grandmothers to pay for a fix have an obvious motive, but what about those where teenage sons kill off their entire family after a tiff about a poor school report? Such cases seem to occur with a certain regularity.

Robberies per 100,000 inhabitants: 1951–60, 540; 1961–70, 748; 1971–80, 2290.
(ISTAT)

71% of shopkeepers in Milan think they are the category most exposed to intimidation and robbery; 33% of all women in the city are seriously afraid of sexual violence, as are 64% of women under 25 – as a result, 50% of female students don't go out in the evenings. (*Corriere della Sera*, 1988)

Despite the general easing of tension, there is a widespread perception of the inability of police to solve crime. Figures show that 75% of reported crimes in 1987 were not solved – an improvement on the 1980 figures (80%), but not on those for 1976 (60%).

In Rome, in the Dolce Vita era of the 1950s and 1960s, bands of gentleman thieves used to do hold-ups in bars, clubs and restaurants in the small hours, when the till was full and the streets empty, for rich pickings and a fast get-away. The police enjoyed the car chases, which were like exciting dog fights, since both cops and robbers

would be driving supercharged Alfa-Romeo 1900s (the criminals were known as *la banda della 1900*); now police have slower, less customized, more production-line cars.

(ii) Criminal chic: the glamorization of evil

In the rest of the world, unsightly themes – violence, wrong-doing, squalor – have always been good box office, ranging from the 16th-century Blood and Thunder genre, via Charles Dickens to Bogart movies. Italy never had much to offer in this field, until the post-war *cinema neo-realista* laid the foundations for a whole new industry, which now strongly characterizes modern Italy and its idea of entertainment. Nitty-gritty issues make for great art, and the early films of Roberto Rossellini, Vittorio De Sica, Luchino Visconti and the films and novels of Pier Paolo Pasolini all did just that.

But the reality that they portrayed – war-time suffering, intense post-war poverty, social and economic injustice, neo-urban alienation, North–South prejudice – were issues that in real life were, thanks to the much lauded *miracolo economico*, fast fading by the mid-1950s. To continue making films and writing novels on these topics would have been anachronistic, and unrealistic: nostalgia as media product wasn't invented until the late 1970s. So Italian movie directors and writers hit on a new, subtler theme: social paranoia. Inspired in part by the classic Russian directors, in part by American semi-documentaries like *The City that Never Sleeps*, but above all by the whole French *film noir* output, they set up a labour-intensive industrial process for converting the mysterious, murkier side of modern Italy into a glistening, sexy, media product.

The raw materials were on hand, and were of a finer quality than in any other country in the world. Post-war Italy was notorious for its organized crime – Mafia, Camorra, 'Ndrangheta (→ 2:iii, below) – and its complex political conspiracies. (→ 3:v, below) The 1970s were to offer yet another gold-plated theme: terrorism – right-wing, left-wing, or international. Soon television was to follow cinema and literature in a massive, three-pronged attack on Italy's social and cultural consciousness.

The works of film directors like Francesco Rosi, Elio Petri and Giuseppe Ferrara, novelists like Leonardo Sciascia, actors like Gian Maria Volonté, Lino Ventura and Michele Placido have created a whole new layer of existence to Italian life, in two different ways.

First, they have created a strange no-man's-land between fact and fiction – anticipating the American genre of 'faction' by over a decade – where real or mostly real events are reproduced artificially: shot on location, with extreme attention to factual detail. To foreign movie-buffs, everything just looks wonderfully exotic and Italian, but to Italians themselves, the location shots all look very familiar indeed. Some films or TV films of the event come out so soon after the real thing, with such convincing look-alike actors, that it is almost hard to tell the two apart. But, unlike the slightly ludicrous American networks' school of faction series, the Italian genre often seems to tell you more than the official reports of the actual event: you end up not knowing whether to believe the newspaper or the film version.

The second effect of this media phenomenon is to render all the squalor and nastiness into something extremely glamorous. Artfully used dramatic effects – from tense, 'detective movie'-style camera angles, razor-sharp dialogues, terse soundtrack music, to sexy actors and actresses – have converted *la malavita* – the underworld – into something intensely desirable. To coin a cliché, designer crime.

In the post-modern late 1980s, when distinctions between reality and fantasy, between past, present and future, are all becoming extremely blurred, all this makes perfect sense. Add to this the Italian predilection for abstract contemplation and intellectual theorizing, and you have a wonderfully captive audience. Increasingly, Italy is becoming a nation which defines itself through fictional re-creations of its own recent history. It is almost as though they don't really mind what goes on in the streets of Palermo, the boardrooms of Milan, or the corridors of power in Rome, as long as it makes good armchair entertainment. It is hard to say whether this form of inverted escapism is any more than social apathy.

There is something of the Frankenstein syndrome in all this: while it was undoubtedly the intention of Rosi, Sciascia and co. that their films and books should be '*di denuncia*' (→ 1; ACCESS, above), they have inexorably become glamour products, irrespective of their authors' intentions. It couldn't be otherwise – most Italians are by nature far more committed to visual glamour than they are to social justice.

Although in real life the terrorist emergency has faded, even if the Mafia one hasn't, there is no indication of this from TV programming. Films on both are relentlessly programmed to tie in with anniversaries of the real events they so accurately reproduce: Giuseppe Ferrara's *Il caso Moro* was on TV ten years to the day (17 March 1978) of Prime Minister Moro's dramatic kidnapping by the Red Brigades (Gian Maria Volonté looking more like him than he did himself), while two other channels had, respectively, a discussion panel and a documentary on him. Ferrara's *Cento giorni a Palermo*, about the Mafia assassination of carabiniere General Alberto dalla Chiesa, timed in nicely with recent, renewed controversy on the Sicilian question.

But while the lead stars are always scripted to die, most of the support cast is still very much alive: modern Italian political and public figures have to live with seeing themselves either directly, or, worse still, alluded to, on television, scheming ruthlessly, and then ratting on the victim.

Cashing in directly on the Italian public's tastes are the new wave of criminal chic TV news magazine programmes. Italy's top TV journalist, the tireless Enzo Biagi, presented a 1988 weekly series tersely called *Il caso* – as in *L'affaire* – which indicated that he had to unearth at least one new *caso* each week: a real cottage industry. Still, he had twenty-seven full-time researchers working for him personally. The current fashion in Italy for shows like this is for a dramatic pitch-black backdrop, but Biagi went one better: he got Giorgio Armani to design something sumptuously austere for the bits of the studio you could actually still see.

Even more dramatic is Giuliano Ferrara (no relation): an immensely fat, pompous man with an Orson Welles complex, who has shamelessly taken the whole *di denuncia* genre to Las Vegas: envious, less vulgar commentators mutter about *la spettacolarizzazione gratuita di cose serie* – making a circus out of serious things – but the punters love it, and his ratings almost match those of *Miami Vice* re-runs. One of his most recent TV programmes, *Radio Londra* on Berlusconi's Canale 5, was named to re-evoke the *frisson* of listening to BBC broadcasts in war-time Fascist Italy – Lord Haw Haw in reverse.

Criminal chic has also been one of Italy's leading exports over the last two decades: although Francesco Rosi's *Mani sulla città* (1963) – *Hands over the City* – an exposé on corruption in 1950s/1960s Naples based on its wheeler-dealing tycoon-mayor Achille Lauro – is undeservedly ignored, his trio of films centring on his conspiracy theories about *il terrorismo di stato*, *Il caso Mattei* (1972) – *The Mattei Affair*; *Lucky Luciano* (1973); – and *Cadaveri eccellenti* (1975) – *Illustrious Corpses* – as well as Elio Petri's classic *Indagine su un cittadino al di sopra di ogni sospetto* (1970) – *Investigation of a Citizen above Suspicion* – launched Italian *cinema di denuncia* as a major international art-house commodity in the 1970s, imbuing Italy with an ineffable glamour a full decade before the Milan designer explosion. This process has since gone much further, with the immense international success of the Mafia TV series *La Piovra – Octopus: the Power of the Mafia* – starring Michele Placido. Even China and the Soviet Union went wild over its unambiguous underworld glamour, showing that cosmetized crime is, after fashion itself, Italy's most fashionable market commodity.

(iii) Organized crime: *la malavita* and its operations

There are few words of Italian origin so well known, or that evoke stronger emotions, than 'Mafia'. Inevitably, it tends to get used in a rather generalized way. In its Italian context, la Mafia refers specifically to Sicilian organized crime, whereas *la malavita* in the Naples area is called la Camorra, and that of Calabria la 'Ndrangheta. Occasionally, 'Mafia' is used as a shorthand term to cover all three without distinction (as is the case among non-Italians), but a generalized reference is usually made to *la criminalità organizzata* – organized crime – or *la mafia*, with a small 'm', may be used.

'Mafia' is also used, both in the Italian media and by ordinary people, in a rather lateral way, to describe certain aspects of the Italian mentality – the way the dynamics of tightly knit family or personal relationships get transferred into business affairs, commanding blind loyalty, giving rise to mutual back-scratching and excluding, often contemptuously, outsiders. The pervasiveness of *raccomandazione* is an obvious example. (→ V, 1:ACCESS) The Italians tend to be their own most lucid critics, and are aware that it is impossible totally to eradicate an evil phenomenon like *la criminalità organizzata* when, specific historical and geographical considerations apart, trace elements of the Mafia mentality can be found in the bloodstream of them all. There is obviously no question of collective guilt involved, but something of the anguish most Italians feel about the Mafia's operations comes from an intuitive understanding of how it is that such a monstrous organization can survive, and prosper.

It is said that the Mafia has existed in Sicily, in some form, for about a thousand years, mostly as some kind of mutual benefit association. Only towards the end of the 19th century did it take on its more sinister aspects. In the 1920s, however, Mussolini wasted no time in stamping it out, and it is one of the ironies of modern times that had it not been for the victorious American army entering Italy at the end of World War II, the Italian Mafia would probably have been extinguished for ever: General Mark Clark, frightened the Communists would take over in cities like Naples and Palermo, imported several veteran *mafiosi* from Brooklyn to get the good old capitalist system working again. The reimported habit caught on again fast – coals to Newcastle, ducks to water.

Despite the immense activity of the modern-day Mafia – it has been calculated that if it were a registered company, it would have the largest turnover and profit margins of any company in the world – its corporate image is a failure; it remains a caricature that is both fifty years out of date, and entirely American. Hollywood has provided the outside world's collective subconscious with a stereotype (invariably recycled by cartoons) – a swarthy, unshaven little man called Luigi, in shades, loud pinstripes and carrying a violin case – so powerful that none of the recent films out of Italy have managed to replace it. In English, the standard imitation of *mafioso* speech is still along the, 'Shaddup, or I-a break-a your leg-a' lines; Italians think of the Palermo accent, with its distinctive slurred 'r' (pronounced like the French pronoun 'je') and slightly sing-song, threatening intonation. Modern Italians think of *mafiosi* as being mostly dressed in shiny nylon designer tracksuits and trainers, since the only time they ever really see them is during the interminable televised *maxi-processi* – mega-trials – from Palermo, when the accused are in their sleaz-ure wear. Until they get caught, however, real-life *mafiosi* dress like other Italians, depending on their social environment. Some may come from the *borgate* – the slums – but many are professionals (lawyers and politicians, for example, with the odd aristocrat too). A scion of one of Sicily's oldest titled families, who hobnobbed with the Queen on her 1982 Italian State visit, has subsequently ended up behind bars on account of his relations with another, more sinister, 'family'.

The Sicilian Mafia takes precedence over the Camorra and the 'Ndrangheta, not only in terms of seniority, and as the undisputed leading brand-name, but also for its capacity for innovation. No sooner have they successfully market-tested a new field of activity, than the other two follow suit, although both the Neapolitan and Calabrian organizations cultivate their own specialities.

The 1990s *criminalità organizzata* functions at various levels, depending on location. In their respective *regioni* of origin, the three main types operate as a fully fledged alternative to the official public authorities. In some local areas, their support is so strong that they constitute the *only* authority. They may provide, directly or indirectly, livelihoods for a majority of the local population. This local, low-risk, labour-intensive system provides the ideal training ground for their junior operators. In the other regions of Italy, Mafia operations tend to be both on a larger scale, and much more discreet, requiring more experienced collaborators. This is even more true of their high-finance operations outside Italy, many of which completely escape detection. The new EC directives on the free movement of capital and the forthcoming Single European Market pose a serious threat to European security, on a scale that few Eurocrats are prepared to admit. In their otherwise commendable efforts to press on with political and economic union, continental politicians are seriously underestimating – in the case of some Italian politicians, quite deliberately – the risks of a huge, pan-European Mafia organization. Geoffrey Case's clever comedy thriller for BBC1, *The Accountant* (1989), in which an honest Jewish accountant stumbles across Mafia infiltration into the City, may not be so funny after all.

Some idea of what the Italian media mean by what they call '*l'emergenza mafia*' can be gleaned from the crime figures. In a country with twenty *regioni*, the three southern ones of Sicily, Campania and Calabria account for some 60% of the total national crime rate.

In the 1970s and early 1980s, there emerged conclusive proof of operative pacts between *la criminalità organizzata* and terrorists, both right- and left-wing, as well as with the subversive P2 organization. These amounted to simple logistical operations, where the two sides had in common methodology and outlaw status. These discoveries allowed the *dietrologisti* – the conspiracy theorists – to have a field-day, launching ambitious new ideas about the Mafia having *un disegno criminoso destabilizzante* – a master plan of rendering Italy ungovernable. (→ 2:vi, below) This is an attractive theory, but implausible. The Mafia have no particular ideology, for they are by nature capitalists, and thus innate pragmatists. If you remove their basic contempt for the rule of law, there is something oddly Thatcherite about the rest of their basic credo: not to depend on the State; to make as much money as possible; to be loyal to their 'family' and dispense charitable works among their loyal inferiors; and to remain indifferent to the feelings of anyone else. Not to forget a marked predilection for capital punishment.

To quote Ernesto Ugo Savona, director of research into organized crime at Washington's National Institute of Justice: 'The Mafia-style criminal organizations have no interest in destabilizing the system. They just want to maximize their profits, and to be able to work and prosper in silence.'

It has been estimated that the Mafia's illegal activities are now worth some 100,000 billion lire per annum (some 12% of GNP), and employ, directly or indirectly, over a million people. Divided down, this sum suggests an average personal income for each Italian Mafia collaborator of 125 million lire per annum, five times the national average.

Profit from the Mafia's principal activities

Spaccio di droga (drug trafficking)	30,000 billion
Estorsione (protection money)	12,000 billion
Tangenti (rake-offs on contracts)	12,000 billion
Intrallazzi/frode (scams/frauds)	10,000 billion
Furto/rapina (theft and hold-ups)	5000 billion
Rapimento (kidnapping)	4900 billion
Contrabbando (smuggling)	750 billion

La Mafia One of the basic characteristics of the Mafia is its capacity to inculcate fear and respect. *L'onorata società* – the honourable society – has become what it is today not just as a result of ruthlessness and hard work, but perhaps above all thanks to an accurate assessment of the Sicilian psychology. The Sicilians are naturally suspicious of strangers, but are loyal to and respectful of their superiors, whatever they may actually think of them. Conventional Italian wisdom attributes this to the number of foreign invasions they have undergone. Whatever the reason, the Mafia are guaranteed, under all circumstances, the absolute acquiescence of the Sicilians: the Mafia can do what they want, and no one will say a word. This silence is called *omertà*. Ask any Sicilian witness to a Mafia crime whether he saw something, and he will answer with a loud tut, and a sharp jerk backwards of the head.

Mafiosi are divided into clans, and are known as *persone di rispetto* – respect-worthy persons. Although there are always warring factions, the Sicilian Mafia is governed by an eleven-person grand council called *la cupola* – the dome. Its current leader, or *Papa* – Pope – is called Michele Greco, and is now behind bars. All the constant internecine murders and arrests seem to have had no effect on the organization's operating capacity. (→ 2:iv, below)

Until the early 1960s, the Mafia proper was almost

entirely restricted to the island of Sicily, with a predominant interest in local business, particularly agriculture. During the 1960s, it diversified into other areas and other interests, investing vastly in real estate, factories, banks and hotels, often using unsuspectable names. In Lombardy alone, it is estimated that they have 350 billion lire invested. From the late 1960s, they moved into international operations in a big way, consolidating their links with the American Mafia, and starting on the drugs racket. Today, it is thought that Palermo is the world centre for drug and arms trafficking. The world's greatest concentration of heroin refineries is certainly in Sicily.

Another major reason for the consolidation of Mafia power during the 1960s was its increased political contacts. Nowadays, it is quite normal for any Sicilian politician to be *in odore di Mafia* – to smell of the Mafia – but the people in question never resign. During the recent preliminary hearings for one of the *maxi-processi* in Palermo, the name of Andreotti's lieutenant on the island, Salvo Lima, came up several hundred times. The current mayor of Palermo, a courageous young *democristiano* called Leoluca Orlando, refuses to serve in the same administration as his fellow Christian Democrat Lima, but the latter's political career is far from over as a result.

La Camorra. The leading figure in the Naples-based Camorra is Raffaele Cutolo, a quixotic individual who runs his empire from behind bars. The Italian papers relate how his carpeted cell has two phones, and that he receives constant visits. Cutolo, who has recently taken to signing extortion notes as 'San Gennaro' – St Janarius, Naples's patron saint – won supremacy in Naples when his clan, '*la Nuova Camorra Organizzata*', bested their principal rivals, '*la Nuova Famiglia*'. Reflecting the Neapolitan character, the Camorra has a much more open but more complex structure, which is consequently less disciplined and less stable than that of the Mafia. Its fluctuating membership, with a constant need of new recruits, makes it more dangerous, too, as the individual *famiglie* have internal feuds which go through alternate phases, but often claim as many as forty victims a month. Apart from the highly profitable drug business, and extortion, the Camorra also has its own specialities in Naples: *rapine* – hold-ups (in Campania, the *regione* around Naples, there were 13,186 in 1988 – some thirty-six a day, the national record); counterfeiting of clothes and leather goods by all the big designer names in its Naples sweatshops; control of the fruit and vegetable market and the *totonero* – illegal football pools; importing illegal cigarettes (no one in Naples, not even the police, buys them at full price from a tobacconist). The relief fund set up after the tragic earthquake that hit Naples in 1980 was effectively controlled by Cutolo's men. The Camorra's domination of the Naples economy is such that the police are reluctant to intervene, since their punitive action would deprive tens of thousands of Neapolitans of a job. In a city already hit by high unemployment, the subsequent social disorders could be incalculable.

La 'Ndrangheta. Probably the smallest of the three, the Calabrian operators of the 'Ndrangheta are definitely the nastiest, and dominate the whole business life of southern Calabria. They have specialized in getting huge *appalti* – tenders to contract – for their construction firms. Calabria, more than other areas of the South formerly sponsored by *La Cassa per il Mezzogiorno* (→ II, 3:vi), is full of *cattedrali nel deserto*, as useless prestige construction projects are known. The most notorious is the gigantic oil refinery at Gioia Tauro, which has never been used. They also specialize in kidnapping, taking their victims up on Aspromonte, a vast, forested mountainous area which is almost police-proof. In the summer of 1989, the Italian police forces launched a massive, month-long raid on Aspromonte, but to little effect. The interior of Calabria resembles in some respects the Wild West – local bandits rule the roost, as most of the road-signs, riddled with bullet-holes, unequivocably show. The 'Ndrangheta recycle their ransom money into drugs: they have a strong Australian connection, where Calabrian immigrants grow marijuana for export.

The Sardinian gangs and the kidnapping business. Totally absent before 1960, kidnapping is now bigger in Italy than anywhere else in the world. It started in Sardinia, and up to 1985 has claimed some 750 people. It is hugely profitable, and involves a relatively low risk factor. Although it has been taken up by both the 'Ndrangheta, and, to a lesser extent, the Mafia, it remains essentially a speciality of Sardinian shepherds, whose knowledge of the rugged inland terrain of the island is unsurpassed. In recent years, Sardinian gangs have been operating on the mainland, mainly in the sparsely populated Maremma area of Tuscany. Many wealthy Italians jump if they hear a rough-sounding Sardinian accent.

There has been a major decline in *rapimenti* in recent years: it peaked in 1970; in 1977, there were seventy-seven cases; in 1987–8, as a result of improved police results, there was a total of only fourteen. On the other hand, there has been an increasing use of cruelty and cynicism in the choice of victims. Between

1987 and 1988, Italians were traumatized by the tragedy of 7-year-old Marco Fiora, who was held for seventeen months, and whose father simply wasn't rich enough to pay the *riscatto* – ransom. Cases like those of Paul Getty Jnr getting his ear chopped off in the 1970s, or the 1983 photo of two of the Bulgari family chained up like animals, made the front page all round the world.

In 1989, after almost thirty years of these atrocious cases, the Interior Minister, Antonio Gava, was prompted to suggest that Italy should introduce legislation similar to that successfully in force in other countries, whereby the families of kidnap victims have their bank accounts frozen, in order to prevent the ransom being paid, thus constituting a powerful deterrent. One wonders why the idea should be thought of so late in the day, after so many devastating results.

Kidnappings 1972–89

Total number of kidnappings	**596**
Ransoms paid	**382**
Kidnappers discovered	**445**
Victims never seen again	**69**
for whom ransoms had been paid	**32**
corpses found	**25**
victims liberated by the police	**81**
total ransom money paid up:	**300 billion lire**

(iv) The State versus the Mafia

Action by the State against *la criminalità organizzata* has been incredibly tardy. Until the institution of the Commissione anti-Mafia in 1963, the official line had been that *Cosa Nostra* didn't really exist; then, in 1968, a major trial was held, with the intention of suppressing it. Despite the attention of the world's Press, it ended in a farce; most of the key witnesses withdrew their crucial evidence; others disappeared abroad; some even committed suicide. Successive trials delivered either 'not guilty' or 'acquitted due to lack of sufficient proof' verdicts. In 1979 Boris Giuliano, the head of the Palermo police, who was on the verge of a major break-through in his investigations, was assassinated. The expression *cadaveri eccellente* – 'Very Important Corpses' – entered popular parlance. Nobody in Rome was prepared to help; it was left to the Sicilians themselves to fight *Cosa Nostra*.

Finally, in 1982, comprehensive anti-Mafia legislation was introduced, modelled on that of the United States. For the first time, it became a crime to belong to the Mafia. In the same year, its promulgator, Pio La Torre, the PCI leader for Sicily, was assassinated. Shortly afterwards, in an apparent change of heart by the State authorities, General Alberto Dalla Chiesa, a veteran in the anti-terrorism struggle (→ 2:v, below) was sent from Rome as a special *commissario* to coordinate the renewed Commissione anti-Mafia. No sooner had he arrived than he realized that his hands had already been tied: the government in Rome had given him almost no back-up – no qualified personnel or equipment, or even the necessary legal powers to carry out his investigations on such things as suspect bank accounts. In September of 1982, he too was assassinated. The Mafia had won an important strategic and moral victory.

In 1984, one of the Mafia's leading figures named Tommaso Buscetta decided to spill the beans; the information he passed on was invaluable to the Commissione anti-Mafia. There followed the first *maxi-processo*, featuring such leading Mafia bosses as Michele Greco and Luciano Liggio. The court handed down some nineteen life sentences, and a total of 2655 years to some 342 *uomini di rispetto* – men of respect. There then followed a series of appeals, with many sentences quashed, or reduced. The findings of the *maxi-processo* turned out a major judicial non-event, as well as very dull TV viewing. TV journalist Enzo Biagi's book on Tommaso Buscetta, *Il boss è solo* (1986) – the boss is alone – became a best-seller, and the only real media event. Despite Buscetta's spectacular confessions, the *onorata società* continued with business as usual.

Since that trial, judges, investigating magistrates and key witnesses have been assassinated with tragic but monotonous regularity. Since 1988, the position of *commissario* of the anti-Mafia commission has been occupied by a brilliant, though controversial, figure called Domenico Sica. He succeeded where Dalla Chiesa had failed, in persuading Parliament in Rome to entrust him with far greater legal powers. The most obvious requirement, though, a change in the law to allow witnesses who testify immunity, and to outlay sufficient funds to guarantee their subsequent safety – like the provisions for the British Crown witness, or the American State witness – have not been forthcoming.

Since 1988, the situation has become even more grotesque. The most conscientious members of the Palermo-based interdepartmental '*pool anti-Mafia*' have either been transferred to other cities, or have become the victims of the most extraordinary whispering campaigns, or have run into complicated feuds and boycotts between rival internal departments. The Italian Press, who should know better, have allowed themselves to be seduced by these essentially marginal events, instead of devoting themselves to the real task in hand – denouncing Mafia members. The summer of 1989 was dominated by a *Dynasty*-style soap opera/ Pirandello tragicomedy, situated in the Palermo Palazzo di Giustizia – Law Department – imaginatively renamed by the medio *il palazzo dei veleni* – the poison palace; this starred alleged insiders (i.e. legal officials) plotting furiously against each other. One was named il Corvo – 'the crow' – on account of poison-pen letters sent by him to the leading State authorities denouncing the star *procuratore aggiunto* – investigator – Giovanni Falcone (whose surname, appropriately, translates as 'the falcon'); another, dubbed La Talpa – 'the mole' – is apparently spying for *Cosa Nostra* from within the Justice department. Whether these figures really exist or not is immaterial. Nor does it matter whether it is all by accident or dastardly design. The only significant fact is that the whole struggle against *la criminalità organizzata* has been transformed into the realm of fiction. (→ 2:ii, above) What is also clear is that out of this embarrassing charade, the only real winners to emerge are the Mafia.

In the police versus the Mafia battle in 1986, two mortars, fifty-seven machine-guns, 4099 rifles, 3300 pistols and 1335 grenades were confiscated. Since 1986, there have been 235 arrests and 741 warrants taken out for members of La Camorra; 178 and 706, respectively, for the Mafia; and fifty-eight and seven for the 'Ndrangheta. Also in 1986, there were 2900 *rapine* – hold-ups – in Campania, 1200 in Sicily, and 1170 in Lombardy. The total number in Italy was 8400, of which 1966 were solved by the police.
(ISTAT)

(v) Left-wing terrorism
Possibly the most significant fact about Italian terrorism, in both its right- and left-wing forms, is that it has disappeared almost as abruptly as it started. There are two quite distinct reasons for this. First, the highly successful police campaign against it, showing that the Italian State can get its act together if it really chooses to; and secondly, the absurdly superficial ideology of its members.

This ideology derived from the collective post-1968 frustrations of the young at what they perceived as the repressive, corrupt régime of their elders, a sleazy, undemocratic political system, and a hypocritical, old-fashioned social morality, based on current Catholic teachings. The role of the Catholic Church in the roots of the left-wing terrorism is ironic, and typically Italian. Whatever the habits of the lumpen clergy, the 1960s was a period of profound renewal at the highest level of the Church. Both John XXIII and Paul VI were open-minded liberals, not only politically, but in many ways socially, and the Vatican Council II represented a clear demonstration of their desire for change. On the other hand, the Italian Church's markedly progressive wing, with its worker priests and trade-union activism, was the ideological cradle for the terrorist movement's original leaders, such as Renato Curcio.

Although Curcio and his friends all became apostates, their *matrice intellettuale* – way of thinking – remained profoundly Catholic. There is a direct link between this and the typically Italian penchant among intellectuals for seeing politics almost exclusively in terms of an essentially idealistic, and hence highly impractical, nature. (→ IV, 3:ii) This coincided with a widespread feeling of contempt among young left-wingers for what they saw as the betrayal by the PCI of the workers' cause, in its increasing embrace of 'the establishment', and hence the need to take it upon themselves to become the workers' champions. The combination of the two became explosive .

All this may have helped generate left-wing terrorism, but the explanation for its appeal for subsequent followers is disappointingly banal. In the absence of modern-day consumer distractions, bored students of the 1970s were simply attracted by the romanticism of violence. The initial public sympathy for the cause at both drawing-room and shop-floor level, soon evaporated as the initially idealistic movement degenerated into an efficient killing machine. The *brivido* – *frisson* – of daring, perfectly executed political crimes, coupled with the glamorous social status of the *fuorilegge* – outlaw – enchanted the more ambitious, while the gut satisfaction of wearing a face-mask on mass demonstrations organized by Autonomia Operaia – Workers' Autonomy – followed up by a pitched street battle with *i fascisti* (alias the police) provided a perfect compromise for those weekend terrorists who still wanted to live with their parents. Tom Wolfe, writing at the time, was the first to spot the sublimely Italian irony of the terrorist/hero who mans the barricades in the morning, and goes home to Mamma for a plate of spaghetti and a freshly ironed shirt afterwards.

However, it has never been fully explained how the real professionals, le Brigate Rosse – the Red Brigades

– and Prima Linea – Front Line – with all their various spin-offs, successfully learnt the techniques of professional terrorism so fast. Target accuracy, tight organizational discipline and relentless hard work hardly seem the primary attributes of a group of spoilt Italian youths.

As the groups proliferated, so did the conspiracy theories regarding their financial and logistical backing. They were linked to everyone from the KGB to the CIA: President Pertini (1977–84) became obsessed by a putative Czechoslovakian connection; PSI leader Craxi, always one for grandiose, poorly thought-through schemes, always talked of some mysterious '*Grande Vecchio*' – an Orwellian Big Brother figure, pulling strings from an unidentified foreign base.

The apex of left-wing terrorism was reached in March 1976, when the Christian Democrat leader Aldo Moro was captured by the Brigate Rosse in a daring ambush in Rome. The following weeks, during which he remained their captive, were the darkest in the post-war political era. Many Italian institutions and individuals showed themselves in their true colours. There were impressive acts of courage and national solidarity – Pope Paul VI personally offering to mediate, while the PCI, overcoming political differences, collaborated closely with the DC-led coalition. There were also other, less publicized, manoeuvres within the government, that went some way to proving the terrorists' point about the innate corruptness of the system. The Brigate Rosse enjoyed two massive propaganda victories. First, they left the car containing Moro's lifeless body exactly half-way between the *sedi* – HQs – of the DC and the PCI ('partners in crime') during the largest man-hunt Western Europe has seen since the war ('all the king's horses, all the king's men . . .') thus showing their tactical superiority to the State's. Secondly, the government scored a resounding own goal by introducing the largely ineffectual but highly repressive *leggi Cossiga* state of emergency laws.

Towards the end of the decade, the terrorists' luck changed, along with the spirit of the times. Quite simply, their cause lost its fashionable appeal, even to most of its followers. Three very Italian characteristics helped it die. First, hyperchoice – the absurd splintering of the terrorists' cause into over a hundred different factions. Second, *il trasformismo*, with the discovery that the terrorists were swapping favours with the Mafia – what kind of ideological purity could there be if they were in cahoots with those arch-capitalists? Third, *il pentitismo* – the emergence of the 'repentant' – saw terrorists reneging on their past and grassing on their former comrades, and having their hefty sentences massively reduced as a result. Despite much soul-searching, the ever pragmatic, indulgent Italian public generally favoured allowing these politically lost sheep the chance to show that they were nice *ragazzi* after all. They came out of it well, as did the Church when, in the early 1980s, with a symbolic gesture that recalled both its role as mediator in the Middle Ages and terrorism's own more recent Catholic roots, some of the last remaining left-wing *brigatisti* laid down their arms by anonymously delivering a couple of bags of Kalashnikovs to the Palace of the Cardinal of Milan, the much respected workers' champion, Carlo Maria Martini.

Like all good fashion-conscious Italians, many *brigatisti*, seduced by the prospect of mini-sentences, shed their political convictions as effortlessly as they had their long hair, flared jeans and Pink Floyd albums. In the long run, it was the adult world of pragmatic politicians and judges (reduced jail sentences) and a crack police campaign masterminded by General Alberto Dalla Chiesa (→ 2:iv, above) that got the better of all the juvenile posturing. In the foreseeable future, *Dark Side of the Moon* is more likely to enjoy a serious revival than slogans about *morte al sistema* – death to the system.

(vi) Right-wing terrorism

Few aspects of modern Italian life have stimulated as much conjecture as the roots of right-wing terrorism. Although it is no fairer to accuse the neo-Fascist MSI of being responsible for right-wing terrorists, than it is to hold the PCI responsible (as does Henry Kissinger) for the sins of the Red Brigades, it is undeniable that some members of the MSI's youth division FdG – Fronte della Gioventù – had direct links with a number of identified right-wing terrorist groups, such as Terza Posizione and NAR – Nucleo Armato Rivoluzionario. (→ IV, 2:ii – Movimento Sociale Italiano) Unlike the Communists, the post-war Italian extreme right-wing has always been characterized by an almost imperceptible overlapping of the various stages of violence. By no means all *picchiatori* – thugs – degenerated into *terroristi*; but it was certainly considered a useful experience.

On the whole, the activities of the young Fascists in the 1970s heyday of political violence were restricted to organized raids and pitched street battles with their leftist rivals. Sometimes these armed clashes left victims on both sides. Since the left-wing groups have all disappeared, their dead have been largely forgotten; but owing to the continued existence of right-wing groups

(principally the FdG), their *martiri* – martyrs – continue
to be celebrated through a series of street posters
commemorating the anniversary of their deaths.

There is something uniquely lugubrious about extreme right-wing Italian mythology. It is dominated by
Celtic crosses, Nordic folklore, burning torches, Gothic
script, and flags that closely resemble the Nazi ensign.
One of the most incongruous elements of fascist semiot-
ics in the 1970s was the piecemeal adoption of Tolkien's
The Hobbit, with posters frequently depicting scenes
from Middle Earth, and referring to *il raduno della
contea* – the county meeting – to indicate their sinister
reunions. With the demise of their left-wing enemies,
the self-appointed task of the right-wing seems largely
over. Many of those most active have themselves been
neutralized – killed in shoot-outs, in jail, in South America or on the run in Italy. Others have been reintegrated
into the system: one *picchiatore* of the period (though
there is no evidence he ever brandished a weapon), the
born-again *democristiano* Pietro Giubilo, even became
Mayor of Rome in 1988. His political sponsor was Giulio
Andreotti. *Naturalmente.*

Unlike the Brigate Rosse, Prima Linea and so on, who
acknowledged their own acts of terror and always aimed
them at individuals in high places, right-wing outrages
were usually bombing raids, with innocent bystanders
as victims,and were almost never acknowledged by their
perpetrators. If the *dietrologhi* (→ V, 1:ACCESS, above) had
fun guessing what foreign power was behind left-wing
groups, when it comes to fascist terrorism they had a
field day. It was unnecessary to look abroad for backers,
since there were plenty of potential candidates at home,
although none of them was owning up. Occasionally,
they gave the game away: ever since the war, long before
Prince Valerio Borghese's attempted *colpo di stato* –
coup d'état – in 1970, it was clear that there were
plenty of people in high places who were sympathetic
to an extreme right-wing putsch. Many of these were
identified as senior members of the two secret police
forces, SISDE and SISMI (→ 3:v, below), and when, in
March 1981, the P2 Masonic Lodge scandal broke, secret
service leaders were among its major names. Generals
Giuseppe Santovito and Pietro Musumeci, along with
their advisor, the still ubiquitous *faccendiere* Francesco
Pazienza, were found to be very close to the P2 *gran
maestro*, Licio Gelli.

The P2 Masonic Lodge was by far the most important
political scandal in Italy since the war. When it was
uncovered, its membership was found to include
major leaders in all the major parties except the
PCI and the PRI, and figures from almost every other

field of public life. In a ludicrous case of protested innocence, almost none of those involved owned up, despite fairly convincing proofs. All of those impugned (including media moghul Silvio Berlusconi: → VI, 2:iv) protested that they had joined only in order to meet all the right people; in 1989, one of Andreotti's leading collaborators, Vittorio Sbardella, rationalized joining this strictly proscribed organization as 'a foolish, but basically extremely human, desire to get ahead in one's career'. However, it was perfectly clear that the long-term plan of Gelli (a notorious Fascist sympathizer) and his friends was to destabilize the status quo, and then organize a right-wing *colpo di stato*. The subsequent parliamentary inquest, conducted by the respected *democristiana* Tina Anselmi, established this beyond any doubt.

More significant than what Anselmi's commission were able to discover is what they weren't. At every turn, her team of investigators was met by *depistaggio* – red herrings – often of a most sophisticated sort. As if the P2 ('P' stood for 'propaganda') organization wasn't large and mysterious enough in itself, it became increasingly clear that the whole *caso P2* was intimately linked to many other *casi*, whose exact relation to each other has never been fully revealed. The death of financier Roberto Calvi, found under London's Blackfriars Bridge after the collapse of his bank, Il Banco Ambrosiano, was connected to the scandal of the Vatican bank IOR – l'Istituto Opere di Religione – which was under the command of Chicago-born Cardinal Paul Marcinkus. The capture, and subsequent death in prison (poison in his *espresso*, of another shady financier, Michele Sindona, also fits into a network of intrigues that remain largely unsolved. There is also plenty of evidence of collusion between the P2, right-wing terrorist masterminds, and the Mafia.

Although it is as hard to get a *mafioso* to talk as it is a *piduista* – a P2 member – at least one knows with the former that he has no ulterior motives (except profit). While all of the proven *piduisti* told this same story, it is harder to believe them – the evidence was not in their favour. Licio Gelli, currently under house arrest after various d'Artagnanesque escapes, still insists he had nothing to do with any of the acts of terrorist violence linked to his name. Despite all the fairly damning evidence against him in relation to the 1980 Bologna station bombing, he not only sweetly protests his innonence, but has even publicly announced that he is 'one of the victims, along with the dead'. Understandably, this remark is seen by the victims' relatives committee as being in poor taste.

Equally honeyed protestations of innocence in regard to all the right-wing terrorist bombings of the last twenty years were heard from the other *faccendieri* currently in captivity, including Francesco Pazienza and Umberto Ortolani. Because of the difficulties in interrogating such professionally unforthcoming men (once they've been captured in the first place), most investigators are obliged to theorize. It is at this point that *dietrologia* takes over from empirical fact.

Indications of connivance between these men and members of the Italian secret services in bombing attacks have led the Italian media to talk of *il terrismo di stato* – State terrorism. This radical theory, also much favoured by certain Italian film-makers (→ 2: ii, above), has over the last twenty years also cost some investigative journalists, such as Mino Pecorelli, their lives. Exaggerated though the theory may seem, its proponents always point out how the accused in right-wing terrorist trials always get acquitted, while the left-wingers always get sent down.

The Italians have a weakness for all sorts of conspiracy theory – they make a good set conversation piece, like the weather for the British. They also have a love-hate relationship with their political figures which means that most of the latter are considered, in a highly generalized way, to be involved in these mysterious conspiracies. This may sometimes, as with the P2 lists, be the case, but mostly it cannot be proved. Indeed, being suspected of plotting to bring down the State does not mean that the Italians go off you.

The name that crops up with the greatest frequency in these vox pop. discussions is that of Giulio Andreotti. Not only has he been the subject of endless parliamentary inquiries into his doings, but, according to popular rumour, he may also be the secret leader of the P2. None of this stops him, as all the opinion polls show, from being easily Italy's favourite politician. Far from being outraged by newspaper cartoons showing him dressed as a *mafioso*, offering Michele Sindona a poisoned cup of coffee, or plotting with Licio Gelli, he appears to be highly amused. This is perhaps the secret of his enormous popularity: not only is he a brilliant politician; he has a great sense of humour, too. Above all, he is so vastly intriguing. He has something of the mystique that surrounded Harold Wilson, the British politician whom Andreotti most resembles – and it never did Wilson's career any harm. But why does Andreotti deliberately surround himself with so many political undesirables? Why has he always hung out so ostentatiously with men like Gelli and Sindona? Was he really in charge of the P2? However much Italians may quite sincerely condemn terrorism and conspiracy, at the same time it is true that many get a kick out of the idea – however implausible

– that their leading politician may lead some kind of double existence.

Right-wing terrorist attacks

		Dead	Wounded
1969	Piazza Fontana, Milan, inside bank	16	90
1974	Brescia, explosion at anti-Fascist rally		8
1974	Brenner, bomb on express train		12
1980	Bologna, station bombing	85	200
1984	Naples–Milan, bomb on express train	12	dozens injured

(vii) Third World terrorism

Italy's geographical and political position has favoured the escalation of international, particularly Middle East-based, terrorism within its shores and territorial waters. Cases in recent years like the hijacking of the cruise ship the *Achille Lauro* and the Rome Fiumicino airport massacre, both engineered by Palestinian terrorists, and the attempted assassination of the Pope by Ali Agca, have made world headlines; many more banal shoot-outs between rival Arab political factions haven't. Although in the heat of the moment, the American Press usually likes to paint the Italian judiciary and security forces as biased or ineffectual in these matters (→ 3:vi and 5:ii, below), the long arm of the Italian law has been doing its bit; in 1988 alone, some ninety-three foreign agents – of whom forty-one were resident and operative in Italy – were tracked down and arrested.

3. The police

Like judges, the police can't join political parties, though unlike the former, they are genuinely quite apolitical. While the Carabinieri are hampered by their military status, the Polizia can, since the major 1981 police reform, be unionized: there are three main ones. Their task is to voice the extreme disquiet felt by Italian police for the conditions they work in, which are generally quite poor, with lack of professional training as the major problem. It is, however, the public who suffer most from this, as all the various police forces are frequently inept and arrogant. The overwhelming majority of them come from the South, where police enrolment represents a fixed employment. Although conditions are not good, southern families will bribe officials to allow their sons into the force. There is consequently enormous competition to join.

The prestige of the various police forces has increased considerably over the last few years, due partly to the decline of anti-establishment ideology, partly to the spectacular defeat of terrorism, even though the police would not claim this as theirs. On the whole, their training and general discipline is also improving, as is their devotion to duty.

Since the end of *gli anni di piombo* – 'the years of lead', as the terrorist period is poetically labelled – the impression of walking on to a Costa Gavras film set every time you went out has now gone: armoured truck after armoured truck of la Celere (→ 3:ii, below) in full riot gear no longer sweep down the streets. Italian cities are no longer in a state of siege. Even the riots at rock concerts have subsided, occasioning a less heavy-handed response. Both the Carabinieri and the Polizia now complain about having to spend too much time guarding party HQs and the homes of notables, when they could be out on the beat, fighting real crime. The problem is in the left arm, not the left wing: heroin-related crime is now responsible for 70% of all reported incidents; terrorism has practically disappeared. (→ 2:i, above)

The parallel existence of four different police forces is a prime example of Italian hyperchoice: apart from history, there is no real justification for it. What lies behind their continued existence is a desire to split power more finely. The 1981 reform should have merged them all; typically, it only recommended close liaison between the respective forces. That exists only in a desultory way, at top level: between the street patrols, there is no contact at all, leading to a ridiculous duplication

Asking the police for help

- Call 113 (*'centotredici'*), the number which summons police help. More help numbers are listed on the front page of the phone-book.
- Be warned: many small crimes are considered too banal to even *fare la denuncia* – report – so slight are the chances of their being solved. Few Italians report muggings, bag-snatchings, house robberies (houses are rarely insured: → 2:i, above); if you are insured, it may be worth it. Go to La Questura (for la Polizia) or the Comando dei Carabinieri to make *la denuncia*. (→ 4: ACCESS – Getting official certificates)
- Police can be very gross with women: even those in distress after serious sexual harassment get treated as though 'they provoked it' themselves.
- They expect you to be very subservient: there is no concept of being a 'public servant' – they're the ones carrying the firearm. You get to call them sir, not vice versa. At a purely human level, they are capable of being quite charming, but this is nothing to do with any consciousness of their responsibilities when in uniform.
- If you are rude, or show irritation, a policeman (or any other public official – that includes postmen) can arrest you for *oltraggio ad un pubblico ufficiale* – insulting a state official. *Il codice Rocco* again.
- Your rights: the *leggi Cossiga* – anti-terrorism laws – mean that you can be held for forty-eight hours without a magistrate's being informed; the police can interrogate you without the presence of a lawyer; and, worse still, you can be legally held for three years

without being brought to trial. Add that to great difficulties in obtaining bail.

• There are also many private police or security forces, many with quite kinky US-inspired fantasy uniforms and logos. The Ministero dell'Interno is trying to regulate these and cut down their number – there are over 500 of them – but in certain law and order breakdown cities like Naples and Reggio Calabria, they are a necessary bastion against crime.

of duties, with rival forces arriving on the scene of one crime, while there is no one at all on the site of another.

Despite their uncouth, often highly unprofessional street manner, it is typically Italian that all the police forces contain men of considerable intellect, the likes of whom would never dream of joining the cops in any other country. One way to discover this is to read the various in-house magazines published by each force: although most of the target readership generally flips through nothing more taxing than *Topolino* (Mickey Mouse), the in-depth assessments of the work of Andy Warhol and analyses of political repression in Central America make them look more like the *New Statesman* or *The Nation*.

But whatever the Italian *forze dell'ordine* may leave to be desired in terms of discipline and training, few other forces in the world match them for stylishness: their outfits, livery and hardware are all matchless. Where other national forces look wimpish or dully functional – the British police look like traffic cops, while war-guilt has prompted the Germans to dress theirs in lumpy green outfits, like municipal gardeners – the Italian police are impeccably macho. Look out for the studied insolence of the younger ones, with their Raybans and cigarettes smoked on duty; you suddenly realize that even a standard issue machine-gun can double as a fashion accessory. Like all Italian men, they are uniform queens: they just love dressing up and showing off.

Such is their vanity, and Italian designer fever in general, that when new summer uniforms were issued to the Carabinieri in 1988, their new look was designed specially by Giorgio Armani. That half the New York Police Department are coke dealers may no longer surprise anyone, but odder still is the fact that not a few of Rome's better looking Carabinieri earn a bit of pocket money in their spare time as rent boys.

(i) I Carabinieri

Standing force (1988): 86,000. Still exclusively male.

Uniform: dark blue with red stripe, ditto peaked cap, which bears a distinctive logo with a flaming torch. Purely decorative leather cartridge box worn over shoulder on white leather belt. Dress uniform features ostrich-feathered admiral hat. Their summer military khakis were phased out in 1988, in accordance with an EC directive on police uniform colours.

Cars: dark blue with white stripes and corporate logo; Alfa-Giulettas and Fiat Unos.

Motorbikes: large-cylinder Moto-Guzzi Californians (850cc).

Street manner: better trained, better behaved, more

helpful than la Polizia; if in trouble, and you have the choice, go to the Carabinieri.

Reputation: stupidity; all the racial minority jokes about Irish, Polacks, Belgians etc. are told about the Carabinieri. Despite this, they are the senior force, with much older traditions and lineage, founded in 1814. Excellent reputation for horsemanship.

Head: General Antonio Vieste.

Structure: technically part of the armed forces, and with military ranks and discipline, they are commanded by the Ministero della Difesa, but also have units that can be leased out to other ministeries.

Police station: il Comando or la Caserma (barracks).

(ii) La Polizia

Standing force (1988): 83,000: now with 5% women.

Uniform: powder blue pants with fuchsia legstripe; navy blue jacket with brass buttons; peaked navy cap. Mounted police wear jodhpurs. Lighter version of same for summer. Women police usually wear uninspiring skirts, but men's jodhpurs when on mounted patrol; they are allowed long hair, which most of them have, worn in plaits – ravishing Amazons.

Cars: same models as the Carabinieri – light blue and white striped, with POLIZIA on the side.

Motorbikes: large-cylinder Moto-Guzzi Californians, like the Carabinieri.

Street manner: usually aggressive; generally poorly trained, driving around at top speed. Rarely on foot, except when standing stationary outside buildings as guards.

Special section: La Celere – found guarding major buildings, in sage green combat uniforms, bullet-proof padding and riot helmets. The '*in borghese*' – plain clothes branch – are even worse, so rough that many flee from their roadblocks, convinced they are being ambushed by criminals. Some get shot in the back for it. Frequently carry red-topped 'lolly-pop stick' baton for allowing them through in a hurry.

Head: Generale Vincenzo Parisi.

Structure: indirectly controlled by the Ministero dell'-Interno through the local *prefetto* (Police Commissioner) at the Prefettura. Local Polizia chiefs are called *questori*.

Police station: la Questura.

(iii) La Guardia di Finanza

Standing force: 42,000, all male.

Uniform: light grey with dark green beret bearing yellow flaming torch badge, hence their sobriquet – *le fiamme gialle*. They are also known as i Finanzieri.

Cars: as above.

Motorbikes: as above.

Reputation: despite their honourable ancestry (they were founded in the late 18th century), they are extremely corrupt – the higher the official, the more often they seem to be had up for astonishing scams, doing exactly what they are supposed to be stamping out. They recently launched a big publicity campaign with the hopeful slogan, *'dalla parte degli onesti'* – 'on the side of the good guys' – trying to remind the public that their brief is to fight *evasione fiscale* – tax evasion – and drug smuggling, not help spread it.

Structure: under the Ministero della Finanza.

Head: Generale Gaetano Pellegrino (former chief Generale Raffaele Giudice was imprisoned for a complex multi-billion dollar oil-refining scam).

Police station: il Comando della Guardia di Finanza.

(iv) I Vigili Urbani

Standing force: varies from city to city.

Uniform: less macho than the previous ones possibly because they don't always pack a gun (about 20% do). Navy blue serge with white jackets and shirts. They usually wear a white version of the London bobby's hat. The Roman ones had their uniform designed by the Fendi sisters.

Cars: as above.

Motorbikes: as above.

Reputation: total slobs, especially in the South. For the most part, patently unprofessional, and cynically indifferent to their work. Now notorious in Rome for their personal feud with la Polizia – streetfights have even broken out.

In 1988, an inquiry showed that 24% of Romans think the traffic police are OK; 53% think them superficial and indifferent; 27% think them arrogant and rude; and 53% consider their general education 'insufficient', though 58% consider their basic training 'passable'.

Duties: Also known as Polizia Urbana, or Metropolitana, they are something like old-fashioned English bobbies: traffic direction, sorting out domestic disputes and minor legislative offences; major ones must be reported to other police; jurisdiction is limited to their own *comune*. They always form the guard of honour when the local mayor or municipality figures are there. On their bikes, they circulate in pairs, and are thus known as *i gemelli* – the twins – or 'cufflinks'.

Structure: under the direct control of each single *comune*, rather than the State.

Police station: il Comando dei Vigili Urbani.

- **In 1988, 45% of Romans preferred to call out il Carabinieri; 38% preferred la Polizia; 16% I Vigili Urbani.**
- **51% considered the speed of arrival on the scene of a crime/accident too slow.**
- **The '999' service, no. 113, carried out 2,700,000 (ISPES, ISTAT) operations.**

(v) SISDE and SISMI: the secret police

Part of a long, sordid history (remember *Tosca*), the post-war Italian secret police forces were grafted almost intact from the pre-war Fascist intelligence forces. Apart from the various intelligence branches of all three main police forces and each of the armed services, there are two main secret police forces:

SISDE (Servizio Informazioni per la Sicurezza Democratica): run by the Ministero dell'Interno, and hence used for domestic espionage; and

SISMI (Servizio Informazioni per la Sicurezza Militare): run by the Ministero della Difesa, for the foreign secret service.

Both are coordinated by CESIS, (Comitato Esecutivo Servizio e di Informazione e di Sicurezza) which is run by the Prime Minister's office.

Although the Italians are politically tolerant of any kind of 'immoral behaviour', in the 1960s Carabinieri Generale de Lorenzo started keeping files on all major public figures. He was seen off, after an abortive though imaginary coup attempt, but the habit grew. There are now secret files on some 18 million Italians.

The secret services are without doubt the rottenest apple on the entire Italian political tree. Almost every major figure in it has been involved in some sordid political scandal. (→ 2:vi, above)

4. Bureaucracy and the denial of access

Bureaucracy and business deals

When in Rome, do as the Romans do: if you are going to stay or do business in Italy, you must embrace this principle to the full, as there is no way you could ever 'go it alone'. There is no one who will admire you for sticking to your principles, and you are set to lose much time and nervous energy if you insist on doing so.

• Always get someone to mediate for you.

• Always be prepared to pay for it.

• Don't feel too guilty about compromising yourself.

The paths open to you are identical to those used by native Italians. The famous *arte dell'arrangiarsi*, which every newspaper article praising the Italian business renaissance never fails to mention, really means:

• Bribery: if you want to do business, you will normally be expected to offer *un regalo* – a gift. (→ VI, 2:ACCESS) If you or your company is rooting for a contract or a tender, be prepared to pay a *tangente* – a 10%–15% rake-off to the contractor. As Pitt the Younger remarked, every man has his price, and the average Italian knows his. You may think this is sleazy, but it's the only way you're ever going to do business, so do it with good grace, like the Italians. Be prepared to pay, but not over-anxious to do so. If it is information you are after, the accepted euphemism is *ti offro un caffè* – let me buy you a coffee.

• Obtaining official documents or services: if you happen to know anyone, or anyone who has a relation, who works in a government office, don't hesi-

If the ease and speed with which you can gain access to information is one of the main yardsticks for measuring the efficiency of the modern democracy, then Italy is rooted firmly in the Middle Ages. Nowhere is this truer than in the whole State bureaucratic apparatus. Although the species hardly recommends itself anywhere in the world, Italian bureaucracy is in a class of its own. The whole concept of readily available information is alien to Italy as a whole, an attitude that is immediately identifiable in the Catholic mentality

Not only the Catholic religion, but also Catholic culture in the widest sense, is based on the supreme importance of the priest figure as the sole means of access to Higher Knowledge. The use of Latin, which most of the faithful did not understand, traditionally habituated Catholics to being reliant on a mediating figure in order to participate in organized religion: someone to show the way, and explain the rules. This changed only in the 1960s, after the Vatican Council II promulgated its own tardy Reformation. Even if the Bible had long been translated into Italian, few Italian Catholics had ever seen, let alone owned, one until then. Access to the source of knowledge (the Bible) is characteristic of Protestant cultures; total reliance on the priest to read out the good bits is vintage Catholicism.

Transposed to a broader context, the consequences of this millenary tradition are obvious. Italians do not expect to understand or gain access to the workings of the State without the aid of a mediator. The language of the State, even now, is an arcane tongue, designed to be understood by the chosen few, and to keep the rest in awe. Throughout history, the survival of an all-powerful ruling class has always been guaranteed by the use of a language different from that of the people. One of the main contributions of Protestant culture to the Western world has been the gradual reduction of the space separating, in linguistic and practical terms, the rulers from the ruled. The Campaign for Plain English in official documents is a typical consequence of this reflex. The 'We're just like you, really' informality of the American presidential fireside chats, Scandinavian monarchs on bicycles, or even British royalty on walkabouts or down mineshafts in hardhats, are another important, if slightly calculated, aspect of this.

Modern Italy, for all the People's Democracy rhetoric of its post-war constitution and cabinet ministers who go to Michael Jackson concerts, faithfully sticks to its pre-Reformation script. Despite its apparently transparent persona, it remains in practice rigidly hierarchical, and highly inaccessible. The arrogance of its administrators is matched on occasion by their personal ineptitude. Complicated, antiquated procedures and the terminology in which they are couched further exacerbate the chronic slowness of bored, under-trained personnel with a second, and possibly also a third, job to think about. (→ 1:vi, above) The workings of what few modern information systems have actually been introduced into government offices will be understood by far fewer staff members.

In most modern democracies, people complain a certain amount about official gobbledegook, or political jargon; but this is nothing to Italy. Italian journalists call it *politichese, burocratichese* and *sindacalese* (trade-union-speak). Only the adept can understand. This process is even more exasperating in the arts, where the intellectual is elevated to a priestly role. (→ VIII, 6)

Post-war Italians have to deal not just with the legacy of a medieval, user-unfriendly State, but also with the even more repressive legacy of the Fascist era. If civil servants in general were encouraged by Fascism to be arrogant and unhelpful, this tendency reaches its apex – or nadir – with the police forces, who are perceived not as public servants, but as oppressors. Given this, the bitterness of the student riots of 1968 and 1977 is understandable: calling them 'Fascist Pigs' was not far off the mark.

In fact, the most part of the 1931 *il codice Rocco* – civil and criminal code, known after the man who was mostly responsible for it – has never been repealed. Mussolini created a repressive, inaccessible, bureaucratic apparatus that sometimes makes Kafka's sinister vision look like something out of Walt Disney. The cult of the all-powerful State apparatus was further underlined by the buildings of Fascist régime architects like Piacentini, who received a specific brief for their work. (→ VII, 5:i) Despite the austerity of their lines, Italian court-houses and police stations of the 1920s and 1930s betray a Baroque, Counter-Reformation inspiration: make it as awe-inspiring as possible. The whole 'criminal chic' school of cinema creates its basic mood out of the combination of the *frisson* created by the monumental marble and chrome court-house corridors and staircases, and the involuntary shudder caused by the sinisterly remote concept of justice dealt out in them. (→ 5, below)

Faced with this chilling prospect, the Italians cope as best they can: with the aid of mediators. No one would think of 'going it alone' – the idea simply doesn't exist

tate to ask their help. Having a phone put in (expect to wait two years), getting permits for your new office premises (very stringent hygiene regulations), as well as any of the services offered by an *agenzia pratiche* will be much easier if you know, or know of, someone who can help. Otherwise, in every neighbourhood you will see at least one sign reading 'AGENZIA PRATICHE'. These rather expensive but very useful agencies will save you a lot of time and nervous energy. Whether you need a renewed driving licence or a residency permit, they will get it for you, or tell you where and how to do it yourself first time round. This service goes even further in Naples and other parts of the South, where *un mediatore* can usually be found hanging around public offices, who will be prepared to stand in a queue for you, tell you where to find a holiday flat, or introduce you to someone 'useful', all for a fee.

Getting basic documents

The Italian bureaucracy loves documents of any kind. In order to survive, you will undoubtedly have to make a few attitude and habit changes. Unlike in English-speaking countries, it is constantly necessary to give proof of who you are. To give your name, rank and number is not enough for Kafka's favourite sons. Whatever you may or may not have just done, the first thing the police or Carabinieri ever say (or bark) at you is: '*Documenti!*' The first few times you go through this little routine you will mentally cast yourself as a heroic Richard Burton in a Nazi war movie. After a bit, the tense glamour of all this wears off, especially if you have left the offending scraps of paper elsewhere. You will soon understand why handbags for men were so immensely popular in the 1970s: you carried all your *documenti* around in them. The Filofax of which you were bored will now come into a new lease of life.

• Even as a tourist, you are in theory obliged to carry your passport around with you wherever you go. Passports are far bulkier than European-style identity cards, which is why the latter are so useful. If you prefer not to bother, keep some photo ID on you at all times. If the police don't like your face, they can give you hell, legally.

• If you intend to stay, bring lots of certificates (or photocopies) about yourself. You may never need them, but if you do and you can't access to them fast, matters will be made far worse. At la Questura – the city HQ of la Polizia – they are always impressed by official-looking certificates. The essential ones are birth and academic (degree, High School, A-levels etc.) certificates.

• By the same token, you should stock up on passport photos. A dozen will probably see you through your first year of official documents. A word of advice: you will have to face these photos innumerable times (curious Italian friends always want to check out the mugshots on your *documenti*), so invest in a professional photographer, who can give you multiple copies. Get it done in Italy, for a mere 15,000 lire: their studios are everywhere. Instead of looking like a bug-eyed, blotchy-skinned Crack victim, your by now paranoid features can be flattered by those 1950s-style soft focus sepia-tinted poses.

• You are best advised to approach an *agenzia pratiche* to help, but the first time you must do some of this mind-numbing queueing yourself.

in Italy. An Italian in need of bureaucratic help, whether to get off paying a parking fine, or to bail out a relation from jail, will not apply personally to the relevant office. It is necessary to find someone important who will do it for you, and who, thanks to their position of influence, is likely to be able to solve the problem much better. This service will cost you: either money (*una bustarella* – a bribe) or, more likely a debt of honour, obliging you to the potentate to a degree, and for a period of time, in due relation to the service rendered. In order to emphasize their position of power over you, they will make you wait an unconscionable amount of time *nell'anti camera*.

In fact, in any form of business dealings in Italy, the party that considers itself the stronger will make the other wait just for the hell of it. (→ 1:iv, above) That is one reason why things are slow in Italy. The person who helps you is your *santo in paradiso* – guardian angel – or *protettore*, and you become their *protetto* – protégé. What is uncanny about the Italians is that, although they loudly proclaim their hatred for the State (which as an abstract entity is hardly to blame for the bureaucratic nightmares they endure), they tend to hold their *santo in paradiso* in genuine esteem. Yet it is the system engendered by the latter that perpetrates the need for all that grovelling, bowing and scraping, all those backhanders. A perfect example of the Stockholm syndrome: ending up loving your oppressors.

For dealing with bureaucracy at a lower, more day-to-day level, there are analogous systems, like the *agenzie pratiche* and the *mediatori* – unofficial Mr Fixits of southern Italy.

The cult of non-information, and having to pay to get it, is not just to be found in the bureaucratic apparatus. Newspapers, too: there is never a summary of contents on the front page, never a quick reference to the TV page; listing of galleries and museums in the more arts-minded papers will tell you the address and some idea of their contents – possibly even the closing date – but not that something has been *chiuso per restauro* – closed for repairs – for over five years. Or go into an Italian post office, and try to find out how much it costs to post a letter – a variable in high-inflation Italy. Nowhere is there a wall chart or leaflets telling you; you are expected to queue up and ask at the counter, which could take you fifteen minutes

Although privately run businesses are usually much more eager to please, sometimes even they treat the punter with disdain. Don't be surprised if you have to queue half an hour at a petrol station, only to find that it doesn't take the normal kind of bank-notes. It would never cross anyone's mind to put up a warning sign saying, 'This machine only accepts the old kind of 10,000 lire notes,' or whatever. There is no sense of the obligation to inform.

Italian bureaucratic-wait horror stories resemble 'the one that got away' modern folk legends. The papers are always carrying stories like the one about the 1987 postal delivery of someone's call-up papers for World War I, or the 1858 Sardinian fishing rights dispute settled in 1981. CENSIS recently decided to monitor the *lentezze* and *lungaggini* – long, slow waits – of the State apparatus in order to establish a working average. They came up with the following:

Average time it takes for an Italian citizen to receive:

- a tax rebate – four years;
- a civil court ruling – seven years;
- an administrative court ruling – eight years;
- a war pension – eighteen years.*
- to see a USL (public) doctor – 27 minutes;
- to pay one's taxes – 25 minutes;
- to collect one's pension – half an hour;
- to get a bureaucratic document – half an hour.

(* There are, however, still some 10,000 cases regarding World War I pension claims before La Corte dei Conti.)

Average time spent in official queues in major cities (Rome, Milan and Naples).

- If you want to stay longer than a holiday, you technically need a *permesso di soggiorno* (permission to stay); if you want to work, in theory you need a *permesso di lavoro* (work permit). Lots of people don't bother, but it is usually worth your while to stay on the safe side. The latter should be obtained with the help of your employers, but in either case you will have to pay a visit to La Questura. For EC members this is automatic, and indeed is technically unnecessary, though old bureaucratic habits die hard. Non-EC members can spend agonizingly long waits at the Questura trying to get these documents.

- Make sure they get your name spelt right at every entry. Even if the fault is entirely theirs, you could be made to pay dear for it in due course. A misplaced letter in your name may mean being denied access to other documents, even on producing other proof of identity. If 'Jane' is entered as 'June' on the town hall computer, you may never be yourself again.

- If you intend to stay long term, you should become a resident. If you want to buy real estate, a car, or open a bank account, you have to be a resident. When letting an apartment, landlords usually specify 'non-residents only', fearing residents, who can lawfully claim *Equo canone* – fair-rent act – treatment. That's fine – you lie to them. Being a resident means becoming by all accounts an Italian, with identical rights and duties, excepting the chance to vote (due to change in 1993) and, for males, the obligation to perform *il servizio militare*. (→ III, 5:ii) The other great advantage is being able to get a *carta d'identità* or a *patente*, which both count as legal documents, and can be used instead of a passport for internal checks, and in practice for travelling abroad in Europe and the Mediterranean. In theory, this is not so, since yours will state '*Non valida per l'espatrio*' – 'Not valid for foreign travel' – on the back, but border guards rarely check, or understand Italian, or, indeed, care. Your *cittadinanza* – citizenship – remains *inglese* (they never use *britannica*, for some reason), *americana*, *australiana*, *neozelandese*, *sudafricana* or whatever, but you now get to be *un residente italiano*. Big deal. What you cannot be is simultaneously a resident at home too. You have relinquished that, now that you are a tax exile, although Americans are traditionally pursued by the IRS wherever they live.

To register as a resident, you go to the city's Ufficio dell'Anagrafe, usually in or near the town hall, armed with numerous passport photos, birth certificate, exhaustive *particolari anagrafici* – passport-style personal details – on both parents (Beria encouraged Soviet children to do this), and much patience. Look for the Ufficio Stranieri (that's why Italians get confused between 'foreigner' and 'stranger'), remembering to specify if you are a Mercato Comune (EC) citizen or not.

The process of checking out yours and your parents' criminal records at home takes on average forty days ('Our computer was down'), but of course they do not inform you by phone or post that your application has been processed: you must go back on the off-chance. Non-EC citizens may have to wait longer, and should solicit further advice/succour from their respective consulates.

● To work, you must also have a *codice fiscale*. This is your employment number, and is really essential. It is based on the consonants in your name, and your date/place of birth. Be warned: if you give your personal details wrong, you can be arrested; they always have sixteen letters/numbers, and you will get a snappy-looking (for Italy) credit-card that should join your now *documenti*-stuffed wallet/handbag/Filofax.

● If you want to set up a company or work freelance in Italy, you will need to get a *partita IVA* – VAT number – just as you will anywhere else in the EC. This essential task is a complicated and now expensive process (there is to be a special new tax on setting up a *partita IVA*). For this you first need to buy the *registro per le acquiste* and the *registro per le fatture* – expenses and invoice registers – from an office stationers' store, because they have undergone *vidimazione* – a special stamping/heat-sealing process.

● When you become a *residente*, or get a *permesso di soggiorno*, you can get on to a doctor's list. Find out from *Tuttocittà*, the phone-book city guide, where your nearest USL branch is. On proof of residency, you can select a doctor from a long list of affiliated local practices. This costs nothing. (→ VIII, 2:i)

● It goes without saying that you should copy out these precious numbers in various different places as you would your credit-card codes. The front of your Italian *agenda* – diary – has a special page for them.

Getting official certificates

Once you have got your basic documents, almost every time you want to do something you will be asked for a *certificato*, which is a sheet of paper stating something about you. Usually, when flashing your identity card is not enough, they will want a *certificato di residenza*.

Certificates have a different rationale to documents. If the latter keep tabs on you, but can be useful, the former are designed simply to fleece your pocket. They have been in existence since medieval times, and, frankly, it shows.

● There are two kinds of *certificati*: those that are issued by *il comune* and those on *carta bollata*. Every time you wish to make *una denuncia* – an official statement of any kind – it must be written down: a phone-call is not enough. What is more, usually you cannot write it on *carta semplice* – normal paper; it must be written on *carta bollata*, which you must buy from a tobacconist's shop (cost 800 lire). This is an ordinary double sheet of lined paper with a sort of official stamp in one corner. Some Italians keep a little store of it, since one never knows when you will need to make your next *denuncia*. Even in situations of extreme personal distress, like having to tell the police you've been robbed (*denunciare un furto*), you will be sent out to get a sheet of it.

● You may be asked to show you have a clean criminal record, and have no trials or debt repayment orders hanging over you. Ask for *il certificato di stato libero*.

● The height of the grotesque is when, as occasionally happens, you are required to prove that you physically exist. For certain bureaucratic processes, it is not enough to show up and look 'there'. For the Italian authorities, you may be like Oakland, Cal., for Gertrude Stein – there is no there, there. Even your hard-won Italian documents will not suffice. During the Fascist era, the fiendish Rocco, of *Codice Rocco* fame, dreamed up the ultimate bureaucratic nonsense: *il certificato di esistenza in vita*

– the 'live existence' certificate. (→ 5:i, below) Don't forget to ask if they want that in *carta semplice* or *carta bollata* . . .

● Married women should remember always to use their maiden name. Adding your husband's surname is optional, to be linked by the preposition 'in' – e.g. Smith in Rossi, Mary. (→I, 3:ACCESS-Women's surnames)

Riempire un modulo – filling in forms

● Always use a pencil, or get several copies of the document: the slightest error makes the document invalid. You may lose your place in the queue, and thus wait hours, if you are told to get another one.

● Numbers can be difficult in Italian, since all those thousands and millions figures have to be correctly written, not just as figures, but also as one long word – sometimes the length of Welsh railway station names, or of Hopi Indian words used in collective psychology. Again, a single cancellation or correction means starting again. If you make a correction on one of your new Italian cheques, remember to initial each correction.

● *Conti correnti* are post office giros used for paying domestic bills, road tax etc. You will need to write the date, your name and address and the number in both figures and words in quadruplicate: a single mistake means back to home base. Never fill in the date until you are actually at the counter: post office queues can be so long that either they close, or you give up before you reach the glass window.

● It is never clear in post offices or public buildings which queue is for what service. Double check before you join it – it may be written up somewhere

– or ask someone. Usually, only when you get to heads of queues do you find that you're in the wrong one.

● After a year's residency, an imported car must have Italian registration plates. If you buy an Italian car, you will also need to pay annual road tax. Finding out how much to pay is hopelessly complicated, since there is a different amount for each different cylinder, expressed down to the last 5 lire – a worthless sum. By law, you have to round that up to the nearest 100 lire. Why, then, you ask, don't they write 102,200 lire instead of 102,185 lire? In the classic Italian confrontation between theory and practice, they will tell you that the law insists on taxes charged to the consumer being exact to the last decimal, while the State accounting system can't cope with fractional figures.

Basic considerations

● Opening times: the golden rule is to find out when the office or wherever you have to go is actually open. As a rule of thumb, stick to mornings only, and go as early as you can. If you can't find out, but go anyway on spec., remember that 11 a.m. is already late for any official *sportello* – counter or window where you must queue.

● Don't always assume that listed information is accurate. Try where possible to double-check: although the *orario estivo* – summer opening hours/timetable – is common in Italy, it is not always faithfully reported. Museums and galleries listed as open may well be closed for repairs. Try calling, but don't necessarily expect a reply.

Useful information

● Municipal tourist information offices: depending on the politi-

cal shade of the ruling *giunta* (→ II, 3:ii), the amount of useful pamphlets available will vary: left-wing councils tend to have more. Before leaving the office, earmark the places you want to visit, and politely cross-question the official as to whether the information is accurate.

● SIP, the phone company, issues a useful guide to each city called *Tuttocittà*, which comes along with phone directories. Not only does it have a comprehensive A–Z list of street-names with corresponding large-scale maps, in its introductory section it has an invaluable series of lists of telephone numbers for:

Civic amenities (expect to wait several minutes) – ACEA (water); Italgas (gas), ENEL (electricity) etc;

airports and train stations;

emergencies (113 – *centotredici* – for Polizia or Carabinieri; *Ambulanza* – ambulance; and Vigili del Fuoco – fire brigade;

churches, schools and libraries etc.;

cinemas, theatres and discothèques etc.;

municipal offices (it even tells you in which government office to get certain official documents; what it doesn't tell you is where that office is, nor the phone-number, though this second omission is justifiable, since no one would ever answer if you did call).

● Most national or local newspapers are now increasing their coverage of useful addresses and phone numbers:

daily editions have a rather sketchy entertainments guide, as well as a brief public service section (especially for August, when so many places close down) listing things like all-night chemists, late-night restaurants and tobacconists (essential to a race of nicotinophiles);

the weekly colour supplements

are, in the absence of any regular listings publication like London's *Time Out, Pariscope* or New York's *Village Voice*, quite a help, though you will find that the information is not systematically updated. *La Repubblica* started the trend with two (*TrovaRoma* and *TrovaMilano*), while *Corriere della Sera* and several others have since followed suit.

● (06) 884 8484 is the emergency telephone line for Rome, its surrounding *provincia* and the *regione* (Lazio), which you can call to help you cope with Italian bureaucracy. This free public service is run by Socialtel, an organization jointly funded by Rome University, local government, the trade unions and the national phone and electricity companies. They will give you precise indications on what *certificati* you need for a specific purpose, where to get it, what it'll cost you, what other *certificati* you need to take along to get this one, and when the relevant *sportello* will be open. Socialtel's intention is to give special assistance to the *emarginati* – the old, the sick, the unemployed, drug addicts, ex-prisoners . . . and foreigners. A friend at last. They are also dispensing helpful advice about finding work (*uffici di collegamento* – job centres – are a nightmare) and information about medical treatment.

5. Justice

(i) The legal system

The Italian judicial system is in a real mess. The law book it is called upon to enforce is a confused, unfinished jigsaw puzzle; where it is not vague and evasive, it is contradictory.

Although Italy (especially the South, and Naples above all) produces some great legal minds, the apparatus which they are called to operate in is stymied by a crippling shortage of trained personnel at all levels, and a devastatingly antiquated environment – from unrenovated 19th-century courtrooms, to court records written out by hand, and a thoroughly inadequate central filing system.

The shortage of personnel is dictated by different factors: partly, chronic lack of funds – Italy spends less than 1% of GNP on all of law and order, despite having the worst, or best, depending on how you look at it, organized crime in Europe; partly, over-exacting standards. The exams would-be magistrates sit frequently leave dozens of posts still vacant.

The lack of personnel, antiquated working methods and uncertain legal code conspire to produce a situation where between the three branches – civil, penal and administrative – there is a backlog of almost 3 million court cases. To go through the three trial' stages guaranteed by the Italian Constitution rarely takes under ten years, with some people spending a full twenty years before seeing justice done.

The scandalous bail system means that one has very little chance of getting out of prison before trial, and no way of getting compensation for one's pains. Since some 60% of cases are then thrown out of court anyway, one wonders why the Italian legal system doesn't allow better bail facilities – above all, because there is no distinction in prison between those awaiting trial and the convicted. If two-thirds of those arrested turn out to be innocent men on entering custody, on release several years later they can be guaranteed to have turned towards crime.

Ironically, the provisions for *scarcerazione per scadenza del mandato di arresto* – release due to expiry of arrest warrant – usually mean that known dangerous criminals and Mafia men, rather than first-time offenders, get freed before their trial. There are currently moves to tighten this loophole, which so favours serious criminals. At present, the law allows a total of six years *carcerazione preventiva* but specifies an ideal maximum of 18 months before first trial, 12 before appeal and

Being up against the law

- *Una communicazione giudiziaria* – when you receive this at home, you know that you are being investigated, but not what for. It doesn't necessarily mean you will go to court.
- *Un avviso di reato* – this legal notice means that, in the view of the Pubblico Ministero – the investigating magistrate – you have committed a crime. You can be fairly sure of the following stage.
- *L'arresto* – decided by the Pubblico Ministero, although the chances of your own case reaching the court are less than 5%. Senior judges are fed up with what they call *l'arresto facile* – the handcuffs-happy arrest – by magistrates.

another 12 before the hearing at the Court of Cassation. The reputation of the judiciary is generally very low also on account of the shamelessly biased trials of right-wing terrorists and *mafiosi*, who are invariably *assolti per mancanza di prove* – acquitted through lack of evidence. This system may satisfy a nice theoretical point, as in the Scots legal system, but in the Italian one, it is a licence to pre-arranged verdicts.

The Italian legal system is based on three main pillars: Roman law; the Napoleonic Code; and *Il codice Rocco*.

The many remaining aspects of Roman legislation refer to civil law, while much of both civil and penal law is derived from the French system, which is still the basis of nearly all European legal codes, and is distinguishable from the Anglo-Saxon legal tradition by almost everything: its absence of Common Law and Equity; the lack of *habeas corpus*; and its strongly theoretical basis. The third, and by far the most sinister, element of Italian law is the Fascist part. *Il codice Rocco* emanated in 1931 from Mussolini's Justice Minister Alfredo Rocco, and laid down the legal basis for a robust, no-nonsense Fascist system. It clearly lists maximum and minimum penalties for most crimes, as well as enacting a series of breathtakingly repressive civil measures, most of which still remain on the books.

So while the post-war legislature and executive were busy promulgating a communist-sounding Constitution, the newly 'reformed' judiciary, composed of the survivors of the pre-war one, were busy conserving everything they could. They saw to it that the *Codice Rocco* was not repealed as a block, limiting the damage to the abolition, in 1945, of the death penalty (Italy was one of Europe's first states to do so) and to laws that openly clashed with the Constitution, like some aspects of censorship. But not all: although the mores of modern Italy are generally very relaxed and tolerant, all it takes is some hotheaded provincial magistrate to have any film, programme or publication banned overnight, across the whole country: no nonsense about applying for court injunctions. All kinds of grotesquely Fascist laws are still regularly applied: for example, the Stalinist-sounding *vilipendio dello stato* – literally, contempt towards the State – loosely interpreted to include institutions, objects and even people, on the whim of any judge.

The examining magistrates of the Napoleonic system in Italy can become little dictators; once they get a bee in their bonnet, they lash out at everything or everyone in sight. One has put out an arrest warrant for Yassir Arafat; another has twice closed down Berlusconi's three national TV networks for a week on a technicality; another, acting on hearsay from a Mafia killer, had a well-known TV presenter with a social conscience, Enzo Tortora, arrested on suspicion of being a drug dealer – Tortora spent several years in prison. There is little to stop them.

But with most of the Constitution so vague itself, most of Signor Rocco's baby has been left intact. Even the Communist Party has never campaigned against its repeal: at best it has been amended, or 'modernized'.

Human rights were further limited by the 1970s' anti-terrorism legislation, known as *Le leggi reali*, and *Le leggi Cossiga*, increasing the rights of police to use firearms without control, and hold people for longer without an arrest warrant. (Police are constantly shooting themselves, each other and members of the public – say, for passing a road block.)

(ii) *La magistratura*

The magistrature, in common with other Napoleonic Code countries, is something you train for: provided they pass the stiff exams, law students can become magistrates in their twenties. All the various kinds of *magistrati* and *giudici* are under the jurisdiction of the Consiglio Superiore della Magistratura. (→ 5:iii, below) A new *magistrato* is appointed to the office of la Procura della Repubblica – a sort of district attorney's office – where they will usually be assigned by the *procuratore* – procurator – of their office to one single area of crime – drugs, corruption, murder – and are called *sostituti procuratori* – assistant procurators. The most important city *procuratore* is obviously the one in the capital: all the juiciest scandals pass that way, as does the heaviest political pressure regarding results. Traditionally, *il procuratore* passes on each case to his favourite *sostituti*, thus 'guiding' the result of the investigation. As of 1989, the new Rome *procuratore* has decided to leave the selection to a computer. There was an uproar.

On the evidence of their findings (usually secret), they decide whether to send a case to trial, or abandon it as not being a prosecutable offence (*il fatto non sussisto*). It has been calculated that under 5% of cases under investigation actually make it into court. Once in court, their title becomes il Pubblico Ministero (il p.m.) or la Pubblica Accusa – prosecuting magistrate. Since each different city *procura* has a different line on certain issues, politicians usually manage to get cases transferred to more convenient cities, in order to change the impact of investigations or findings. This has happened frequently with right-wing terrorist trials.

Some magistrates love the glamour, others are simply very courageous, but many *sostituti procuratori* are well-known media figures, mythologized as the man struggling against the odds, frequently gunned down in the course of duty, as in Francesco Rosi's film *Tre fratelli – Three Brothers* (1981). Judge Falcone of the Commissione Anti-Mafia di Palermo has twenty-eight full-time bodyguards, which makes his movements rather noticeable. Every time his murder-proof motorcade leaves his home or his office, it sends Palermo's already fragile traffic ecosystem into paroxysms.

(iii) Trial procedure

Important trials are now televised, and edited highlights always liven up the TV news. Ordinary Italians thus have a very clear visual idea of the whole criminal/legal system. Mafia and terrorist trials always have the accused in huge zoo-like cages, in which they prowl or strut around, according to mood. Both the Naples Camorra and the Sicilian Mafia are flashy dressers – designer tracksuits – while some *mafiosi* tend to be more conservatively dressed, perhaps with the Lacoste and blouson jacket look. Recently, a couple of terrorists managed to conceive a child in court. No one noticed, and the baby was born in prison, nine months later.

The **civil law system** has five different arenas:

(a) Il Giudice Conciliatorio is an arbitrator, who tries to convince the parties to settle out of court, failing which they go to:

(b) Il Pretore – something like the small claims court.

(c) Il Tribunale is a regular court, with between one and three judges, depending on the case.

(d) La Corte d'Appello is the Appeal Court, with five judges.

(e) La Corte di Cassazione is a sort of Supreme Court of Appeal, but which can argue only points of law, and not the specific case, composed of many judges: a typically Napleonic invention.

Three phases are the maximum possible. The Appeal Court is more like a complete retrial, with fresh evidence.

The **penal law system** is as follows:

(a) Il Pretore.

(b) Il Tribunale.

(c) La Corte d'Assize.

(d) La Corte d'Assize d'Appello.

(e) La Corte di Cassazione.

Appeals in the penal courts are also effectively retrials, and consistently overturn previous findings. To go from guilty in the Tribunale to innocent at the Court of Appeal and thus to have the case thrown out of court at the Court of Cassation is a regular occurrence. Unfortunately, it takes at least ten years.

I Giudici Popolari are like our jury, and are selected by the head of La Corte d'Assize to sit on penal law cases. However, jury service is voluntary, and out of 250 chosen, fewer than a dozen accept: particularly for cases against the Mafia or terrorism, people are far too scared of reprisals. A pity, since these are the trials when they are most called for.

The **administrative law system** is as follows:

(a) Il Tribunale Amministrativo Regionale (TAR): TAR courts have jurisdiction only within the same region, and examine conflicts between the various regions, between single regions and the State and between individuals and the State.

(b) La Corte dei Conti is a court of auditors, which examines how the State spends its money. Pensions cases end up here. Parliament doesn't much like it, because it tends to be over-critical of their spending profligacy etc.

(c) Il Consiglio di Stato is the Council of State, the supreme court of administrative law. It has, above all, a consultative role, offering opinions on drafts for new laws, and presidential decrees before they are enacted. It is closely modelled on the French Conseil d'Etat. Over recent years its powers have been significantly reduced, with some of them being handed over to the lower level TAR (Tribunali Amministrativi Regionali).

(d) La Corte Costituzionale invigilates the workings of the Constitution and the doings of Parliament. (→ III, 3:iv)

(e) Il Consiglio Superiore della Magistratura (CSM) was set up to administer the Italian magistrature as an autonomous body, free from political pressure. In this, being divided up according to *lottizzazione* principles, it has notably failed, but it still manages to do a reasonably good job. Like the Constitutional Court, in recent years it has become less timid towards Parliament.

(iv) Legal reform

After a gestation period lasting over twenty years, the *Nuovo codice di procedura penale* – the new code of procedure – was introduced in September 1989. Since so much of it depends on a vast injection of cash and investment into the whole legal system, it is most unlikely that it will be, especially since its (for Italy) revolutionary contents will oblige the entire judiciary to retrain: most unlikely. Typically, although all the political parties pay lip service to it, they are secretly very reluctant to see it introduced, as it will inevitably reduce much of their illicit power of influence over legal proceedings.

The *Nuovo codice* is modelled largely on the British

system, and is designed to simplify and speed up the course of Italian justice. It involves drastically curtailing the powers of the *Pubblico Ministero* – the examining magistrate – who plays detective (investigates), policeman (arrests), lawyer (interrogates) and judge (decides verdict).

In theory, it should mean the following:

(a) *Segreto instruttorio* – secret investigations – carried out before the case reaches court are to be banned, to reduce political pressure to drop the case, trump up charges etc. Formerly, the arrested didn't know what the charges were until they were in court. Now the Defence will have time to work up a case.

(b) He or she will no longer be able to order phone tapping.

(c) The *Pubblico Ministero* will no longer have the power to arrest, but will have to ask the judge's permission. He or she will have the power to release unfairly arrested people, as well as still be able to recommend that the case goes to court, or is shelved.

(d) The *Pubblico Ministero* will now have to gather evidence, not 'proof', which currently the Defence have to prove wrong.

(e) Prosecution and Defence will have equal standing in court, with cross-questioning by lawyers, not the judge.

(f) Preliminary investigation will no longer be carried out outside court. All cases will be decided on their merits in court, not from the pre-gathered 'proofs'. This also means Italian lawyers will have to learn to be succinct and actual, rather than rhetorically spouting endless theoretical points.

(g) Arrests will no longer be mandatory for certain crimes.

(h) Plea bargaining is to be introduced – perfect for the Italian mentality.

(i) Sentencing will have to be guilty or not guilty: the ambiguous old formula of *assoluzione per insufficienza di prove* can no longer be used by judges as a way to let themselves off the hook.

Francesco Saja, President of the Corte Costituzionale, thinks that the new penal code still 'doesn't sufficiently guarantee the personal liberty of the accused'; he also thinks the 'judge is not a policeman, he wasn't born to carry out investigations, but to guarantee the impartial observation of the law'.

(v) **Prison conditions**

As elsewhere in the West, prison conditions are critical. In 1988, there were 31,382 prisoners in cells built to accommodate 27,000. This is under half Britain's current prison population. If severe overcrowding is no longer a problem, preventive custody is: 52% of the 1988 prison population were awaiting trial; only 43% were actually sentenced; the other 5% were simply 'interned'. Prison reform over the last decade has been largely unsuccessful, though convicts now get to wear their own clothes. Drugs circulate fairly freely, as do seditious ideas, since there is no segregation of terrorists and common criminals. In 1988 it was estimated that, as a result of heroin use and promiscuous sexual relations between prisoners, over 80% of inmates were HIV positive. A 1987 constitutional ruling stated that having relationships with prison warders was 'an inviolable part of their emotional rights'. A similarly compassionate view is taken of Mafia bosses, who conduct their empires from their cells, over the phone. (→ 2:iii, above)

There is currently a massive new prison-building programme in progress, with seventy-eight planned since 1971, of which some fifty have already been completed, though at immense cost. A scandal has blown up over *le carceri d'oro* – the golden prisons – which are now costing 1250% more than originally expected: several ministers are currently under review as a result. Over 16 billion lire has been allocated for prison building in the triennial 1987–90 alone, presumably to make things even more comfortable for the likes of Raffaele Cutolo.

The 1980s was an era of enormous economic success for the Italians. Italy started the decade as the proverbial poor man of Europe, with lame duck industries, the highest strike record in the West and incompetent political meddling; it emerged at the other end as the capitalist world's fifth largest economy, poised to overtake France into fourth place.

Although the subsidizing of the economically backward *Mezzogiorno* continues to be a drain on the national economy, Italy's overall lateness in entering the world's industrial forum has in other ways been an advantage. Unlike Britain, weighed down by its depressing legacy of rusted plant from Victorian smokestack industries, the Italian post-industrial economy has been able to enter the field at a sprint.

It would be misleading to say that the government has difficulty in running the economy; on the whole, it runs itself, to advantage. Even the enormous para-statal sector is now managing to be competitive, despite government interference. However, for all the successes of manufacturing industry, there remains the ominous lack of any overall economic policy, plus a national debt now greater than GDP, and a budget deficit running at over 12% – a situation which the advent of 1992 threatens to worsen.

Italy's economic success has been aided by the courage, hard work and innovative flexibility of its entrepreneurs, both the major names, which regularly appear in the world's financial Press, and those tens of thousands of minor ones that don't. There seems to be no middle ground: companies are either enormous, or minuscule. The family firm – whether large or small – remains, with its old-fashioned loyalties in a modern business environment, the archetypal successful economic structure.

In a way that no other world economy has managed to do, Italy's goods seem to have a built-in, glamorous corporate image, embracing everything from designer furniture and fashion to industrially produced foodstuffs and cheap automobiles. Even when simply repackaging other countries' ideas, they manage to make them look original and exciting. Italians call this useful phenomenon il 'Made in Italy'.

The Milan stock exchange is still the fastest growing in Europe, and although the principles on which it operates would cause any British or American investor to blanch, it remains a useful barometer of the country's almost limitless financial optimism. In the current mood, it would be easy, but unfair, to credit Italy's industrial renewal entirely to its managerial class. The 1950s'–early 1960s' economic boom was founded on the South Korean-style exploitation of an ingenuous workforce subsisting on low wages, while the 1980s boom was made possible by a new pragmatism among the unions, and a rediscovered hedonism among the workforce. However, high unemployment and limited welfare benefits render claims of '*il sorpasso*' slightly more dubious.

---

1. Government and economic management

(i) Playing with figures

There are three ministries in direct control of the economy: il Ministero del Tesoro – the Treasury – il Ministero della Finanza – the Ministry of Finance – and il Ministero del Bilancio – the Budget Ministry. Italy's

Doing business with Italians

● **Establishing contact**
When to make contact – Italian business hours need mastering. As a rule of thumb, always call

before 12 noon. Government offices keep a 8.30/9 a.m.–1.30/2 p.m. day; some offices stick to the Mediterranean hours of 9 a.m.–1 p.m. and 3–7 p.m., but most larger companies, especially in the more industrialized Centre /North and North, have adopted '*l'orario americano*' – i.e. 9 to 5; many hyperactive Milanese *bizfolk* are still in their shirtsleeves at 7 or even 7.30 p.m. Calculate for time difference – the UK is usually one hour behind, except for two or thr ee weeks in October; most of continental Europe is on the same time-zone as Italy; New York/Montreal is six hours behind, California nine; Japan is eight hours ahead, Western Australia nine.

• When no one answers the phone: it may be a *festa* – national holiday (→VII, 2: ACCESS – National holidays) – or a *ponte* – the 'bridge' day between a *festa* and *il weekend*. Most businesses simply close down for the entire month of August, unless they indicate to the contrary.

• When they do: although most firms employ telephonists who are proficient in English, you may get the one who isn't. In that case, you will hear them use: '*Pronto?*' – 'Hello?' '*Mi dica!*' – 'Yes, what is it?'/ 'Who would you like to speak to?' '*Attenda in linea, prego*' – 'I'm trying to connect you.' If you have to receive business correspondence in Italian, you will obviously need a translation service, but notice the courtesy titles: *Spett.- le* (*Spettabile*) on a line of its own over the name/address of your company; *Egr.* (*Egregio*) on a line of its own, and corresponding to Esq./Ms over your personal name; and the sign-off formula *Cordiali saluti* – yours faithfully.

• The summer lull: don't ever expect to get anything done

huge and complicated public sector is controlled by il Ministero per la Partecipazione Statale, while foreign trade is the responsibility of il Ministero del Commercio con l'Estero. Italy's delicate coalition governments usually mean that these ministries are held by politicians of rival parties, whose plans rarely fit in with each other's.

GDP figures for 1986 (1 and 2 refer to different dollar exchange rates: Italy prefers the first)

	GDP in $bn		GDP per head	
	1	**2**	**1**	**2**
USA	$4195	$4195	$17,360	$17,360
Japan	$1520	$1963	$12,210	$16,150
West Germany	$781	$ 892	$12,793	$14,610
Italy	$673	$ 600	$11,760	$10,490
France	$670	$ 724	$12,100	$13,070
UK	$655	$ 548	$11,540	$ 9,650
Canada	$407	$ 367	$15,910	$14,200

(OECD)

The two most pressing economic problems are the vast budget deficit, still over 12% ($100 billion; it is forecast at $150 billion for 1992) – the Americans worry about a 3% deficit – and the enormous public debt, which in 1989 – at around 1000 trillion lire and forecast to double within twenty-one years – has almost reached 100% of the GDP. Although in the early 1950s it stood as low as 27%, in 1921 it reached a disastrous 123%. The Banca d'Italia and, to a lesser extent, the government issue shrill warnings about the consequences. An economist recently produced the lugubrious abstraction that every Italian child is born with a 17 million lire debt on their head.

Bottom of the class: Sorting out the national debt in the public sector as % of GDP

	1986	1987	1988
USA	4.4%	3.3%	2.7%
Japan	1.1%	+ 0.4%	+ 1.2%
West Germany	1.3%	1.8%	2.0%
France	2.9%	2.5%	1.6%
Ireland	11.0%	8.9%	3.4%
UK	2.4%	1.4%	+ 0.8%
Italy	11.7%	11.2%	10.6%

OECD forecasts for the Italian economy, 1988–90

	1988	1989	1990
Consumer prices*	5%	5.25%	5%
Internal demand		2.5%	3.5%
Investments		4.25%	4.25%
GDP	3.9%	3.5%	3.25%
Exports	5.8%	5%	5.25%
Imports	7.3%	6.5%	5.7%
Balance of trade		US$8 bn.	US$10bn.
Current account deficit	124,000 bn. lire	124,000 bn. lire	

(* the figure for inflation was the result of heavy pressure by the Italian government on the OECD; OECD's 'independent' figures were as follows: January–August 1988: 4.3%; September 1988–May 1989: 7.9%.)

Given the gravity and chronic character of these figures, it is surprising that there remains such general confidence, both at home and abroad, in the Italian economy's short-and long-term viability. *The Economist* (1988) suggested that the answer may lie in the following facts. First, only 3% of the public debt is in foreign hands, being funded to a great extent by government bonds: Italian families are the world's most avid savers, and are very happy to invest in them. Their savings are worth 26.6% of GDP, compared to 17.7% in the UK (1988). Whatever the vagaries of Italian politics and its stock exchange, the Banca d'Italia continues to inspire investor, and international, confidence. Also – until July 1990 – Italian investors are subject to severe restrictions on the export of investment capital, thus preventing a possible flight from the lira. The Italian Treasury is currently engaged in a delicate balancing act: trying to reduce capital controls before 1992, as well as lowering the high interest payments (10%–12% per annum) on its extremely popular short-term CCT, BOT and BTP Treasury bonds, while maintaining investor confidence. However, despite all the macho posing about *il sorpasso* – overtaking Britain – Italy has requested a six-month safeguard period from the EC in the event of panic export of capital.

Of the 12.5% current account deficit, 8.5% is caused by interest payments, while the remaining 4% is caused by government spending, which exceeds

in the weeks leading up to August, any more than you would in those leading up to Christmas: the business motto 'we never close' is not appropriate for Italy.

● Making contact: the vagaries of the Italian postal system make regular mail an unwise choice for anything they need to see within three weeks. Sending express mail makes little difference. The fax is a godsend for communicating with Italian businesses, as they themselves are discovering.

● Who calls whom?: one of the most irritating aspects of doing business with Italians is their habit of making you do all the running. Italians are famous for their 'out of sight, out of mind' ethic in love affairs; that's how they run their business affairs, too. Unless they want something desperately badly from you, don't expect them to call. The common Western practice of courtesy follow-up letters/calls doesn't exist there; having such a lousy postal service is no fun, but they could always call/fax you. The danger of maintaining your regular policy of 'keeping in touch' may be seen by your Italian counterparts as proof that you want something badly.

● On the spot

Power dressing – in case you've not noticed, Italians are very clothes-orientated. Visiting foreign executives are often intimidated by seeing Italian office clerks better dressed than they are. Italians automatically expect people to dress the part, even above their station. This can be tricky for you, because you'd never know from their confident outfit and general mi en if their company was on the edge of a serious collapse. Britain's Department of Trade and Industry and the American equivalent should give their Italy-bound business people a mandatory clothes-screening, such is the difference of impact on the Italians they deal with. Do not make the common mistake of wearing what you think is a 'sharp Italian suit': at best, you will remind them of their local barman in his Sunday best. They will expect you to look very preppy, or very 'English gentleman'. and they will be exceedingly impressed if you do. Women have more leeway, but unlike for men there is no real British look for them to emulate: your Italian business colleagues would laugh if you turned up looking like Princess Anne. (→ II, 6)

Backhanders – if you are after a tender, you should be prepared for expectations of something on the side: anything up to 10%, depending on the field. However you personally, or your company, feel about graft, remember that most Italian businesses work that way, and if you want their custom will expect you to consider that in your overall reckonings.

Relating to Italians in business – however much Italian bizfolk may dislike the people they are dealing with in their absence, the convention of appearing to be old friends in their presence is extraordinarily strong. The idea of being simply cordial but businesslike, which you are probably more used to, doesn't have much currency in Italy. Consider this weakness for crocodile smiles and gushy familiarity in the light of two things: the Italians' natural ability to strike an attitude at will, and the widespread notion, common to all activities, that you always do business with 'family'. (→ V, 2:iii) And all those offers to 'show you around Milan on Saturday' and 'come back next time with your wife/husband, and I'll take you to my house in the moun-

revenues (except the interest payments) and is called the primary deficit. The Italian government is hoping to eliminate the primary deficit before 1992, hoping that the interest deficit will gradually cancel itself out. So far the results of this campaign have been meagre. Government spending probably need not be cut at all: if all tax revenue that is theoretically owed were to be collected, the deficit could be reduced very substantially. There are signs that the tide is turning on *l'evasione fiscale* (→V, 1:ii) – September 1988 revenues were up 12% on the previous year, and the 1989 figures show an even bigger improvement.

Thus, the Italian economy is basically healthy, even though it displays symptoms that would be extremely worrying in other countries. (1:ii, below) One recent cause of extraordinary gloating in the media (and, subsequently, among the public) was the discovery that since 1986 the Italian economy had overtaken Britain's and is only a fraction behind France's. This act of overtaking – *'il sorpasso'* – was achieved as much by juggling with the figures as by charting a heroic growth rate: for the first time, the entire black economy was included in the State's official calculations (made by ISTAT), adding 18% to the sum total (though this would appear to be a very conservative estimate of undeclared income). In any case, GDP growth in Italy in the period 1978–86 was remarkable: as opposed to Britain, France and West Germany's 16%–18%, Italy could boast a full 25% growth rate.

Il tasso di sconto – discount interest rates, September 1989

UK (bank base)	14%
Italy	13.5%
Belgium	9.25%
France	8.75%
USA	7%
Holland	6%
Austria/Switzerland	5.5%
West Germany	5%
Japan	3.25%

(ii) Foreign trade

Moments of success and crisis in Italy's post-war economy are more intimately linked to the balance of trade than in most countries. During the 1950s and 1960s, the *boom economico* was based on the same formula as that of Far Eastern nations today: high exports and low imports; maximum quality goods for minimum possible labour costs. Particularly since the mid-1970s, Italian exports have been aided by a phenomenally successful marketing image. More by accident than by design, the discerning (and not so discerning) around the West perceive Italian style as something quite tangible – extremely chic, but also quite practical. Over the last decade, it has become irredeemably linked with the buzzword 'designer'. (→ 3, below; VII, 5:ii)

Apart from a positive image, Italian export-orientated industries are also blessed with being able to think on their feet. Economic analysts have long admired their capability to switch production towards sectors more in tune with international demand. The overall decline in British exports is the result of its singular failure to anticipate new trends, at a time when Italian producers were jettisoning unrefined food products and raw textiles in favour of automobiles, finished clothing and precision machinery.

Another useful element in Italy's overall export strategy has been the hands-off attitude of the government. Although there are numerous ministries and agencies officially connected to the export drive (notably il Ministero del Commercio con l'Estero), they have no concerted export policy, and, in truly Italian pragmatic style, rather let *l'industria italiana* get on with it. The most famous case of this extremely *laissez-faire* attitude was when ENI boss (→ 1:iv, below) Enrico Mattei, in the 1950s and early 1960s, formed his own foreign policy. Unlike the US, Britain and France, Italy avoids letting international disagreements get in the way of trading: while maintaining excellent trade links with Iraq, Italy seems set to beat both West Germany and Japan to the lion's share of Iran's industrial reconstruction; in his recent book on Agnelli (1989), Alan Friedman shows how Fiat seem, in the face of considerable American displeasure, to have been busy supplying arms to Libya and Argentina. (→ III, 4:vi)

National character also helps a lot, particularly in Middle Eastern or Third World countries, where governments prefer a language problem with Italians to the patronizing attitude of ex-colonial powers. Italy's extremely efficient public works sector, led by IRI offshoot Snamprogetti (→ 1:iv, below), has won many contracts for motorways, bridges and tunnels, and hydro-electric engineering: this is reflected in the trade figures with OPEC countries, which rose from $500,000 in 1970 to over $10 billion in 1980.

Favourably impressed foreigners from all over the world have contributed handsomely to Italy's income in tourist spending (but → 3:vii, below). Added to remittances from Italian workers abroad, non-illegal invisible exports (→ V, 2:iii) amount to about $15 billion annually. However, a variety of factors, from the fall in the dollar to

tains/at the sea to do some skiing/sailing' needn't be taken too literally.

Office etiquette – despite an apparently free and easy atmosphere, Italian places of work are in fact much more hierarchical and sexist than you are used to. The English-speaking countries' business community's habit of treating their opposite number's female p.a. as an equal is unheard of in Italy, and may give rise to misunderstandings. Rather than ask their names, feel safe to use the blanket courtesy title 'Signora'. Presuming that you are not going to experiment with your Italian, at least during business meetings, you will be saved any awkwardness over using the intimate '*tu*' form, or the politer '*lei*' form to say 'you'. You can, however, easily strike the wrong note with simple greetings: remember that however easy you find '*Ciao*' for hello/goodbye, it is highly inappropriate in a formal business context, when you should stick to '*Buon giorno*'/ '*Buona sera*' – 'Good morning'/ 'Good afternoon-evening' – and '*Arrivederci*' and '*Ci vediamo*' for 'Goodbye'. Italians are always delighted when you make an attempt to use their language, but they are also liable to treat you as an inferior if you say something stupid, something most business people could probably do without during negotiations.

● **The meal** – socializing for business: don't expect to conclude much on the phone, or in an office/factory environment: save it all for *The Meal*: this is more likely to be dinner than lunch, and is thus likely to be more protracted than you are used to. The meal with the client is also the classic moment when Italian business folk get their foreign clients where they want them. Mesmerized by the folksy Italianness of it all, you may give away more than you had intended. Be prepared for the following:

Italian meals have at least three consecutive courses, of which the *pasta* is the first or second. However much you enjoy the *pasta*, remember there is the *secondo* – main meat/fish course – to follow. It is fine to skip the *primo* or the dessert, but not to have the *secondo* – or at least a salad – is bad form, and will make you look an unsophisticated tourist.

However much you like good Italian wines, go easy on alcohol during the meal. Few Italians drink more than a couple of glasses at dinner; at lunch, none at all. They will thus notice it more if you get carried away. If they're trying to squeeze a deal out of you, watch how they keep getting the waiter to fill your glass. What they will do is smoke between courses: grin and bear it.

Apart from restaurants, Italy has no sophisticated nightlife to speak of. Therefore, do not be surprised if you are not tak en to the kind of show/club you'd expect to be taken to in London/New York. If you end up somewhere tacky like '*un pianobar*' or '*un night*' (club), don't think it's because they're cheapskates; it's just that there's nowhere better to go. (→ I, 4)

• Punctuality: although the Milanese and Turinese pride themselves on their North European efficiency, don't always presume they will be on time for appointments. Central and southern Italians operate on a flexi-time principle which the northern Italians have had to adjust to. The chaotic traffic system of most Italian cities offers a good alibi, but much of it is simply a state of mind. Do not be over-judgemental about impunctual business partners: it

fears of terrorism, makes the tourism industry extremely vulnerable to the blips Italians call *una crisi*.

After continuous complaints from industry, there are signs that ICE – l'Istituto di Commercio Estero – is now co-ordinating the Italian trade offensive more effectively than in the past. Thanks to their efforts, Italy became in October 1988 the first European nation to mount a major trade exposition in the Soviet Union. In the absence of a royal family to do the hard sell, Italy's entire political and economic *nomenklatura* turned up at 'Italia 2000', along with hordes of suitably impressed Muscovites.

The enormous sense of self-confidence (→ III, 6:iii) is currently doing wonders abroad as well as at home, but many Italian economists are increasingly uneasy: all this climate of 'eat, drink and be merry' seems increasingly to be pointing to a lugubrious prediction for the future. Indeed, the Italian economy currently faces several extremely serious, and apparently insurmountable, problems. The trade deficit for 1987, at $8.6 billion, was over three times greater than for the previous year, while the third quarter alone of 1988 was $2.8 billion.

(*a*) The staggering amount of Soviet-style red tape that surrounds the Italian Customs is getting no better, and both loses valuable time for exporters and exasperates foreign buyers.

(*b*) Although the economy was greatly aided by the fall in oil prices over the last few years, Italy's underlying dependence on imported energy is so acute (well over 80% comes from abroad) that drastic measures should by now have been taken. On the contrary, though, gas-guzzler Italy has managed to make only half the energy savings of its industrialized rivals, and has indulged in the (economic, if not environmental) luxury of voting in a national referendum to dismantle all nuclear power stations immediately.

(*c*) Italy has an even larger imported food bill, which speaks a lot for the inefficiency of its agricultural structures, despite the blandishments of the EC Common Agricultural Policy towards *i contadini* – peasant farmers.

(*d*) There is a worrying Italian propensity not to invest in R&D, particularly in the field of advanced technology; at 1.5% of GDP, this is half the figure invested by each of the West's leading three economies. Although Agnelli and De Benedetti continue to preach its importance in terms of export competitiveness, most companies aren't listening. (→ 3:ii, below)

(*e*) In Italy's most famous trade export sector (clothes, shoes and textiles), imports are booming while exports are slumping. This crisis is in some ways a measure of the Italians' overall material well-being – their rag- trade workers, though still Italy's worst-paid category, can no longer compete with those in the dark satanic mills of the Orient and Eastern Europe in offering rock-bottom export prices; while a combination of two of the Italians' most endearing characteristics – their hedonism and their *xenofilia* – is having a particularly worrying impact on imports, which rose by 22% in the first quarter of 1988 alone. Shoemakers continue to export a massive quantity of shoes, but 35% of those sold in Italy now are foreign: some cheaply made in the Far East or in Eastern Europe; others, like the highly fashionable Timberland boat shoe, imported from America. The fashion export boom seems to be definitely over. Exports of clothes and textiles rose from a value in 1970 of 7712 billion lire to 18,227 billion lire in 1986, but slumped by 15% in the following twelve months, reducing the sector trade surplus by a massive 1 trillion lire.

Typically, hitherto complacent producers are crying about dumping and calling for protectionist measures. The clothing and shoes sector was the one that most witnessed the extraordinary growth of import/export firms over the last twenty years, growing from 16,000 in 1967 to 100,000 in 1980. Most of these outfits were operating in the shadows, breaking all commercial laws, their suppliers ignoring all standard employment regulations, all with a blind eye turned by the authorities. Now the boot is on the other foot. It is one thing for top Italian designers to have much of their collections run up in the Far East; now, however, the West Germans, who traditionally receive 25% of Italian rag-trade exports, have set up a decent one of their own with prestige labels like Hugo Boss, and are now cutting costs too by having things made up in Eastern Europe.

doesn't mean that they can't get their act together at work.

● The two main financial dailies are *Il Sole /24 Ore* (the pink 'un) and *Italia Oggi*; otherwise, all national dailies have ample business sections, as do the TV news programmes. Notice how many yuppie-style business glossies there are: *Capital*, *Class*, *Gente Money*, *Fortune Italia* are the biggest sellers. (→ VII, 7:ii–iii)

Import/export with the EC, the rest of Europe and the USA, 1986

	exports	imports
EC	**56.1%**	**56.5%**
West Germany	**18.6%**	**21.1%**
France	**16.3%**	**14.6%**
UK	**7.4%**	**5.3%**
Switzerland	**4.7%**	**4.8%**
EFTA	**9.9%**	**9.4%**
Comecon	**3.2%**	**4.1%**
USA	**9.6%**	**5.3%**

● 1986–7: trade surplus with USA reduced by 19% from 7160 to 6514 billion lire; trade deficit with EC increased by 2294 to 7160 billion lire.

(iii) The naughty child of Europe: waiting for 1992

Italy is never, never going to be ready for 1992; despite all the chat, it hasn't got its act together at all. It has always been the most enthusiastic member in favour of economic unity, but it is also the member that hides behind the most protectionist measures. It is also always the blackest of the EC sheep in regard to implementation of EC regulations. (→III, 4:iii) Like the UK, it may no longer be the poor man of Europe, but if the UK has managed to turn itself into the *bête noire* of Brussels, then Italy is without doubt the naughty child of the EC. Unlike the UK, however, which makes no secret of its opposition to much European legislation, Italy agrees willingly, and then does nothing about it. 40% of the cases before the European Court for non-implementation of EC directives are against Italy: in 1988, the Italian government received over a hundred warnings – almost twice that of any member state – from the European Commission. While the rest of steel-producing Europe has been cutting its quota fiercely, the IRI-owned Finsider (now called Ilva) was actually *increasing* production, much to Brussels's annoyance.

With their characteristic grasp of abstract issues, the Italians *en masse* all understand the economic, political and social challenge presented by the Single Market Act, and are far from bored by the non-stop, five-year media event currently being dished up to them. Unlike the total indifference, even ignorance, displayed in Britain, even the Italian in the street is aware that 1992 represents the third successive major appointment with Europe, after adhesion to the EEC in 1957 and the EMS in 1979, and thus requires a serious effort of restructuring in order to meet it. But unlike the French, the Italian government doesn't seem to be getting there.

In fact, judging by the pronouncements of Treasury Minister Giuliano Amato, it seems likely that Italy will request an extra period of grace before harmonizing all its trade, banking and investments procedures to the standards agreed on by the Twelve. One of the things that the government most fears is that, in allowing Italians to invest abroad after July 1990, the State could lose out on its valuable source of income through government bonds. Il Tesoro is partly trying to ensure this does not happen by aiming to reduce the primary deficit by 1992. The Italian banking system also seems quite incapable of making the quantum leap necessary to remain competitive, especially with a 30% tax on bank interest – the highest in Europe; top German bankers are now publicly telling their Italian rivals that they will eat them alive. Some sectors of industry seem far too complacent about the chances of il 'Made in Italy' without the safety net, imagining that practical problems like standardization and distribution can be solved with an Italian shrug of the shoulders. Fortunately, most of the major Italian industries seem prepared for 1992 to a degree beyond any of their neighbours. This strategy may be detected in terms of firms anticipating Pan-European consumer demand, like Fiat (whose new Tipo model was specifically designed to meet Euro-tastes) and Benetton (whose entire distribution philosophy is based on synthesizing Euro-taste); in those of business magnates like Carlo De Benedetti and Raoul Gardini, who are busy buying their way into the other European markets to ensure an even, major presence by 1992; and, indeed, in those who do both, like Fininvest's Silvio Berlusconi, with his ambitious plans to operate private television stations all over Western Europe.

Buying and selling firms in the shake-up prior to 1992

(no. of firms, followed by price in millions of ECU: 1989)

	bought	sold
France	86 (4149)	91 (2299)
USA	68 (3615)	-
UK	160 (3287)	101(5956)
Italy	27 (1071)	52 (2039)*
West Germany	46 (300)	90 (1774)
Spain	11 (298)	65 (1084)
Sweden	45 (757)	16 (206)
Japan	24 (532)	-

(*The 52 Italian firms have been mostly bought by French and West German interests; the 27 firms bought by Italian firms were mostly in Spain and Portugal.)

Even more absurd, and potentially a cause of even worse problems for Italy's post-1992 integration into a harmonized European economic sphere, is the state of its taxation system. It is incoherent, inconsistent and unfair: in short, a mess. A series of reforms launched in the early 1970s, which had been conceived as long ago as the war, but never fully implemented (perhaps only Italy could invent an unfinished anachronism), has subsequently been adorned with a series of chaotic, even contradictory, amendments. As a result, overall tax pressure (on those who actually pay it) is higher than almost anywhere else in Italy. The increase in taxation is way ahead of both GDP growth and the inflation rate;

in 1988, it grew by 14.7% compared to 1987. It is further complicated by a parallel régime of tax deductions and exemptions that is blatantly weighted in favour of some, and grossly penalizes others. Many European firms contemplating expansion into the Italian market have discovered that they fall into the 'others' category.

(iv) State industries and privatization

Characteristic of Italy's economically hybrid post-war profile is the mammoth State holding company IRI – Istituto per la Ricostruzione Industriale – which is Europe's largest single company, excluding oil companies. It was set up in 1933 under Mussolini to bail out industry in the aftermath of the Depression, and then started gradually absorbing other chunks of the economy too. This classic Fascist-corporativist statement not only survived the war, but flourished in the new, somewhat wheeler-dealer, liberal, but Soviet-inspired, State. It even multiplied after the war, when three new companies, Ente Nazionale per Idrocarboni (ENI), Ente Participazioni & Finanziamento Industria Manifatturiera (EFIM) and Società di Gestione & Participazioni Industriali (GEPI), were established on the same lines.

IRI is based on a highly successful formula of joint holdings, some of which are controlled entirely by the State; others have only a 51% State holding, and so on, but all are run like private companies, with a board of directors, and shareholders. The whole operation is overseen by the government through il Ministero per la Partecipazione Statale, the Ministry for Nationalized Industries, – but it is business managers, not State bureaucrats, who have the final say. This ideological flexibility has permitted Italian industry since the war to develop by exploiting the best of both worlds: the finest entrepreneurial talents directing major business ventures underwritten or financed by the State, Unfortunately, each one of the 1000-odd companies controlled by the IRI complex is subject to meticulous *lottizzazione* (→IV, 4:i) and thus all appointees have to receive the backing of their party to get a job. However, the system as a whole works, with many of the individual companies reasonably profitable.

What the State owns

● **IRI has a total of some 600 subsidiaries, including:**
Ilva (founded 1937 as Finsider) – most of Italy's steel industry;
Finmeccanica (1947) – engineering;

Finmare (1936) – maritime insurance: Mussolini nationalized the four leading companies, Adriatica, Tirrenia, Italia and Lloyd Triestino;

Stet (1933) – the telecommunications industry, including SIP, the notoriously inefficient phone company, and Italtel, the now profitable telecom equipment makers; Stet is liable for merger with Italcable, Telespazio and ASST *enti* – i.e. public utilities – to create a major Italian telecom group, jokingly called Superstet;

Alitalia – the State air carrier, one of Europe's biggest five: currently working on a global agreement with British Airways and the US United;

RAI – the broadcasting corporation, with 49% of total audience share: 3 TV channels, 3 radio channels.

SME – food group: De Benedetti wanted it; now the multinationals would like to carve it up;

SACIS – the television advertising agency;

ERI – RAI's publishing arm;

most of the *autostrade*;

four major national banks, B.I.N., *Banche di Interesse Nazionale* (Banks of strategic national importance) – Banca Commerciale Italiana, Credito Italiano, Banco di Roma, Banco di Santo Spirito and CARIPLO, la Cassa di Risparmio delle Provincie Lombarde, the world's largest savings bank.

CIT – the State tourism holding: Berlusconi would like it.

● ENI – Ente Nazionale per Idrocarboni – the State Agency for Hydrocarbons – though smaller than IRI, is more profitable. According to *Fortune* magazine (1987), it is the world's ninth largest company in terms of sales. It controls a total of 300 *enti*, with about fifteen important companies, including:

AGIP – Italy's leading, and the world's fourteenth largest, petrol company;

SEMI – tourism and catering section;

Snamprogetti – the successful international engineering concern;

Enichem (chemicals) – merged (1989) with Montedison to create a 50%/50% controlled Enimont.

● The Italian State, as opposed to IRI, also owns two huge financial agencies, EFIM and GEPI, as well as six of the other national banks; Italy's thirty-one lending banks; and Italcasse: a group of eighty-five regional savings banks (vulnerable through often incompetent management): as well as various other major credit organizations, like IMI – Istituto Mobiliare Italiano – which funds the majority of Italy's public works projects. The

entire banking and finance sector is thus organized as autonomously managed individual public corporations.

● **Between them, IRI, ENI, EFIM and GEPI are responsible for almost 30% of sales and almost 50% of fixed investment in Italy.**

With such a massive spread of business interests in so many socially sensitive areas, it is hardly surprising that IRI as a whole had an extremely bloated workforce, and was running huge losses, culminating in a loss of between 2 and 3 trillion lire in 1982–3. IRI's new minder is Romano Prodi, one of Italy's best business brains. While sacrificing nothing of IRI's basic social characteristics, he managed in 1986 to turn over a decade of losses into a slight profit. IRI's overall profitability has been increased even more dramatically since then, with the 1988 turnover up thanks to 6.4% on 1987 and to Prodi's coherent restructuring of the various *enti*. However, as a result of *lottizzazione* agreements between various DC *correnti*, Prodi was being forced to resign in 1989.

The worldwide move towards privatization has also hit Italy, but typically it is less doctrinaire and more pragmatic in spirit. The current thinking that the Christian Democrat, but essentially neutral, Prodi has inspired seems to be one of reducing or eliminating the State holding in a company that can be demonstrated to be more effective as a private one. Given the 100% politicization of IRI appointees, the various parties are reluctant to see another slice of their power falling into the hands of the Big Three, just as the reverse is true. Most Italian political leaders would be prepared to adopt the Thatcherite 'shareholding democracy' theory as their own, if wholesale, or even partial, privatization meant that ordinary citizens ended up in control. However, Milan's dodgy stock exchange set-up practically guarantees that the Big Three would simply replace the State in command. Socialist leader Craxi blocked the IRI's sale of food group SME to De Benedetti, but was furious when Agnelli refused to accept Craxi's protégé, the late Marisa Bellisario, as head of a joint State/private telecom venture, made up from the fusion between Fiat's Telettra and IRI's Italtel. In 1987, Agnelli's Fiat gobbled up the State's almost bankrupt Alfa-Romeo in a deal that recalled British Aerospace's advantageous purchase of Austin Rover. Both cases are being examined by the EC Commission. Both Prodi and Raoul Gardini made a good deal by the fusion of IRI's Enichem with the latter's Montedison: Italy now has a united chemicals colossus capable of holding its own on the world market. Prodi was equally wise in reducing the State's share in the leading merchant bank, Mediobanca, a move also instigated with the high-street banks in IRI's control. (→ 2, below)

What Prodi is really trying to shake up is the disastrous steel industry, with its annual losses of over 1 trillion lire. Known until May 1988 as Finsider, but now rechristened Ilva, it is trying to close plants in Genoa, Taranto and Bagnoli near Naples, and to shed some 50,000 staff before 1992. (→ 1:iii, above) Ilva is caught between the two fires of the EC Commission – who have already imposed massive fines for insufficient 'transparency in corporate planning' (for which, read,'conning the European Commission about its real intentions') – and a coalition of the government and the unions, respectively restless and furious over the prospect of mass unemployment. Equally annoyed are Finsider's 2% of private shareholders, who have just discovered that their shares are worthless after asset stripping.

IRI also has its star performers: telecom giant Stet can boast a 61% jump in profits from 1986 to 1987, and is about to be launched by Prodi on the world's stock markets; its equipment manufacturing subsidiary Italtel underwent an extraordinary reversal of fortunes after being entrusted to Italy's most powerful businesswoman, the charismatic Marisa Bellisario, who died unexpectedly in 1988. In the six years between 1981 and 1987, she converted a $650 million debt and a $220 million annual operating loss into a $90 million profit, managing to reach agreement with the unions to shed 40% of the workforce, and completely renovating the product range.

La Thatcherizzazione dello stato:
selling off the family silver

In 1987, the Cassese Commission estimated that Italian State property was worth some 650 million billion lire; this left out most of its real estate – hospitals, USL property, schools and universities and *le case popolari*. With all this, the figure could almost reach 1000 million billion – which is the same figure as the national debt. The idea is tempting, but of course the State could never sell most of it, for all the obvious reasons. However, in 1989, the Andreotti government decided to examine the idea of selling off some of the State's financial holdings; none of them have ever been quoted on the stock exchange. Already, by law, as much as 49% of any State holding can be in private hands. The income from all this could help balance out something of the current account deficit.

What the State's goodies are worth (in billion lire)

Land	431,000
Buildings	220,000
IRI/ENI/EFIM	80,000
ENEL	47,100
IMI	9900
INA	6800
RAI	6000
Cariplo	5600
Banca Nazionale del Lavoro	5100
Monte dei Paschi di Siena	4700
San Paolo di Torino	4500
Banco di Napoli	1700
Cassa di Risparmio di Roma	1300
Cassa di Risparmio di Torino	1300
Banco di Sardegna	1000
Banco di Sicilia	735
	total 917,335

(Cassese report: Mondo Economico)

2. *L'economia spettacolo*: the big Italian dynasties

Although the Italian economy has expanded and restructured itself beyond recognition over the last decade, in one way it hasn't changed at all. It is still completely dominated by tiny handfuls of men, usually representing a dynasty. The novelty consists in a few new names – and in the extraordinary degree of deference, even hero worship, shown them by the public at large. This new attitude has obviously coincided with the decline of left-wing ideology and the corresponding increase in enthusiasm for business and 'doing well'. Gianni Agnelli, once the pet hate of Italian students, was recently mobbed by a student anti-educational cuts demonstration with enthusiastic cries of 'Viva Agnelli! Bravo Gianni!'

Italy's small number of captains of industry have become real stars in their own right. Like politicians (→ IV, 3:i), they are now much in demand for Italy's relentless TV chat-shows. TV has played along. In a way that was implicitly critical of his colleagues, RAI programme presenter Gianni Minoli put it like this: 'Quite frankly, business figures like Gardini, Schimberni, De Benedetti and Agnelli are now more popular and glamorous than our regular showbiz figures.'

Their faces help sell a whole generation of glossy business magazines. One of these, the immensely popular *Capital*, recently polled Milan ad-men for their ideal testimonial presenters: the top ten contained no footballers, actresses or singers; they all chose business leaders. *Il Giornale* editor Indro Montanelli put it, with characteristic sharpness, into a sexual context: 'The literature and iconography of business and financial success have now overtaken in popularity that dedicated to women's breasts.'

The servility of Italians to those in power is not the only factor involved; nor is the natural charisma of their idols: they have been working on it hard. A survey commissioned by Pirelli shows that in 1976 Italian executives dedicated a mere 10% of their time to PR; following US Chrysler boss Lee Iacocca's lead, they now dedicate 54% to it. Italian big business may be feudal, but that doesn't mean it is not also up to date: thus its great dictators wish to be seen as benevolent dictators, a job description that is more reasonable than many.

In order to handle the chat-shows and TV news on which they so heavily feature, several thousand top managers have been on extremely expensive media training courses. Perhaps most of these needn't have bothered, since the *dramatis personae* of Italy's *economia spettacolo* are so few. The real superstars even have nicknames. Their doyen, Gianni Agnelli, has always been known as *l'avvocato* – the lawyer; Leopoldo Pirelli used to be known as *l'ingegnere* – the engineer – until eclipsed in fame by Olivetti's Carlo De Benedetti, who has the same kind of degree; the subsequent rise to notoriety of Raoul Gardini (Ferruzzi, Montedison) left pundits stuck: since he had no degree, his modest provincial origins and agribusiness involvement led him to be lumbered with *il contadino* – the peasant farmer. Media moghul Silvio Berlusconi is commonly known as *Sua Emittenza* – a clever pun on the religious courtesy title and the Italian word for 'broadcasting station'.

The influence on the public of these superstars is evident in several sectors, their celebrity status consisting not simply in reaching magazine covers, but mostly in creating a climate of total business confidence, especially among small, first-time investors, thanks to whom they can now raise abundant equity. Even how they dress is a matter of sartorial inspiration for Italy's legions of would-be business heroes.

With the exception of Berlusconi, the big families all have incestuous, though cut-throat, relations, with shareholdings in each other's firms and public declarations of mutual good will accompanied by furious boardroom rivalry. The Italian public seem to have been trained to admire their ruthless, swashbuckling business techniques. The Press gushingly compare them to the Renaissance *condottieri* – soldiers of fortune – implying that their glamorous appearance excuses them for riding roughshod over shareholders' (or the public) interest. In his paper, Indro Montanelli has described Agnelli as 'admirable, but cynical ... an aesthete but not a moralist'. He adds that in Italy there is 'no tradition of public service, no Rockefellers or Kennedys going into politics to pay society back for the fortunes their grandfathers made. Here they simply continue to pursue family interests.' 'Family' is the operative word. For all Italy's financial and industrial restructuring at corporate level, it is the families, not the shareholders, that are still in command. Mario Schimberni, before being ruthlessly evicted in 1987–8 by the dynastic Gardini from Montedison which he'd tried to make into an exemplary public company, observed that 96.2% of Italian companies were still family run, even though many may have a corporate structure that camouflages this. When Gardini first won control of Montedison, Agnelli patronizingly gave his approval, since he was from 'a grand old family' – so presumably his hostile take-over was fine.

Although some of the big Italian companies have been founded only recently, the archaic family structure is common to all of them, as is the arrogant indifference to their shareholders. Most of the old firms went through serious crises in the 1970s, which were reversed due to heavy capital reinvestment and massive cuts in the workforce. Possibly more than in any other EC country, the understanding that European and international co-operation (joint ventures, foreign investments) are imperative for survival into the 1990s now characterizes their overall strategy. (→ 1:iii, above) The first three names – Agnelli, De Benedetti and Gardini – are definitely in a class of their own: the Big Three. Although Berlusconi represents a powerful challenge, his absence from the stock market limits his overall impact, while Pirelli can no longer be considered in the big league.

(i) Gianni Agnelli – Fiat

The Agnelli empire controls some 20% of the total stock listed on the Milan stock exchange. The Agnellis own a controlling 41% share of Fiat, which is Europe's largest automobile producer, the world's sixth largest. In 1989, it has a 52 trillion lire turnover (of which 18 trillion lire was abroad), with over 4 billion lire profits. The Fiat group constitutes 4% of Italian GDP, and has 64% of the domestic automobile market – by far the largest domestic share in Europe. The Fiat car division (including Lancia, Alfa-Romeo, Ferrari and Autobianchi) represents 50% of sales, with Iveco trucks, railway and farm vehicles, buses and components comprising the rest. Then there are Fiat's subsidiaries – helicopters and aircraft engines, civil engineering, chemicals and scientific research, and telecommunications equipment (Telettra).

Stock exchange equity loans have helped reduce a 1980 debt of 8 trillion lire to less than 1 trillion lire, as well as financing massive automated plant reinvestment, accompanied by a large shredding of the workforce, helping to double productivity, in less than a decade, to Korean levels.

Agnelli is now president of Fiat, having delegated day-to-day responsibility to the extremely able Cesare Romiti (managing director) and, until 1988, Vittorio Ghidella (in charge of the car division).

Through IFI, Istituto Finanziario Italiano, the family finance holding, the Agnellis also control the Rinascente department store chain, as well as Prime, which is Italy's second biggest mutual fund; they also have major stakes in the Gemina finance company and Mediobanca, Italy's only merchant bank. Even more high-profile is the Agnelli grip on the media: they own Turin's *La*

Stampa, now effectively control Milan's *Corriere della Sera*, having bought into the publishing group Rizzoli, and seem poised (despite Agnelli's denial) to take over 50% of Italy's semi-official TeleMonteCarlo TV service. It is typical of the Agnelli style that, despite a rather Fiat-orientated business section, *La Stampa* remains Italy's best newspaper. (→ VII, 7:ii)

The dynasty was founded by Gianni's grandfather, senator Giovanni Agnelli. The brilliant, charismatic Gianni is aided by his less bright brother Umberto. They are married to two beautiful sisters from a prominent noble family, Marella and Allegra Caracciolo, whose brothers, Nicola and Carlo, are on the board of *La Repubblica*, Italy's third leading daily paper. It is Umberto's son, Giovanni, who is being groomed to take over the business, while Gianni's son, Eduoardo, is being groomed to take a very back seat. Gianni's sister, Susanna Agnelli, is junior Foreign Minister; her best-selling autobiography, *Vestivamo alla marinara* – 'We wore sailor suits' – is being made into a major film. Another clan member, Luca di Montezemolo, in his early 40s, is organizing the 1990 Italian World Cup.

In his 60s, Gianni Agnelli is still considered the supreme paragon of Italian male elegance; his almost regal presence at any event, professional or social, confers it with a dignity unmatched even by anything the President could provide. Indeed, over 60% of Italians polled indicated him as the ideal candidate for an executive presidency. The Agnellis sponsor numerous cultural events and sites through the Fondazione Agnelli, as well as individually; Venice's Palazzo Braschi, owned by the Fondazione, is certainly Italy's finest private art exhibition space. (→ VII, 3:ii)

Despite his unparalleled power and influence in Italy, he resists the temptation to bully the nation. He is aligned to the Partito Repubblicano, but has always shown a conciliatory attitude to other parties, especially the Communists. His relatively enlightened attitudes have in recent years helped install some revolutionary agreements with the unions. (→ 5:i, below) Controlling two of the nation's leading three national newspapers does mean that little hostile comment to him appears, but he is not beyond admitting on TV: 'Italy does consume rather too much, although it's hardly in my interest to say so.'

(ii) Carlo De Benedetti – Olivetti

Formerly Fiat's managing director, De Benedetti moved over to this formerly prestigious typewriter company in 1978 to save it from spectacular collapse. By persuading the unions to accept massive cuts, and by switching rapidly from manual/electric typewriters to computers and software, he transformed Olivetti into Europe's largest data-processing and office automation equipment company, and the world's largest producer of office standard home computers. The massive debt of 1978 was rapidly reduced, with profits in 1985 up by 41.5% over twelve months. The first of Italy's business stars to see the importance of international deals in overcoming problems of size on the world market, and of producing abroad to avoid Italy's cumbersome labour laws, he sold a 25% share to America's AT&T. With only 33% of Olivetti sales in Italy, De Benedetti's international strategy is reflected in the deals he has done with other office equipment/data-processing firms; first, with Toshiba; secondly, when he bought the ailing Nuremberg-based Triumph Adler for $260 million, followed by 80% of the UK's Acorn Computers, and in 1988 Norway's Scanvest Ring Computers.

Through his three holding companies, CIR, Cerus and Cofide, he has built up the classic three F's empire: Food, Fashion and Finance. In 1988 he sold the Buitoni food conglomerate (pasta, chocolate etc.) to Swiss Nestlé; he owns 50% of Yves St Laurent, and 47% of Belgium's largest company Société Générale de Belgique (SGB). His Paris-based Cerus group has finally reached agreement with the previously hostile Suez group regarding the management of SGB, which he sees as an ideal vehicle for his 1992-orientated plans.

In Italy, where his holdings include control of the finance corporations Italmobiliare and Euromobiliare, and Credito Romagnolo, Italy's second largest all-private bank, he first pressed for the need for high-risk venture capital operations. In a sly move, which apparently gained him nothing, he co-operated with rival Gardini to wrest control of Montedison from Mario Schimberni. In 1989, he increased his holding in Mondadori, Italy's largest publishing house, and in a notable coup persuaded the previously independent-minded Eugenio Scalfari to give him a controlling interest in the latter's daily, *La Repubblica*. This move was fiercely contested by the paper's staff, who did not approve of the Agnellization of their editorial independence. (→ VII, 7:ii)

Altogether, the turnover of his empire is almost 18 trillion lire, while he controls almost 5% of the stock market. Like Agnelli, his political sympathies are with the Repubblicani, although he is less socially *presenzialista* than the Turinese clan. La Fondazione Olivetti – Olivetti's arts and research foundation – and the sponsorship of numerous international art exhibitions maintain a suitable PR profile.

(iii) Raoul Gardini – Ferruzzi and Montedison

Gardini's rise to power has been the fastest and most spectacular of all the new breed. Married to Ida, daughter of Serafino Ferruzzi, owner of an agribusiness empire based in Ravenna, he took over the firm in 1979 on his father-in-law's death. Ferruzzi is now the world's largest agro-industrial group, controlling 2.5 million acres of farmland worldwide, dominating the European sugar market and the Atlantic cereals trading. Ferruzzi had revenues of $18 billion in 1987, with a larger share of business in France than in Italy. Ferruzzi's biggest gamble is trying to persuade the EC to adopt his plan for producing biethanol out of the European grain mountain, as an octane booster in petrol instead of lead. His rivals protest that it is far too expensive, although the French still look interested, and seem set to allow him to open a factory there, with plans to invest $700 million.

His most audacious move was to win control of Montedison – the recently privatized chemicals, pharmaceuticals and plastics giant, with $12.8 billion annual sales – by routing chairman Mario Schimberni. His ruthless restructuring methods between his two companies cause stock market panic, and considerable criticism. He now controls over 200 companies, with a total 25 trillion lire turnover, and just over 10% of the stock market, although in 1988 he engineered a merger between Montedison and the State-owned Enichem, to create Enimont, a force large enough to compete internationally with Dow Chemical, ICI and Bayer, who have all cast predatorial glances towards Italy. Enimont is now the seventh largest chemical firm in the world, and Gardini is attempting to run the whole company.

Leading the vanguard of Italian businessmen casting, in their turn, predatory glances at the Soviet Union, in 1988, Gardini signed a mega contract with Gorbachev which enabled him to set up an extraordinary one-man New Economic Policy to match Lenin's: to run 0.5 million hectares – the site of Lombardy and Piedmont combined – in four separate agro-industrial complexes, thus aiding the recovery of the Soviet economy, of which he was already the largest single grain provider. He owns the Rome-based daily *Il Messagero* outright, and a significant share of the business daily *Italia Oggi*.

Living up to his country farmer image, Gardini cultivates the Anglo sports look, and likes to be photographed duck-shooting in a Barbour and wellies. He is also an accomplished yachtsman, and a well-known socialite.

(iv) Silvio Berlusconi – Fininvest

Berlusconi was first successful, in the early 1970s, in construction – he built the huge Milano 2 development. Shortly after, he moved into the new world of deregulated TV (→ VII, 6:i); but Fininvest continues to be Italy's largest private construction firm.

The immense, and immediate, success of his three TV channels was underscored by his Publitalia advertising agency, which soon became larger than the State-owned one and now handles advertising for yet three more semi-national channels, Junior TV, Italia 7 and Capodistria, making six channels that he effectively controls in Italy alone. He has expanded abroad with mixed results; his La Cinq, France's first private station, has been bugged by government feuds, though this has not stopped major incursions into the international TV field. In Germany, Tele 5 started in 1988; in Spain, he has been granted a 25% share – the maximum possible for foreigners – in TeleCinco, one of the new private channels, by a friendly Gonzalez. He has similar plans for Belgium and Canada.

Berlusconi has also built up an enormous cinema empire, with ReteItalia emerging as one of Italy's largest producers, as well as the largest cinema circuit in most major cities. His media interests also include the national daily *Il Giornale* (which he may be forced to sell, to comply with proposed government legislation on media monopolies) and Italy's best-selling weekly, the TV listings guide *TV Sorrisi e Canzoni*. Recent well-publicized buys include La Standa, Italy's largest chain-store, and the once struggling Milan football club, which he has not only put back at the top of the Italian league table, but has transformed into one of the three or four top European sides (→ VIII, 4:ii), buying world-class players like Dutch Ruud Gullitt and Marco Van Basten and introducing American razzmatazz to the stadium. What makes his 150-company empire, with its 10 trillion lire turnover and 750 billion lire annual profits, so remarkable is that he has done it entirely without stock market capitalization.

He too has penetrated the Soviet market – setting up a 45-minute weekly showcase TV programme profiling Western (largely Italian) know-how in a style that is a cross between Walt Disney's *Look at Life* and his slick, aggressive advertising arm, Publitalia.

He shuns the world of Milan high finance, holding a low opinion of its leaders, and generally keeping his own council, running the shop with his brother Paolo and a cabal of assistants who display all the blind devotion of an oriental sect. His charismatic, workoholic presence is mirrored by the sleek (8000) workforce which runs all three TV channels. He strenuously denies that his close friendship with Socialist leader Craxi has permitted his rise to power, insisting that his only ideology is profit. Although he shuns, and even despises, Milan's business *salotti* – drawing rooms – his carefully rationed social appearances make him appear the peerless playboy.

(v) Leopoldo Pirelli – Pirelli

Like the Turinese Agnelli, Milanese Leopoldo Pirelli is the scion of a three-generation industrial dynasty. Now in his 60s, he has done slightly less well, having lost his press sobriquet of *l'ingegnere* to the more dynamic De Benedetti. Pirelli was falling behind in the technology war in the early 1970s, but subsequently managed a complete turnaround, aided by Mediobanca and Gemina financing (Agnelli). They are now the world's fifth tyre producers, and the largest makers of fibre-optic cables. Leopoldo has recently consolidated this lead by buying into several American hi-tech. firms. With 110 factories in sixteen countries, two-thirds of its annual $3.7 billion sales are outside Italy. His recent hostile takeover bid of US Firestone didn't succeed.

Pirelli is a complex figure, both patriarchal and enlightened. In the 1970s, he assembled the Pirelli board to instruct them to vote for divorce in the referendum; he wonders, Hamlet-like, whether a good businessman can also be a good citizen, and calls for ethical business dealings – yet his company still refuses to present a consolidated balance sheet, playing around instead with the Russian doll firms-within-firms structure, which effectively disguises what degree of control his family exercises.

Pirelli's corporate prestige is enhanced by the Pirelli calendar and by leading post-war architect Giò Ponti's breathtaking Milan skyscraper HQ. (→ VII, 5:i)

(vi) Fashionable Milan families

Not all the big family dynasties have remained united and/or successful.

While the firm that bears their name remains Italy's largest, the **Mondadori** have fallen out, with former boss Leonardo ejected in 1988. The **Rizzoli** publishing empire, which owned *Corriere della Sera* for a decade from the mid-1970s, dissolved after Angelo's foolish and illegal dealings landed him in jail. The family he bought it from, the **Crespi**, once Milan's grandest, are now practically powerless, their doyenne, Giuliana Maria, living in country exile. The **Bonomi** finance clan, run jointly by mother Anna and son Carlo, have also lost much of their former power, although Carlo has become quite active on the London stock exchange.

(vii) The Mediobanca club

Northern Italy's main industrial dynasties are represented among the shareholders of Mediobanca, until
the law changes, Italy's only merchant bank. Even
though their total holding is 6%, as opposed to the
57% held by the three IRI banks (→ 1:iv, above), it
is they, not the majority shareholders, who control
Mediobanca's operations. In this way, the now dis-
credited chairman Enrico Cuccia was able to influence
the Italian financial world almost absolutely for forty
years. Although Cuccia was briefly replaced by the
reliable Antonio Maccanico, the latter has now been
supplanted by Francesco Cingano, who, like Cuccia, is
under investigation for 'financial impropriety'./

Mediobanca is still awaiting its long promised reform,
with both the State's share and the élite financial
club's share to be fixed at 50% with 50% being
held publicly.

(viii) The rag trade and its ruling families

Benetton was founded in the 1970s by five siblings
who discovered a way of producing woollen garments
before dyeing them, so as to avoid wastage and to be
able to meet market demands much faster. They have
grown in a decade to be the largest wool purchasers
in the world. Sharing the responsibilities between them,
with Luciano Benetton as front man and Giuliana as
designer, they now have 4000 shops worldwide, run
from their restored *palazzo* in the Veneto.

Stefanel is of almost identical origin, although having
been founded more recently it is somewhat smaller than
Benetton. It is run by siblings Giuseppe and Giovanna
from *their* restored *palazzo* in the Veneto with around
1000 shops worldwide.

Marzotto, a sixth–generation family of business-
minded counts from the Veneto, whose textile empire
now controls 50% of world linen production, is the
joint largest wool producer in Europe. They have
now swallowed up two rival companies, Bassetti and
Lanerossi (obtained from IRI at knock-down price), to
make them one of the world's ten largest textile groups.
Their holdings also include Santa Margherita wines in
the Veneto, and the Jolly hotel chain (second largest in
Italy), which was started by the current seven siblings'
father Gaetano so that he could have somewhere decent
to stay on his travels. Paolo's ex-wife, Marta Marzotto,
is Italy's best-known society hostess, whose *salotti*,
whether in Sardinia, Cortina d'Ampezzo or Rome, are
the most fashionable.

Ermenegildo, the thirty-year-old grandson of the
founder of **Zegna**, now runs this $2000 million cloth

and clothing firm, the world's largest buyers of luxury wools, and producers of 30% of the world's up-market men's suits. Their wool ideas were copied from Scots weavers and reproduced in Piedmont.

(ix) Iron and steel families: the Italian Krupps
Ugo Gussalli Beretta is the thirteenth-generation descendant of Pietro, the founder of **Beretta**; they have been making guns for 300 years, of which 60% are sports guns. They recently won a huge contract to supply the US Army with 316,000 9mm. as the standard sidearm issue to replace the Colt.

The steel empire **Danieli** was founded in 1900 by Mario Danieli and is now controlled by granddaughter Cecilia. Their base in Udine controls twenty companies worldwide; their speciality mini-mills are found in twenty-seven countries. They produce 50% of the world total of them.

The other, even larger, Italian steel dynasty, based in Lombardy, is **Falck**. They are in their third generation.

3. Il 'Made in Italy' and its characteristics

(i) Mega-big versus small

Business companies, like so many other things in Italy, go in for extremes: they are either enormous, or they are tiny. The public sector itself is so big (→ IV, 4:iii) that the purely private sector (35% of output) is the smallest of any non-Communist state. The State holding company IRI may be the largest non-oil firm in Europe, and Fiat Europe's largest and the world's third most profitable car manufacturer, while Benetton are the world's largest wool buyers, but some 90% of Italian firms have fewer than 100 workers. In the FORTUNE (1987) league of the world's top 500 non-American companies, Italy boasts a mere seven: IRI (4th), Fiat (8th), ENI (18th), Ferruzzi (28th), Olivetti (123rd), Pirelli (200-ish) and Esso-Italia (327th). France has thirty-nine, West Germany fifty-three and Great Britain seventy-five. Even the relatively under-developed Spain has eight. Note that besides the six in the top 200 and 500, only Esso-Italia features between 200 and 500. There are simply no medium-sized Italian firms at all.

Elsewhere, conventional wisdom states that company takeovers, hostile or not, are generally necessary to guarantee survival, especially as an export force, for small firms. There are many reasons why this does not hold in Italy.

The propensity for family businesses tends to exclude incorporation, despite notable exceptions to this rule. Compactness tends to favour loyalty and meticulousness. There may be a limit to the number of sons-in-law one can acquire for the sales team; there is none to the amount of overtime an Italian patriarch can force them to work. This intensely family dimension makes the whole idea of takeovers between small businesses more social, and thus more delicate, than one might wish.

Italians are still used to a localized system of production and distribution almost forgotten in other industrialized countries. There are very few nation-wide retail chains, and most of the food industry is locally organized. The plethora of small local banks is ideally suited to the 'personal touch' necessary for lending to equally minuscule companies: one of the problems for small firms in Italy is being taken seriously by the big banks. In the early 1980s, a group of small industrialists in a wealthy village in the Po valley mustered together the $750 million sufficient to buy up the floundering *elettrodomestici* company Zanussi; they were turned down in favour of Swedish Electrolux because the Milanese bankers handling the sale had never heard of them or their syndicate.

Italy's fragmented political system plays its part: the power of local politicians is such that most small companies can find *un santo in paradiso* – a political guardian angel – to help for a *tangente* – a rake-off – in the way that usually works only for far higher stakes elsewhere. Hyperchoice works in commerce as well as in politics or the media: Italy's 1250 local TV stations are ideally complementary to the small companies who can afford their rock-bottom advertising rates. If independent TV stations with a few thousand viewers, or the Partito Liberale with 2.1% of the nation's votes, are happy with their minute share, why shouldn't tiny, un-economical-looking businesses also be content?

Learning from the negative experience of the large production-line industries, many of the new wave of small company bosses have tried to keep unionization, and expense-provoking industrial safety inspectors, off their shop floor. In the case of the rag trade, this means unregulated low-wage cottage industries, while the mechanical and electrical manufacturing industries try to farm out as much as possible to neighbouring firms. Playing footsie with employees' statutory employment rights is often described favourably as 'flexibility'.

The most valid reason relates to quality, something that small, artisan firms are usually more capable of offering. Over the last decade, there has been a remarkable renaissance of artisan traditional skills throughout Italy, to meet the sybaritic tastes of the general public. Some 1.5 million small companies have sprung up, encouraged by government grants of 90 billion lire aimed at spreading the area of industrial activity. Despite the efforts of the government aid body for the economic regeneration of the South, *la Cassa per il Mezzogiorno*, and the fact that 23% of Fiat cars are made in their southern plants, nearly all Italy's big industry has remained firmly located in the triangle formed by Milan, Turin and Genoa.

Thanks to the emergence of these small firms, the last decade has seen Italy's economic growth being spread much more evenly over the rest of the country, although particularly over the rest of the North and in the Centre. The Chamber of Commerce admits some 80,000 new small firms a year.

(ii) Creativity and adaptation

There are certain virtues common to most areas of Italian industrial creativity, and some similar structural defects. The ability to think quickly, adapt to meet demand and work extremely hard, coupled with a high degree of flair for visual detail and artisan skill, is common to automobile and clothes design alike; so is the knack of recycling other people's ideas. The Japanese are famous for being design hijackers; the Italians are not, because they do it more subtly, and end up giving the product a highly Italian feel.

The extremely low percentage spent on R&D (1.5% of GNP) and the reluctance to initiate international collaboration projects are likely to affect many sectors of advanced technology in the future. Most R&D is government-funded, with only 45% funded by private concerns (compare the USA's 72%); over 80% of inventions are made by the big groups, Montedison, Pirelli, ENI, Fiat, Olivetti and Stet. Italian industrial creativity is limited to a few inventions in auto technology, some chemical processes, but above all new leather and textile machinery. Of patents deposited in Europe, their 3% is less even than Switzerland's 5% – is it possible to invent less than a cuckoo clock?

Despite this general lack of invention, morale is generally high, although there is a danger of Italian industry resting on its laurels, as though the label 'Made in Italy' were enough, on its own, to sell anything.

(iii) The automobile industry

The continued success of Italy's automobile industry at home is due not just to good technology and a flair for design, but also to a high degree of brand loyalty and a virtually total ban on Japanese imports. The Italians' lack of enthusiasm for ecological and safety considerations (seatbelts and lead-free petrol) gives the entire sector a curiously 1960s innocence, which is great for sales; the 1950 total of 118,000 vehicles has been transformed into Europe's fourth largest market, just after France.

Fiat has enjoyed a total turnaround in every field since the mid-1970s: quality of production, industrial organization, sales. Extensive R & D into both production methods (Fiat's robotics unit is unequalled outside Japan) and vehicles has led to an ever-improving market position – some would say stranglehold – on the home market, with 64%; they have the highest European sales figures, at 16.2% beating both Volkswagen (12.4%) and Peugeot (11.4%). All the models over the last decade – the Ritmo (UK = Strada), the Panda, the Uno, the Regata, the Croma and, most recently, the Tipo – have had considerable success.

In buying up smaller companies, like Autobianchi, Lancia, Alfa-Romeo and Ferrari, Fiat have been careful to preserve their traditional identity, and hence customer loyalty: compare this to the British motor industry, a veritable graveyard of forgotten marques. Rather more subtle has been the crossover of technology employed by Fiat for each of its offshoots: hence the new Alfa-Romeo 164 has not just a great engine, but, at last, a comfortable interior; the Lancia Thema has a Ferrari engine that finally matches the luxury of the styling details; the Autobianchi Y-10 uses the same 'Fire' class engine technology so successfully employed in the cheaper Fiat Uno.

Italian car body designers, like Bertone, Pininfarina and Giugiaro, are still in a world class of their own. Giugiaro has not only been behind recent Fiat successes, but was responsible for the first version of the VW Golf, the Spanish Seat Ibiza and the Korean Hyundai. Similarly, Sergio Pininfarina has designed not only most recent Ferraris, the Lancia Thema, the Alfa-Romeo Spider and the beautiful new Alfa 164, but also the Rolls-Royce Camargue, Austins 1100 and Cambridge, Peugeots 205 and 405 and the new Cadillac Allanté. Faithful to the spirit of his father, Battista Farina ('Pinin' was Sergio's nickname; it is Turin dialect for small), who founded the firm in Turin in 1930, he now runs the firm with three of his children, as well as being the current leader of Confindustria, the Italian confederation of industrialists.

Independent hand-crafted car firms, like Lamborghini (1986 production 238 units) and Maserati (1986 production 4133 units), are booming. Maserati are also collaborating successfully with the American market, with their Q Coupé.

The Italian motorcycle industry has kept its head in the face of Japanese competition (much better than British firms like Norton and BSA with their Alamo co-op last stand) by thinking on their feet. Moto-Guzzi went for the quality, high-volume end of the market, left wide open by the Japanese. The styling and thinking behind the Carabinieri–approved Moto-Guzzi Californian may be unashamedly American, but at least 50% of the bikes on Italian roads are Italian made.

(iv) Fashion and textiles

Several of the general virtues listed above apply particularly to the Italian fashion industry, which has a few other aces as well. A centuries-old artisan tradition in working every conceivable variation of fabric and leather, added to extensive recent research on novel ways of treating or developing them, allows Italian designers to adopt a 'total look' strategy foreign designers can only dream about. The proverbial Italian eye for 'what looks good on a man / woman' permits them to transform fabrics or styles from abroad so that they look 100% Italian. This tendency to elaborate other people's ideas is admitted by only a few designers: Armani has basically re-elaborated the classic Anglo-American adult male wardrobe. The same fact is truer in youth fashion, which apes the Anglo-American street style, repackaging it as something utterly Italian looking. Most international fashion buyers are happy with this, though the highly influential *Women's Wear Daily* editor John Fairchild now boycotts Milan (except Armani), denouncing all Italian designers as brazen copy-cats.

As competition from new rivals, like the USA, Germany and Japan, as well as the traditional France, hots up, Italian designers are exploring every available avenue in order to survive and prosper: market flotation, expansion into other manufacturing fields via franchises – even the financial market.

Top-earning Italian fashion designers

The grossly inflated column 1: sales for all products sold under a designer label, but not produced in-house (not just clothes, but accessories like bags, sunglasses, perfumes, household linen and ceramic tiles); column 2: sales of own-label clothes; column 3: what they spend on advertising annually. (Turnover in billion lire)

(1) Valentino	500	40	18
(2) Versace	440	110	8
(3) Armani	340	55	4
(4) Ferre	280	120	10
(5) Trussardi	214	88	13
(6) Krizia	200	20	6
(7) Enrico Coveri	150	20	4
(8) Laura Biagiotti	115	14	-
(9) Missoni	115	35	7
(10) Mario Valentino	90	80	-

There is another important element behind the success of Italian fashion that is rarely credited: the role of the big textile groups. It is their combination of modern technology, access to large markets, investment capability and, above all, sheer size that has permitted nearly all Italy's fashion designers to expand and prosper. Also not generally recognized is the hold they have over designers, dictating marketing strategy and product development to a great extent.

The most important is the 100-year-old Rivetti family GFT – Gruppo Finanziario Tessile – of Turin, now run by the dynamic Marco Rivetti, in his 40s. It has 7000 work-ers making over 5 million garments a year for customers including Valentino Armani and Ungaro, with a $900 million annual turnover. Marzotto and Zegna (→ 2:viii, above) are among other important names.

Italy is also one of the world's premier jewel-lery manufacturers, of which Balestra 1882 is the world's second largest working in gold. Their 200-strong workforce combine traditional gold-working methods with laser-welding technology. The other giant, Uno-a-Erre of Arezzo, have adopted a Benetton-style last-minute manufacturing system which is revolutionizing production.

(v) The electrical and mechanical industries

Italian producers of *elettrodomestici* – literally 'electric servants', i.e. household appliances – like Zanussi, Candy, Indesit and Ariston, more than hold their own in Italy, with its high domestic demand: the Italians have quite American expectations, changing their entire kitchen armoury with regularity. Without enjoying quite the kudos of certain German rivals, their export figures remain healthy. Italy's hi-fi industry is also fairly buoyant: Brionvega radios, Seleco TVs and Autovox car stereos all have as good a name as imports from Northern Europe or Japan, as does the entire Olivetti office equipment range.

Italy is the world's fifth largest exporter of machine tools, with an internal annual rate of over 12%. Especially successful are the metal-bending equip-ment firm Pedrazzoli and the food-processing machine firm Braibanti. Similarly, Italy features well in various advance technology sectors, like robotics, radar sys-tems and aerospace. Fiat's Comau subsidiary makes industrial robots which are used as much worldwide (General Motors is a major client) as in Italy, where they have successfully automated much of the Fiat auto production line and the gigantic Benetton warehouse stock systems.

(vi) Defence and space technology

Italy produces an almost complete range of defence technology, from warships by Fincantieri to advanced electronic weapons by Contraves, with annual sales peaking in the early 1980s at $6 billion. IRI-subsidiary Selenia employs 13,000 and produces world-class radar systems and advanced military and civilian technol-ogy; ironically for a country with such a poor postal service, they have sold the US Post their patented postal sorting system in a $111 million deal: space technology developed by Selenia Spazio is present on over seventy satellites and forty earth stations. International co-operation has produced even more spectacular results: IRI-owned Agusta and Aeritalia (they are shortly to be merged) are respectively involved in the EH101 helicopter with Britain, and the new Airbus and the pan-European Tornado fighter project.

(vii) Tourism and catering

Italy's natural and artistic beauty, excellent but varied cuisine and climate have long been considered sufficient attractions for tourists; perhaps they were once. The Italian tourist industry is now *in crisi* as a result of the cupidity and unprofessionalism of its operators. World tourism grew by 6.5% in 1987, but only by 4.4% in Italy. Countries like Spain and Yugoslavia may have less overall appeal, but by offering better, more reliable services and lower prices they are beginning to give the Ente Nazionale Italiano di Turismo (ENIT) – the Italian tourist board – serious problems. Foreigners are still drawn by the romantic myth of the simple 'Room with a View' family-run *pensione* or *trattoria*, but are as shocked by the increased prices and decreased quality as other Italians are. There is a perceptible decline, particularly in Italy's restaurants, commensurate with the massive proliferation of American fast food outlets and Chinese restaurants. The Italian Press frequently publishes warnings to the tourist and catering industries, advising them not to kill the goose that laid the golden egg.

Just as with other businesses, hotels are predominantly family run. There are very few big chains. In 1989, the State-owned ENI entrusted its hotel/catering division SEMI to the UK's Trust House Forte, in the hope that it might stop losing so much money (100 billion lire deficit to 1987). Charles Forte already owns two prestige hotels in Italy, Milan's Hotel Gallia and the Eden in Rome. (→ also 2:viii, above)

4. Financial services

Understanding business terms

* *Ente* (literally 'entity'): a State-controlled company, usually a public utility and hence not expected to be that profitable.
* Italians use 'holding' a lot when they just want to say company.
* SpA – Società per Azioni: stock market listed company.
* SRL – Società di Responsibilità Limitata: limited company.
* Names that start 'Fin' indicate finance companies.
* Conf. indicates 'Confederazione', i.e. business confederation.
* *Azienda*: 'firm', in a non-legal sense.
* *Presidente*: chairman
* *Amministratore delegato*: managing director.
* *Consiglio d'amministrazzione*: board of directors.

(i) The stock exchange and investment

Italy's financial capital is very emphatically Milan, so, fittingly, it is Lombardy's *borsa* – stock exchange – rather than Rome's that is the important one. For years it was a small, unexciting but corruptly run floor, where almost three-quarters of total shares were controlled by a small handful of economic dynasties – the Agnellis, Pirellis etc.

Since the mid-1980s, its fortunes have changed considerably. It is still corruptly run; insider trading is quite legal, as it is in France and Spain, it is controlled by the same dynasties (plus a few new ones); it remains small – but it is Europe's fastest growing stock exchange, and arguably the most exciting. It is also extremely volatile, going from bullish to bearish almost overnight; it has a quite hysterical reaction to news. When Black Monday hit Milan in October 1987 to the tune of 25% (similar to London and New York), it provided merely a second instalment to the 28% drop incurred by prices over the year, after a euphoric 1985–6 high, largely stoked by the launch of unit trusts in 1984. Many of the takers were first-time investors who had just discovered the wonderful world of shareholding; they helped shift $54 billion unit trusts in three years. In 1985, there were only 250,000 investors, but by 1988, there were ten times that figure.

The top six European stock exchanges (in billions of US$)

		monthly turnover
(1) Great Britain	796.5	55.3
(2) West Germany	268.0	59.0
(3) France	267.6	15.5
(4) Switzerland	174.0	9.3
(5) Italy	157.1	19.3
(6) Spain	107.2	4.8

(*Financial Times*, Sept. 1989)

However, despite its dynamic profile, *la borsa* is run on thoroughly antiquated lines, and is so unregulated that almost anything goes. There is still a dealing floor, but prices are fixed not continuously, but only once a day, at the end of trading, thus enabling much information to be withheld from buyers. Most dealing takes place illegally outside the floor; Italian brokers don't see what all the fuss about insider trading is about. Share prices are also manipulated, since less than 50% are available to the public; they are in the hands of élite syndicates like Mediobanca. When the big firms ride roughshod over smaller investors – as Gardini did in rearranging the assets of his two companies, Ferruzzi and Montedison – it caused serious panic at the *borsa*, yet no one really criticized him.

Although there has been a vast increase in stock market capitalization over the last ten years, more than doubling to 13% of GDP (bringing it nearer the level of France and West Germany, though still well below other major markets: USA 45%, UK 88%, Japan 110%), the Milan trading floor has not yet reached its full potential. This state of under-capitalization is due mostly to the attitude of company owners, who are reluctant to relinquish even the slightest degree of control of their firms. A fairly common characteristic of Italians, of whatever economic status, is that they greatly dislike the idea of being in debt. The family dynasty approach is closely linked to this reflex; so is the highly unfair preferential shareholder vote system. Less than 50% of Fiat is quoted, while Berlusconi's massive empire remains strictly out of bounds to non-family. As a result, Italy's stock market is much less representative of the national economy than is that of almost any other industrialized country: only about 200 companies are actually listed on the COMIT index. This index measured 100 in 1972, and 709 in September 1989. This figure is also rather misleading in real terms, since only about 10% of these 200 companies actually engage in normal trading. They are almost all controlled by five families/groups.

Some three-quarters of *la borsa* is controlled by a mere nine companies, six of which are family run. They represent a stock exchange within a stock exchange. *La Republica* publishes a weekly graph called 'I signori del Listino', the Lords of the stock market, made up of these leading groups:

Agnelli-Fiat	**26.5%**
IRI	**26.2%**
Assicurazioni Generali	**16.8%**
De Benedetti-Olivetti	**8.8%**
Ferruzzi–Montedison	**7.6%**
Presenti (construction)	**2.8%**
Pirelli	**2.7%**
ENI	**2.4%**
Orlando (steel)	**0.6%**
	9-company total: 99.6%

La Republica, 1989

Consob, the Italian stock exchange control commission, headed by the energetic Franco Piga, has been trying for several years to put Italy's economic house in order. Piga has met with predictable pressure from all sides – the political parties, big business and the brokers – *agenti di borsa* – who all feel (and they are right) that their occult powers over Italian finances will be eroded by his planned reforms. Piga proposes to put the Milan *borsa* on an equal footing with other world markets, and thus, by introducing more transparency and professional behaviour, encourage further investment. This means banning insider trading; obliging companies to furnish clear information regarding mergers and buy-outs, as well as details of financial restructuring; and publishing far more detailed annual reports, clearly explaining profits and investments. The relationship of many companies is quite arcane: Italian newspapers often publish complicated graphs resembling molecular formulae in order to explain the incestuous hierarchical links between apparently different firms.

The Italian public of small investors are generally taken for rather a ride. The enthusiasm for popular capitalism has been intensely generated by the media, with the express backing of business interests, and thus the average punter has little idea of what goes on behind the scenes. Even the sports paper *Corriere dello Sport* has a business page, and the Communist daily *L'Unità* now carries a stock market report; the lunch-time TV news on all channels has a very animated 'live from the stock exchange' report. (→ 1:ACCESS, above)

The ten Italian firms with the highest share value (in billions of lire)

(1) Generali (insurance)	18,310
(2) Fiat (automobile)	18,248
(3) RAS (insurance)	5,311
(4) Stet (telecom)	5,248
(5) Olivetti (computer/data)	5,280
(6) Fondiaria (insurance)	4,435
(7) SIP (telecom)	3,557
(8) Montedison (chemicals)	3,530
(9) Alleanza (insurance)	3,479
(10) Mediobanca (banking)	3,193
(Morgan Stanley Capital International, Geneva 1988)	

Europe's ten firms with the highest share value (in billions of lire)

(1) Royal Dutch	Holland	39,000
(2) BP	UK	38,100
(3) British Telecom	UK	33,800
(4) Shell	UK	26,300
(5) Daimler Benz	West Germany	20,000
(6) Assicurazioni Generali	Italy	18,300
(7) Fiat	Italy	18,200
(8) Nestlé	Switzerland	17,200
(9) Glaxo	UK	17,000
(10) Allianz	West Germany	15,600

Only 40 out of the top 500 firms quoted on the stock exchange are Italian, so few are fully capitalized. The best period for *la borsa* was in May 1986, when Fiat was worth 30 billion lire. If the top six stock exchanges table had been made then, Milan would have been in third, not fifth, place. These figures obviously do not reflect turnover or profitability: contrast Fiat's position.
(Morgan Stanley Capital International, Geneva, 1988)

(ii) What the Italians are buying

The Italians are enthusiastic investors: they traditionally save some 22% of their incomes (compared to 16% in Japan, 11%–12% in Great Britain and France, 3% in the USA), either in the bank or in real estate. Now Italy has been bitten by the stock exchange bug, and investments in government securities, mutual funds (introduced in 1984), bonds and shares have almost trebled since 1975, to around 48% of all family financial assets.

Many first-timers were attracted by the no-nonsense mutual funds, while others went for '*i titoli di stato*' – State-issued bonds: CCT, BOT and BTP. Although inflation is now well within single figures, Italians still have a folk memory of the telephone number inflation of the past, and thus go for short-term bonds, with their extremely high interest rates. The most popular are the three- and six-month BOT loans, which render 9%–10% yields. Their other great attraction is that they are completely tax-free. Despite the government's attempts to render them less attractive, quarterly auctions for them are always sold out, while the capitalization or fresh equity issue of many private firms goes relatively unnoticed, and unbought.

The government is currently involved in a delicate balancing act: on the one hand, trying to lengthen terms of bond maturity and reduce interest rates on CCT, BOT and BTP in order to cut the national debt; on the other, hoping that, come 1992, Italian investors' money will not fly the coop. (→ 1:i, above)

Jolted by big losses sustained during 1987, many first-timers have retired hurt, some putting their money into trust funds or back into their deposit accounts, but most investing in property (not building societies: they don't exist in Italy).

(iii) The banking system and insurance

It seems extraordinary that the people who practically invented banks and finance should be served now by the worst banking system in the industrialized world. The Tuscans can boast the oldest extant bank in the world, Monte dei Paschi di Siena; the Venetians invented double entry book-keeping; while Lombardy became synonymous with long-term investment loans during the Middle Ages. Nowadays, the entire Italian banking system is caught in an unfortunate vicious circle; Italians are among the least convinced bank users anywhere, and are made even more suspicious by the low-grade, high-cost facilities on offer. The peasant-like 'money under the mattress' syndrome means that few Italians have current accounts; the high taxation on bank savings deters most from having deposit accounts; and the general climate of financial mistrust makes cheques, let alone credit-/debit-cards, hard to use. Italians dislike borrowing money, except from within the family circle, and will pay cash even for houses.

With over 80% of the banks in the public sector, and all appointments, from the chairmanship down to tellers, subject to political negotiation, it is not surprising that the service offered is so poor. Not only the bank as institution, but cashiers too, display an arrogance as breathtaking as their inefficiency.

However, to be quite fair to the banks, they have been extremely hidebound by rules and regulations ever since Mussolini acted to stem the damage of the post-Depression banking crisis. There are many services they are not allowed to offer; only recently have controls been relaxed over credit, allowing loans to be longer than eighteen months. They are now allowed to go into merchant banking. Such is the diffidence of Italians towards the banks, that the efforts by regular trading companies like Fiat or even Benetton to set up finance leasing and insurance services have met with considerable success; even Versace is about to jump on the bandwagon.

Italians are also hampered by extremely stringent

Using cheques and credit-cards

Until 1988, you might almost have left your credit-cards at home, so restricted was their usefulness in Italy, and resign yourself to the annoying, old-fashioned practice of travellers' cheques. A massive campaign by American Express, Visa etc. since 1986 has, however, considerably increased the number of places where you pay with plastic; in the early 1980s, there were fewer than in some Third World countries. Still, old habits die hard, and what with the unacceptableness of incorrectly filled-out slips and for purchases under 20,000 lire, their daily use is still too limited. Likewise, all motorway tolls and nearly all petrol stations only take cash. Beware of paying in restaurants and shops with travellers' cheques – the exchange rate they calculate on is invariably way below the official one. Eurocheques are probably the best solution, although many Italian banks impose a 1500 lire duty on each one you, as a foreigner, use. This, however is against EC fair competition rules, and you should protest if they try to charge you.

Dealing with banks

Even in the more modest branches, security measures are impressive – armed guards, double doors which filter you in – but exchange controls, which are currently being loosened up for 1992. It is illegal for Italians to have a bank account, to hold shares or to own property abroad; there are still restrictions on using credit-cards or taking cash for a sum over 2 million lire. Although the Banca d'Italia is trying to prevent the illegal export of capital, it is naturally the small man that these measures hurt, while the *abusivo* practices of the hyper-rich go on undetected.

There is an inordinately large number of banks, yet most of them are very small, and may have as few as one branch. There are still considerable bureaucratic difficulties involved in opening new ones. According to the Banca d'Italia, there are only 2.3 branches per 10,000 Italians, half the rate in other industrialized countries. Many are savings banks – *casse di risparmio* – with each small town having its own. The Banca d'Italia is now encouraging mergers to face 1992, but local political interests tend to count for more than pressing economic necessity. German banks are finding their way into the Italian market already, but the Italian banking institutions still seem only vaguely aware that, as foreign banks move in on a national scale, offering far superior facilities for a lower cost, they will have to get their act together much better in order to survive at all.

The big banks
Banca Nazionale di Lavoro (State-owned: the largest bank in Italy, but 15th in Europe)
Banca Commerciale Italiana (IRI)
San Paolo di Torino (State-owned)
Credito Italiano (IRI)
Banco di Roma (IRI)
Banco di Napoli (State-owned)
Monte dei Paschi di Siena (State-owned and the oldest bank in Italy)
Banco del Santo Spirito (IRI)
Credito Romagnolo (private)
Ambroveneto (private)

Italians have .25 current accounts per head, compared to 1.5 (USA), 1.9 (UK), 2.0 (Japan); they boast 0.1 credit-cards per head, compared to 2.0 per head in the US; only 22 non-cash payments are settled annually in Italy, compared to 75 (UK), and 172 (USA).

Insurance is another sorry field. According to Tests

that's where it ends. Every transaction, however simple, takes an inordinate length of time. Even in the largest branches, queueing is haphazard; you have to take a chance on any window. Despite massive personnel deployment (each branch has an average of twenty-three employees, almost double that of the other main industrialized countries), technical training is limited, and the computer terminals are constantly down. With over three-quarters of the banking sector State-owned, employees have a secure, well-paid job – to be an *impiegato bancario* – bank employee – is a great ambition in Italy – and treat customers with disdain. Hours are short, though they vary slightly from bank to bank: either 9a.m.–1p.m. and 3–4p.m. or straight through to 2p.m.

● To open a bank account in Italy you will need *la residenza*. (→ V, 4: ACCESS – Getting basic documents) Unless you have a personal introduction, you will end up choosing your bank for convenient location rather than for favourable facilities: they are uniformly bad throughout Italy. The awfulness of service has been elevated into a kind of religion. For example, try cashing a personal cheque in a town where your bank has no branch (since nearly all banks are regional, this is most of the time); not even a covering phone-call from your branch will help. This is why Italians often travel with vast wads of notes on them.

● The new alternative is the Bancomat system – automatic cash dispensers which allow you to use the machine of another bank subject to certain conditions (before 10p.m. during weekdays, for a 1000 lire surcharge). Unfortunately, so few Bancomats actually work, above all outside banking hours, that many Italians feel them to be worse than useless: the Press has carried on a lively debate on the matter since their introduction. Since 1989, however, the service has greatly improved.

• Equally annoying is waiting for an incoming cheque to be cleared: the Banca d'Italia estimate that on average this takes a month, though it depends if it is *su piazza* – in the same city – or not. Money-drafts from abroad may be wired into the head office of your Italian bank within hours, but they may take two or three weeks to reach your local branch, at which point you must explain why you are receiving the money: it is always best to say *per regalia* – a gift – whatever the circumstances. Try and get your British bank to send the draft to the London branch of your Italian bank and transfer it that way – it seems to be quicker. For this reason, few Italians have their pay cheque paid into their bank: they go personally to pick it up and then cash it in, regardless of time wastage.

• In the same way that the Italian banks got together to install an almost useless automatic till network, they have also put out a completely useless credit-card – the CartaSì. So few shops accept cheques of any sort, they won't accept ones covered by a card either .

Exchange rates, 1989

The lire is worth:
UK£ = 2209 lire
US$ = 1401 lire
Aus$ = 1097
Can$ = 1183
Punt = 1921
NZ$ = 832
Rand = 501
DM = 720
F.Fr. = 213
S.Fr. = 831

Achats, Brussels, Italy's insurance premiums are the most expensive, bar Greece and Portugal, in Europe, several times more than those in Britain. The Italians are simply not used to the idea: very few houses are insured (→V, 2:i); car insurances rarely go beyond third party (→VIII, 3:ii); and so too life assurance policies have as yet made very little headway. There is currently a concerted attempt being made to pump the market before the influx of foreign competition in 1992, along with private pension schemes.

B.Fr. = 34
Swedish Kr. = 213
Danish Kr. = 186
Norwegian Kr. = 198
Schilling = 103
Florin = 638
Yen = 9.64

5. The social dimension

(i) The trade unions

Italy, like various other European countries, has trade unions that are grouped by political loyalty rather than category of work. The vast majority of union activity is channelled into a mere three unions, and each one is closely linked to a party. The CGIL (Confederazione Generale Italiana del Lavoro) is predominantly Communist, with a Socialist minority faction; UIL (Unione Italiana del Lavoro) is Socialist; while CISL (Confederazione Italiana Sindacati del Lavoro) is Christian Democrat. *Il sindacalismo* – trade unionism – has also witnessed some unusual extremes, in terms both of political attitudes and of working conditions. An imposing political force since the war, during the angry years following *il sessantotto* wide sections of trade unionism became extremely radical, almost revolutionary; yet during the 1980s it has been tamed to a remarkable extent, adapting to the aggressive new capitalism much less painfully than elsewhere in Europe.

From the end of the war until the late 1960s, Italian workers were among the worst paid in Europe, yet in 1972 labour costs became the highest in the world; from 1970 wages increased by 25% per annum, while fringe benefits added 50%–60% to their value. In the decade between 1969 and 1978, real wages rose by 72%. Furthermore, *la cassa integrazione*, an unemployment benefit fund for the temporarily laid off, paid out 90% of earnings. The political climate of the time caused productivity and workmanship to plummet, with catastrophic effects on exports. No one in Italy will touch a used Alfa-Romeo from the early 1970s: at that time, they were deliberately made badly by a sullen workforce. Between 1970 and 1977, Italy had the world's worst strike record, with its worst year in 1975, when seven times as many man-hours were being lost through strikes as in that other strike-prone nation, the UK. Employers were desperate; many were going out of business.

However, the mood changed quite rapidly in the early 1980s. The government relieved hard-pressed employers of some of their responsibility for funding welfare benefits, which passed to a further indebted State; in 1980, 40,000 Fiat workers marched through Turin actually wanting to return to work. Perhaps relieved that the worst was over, Agnelli, in moves later imitated by his colleagues, managed to show considerable flexibility in reaching an agreement with his workforce. In 1988, he signed a union deal, which has revolutionized industrial relations in Italy, guaranteeing Fiat workers ample profit shares in the company. Over the last decade, union leaders have accepted mass lay-offs from tough but reasonable bosses like Marisa Bellisario of Italtel and De Benedetti of Olivetti as an alternative to total corporate bankruptcy. This has been achieved through tact and diplomacy, not, as in Britain, through confrontation. Similarly, union leaders in the 1980s have acceded to many of their legal rights and privileges being whittled down, above all *la scala mobile* – their index-linked salaries – in force since after the war. Even the CGIL leaders, who in 1984 most opposed the abolition of *la scala mobile*, now admit that it was hopelessly inflationary. Union leaders – '*le forze sociali*' – are still consulted on all major economic and social policy issues, giving them at least the impression that their opinions are valued. Italy's largely classless and culture-orientated society of the late 1980s also confers on *i leader sindacali* a far greater degree of social and intellectual respectability than their brothers would receive in other countries.

This is in stark contrast to the post-war years. Low wages and tough, often illegal, working conditions have always presented a particular dilemma to Italian unions, since the entire *boom economico* of the 1950s and 1960s was founded on 'stable' labour costs, as is currently the case in the Far East. People were also quite prepared to accept exploitation, since many of them had just moved from the country to the town, from agriculture to industry, and were grateful for any job they could get. To have fought too hard would have meant mass unemployment.

Union membership has also fluctuated considerably, although Italy still remains, after the UK, the most unionized country in Europe. In 1987 there were 2.8 million members, down from 3.6 million in 1977. However, the general trend is downward: from 60% in 1947 to 33% in 1967, with quite big increases during the politicized *sessantotto* period, falling again in the mid-1980s. Between 1985 and 1986, the *Confederazione* lost an average of 3% of its members. Fiat is less than 30% union-staffed, the new post-smokestack industries even less. Decline is further aided by the lack of a closed-shop law.

Relations between the three components of the federation also change. The Communist-inspired CGIL was founded in 1944, as the only union; during the 1948–50 Cold War period, after the PCI had been excluded from government, America persuaded non-Communist elements to leave CGIL, and set up two rivals, CISL and UIL, funded with American money.

Although their relations pass through stormy patches, all three generally go around in a posse. In the early 1960s, they progressively detached themselves from party control, and thus created a largely successful *confederazione sindacale*: they continue to display a degree of concerted action surprisingly coherent for Italian politics.

There are also other unions: the neo-Fascist CISNAL, largely snubbed by the others, and a series of bite-sized maverick unions – *sindacati autonomi* – which specialize in awkwardly timed strikes in sensitive sectors, like public transport and the postal service. The most recent, and potentially worrying, evolution in Italian trade unionism has been the emergence of the *cobas* – *comitati di base* – non-union grassroots committees in many public sectors, which complain that the CGIL–CISL–UIL confederation has let them down. Although unions and government alike refuse to recognize them, their impact has been catastrophic; private sector bosses are now praying they won't spread to them too.

Labour relations get strained in Italy when the tri-/bi-annual contracts are renewed; whole sectors are negotiated at the same time. La Confindustria, the CBI-like employers' confederation, has a nasty habit of letting the expiry date pass without opening negotiations for the fresh contract, thus leaving workers in an entire sector technically without contract. This is traditionally used as a scare tactic to pressurize unions into moderating their demands. *Il rinnovo del contratto* – contract renewal – is usually the key phrase on striking workers' banners.

Who's who in *I sindacati* (1989)

Current *segretario generale* – leader
- **CGIL: Bruno Trentin (PCI); with *segretario generale aggiunto* – 'additional' general secretary – Ottaviano del Turco (PSI).**
- **CISL: Franco Marini (DC).**
- **UIL: Giorgio Benvenuto (PSI).**

(ii) The employers' federations

These are, in the 1980s, a much more conciliatory bunch than in some European countries. Most are members of Confindustria, founded after World War I as an independent body, which after World War II

has always been close to the Repubblicani and Liberali
– the business parties. Employers in the State sector
belong to Intersind, while those in commerce, agriculture and small firms are members of Confcommercio,
Confagricoltura and Confabi. The cause of most tension
between them and the government, with the unions
jeering loudly from the sidelines, is *evasione fiscale* –
tax evasion – openly advocated or strenuously denied
by turn, but always practised. (→ V, 1:ii)

(iii) Unemployment and underemployment

According to the figures, Italy suffers the worst unemployment of the group of the seven most industrialized
nations. From 11.3% in 1977, it peaked at 14.2%
in 1985 and currently stands at around 11.9% (1989
figures). The categories most hit are women, the
young, and the South: being all three gives you a
30% chance of finding work. On the other hand, for
men over 30 living in the North, there is almost full
employment (fewer than 5% without work). A 1988
CESPE report shows that unemployment increased by
85% between 1977 and 1987, with a total of 3 million
Italians searching for work, nearly half of them for their
first job. That figure has since been slightly reduced. In
fact, since hire/fire laws are so stiff, many bosses are
reluctant to take on fresh staff, penalizing the under-24s
(40% without work) in particular. Much of the political
rhetoric focused on *i giovani* (→ I, 2) derives its strength
from this grim statistic.

Statistic it remains, since there are other factors
involved. First, Italy's huge black economy – by some
estimates up to 25% of GNP – which finds work for
many of those officially out of work (→ V, 1:vi): unfortunately, in the South that tends to mean organized
crime. (→ V, 2:iii) Secondly, the national pension scheme,
INPS (→ 5:iv, below), pays out to an estimated 4.5 million
fairly able-bodied folk, who are prepared to be officially
'invalidi' to keep others in work. (→ IV, 4:ACCESS-Welfare
facilities) All sides propose part-time work as a solution,
though Italy still has only 5.5%, far below most other
industrialized nations, on part time.

(iv) Incomes and pensions – *il sorpasso*?

Official salaries in Italy are surprisingly low; this perhaps
explains why many people supplement theirs with
second or third jobs. (→V, 1:vi) The government-
commissioned Carniti report (1987) made some fascinating findings about income distribution: namely, that
workers in 'unprotected sectors' – i.e. that don't export
goods, and thus suffer foreign competition – earn far less
than workers in monopolistic 'protected sectors'. The

1987 average hourly wage is 11,000 lire, with bank and insurance company clerks earning double the national average (some 21,000 lire per hour), while internationally competitive sectors like hotels and footwear/clothing earn a mere 9000 and 8000 lire, respectively. Contrary to expectations, there is only a marginal income discrepancy between the prosperous North and the impoverished, underemployed South. Other surveys prove this point: the difference in average income between the richest *comune* (all in the North) and the poorest (all in the South) is of some 27 million lire.

Those with *la maturità* – high school certificate – have a notably higher income: in banking, 73.8% have *la maturità*, and earn 21,000 lire an hour; in metal, this drops to 17.5% and 10,000 lire per hour; in clothing, to 6% and 7265 per hour.
(CESPE, 1988)

A Milanese metal worker takes home an average of 1,220,000 lire per calendar month, while his/her fellow office worker takes home 1,430,000 lire.

Monthly expenditure per head is 620,000 lire.

22% manage to save, as compared to 3% in the US.

52% of families live on one income.
(ISTAT, 1988)

Italy, like Japan, pensions off men at 60, women at 55, though in the wake of the massive payments crisis, this looks likely to be shifted upwards towards the British or American level. In 1960, Italy spent some 5.5% of GDP on its old people, rather above the OECD average, but by 1985 this figure had already reached 15.6% – way higher than any other state; this sum represents 30% of total government spending. By the year 2000, this will be 20% (UK 7.5%, US 8.2%), unless serious steps are taken soon. As it is, INPS – Istituto Nazionale della Previdenza Sociale – maintains almost one pensioner for every person in work. Not that pensions are that generous. According to the Carniti report (1987), bank workers top the scale with 23.2 million lire per annum, 4 million more even than doctors, while private sector manual workers have to scrape by on a mere 8.2 million.

From the official figures quoted above, it is hard to imagine how the Italians can now be better off than the British, or, indeed, the French, as their government has been insisting since 1987. But there are so many different statistics available, and these can be read (or manipulated) in so many different ways, that a truly non-partisan verdict is difficult to reach. Italy's official GDP (which now includes a conservative 15% estimate for the black economy) now easily tops Britain's, but fluctuating exchange rates can easily alter that. The 'purchasing power parities' approach, favoured by economists, which tots up the cost of common items, may show different results again.

Rising labour costs

Country	1988	1989 (estimate)
Italy	8.4.%	10.5%
UK	7.8%	8.0%
USA	6.0%	6.0%
France	4.5%	3.8%
West Germany	3.8%	3.3%
Japan	3.3%	4.3%
(Confindustria)		

Another yardstick used is that of consumer goods: in the battle of the dishwashers. Italy boasts substantially more of these, and of washing machines, cars and second homes, while Britain wins effortlessly on VCRs, insurance policies and credit-cards, and, just, on TV sets. Without question, Italians have far more expensive new clothes, but then again, the British take many more foreign holidays.

Although this may seem rather a pointless argument,

The cost of living

Denmark	136.5%
Japan	134.5%
West Germany	113%
France	104%
Belgium	100% (used as reference point)
Ireland	96%
Italy	95%
Holland	94.5%
UK	94.5%
USA	93.5%
Luxembourg	91%
Spain	80%
Greece	71%
Portugal	59%
(Eurostat, Brussels, 1989)	

the Press of both countries (particularly Italy's) don't see it that way at all. It seems to matter very much to the Italians to show that they are better off than the British, who in turn don't seem to appreciate the comparison. But even if Italian salaries are considerably lower than British ones, they certainly seem to have more money in their pockets, even though they generally have to pay out more for most things – transport and housing excepted – than the British do. Having a wonderful climate gives the average Italian the kind of lifestyle far richer English people have to pay for, but on the other hand, many of the community services still offered in Great Britain cost very dear in Italy.

La manodopera – The work force

Total	**23,642,000**
Employed	**20,820,000**
Men	**13,732,000**
Women	**7,088,000**
Unemployed	**2,822,000**
First-job seekers	**2,302,000**
Previously employed	**518,000**
Men	**1,208,000**
Women	**1,614,000**
(ISTAT, April 1989)	

Employment and unemployment: men / women

	year of survey	Italy	UK
Population	(1987)	57.3 million	56.9 million
Female as % of total	(1987)	51.4%	51.3%
% of women in civilian employment	(1986)	33.8%	42.9%
Women's earnings as % of men's	(1985)	83.9%	69.3%
Male unemployment rate	(1988)	8.2%	8.0%
Female unemployment rate	(1988)	19.9%	7.0%
Women as % of total unemployed	(1988)	57.6%	38.7%
(Eurostat, Brussels 1988)			

La disoccupazione: unemployment

The overall national rate is 11.9% (ISTAT, July 1989)

Centre/North	Men 5% Women	13%	Aged 14–29 45%
Mezzogiorno	Men 14% Women	32%	Aged 14–29 22%

the richest countries in the world

	Incomes per capita
Switzerland	**$21,330**
USA	**$18,530**
Norway	**$17,190**
United Arab Emirates	**$15,830**
Japan	**$15,760**
Sweden	**$15,550**
Canada	**$15,160**
Denmark	**$14,930**
Kuwait	**$14,610**
Finland	**$14,470**
West Germany	**$14,400**
France	**$12,790**
Austria	**$11,980**
Holland	**$11,860**
Belgium	**$11,480**
Australia	**$11,100**
UK	**$10,420**
Italy	**$10,350**
Hong Kong	**$8070**
Singapore	**$7940**

If the Italians' use of their leisure time still looks rather passive, the way they spend their money certainly isn't. The demand for consumer services as well as goods, together with the widespread respect for *la cultura* in a mostly classless society, has created in Italy an even greater appetite for the arts as a prestige leisure activity than in other countries. Italy's often strident media bears a large responsibility for this relentless flaunting of wealth, while the Italian cultural and social tradition has always had a strong propensity for anything visually spectacular. It is now beginning to be clear to everyone that the boundaries separating good taste from vulgarity need redefining.

For all the noisy attention paid it, the Italian contemporary arts scene has a curiously patchy record. Part of the problem seems to be that Italy tends to be a victim of its own success. Conscious of its enormous cultural heritage – UNESCO estimates that over two-thirds of the Western world's visual arts heritage is in Italy – the Italian arts community gives the distinct impression of feeling it need not make any further effort. During the 1980s, this effect was heightened by the tendency to apply the prestige-laden 'Made in Italy' label to cultural as well as industrial products. Quite separate from the quality of current output is the quality of arts administration. Private arts sponsorship is now more widespread in Italy than in the rest of Europe, largely the result of the State's disastrous record in caring for the entire arts sector. This is due to a lack of sufficient funds, to political meddling, and, partly, to technical incompetence.

On account of their more commercial basis, and the more immediate nature of their output, the media offer a more accurate reflection than the arts of Italy's current state. There is a great divergence between the audiovisual régime, which has permitted over the last decade the proliferation of radio and TV stations – creating a very modern sense of cut-throat competition, of the sort that Britain has not yet experienced – and the world of newspaper publishing, which seems to have stood still for decades. This is not altogether a bad thing, since the dailies tend all to be 'quality' – low in circulation, high of brow, and very wordy. The same thing could be said for book publishing, although the burgeoning market for magazines is indicative of a radically different, much racier tradition, one that has been emulated with considerable success by television. The formerly cosy world of the old publishing empires is now crumbling, as the business moghuls add titles and imprints – as well as TV stations – to their own, much larger empires.

1. Consumerism and hedonism

(i) *Il lusso di massa*

In Chapter VI, we saw how the Italians make the perfect exponents of the Thatcherian enterprise culture, with their traditionally frugal, hard-working business acumen, and their recent embracing of investments and share-owning. By the same token, the Italians *en masse* have become Europe's greatest consumers, with a carefree, luxury-loving materialist ethos that brings them far nearer to North Americans than to most of their continental neighbours. The predominance of an intentionally American-derived lifestyle in advertising and the media is evidence of this.

The 1980s were pretty hedonistic everywhere in the West, but somehow in Italy it went further. There seem to be several quite separate reasons for this. Italy's economic growth since the 1950s has created an entire class of *nuovi ricchi* anxious to enjoy the fruits of their success. The explosion of what Italians call il 'Made in Italy' – the Milan-based fashion and design industries – coincided perfectly with the rise in people's incomes and expectations, from the businessman who can still remember his barefoot childhood, to the growth of Italy's economy since the war, to the increase from 150,000 automobiles on the roads in 1948 to over 24 million in 1988. It is thus unsurprising that many Italians' social attitudes should resemble the brassy, optimistic ostentation of mid-19th-century English society.

Italy's climate, environment and traditions also contribute to the new mood. The plethora of yachts and boats jamming Italy's leisure ports, and the overcrowded ski resorts and restaurants, may suggest untold wealth and luxury to many foreigners, who have to travel, and thus spend, much more to enjoy what the Italians see as quite simple pleasures.

But it is the recent shift in the West's political mood that has perhaps had the most impact. If the 1970s were generally a period of liberal ideas and economic stagnation worldwide, symbolized by the decline of the Carter administration, in Italy the ravages of *il sessantotto* and *il terrorismo* (→ V, 2:v–vi) went much further – and consequently the Italians were much keener to throw them off. The international, hard-nosed New Right era, epitomized by Reagan and Thatcher, scarcely affected Italy's stagnant consensus politics at official level, but their vision of individual enterprise and economic well-being was embraced by Italian society at large with considerable enthusiasm. Around the end of the 1970s, the collapse of Italian post-1968 left-wing ideology and social attitudes was followed by a wholesale rehabilitation of certain traditional social reflexes, like *la bella figura* and *la dolce vita* (→ 2:ii, below), with indecent haste.

Liberal newspapers and magazines like *La Repubblica* and *L'Espresso*, once full of buzzwords and phrases like *impegnato* – politically committed – and *la cultura alternativa*, suddenly replaced them with keywords like *raffinatissimo* – sophisticated – and *i salotti dorati* – gilded salon society. At the same time, encouraged by the remarkable success of the business-chic magazine *Capital* (the title was deliberately ironic and ambiguous), publishers have flooded the news-stands with glossy luxury lifestyle titles like *Il Piacere* – pleasure – *Dynasty* and the outrageous *Class*. (→ 7:ii–iii, below) Thus one of the most popular cult catchphrases of the mid-1980s was coined by media pundit Roberto D'Agostino: '*edonismo reaganiano*' – Reaganite hedonism.

There are now signs that some Italians are beginning to tire of this decade of unadulterated pleasure and consumerism. *Corriere della Sera* recently ran an acerbic front-page leader criticizing the obsessive pursuit of perfect summer holidays, poetically entitled 'L'INFERNO DELLA GOIA'. In contrast to certain other nationalities, the Italians have developed very exacting standards in the pursuit of pleasure. They may be stoical and determined in their work (if self-employed), and put up with the lousiest postal service and public adiministration in the West with a resigned shrug of the shoulders, but as consumers they always go for the best.

Italians have an almost New World impatience with class restrictions, while what left-wing sentiment in other European countries (like Britain) would grumblingly classify as bourgeois or self-indulgent is enthusiastically aspired to by every social class. If people can't afford luxury, then they will work until they can. It was the Italians more than the French who went in for designer labels everywhere (the rest of the world copied), recognizing that a shop assistant had every bit as much right to a Louis Vuitton bag or a Bulgari watch as a top fashion editor, and that a car mechanic was as ideal a target customer for imported luxury clothes like Lacoste and Timberland as a rising young executive. (→ 1:ii, below) The thinking behind this reflex is called *il lusso di massa* – luxury for everyone.

The consumer boom in Italy is directly affected by the *abusivismo* mentality. A vast proportion of the nation's income is undeclared, and is thus free to be spent on more luxury goods. Although some 20% of the economy is calculated to be black, thus losing countless millions in tax revenue, the government implicitly accepts this state of affairs, since the resultant increased consumer spending renders the economy so buoyant. (→ V, 1:ii) In a country where the lifestyle (quite apart from climate considerations) is among the most attractive in the West, but where official figures speak of an average single income as 1.2 million lire per calendar month, with some 22% of families earning less than 1 million and only 4.5% families more than 4 million (→ VI, 5:iv) this has to be the explanation.

Although the cost of living is now higher than in most other European countries, with wages apparently lower, Italians are both spending – and, surprisingly, saving

– more than anyone else. *La borsa* – the Milan stock exchange – is now all the rage with first-time investors, who have embraced the Thatcher dream of popular capitalism with even greater conviction than the British. (→ VI, 4:i) Although the media continues to talk of *la crisi economica*, just as it did ten or fifteen years ago, most Italians feel they've never had it so good.

• **To buy a colour TV, the average Italian worker has to work 134 hours; the average British worker has to work 56 hours and the average Japanese 85 hours.**
• **To buy a chicken a US worker has to work 9 minutes, but an Italian worker 45 minutes.**
(International Federation of Metalworkers, 1988)

(ii) The Italian dress sense

According to popular modern myth, most Italians – of either sex – are so naturally stylish that they would look stunning dressed even in a plastic bag. In theory, this may be true: their sense of physical presence is the envy of all nations. (→ II, 6:iv) In practice, it is meaningless, since many Italians wouldn't leave their bedroom, let alone their apartment, unless they were sure they looked like a million lire, and were clad in the smartest clothes they could – or even couldn't – afford.

The bottom line of *bella figura* is concerned less with elegance than with implied wealth. The Milanese designer boom took off in the 1970s not so much because there were enough Italians who were committed to being superbly dressed (there might have been a run on refuse bags instead) as because there were enough people prepared to spend vast sums of money in order to look as though they'd spent even more.

Consequently, Milan took over from Paris as the centre of world fashion not because their designers were better (though, arguably, many were), but because they opened up two new markets: men; and the less well off. The 1980s' economic boom then ensured that many of these people became well off, thus encouraging a new wave of customers. The rhetoric surrounding il 'Made in Italy' then persuaded Italians that being extravagant in clothes shops was a new form of patriotism. (→ III, 6:iii)

Although Italy's plethora of self-appointed style warriors (often the designers themselves) continue to lecture their audience on achieving stylishness with inexpensive or even second-hand clothes, the punters want none of it. If something, however well made or stylish, isn't *firmato* – designer label – they don't want it. This is as convenient for the counterfeiters as it is for the designers themselves: faced with the choice between a shoddily made rip-off Lacoste and a generic but well-made polo shirt, 95% of Italians go for the croc.

In fact, it is more this label snobbery than discerning fashion sense that typifies the worldwide export success known as 'Italian style'. Label fetishism breeds a safety-in-numbers neurosis that foreign fashion hounds find most disconcerting on hitting Italy for the first time: everyone (each according to their age/peer group) is wearing the same thing. They are dressed expensively, but identically. This is particularly evident among the young. While the essential philosophy behind most hip Anglo/American street fashions is a funky DIY approach, which spurns chain-store straightness, all but the most individualist young Italians want to look all shop-bought, even when they are trying to copy funky street fashions. Increasingly, this Italian clean-cut ethos has sold well abroad, often to the very kind of people whose approach Italian designers have tried to copy. The double irony of this is particularly acute in Giorgio Armani's Emporio Armani youth-orientated (but still very expensive) shops: first, because most of the clothes stocked are merely lookalikes of earthier prototypes that bourgeois-minded young Italians wouldn't touch – from thrift-shop tweed jackets to Californian cut-off jeans; and secondly, because this stuff is considered real hot by hip foreigners who have been penetrated by Italian-style label fetishism.

The 1980s' economic boom in Italy has seen an interesting case of the clothes making the man: to be a yuppie in Italy has to do not with what you do, but with how you dress. this observation seems less remarkable now than it did a few years ago, because this attitude has been widely exported and now affects how men dress all over the West. The so-called yuppie chic (stripy shirts and ties, double-breasted Prince of Wales suits, smart leather jackets and moccasins) currently flooding the world's chain-stores (like the UK's Next) is consciously moulded on an Italian model. The curious thing is that, for the Italians, this look is either American or British. What has really happened is that British notions on male grooming have been re-elaborated by the Americans (most notably Ralph Lauren) and then imported by the ideas-hungry Italians. Much of the so-called Italian Look as championed by Giorgio Armani originally derived from traditional British tailoring. Indeed, many fashion-conscious Italian executives affect to make up much of their wardrobes from imported semi-bespoke tailored clothes with British or American names, even though Italy has plenty of its own.

Italy has become famous for its big name designers rather than for a more discreet tailoring tradition, which is as good as anything elsewhere in the world. It is exemplified by: Domenico Caraceni, who lost his sight in World War I and had half of the vision of one eye restored by surgery. Nonetheless, he opened a *Sartoria* in Rome and his suits soon came to be worn by the entire aristocracy, D'Annunzio, the last two Italian Kings and Edward, Prince of Wales (who kept it quiet so as not to offend Savile Row). He opened ateliers in Paris, Naples and Milan. His son Augusto, and now his granddaughters, have carried on the tradition. Perfect copies of his original models from the 1930s are now made by Lubiam.

● Angelo Litrico: the Rome salon of this remarkable fisherman turned bespoke tailor was an early temply of sartorial détente, since he dressed Kennedy and Khrushchev, Brezhnev and Gorbachev, as well as generations of the international jet set. As London Underground users may have noticed, his heirs have done a franchising deal with C & A.

● 20% of Italian men have shirts made to measure, and 43% of both sexes have bags, shoes etc. made to measure.
● 92% of all Italians have a new, best outfit.
● 22.5% go to a tailor/seamstress.
● 45% have mostly non-designer-label casual clothes, 34% have some designer-label stuff, and 17.5% have *abbigliamento classico firmato* – designer smart/conservative clothes.
● 18% have mass-production jewels; 3% have exclusive-name jewellery (Bulgari, Gucci etc.).
(CENSIS)

2. *Ozio* and free time

There is an essential difference between Mediterranean and Anglo-Saxon attitudes to life in the use of free time. Our tradition of having two mandatory days' rest a week has been imported into Italy, as in many other countries, in name at least, as *il weekend*, though it is still partial: schools and most public offices still work Saturday mornings. Our 9–5 working week is something of a novelty to Italians, who call it *l'orario americano*: schools, shops and businesses often start earlier than we could handle, at 8 or 8.30 a.m., but usually finish earlier: government offices and public buildings close down for the day from 1 to 2 p.m. Shops and other offices have traditionally had the long 1–4 lunch-break, incorporating *la siesta*, although increasingly *l'orario americano* is taking over – busy cities like Milan have little time for a *siesta*. (→ VI, 1: ACCESS – Doing business with Italians)

The advantage of clocking off at 2 p.m. is perceived by most Italians as permitting one to do a second or even third job, much more than to sand down the floor boards or join a pottery class. The English-speaking world, famous for its sense of guilt about idleness, often transform leisure time into an alternative existence – different, but purposeful and practical. Italians do not subscribe to this work hard, play hard notion, and don't see anything intrinsically slobbish about doing nothing all weekend, or in the evenings. Times haven't changed from when Stendhal observed that 'a Roman Matron in her whole life will go only about as far as a young English girl does on a single country walk'. Similarly, most Italians view our enthusiasm for gardening, DIY and yoga classes with a bemusement derived largely from the pre-war peasant attitudes, and still common in developing countries, where people are probably too tired after work to think about doing anything except hanging out. Any form of gratuitous bodily exertion out of work, especially by males (thus excluding exhausting processes like housework and cooking: → I, 3:iv), are still seen as a loss of *bella figura*. The acceptance of sports as a smart pastime is very recent. (→ VIII, 4)

Once again disproving the Italians' theory that all their habits derive from the ancient Romans, it has to be said that there was also a strong classical tradition in favour of active leisure along Anglo-Saxon lines, which was much praised by the ancients. The Romans, whom we rightly never think of as a lazy people, considered leisure – *otium* – as the optimum pursuit, and for them it meant doing the things they actively

Nightlife

To punters used to the nightlife of London, New York and Paris, Amsterdam or Sydney – and many far smaller foreign cities – going out clubbing in Italy is surprisingly disappointing.

● **Company:** To the Italians, the whole idea of entertainment and enjoying oneself is so closely linked to the company of others that most of them would far rather stay at home than see a show or eat out alone. However used you may be to going out by yourself, you will be made to feel weird doing so in most of Italy: people will look at you with surprise, or even pity. If you can't beat 'em, you may as well join 'em. This unspoken imperative about going out in company makes it correspondingly easy to call people up, even if you've met only once, and suggest meeting. (Just don't be surprised if they don't remember you or say they're already booked up for the coming weekend.) (→ I, 2 and ACCESS – Dealing with friends and Breaking the ice) Most Italians are very *disponibile* – amenable – so even if they're not that wild about you, they'll probably agree out of habit. That way, you will meet their friends. The fact that people rely on each other so much more for entertainment partly explains why the *locali* – nightspots – you may visit seem so stale.

● **Alchohol:** drinking is not a central part of conviviality: in a bar, Italians will nurse a beer for hours; aperitifs are usually downed in minutes. Getting drunk is a total no-no: remember your *bella figura*. Tipping is optional; some small change is enough. (→ VIII, 1:ii)

● **Finding out: in the absence of listings magazines, rely on newspapers.** *La Repubblica* **and** *Corriere della Sera* **carry fairly exhaustive daily accounts, with a fuller version in their weekly magazine. (V, 4:**ACCESS **– Useful information)**

● *Locali* **– nightspots: the social atrophy that infects Italy means that there is an extremely low turnover of venues, as with pop singers. For all the Italian obsession with visual impact, even the décor doesn't seem to change for years on end. Discothèques are several seasons, if not whole light-years, behind London, New York, and Paris. The idea of specialist music, or nightly residencies, doesn't exist; if something like House, Rare Groove or anything internationally current does appear in Italy, it gets swallowed up inside a bland generic disco formula. The absence of a black community (what few there are tend to go to their own places) robs the clubs of the funky atmosphere you're probably used to.**

Italy hasn't discovered dress codes, since there are no specialist clubs. The general rule is to over-dress: *bella figura* **again. Not having to pay to get in is a point of pride: many punters will hassle the bouncer for hours. However, to encourage business, some places are free on weekdays anyway. Entrance is otherwise expensive, considering how little is offered inside: it starts at 15,000 lire, but includes** *prima consumazione* **– your first drink; after that, they're expensive.**

Gay clubs and bars are relatively scarce on the ground, but popular with straights – the music is generally better. People go there to pose rather than to score: Italian gays are often too hung up on themselves to want to talk to strangers.

enjoyed. Significantly, they designated work or business as *negotium* – literally absence of leisure, since they *had* to work. However, in modern Italian *ozio* indicates a more passive form of leisure, which in English usually translates as sloth. (*Negozio* is a shop: cf. the English 'negotiate'.) Cicero, on the other hand, theorized a lot about doing interesting things as in his phrase about *cum dignitate otium* – leisure with honour – being the best thing.

The idea of sleepy Italian villages peopled with old peasants sitting on wooden chairs in the street is easy for foreigners to assimilate; what always surprises them is seeing the same thing in a modern urban context. Witness those young people all dressed up, but with nowhere to go. As mentioned earlier, *stare insieme* – just being together – is the important occupation for your spare time; not doing anything special. (→ I, 4:i) That is why Italian cities offer comparatively little to do in the evenings, apart from strolling about or eating out. Nightspots for all ages are dull and unimaginative; there is no real sense of initiative. Most young Italians find the idea of actually having to do something themselves, from organizing a pursuit-orientated weekend somewhere to dressing up for a *carnevale* party, *troppo impegnativo* – too much trouble – and thus prefer to stay at home or turn up in their street clothes. Making an effort in spare time is not what it's about. This all seems to contrast sharply with the common idea of Italians as being exuberant and rising to the occasion: that happens, but only on the spur of the moment; if it involves planning, forget it.

(i) *Locali* – nightspots

A 1988 ISTAT survey confirms what is evident even to the dullest observer – that the number of registered *locali* (premises licensed to offer any kind of entertainment or refreshment) is rocketing, by about 10% a year. Surprisingly, Italy discovered American hamburger joints only recently, but since 1985 *il fast food* – take-away places – has been challenging eating at home, or at *la pizzeria*, as teenage Italians' favourite place for gorging themselves. Correspondingly, there are more discothèques, billiard halls, piano bars and clubs of all descriptions than ever before. (→ I, 3:ACCESS – Meeting other men; VI, 1:ACCESS – Doing business with Italians; VIII, 1:i)

(ii) *Mondanità, La dolce vita* and all that

Rome's Via Veneto, object of many a 1950s-style nostalgia pilgrim, is an anti-climax. Attempts over the last decade to revive its former splendour have not worked. The media endlessly profile the former protagonists of *la dolce vita* (itself a media invention at the time), hoping that something exciting will reproduce itself. It won't, because in the 1950s Italy's high society could hang out in clubs without fear of meeting *hoi polloi*, beyond the odd *paparazzo* hassling them with a camera. There has been a social, and media, revolution since then. As a result, everything takes place in private homes. The names are always the same, from four distinct groups – aristocrats, intellectuals, politicians and industrialists. *Il salotto* – the drawing room – is the key venue; Marta Marzotto, Bona Frescobaldi (friend of Prince Charles) and Marina Ripa de Meana are the most hyped hostesses. Milan and Turin provide the industrialists (the Agnelli clan; the fashion designers; lots of bankers: → VI: 2) Rome is home to most of the politicians and aristocratic families that mix (Colonna, Sforza, Barberini, Chigi, Ruspoli, Giovanelli, Torlonia, represented at several generations: (→ IV, 3:i) chic intellectuals can be from anywhere.

Ideas are sexy in Italy: to have author Umberto Eco or *La Repubblica* editor Eugenio Scalfari in your *salotto* is considered a bigger deal than getting a billionaire.

(iii) Gambling

Despite very restrictive laws, which permit a mere four casinos in the whole of Italy, the nation is in the throes of a mass gambling psychosis similar to Spain's.

In a recent report entitled '*Giocomania*' – gaming fever – CENSIS showed how Italians, after the Americans and the oil-rich Arabs, are the world's top gamblers. They play for some 28 billion lire a day, amounting to 10,000 billion a year. Apart from the 2 million who frequent the tables at the four northern resorts of San Remo, San Vincent, Campione and Venice, there are even more assiduous Italian visitors to casinos beyond the borders – the Côte d'Azur, Yugoslavia, Germany and North Africa. San Vincent has the dubious distinction of being Europe's largest casino, in terms of size, entrants and turnover.

The State monopoly football pools, Totip, are a national institution, with a significant portion of news and sports media devoted to them. Since the invention of numerous computer-based systems made winning much easier, *il tredici* – a clean sweep of thirteen answers – now nets much smaller winnings. Both the State and individual regions or city councils organize annual lotteries with multi-billion lire prizes. Vast armies of the halt and lame are employed around Italy selling *lotteria* tickets in the street – at around 5000 lire – while numerous variety TV programmes feature games linked to a certain *lotteria* throughout their season,

(→ I, 3:xi)

Fashionable bars with tables outside constitute the basis of summer city social life. Many people sit there without even drinking anything all evening. Wine bars do not exist, but fake English pubs do.

In summer, Italians go to a *gelateria* after dinner the way the British go to the pub; they have a quick one, then leave. Teenagers now like to hang out at *il fast food*.

Piano bars are the expensive, seedy descendants of pre-war jazz clubs. A must to avoid. Videobars are something of a hype, and unnecessary, seeing that Italy has so much rock video on TV. They are regular bars with a couple of VCRs relaying Video Music. (→ 6:i, below)

There are lots of jazz clubs, ranging from the stale and corny to the authentic 1950s' feel; most are to be recommended, provided you like that style of jazz.

● Summer events and fêtes: provincial towns and villages often put on an annual *sagra* – harvest festival – for their local prize product – strawberries, truffles, sausages; outdoor banquets are organized. (→ II, 3: ACCESS – What is still regional in Italy) The Communist Party has something similar, *la Festa dell' Unità*: one is put on in every area each summer, and includes concerts, open-air meals and funfairs, as well as some discreet political propaganda.

including the final prize-winning draw. Betting on the horses and the dogs is common, but neither so lucrative nor so well established in Italy as in France or Britain: flushed with success after their takeover of *le Tiercé* in France in the mid-1980s, Britain's gaming colossus had been tempted to repeat the strategy in Italy, but were warned off when they saw how poorly developed the sector was.

Inevitably, gambling of all sorts in Italy is intimately associated with *abusivismo*, most prominently with the activities of organized crime, in terms both of laundered money and of illegal gambling networks. (→ V, 2:iii) In all its various forms, but most notoriously *il totonero* – the illegal football pools – and especially in cities like Naples, it accounts for almost half the legal takings again: 4000 billion lire a year.

(iv) *Feste*: holidays

Institutionalized whooping it up or mellowing out has been drastically reduced over the centuries: towards the end of the Roman Empire, there were some 200 feast-days a year. During the Christian era, these have been gradually reduced: a century ago there were forty; there are now only ten. With Spain clocking up fourteen, Austria thirteen, Germany twelve, Sweden eleven, and France, the Netherlands, Belgium, Norway and Denmark also ten, only the US (nine), Britain (eight), and Switzerland (six) have fewer.

If they occur on a Thursday or a Tuesday, it is very common for Italians to take the intermediate day off too, often without permission. This time-honoured tradition (officially discouraged) is called *il ponte* – the bridge.

(v) Summer holidays

As in France, August is the sacrosanct month, when everything in the major cities seems to close down. Tourists, who arrive above all during August, experience great difficulty in finding hotels, restaurants and bars that are open, with about 75% being closed at any one time. Only very recently, in the late 1980s, has it crossed the minds of newspapers to do their readers the service of publishing comprehensive lists of chemists, petrol stations or restaurants open over the summer period: tourists should read them too. (→ V, 4:ACCESS – Useful information)

However, the habit of the inconvenient August curfew has declined quite considerably over the last five years, since far more Italians now spread their holidays, and, partly as a result of the vigorous cultural programmes dreamed up by the *estate romana* and its offshoots (→ 3: ii, below), no longer feel beyond the pale if they stay over

---

National holidays

1 January: New Year – *Capodanno*

6 January: Epiphany – *La Befana* (movable) Easter Monday – *Pasquetta*

25 April: Liberation Day – *Anniversario della Liberazione*

1 May: May day – *primo maggio*

15 August: Assumption – *Ferragosto*

1 November: All Saints' – *Ognissanti*

8 December: Immaculate Conception – *L'Immacolata Concezione*

25 December: Christmas Day – *Natale*

26 December: Boxing Day – *Santo Stefano*

While Christmas Day, Boxing Day, New Year's and May Day and Easter Monday are common to most Western countries, Italy does not celebrate Good Friday, Ascension Day or Whitsun, when business is open as usual.

4 October is technically the national day, being the feast-day of St Francis of Assisi, Italy's patron saint, but it is not a holiday.

25 April, Liberation Day (World War II), however, is while 6 January (*La Befana*) and 15 August

in the city while 'everybody' is elsewhere. It is now quite fashionable to do the reverse and appreciate the joys of easier parking and driving, less noise and people etc.

Driving, especially on motorways, is hazardous around the beginning and end of the holiday periods: now pamphlets, often calculated several months in advance (available at motorway toll-booths and service stops), are published advising Italians when to travel. The 1988 introduction of the 110 k.p.h. *autostrada* speed limit for the summer months produced sensational protests, but it also saw a vast reduction in accidents (30%) and in petrol consumption.

(*Ferragosto*), though religious days, have far stronger pagan connotations. Only *Ognissanti* and *L'Immacolata Concezione* retain a largely religious significance.

Each city has its own *santo padrono* – patron saint – whose feast-day usually involves some kind of religious and civic celebration.

Italians abroad

● **Eastern Europe: far closer and more appealing to the Italian mentality than to the English-speaking one, and enjoying a particular boom in the late 1960s and through the 1970s: the enthusiasm is still there, especially since the political changes. Italian intellectuals have a fondness for what they call *la cultura mitteleuropea*, which makes all corners of the former Habsburg Empire a pilgrimage area.**
● ***Tossicodipendenti* – heroin addicts – head for Thailand/Bali/Goa.**
● ***Nuovi ricchi* hedonists go tropical – the Seychelles, the Maldives or, latterly, Kenya.**
● **Paris/Barcelona/London: there are perennial arguments about which is the all-time favourite European city: Barcelona wins with a trendy minority; Paris with the more traditional intellectual, nostalgic for a Latin capital of culture and wishing Italy could be like that; London with those who want to do a course – language or street culture.**
● **The USA comes and goes, depending also on exchange rates; the States is so much a part of the Italian mental fantasy geography that to go there is like a medieval pilgrimage.**
● **Working holidays: impossible. Grape-picking in France, archaeological digs in Tuscany or student camp overseeing in the USA are all quite foreign to the Italian nature.**

(vi) Where the Italians go for their holidays

Foreign travel is still far from being the massive industry it is elsewhere, for numerous reasons. The Italians are neither particularly adventurous nor prepared to go without creature comforts; there is no tradition at all of bargain/charter tours and flights; their own country has quite enough sun and natural beauty to keep them going; as a result, many people have second homes – either of their own, or of relations, who expect them to visit – at the beach, in the country or in the mountains.

The Italians' rather unimaginative, lazy tendency to spend a month sprawled on the beach was widely criticized in the 1970s and early 1980s, when it was fashionable to be *impegnato* – committed. The left-wing news magazines exhorted their readers to embrace the idea of *la vacanza intelligente* – the thinking person's holiday – visiting off-beat sites at home, but, above all, abroad.

In case you've never noticed, the Italians who do go abroad stick together like clams, and go only to places that are fashionable. This explains why in certain places, they seem so ubiquitous although far fewer go abroad than, say, the Germans.

- **In 1988, 55% of Italians went away for at least four days (in 1985, it was 49%); 33% had only one holiday, while 13% went away twice a year, and 7.8% three times. 60% preferred the sea; 20% the mountains; 56.5% preferred August; 25.5% July; 12% September.**
- **Among Italians who went abroad to Europe in 1987, 47% went to France, 16.2% to the UK, 9.9% to Spain, 8.7% to Yugoslavia, 3% to Austria and 2.7% to Greece.**

3. The keepers of the arts

(i) *La cultura* as a popular commodity

In Chapter VIII, we will see the reasons for the Italian devotion to the *idea* of culture, rather than to its practical appreciation. Here we see what this means in concrete terms. Common to all Latin countries is the perception that the arts are for everyone, not just for an intellectual élite, while at the same time the category of 'artist' is treated with popular respect. A garage mechanic is thrilled if his son gets to play in a major orchestra, just as popular gossip magazines like *Oggi* and *Gente* carry weighty film reviews and colour features on art exhibitions alongside shock horror exposés involving naked politicians. Nearly all Italians aspire to having some *cultura*. Emblematic of this is the fact that *la terza pagina* – page three – of Italian newspapers does not automatically suggest tits 'n' bums, as in the UK popular Press, but is on the contrary dedicated to sometimes impenetrable articles about *la cultura* – the arts.

Even those Italians who left school at 13 possess strong chauvinistic feelings about their national cultural heritage: classical ruins and Baroque churches, Dante and Michelangelo, Verdi and Manzoni inspire a collective confidence on a par with the gung-ho patriotism that inspires countless Britons and Americans.

However, this attitude of reverence has little in common with a mass 'hands-on' approach to the arts. There is further evidence of this in the '*Maestro*' syndrome. (→ I, 6:ACCESS) For all that touching of forelocks to literally anyone who can play the piano or has had a couple of paintings exhibited ('*Buongiorno, Maestro*'), there are far fewer Italians who take up an instrument or go to evening school painting classes in Anglo-Saxon countries, where *Maestro* frequently translates as weirdo.

The same purist attitude linked to a consumer dilemma is typical of reading activities: there is no middle ground. Italians constantly berate themselves for buying, or at least reading, far fewer books and papers than their fellows in other countries; but Italian newspapers are all very ponderous and wordy, and the books on the best-seller list tend to be heavy-duty reading. (→ 7:i, below)

In its extremely central role in Italian society, *la cultura* displays another, apparently paradoxical, side to the coin: along with all the deep respect for 'art' comes a violently superficial blasé attitude. All those unabashedly noisy concert audiences and befurred, bejewelled *presenzialisti* – professional liggers – at art

Audience behaviour

● **Dress code:** it may seem odd, when so many Italians wear furs and high heels to the supermarket, to find so many still in *lo stile casual* at the opera or the theatre. This is the tail end of the paranoia that characterized the post-1968 *contestazione* – the left against everything – period, when mink and dinner jackets attracted eggs and rotten tomatoes like heat-guided missiles. However, the majority now dress up.

● **Applause:** Italian audiences often seem to be clapping themselves as much as those on stage – if a concert is being televised, applause is tripled. Particularly at the opera, *la claque* – paid applauders – are much in evidence, despite official denials. If you want to participate in all that slightly self-congratulatory *bravo*-ing, at least get the gender endings right: *bravo!* and *brava!* are for a single male or female, respectively; *bravi!* is generic plural; while *brave!* would apply only to an all-female cast.

● **Negative reactions:** people can be equally quick to boo. In the cut-throat world of Italian opera, *la claque* is often paid by one singer to boo a rival. Whistling is always a negative response. On the other hand, loud talking during performances of whatever kind, or walking out at the end without applauding, are so common as to be no longer considered rude. This is often the effect of too many free tickets per show: what you don't pay for, you often don't appreciate. (→ V, 1:ii)

● **Paying for it:** Italians mostly think the arts are there by divine right, seats are often mostly filled by give-aways and office subs. Move forward where possible. Not that Italians love freebies more than others; they just try harder for them, and are less embarrassed by put-offs.

Going to museums and galleries

• Finding out opening times, and checking that the museum or gallery is actually open, is an arduous process. In keeping with the Italian non-access tradition, newspapers and specialist magazines don't usually list *chiuso per restauro* – closed for repairs – so it's often worth checking first by phone, provided that someone answers the phone, and can speak English. (→ V, 4:ACCESS – Useful information)
• State-owned museums and galleries have free entrance for the under-18 and over-60, from all EC countries: you'll need a *documento valido* passport or a driving licence with photo to prove it.

Music and arts festivals

• Florence: Maggio Musicale (May, June) – international level opera, ballet, concerts; fairly patchy, with great highs and a few lows; excellent experimental tradition.
• Siena: Festa Chigiana (August) – fairly traditional fare, with accent on chamber music and symphony concerts.
• Taormina and Syracuse: classical drama festival (May/June) – both Sicilian towns have beautiful Greek amphitheatres, used to great effect for Greek drama; often televised.
• Spoleto: Festival of the Two Worlds (June/July) – Italy's best-known arts festival, set up by composer Gian Carlo Menotti to honour his friend Thomas

exhibition *vernissages*, too busy greeting each other and being seen to look at the canvases, makes one wonder whether many Italians actually care for the arts at all. If arts events are commonly used as a springboard for fashion in Italy, then so do the arts become a fashion commodity in themselves. Fast-moving literary, painting or musical trends are common to all countries with a vigorous arts tradition, but in Italy they rise and fall with the ruthlessness of the 1950s hemline. Single writers or whole schools of painters may find that *vanno di moda* – they are in (or out of) fashion – as quickly as Los Angeles cross-ethnic cuisine restaurants.

(ii) How the arts are administered

There must be few countries in the world where no one grumbles about insufficient funding, government indifference and administrative incompetence. Italy is certainly not one of them. In fact, its fully justified reputation in the forefront of international culture tends to raise people's expectations and, consequently, put the country's insufficiencies under a spotlight. Italy also has a special, if in some ways enviable, problem, which is that it contains, according to UNESCO, somewhere between two-thirds and three-quarters of the West's entire artistic heritage, which requires a massive budget for upkeep and conservation. Having even more valuable paintings, sculpture, churches, *palazzi* and classical sites than the rest of the world put together is all very well, if you can afford to look after them.

Since Italy's *patrimonio culturale* – cultural heritage – is so enormous, it gets a ministry of its own, il Ministero dei Beni Culturali, which is quite separate from the one that administers the performing arts. Presumably in recognition of its inferior quality (and quantity), the latter arts category is lumped together with tourism in il Ministero del Turismo e dello Spettacolo.

Although having quite distinct functions, the twin arts ministries have much in common. They are both chronically underfunded and inefficiently run, both ministerial posts being regarded as political sinecures reserved not for *cognoscenti* but for party hacks, who are then reshuffled on average once a year. Some of their aides may know more about their job than their bosses do, but few have any managerial training: local ground staff seem to vacillate between comic incompetence and militant trade union intransigence (→ 4: i, below).

Although senior administrative posts are frequently held by people with excellent academic qualifications, the total lack of professional training courses for arts management in Italy guarantees inefficient and outmoded organization. *Raccomandazione* is the other main problem: all arts appointments, from theatre or museum director down to janitor, are essentially a question of political patronage.

(a) Museums and galleries are in a real mess. There are frequent international rows over the Italian government's cavalier attitude to its arts treasures; most recently, in 1988, John Russell, the distinguished *New York Times* arts critic, caused a near diplomatic incident after a carefully detailed denouncement of Italy as an arts disaster area. The problems are both intrinsic and self-inflicted: insufficient government funds, lack of clear ministerial direction and overflowing storerooms make life difficult. Considering that Italy's visual arts heritage is one of its largest tourist draws, it seems incredibly short-sighted to have most museums and galleries closing daily at 1.30 p.m. Since 1988 there has been a policy of summer afternoon opening, from June through to September. But the ministry couldn't even get this right: having hired some 650 part-time janitors for the Rome area, they forgot to publicize the change, and so most tourists stayed away anyway.

Despite an excellent restoration tradition in Italy, hopelessly few works get treated, as a result of lack of funds allocated, poor organization or disagreement on restoration technique. Layout, lighting and labelling is generally poor, and frequently singled out for criticism by local and foreign experts. Particularly infuriating is the habit of labelling exhibits with unending academic tracts or, presumably assuming the viewer already knows it already, nothing at all; marketing the arts to a mass middlebrow public is unheard of, in keeping with the conventional Italian wisdom that only the *super cognoscenti* should be interested. This philosophy runs counter to the practice of low admission prices, although this is being gradually rationalized to help make ends meet.

Theft is a serious problem, not aided by careless janitors. In 1988, *La Corte dei Conti* (→ V, 5:i) admonished the State for allowing some 400 works of art and 40,000 art objects to disappear from public view in the first eight months of 1985 alone – and that's counting only the ones that actually got noticed. Some custodians think the gaps in walls are a result of works having being removed for restoration. The favoured technique is simple – as old as art itself: walking out with small paintings under your coat. This happens to archaeological works, too: the head of Mars on Rome's Septimus Severus Arch disappeared in 1984, but was noticed only three years later, by Federico Zeri, the art critic.

(b) Some of Italy's arts festivals and exhibitions are

Schippers; attracts arts festival lovers from Rome, Florence and further afield; although it has been fairly influential in the past, its heavily politicized nature now means wildly varying levels of quality.

● Torre del Lago (near Viareggio): Puccini Festival (August) – small and select performances at Puccini's old house.

● Pesaro: International Rossini Festival (August/September) – now a major international event, with top quality singers from around the world coming to sing minor league Rossini operas. So many never performed, or almost never performed Rossini scores, keep coming to light, that this festival could go on for ever being novel.

● Verona: opera festival in the Roman amphitheatre (July/August).

● Macerata: opera festival in the Sferisterio theatre (July/August).

world-famous, notably the Spoleto Festival of the Two Worlds, set up some thirty years ago by the Italian American composer Gian Carlo Menotti as a showcase for his friend, the American conductor Thomas Schippers, but now a moderately distinguished international venue for all the performing and visual arts; the Venice Biennale for painting and sculpture (→ 5:iii, below) and the annual Venice Film Festival (→ 4:ACCESS–Going to the cinema) are also deservedly world-famous. Unfortunately, both these events, and the thousands of smaller or lesser-known ones laid on by other cities or *regioni*, are hopelessly paralysed by political in-fighting.

The late 1970s and early 1980s were characterized by summer arts festivals in almost every *comune*, especially those ruled by a *giunta di sinistra* – a left-wing council – and were run by the *assessore alla cultura* – the arts councillor. These followed the invention of *l'estate romana* – the Roman Summer – by innovative young Communist *assessore* Renato Nicolini, who in the late 1970s emptied the *comune*'s coffers by filling the capital's streets, parks and ancient *palazzi* with John Cage, Noh Theatre and old movies, at highly accessible prices. His post-modern theories about *l'arte dell'effimero* – the ephemeralness of art – fitted in perfectly with the 17th-century Baroque tradition of street spectacles, making him a national household name for several years (personal reputations are ephemeral, too) as well as providing an inspiration for a whole generation of European arts moghuls like France's Socialist Arts Minister Jack Lang.

The pendulum has recently swung back towards less ambitious, more traditional arts presentation, especially since private sponsorship began to make a serious impact in Italy. Thus it is now sober, right-wing businessmen, rather than maverick, left-wing politicians, who are perceived as the real arts patrons. Fiat's Fondazione Agnelli have made the Palazzo Braschi in Venice (redesigned by modish Gae Aulenti) into one of the best arts centres in Europe; Carlo De Benedetti's Olivetti tirelessly sponsors international arts exhibitions in all fields; while la Confindustria, Italy's Industry Federation, has now organized a massive coordinated arts sponsorship trust.

Italy, with 5.2% now enjoys the largest percentage of private arts sponsorship per GNP in Europe, over France (4.9%), Great Britain (4.7%) and Germany (3.1%).

---

4. The performing arts

(i) Classical music, opera and ballet

The fact that Italy has had such a central role in the birth and development of serious music – from the Schola Cantorum – song school – in Rome in the 4th century, to Guido of Arezzo, the 11th-century monk who devised modern musical annotation, to the polyphony of Palestrina in the 16th century, to Verdi's operas in the 19th – seems, paradoxically, to be a disadvantage today. Italy seems to be resting on its laurels, in terms both of musical training and of live performance lagging behind the US, the UK and West Germany. There are relatively few orchestras in Italy, and far fewer good ones. There are plenty of reasonable conservatoires, producing acceptable soloists and conductors, but most of the good ones want to work abroad. It is a case of too many chiefs and not enough Indians – musicians want to be individual stars, not to work together in an orchestra.

Going to concerts

Finding out about concerts is easier than most things in Italy: the streets tend to be plastered with posters advertising location, programme etc. Following the trend set by *l'estate romana* (→ III, 2) many are given in churches, ancient *palazzi* or in the open air. They are usually very cheap, or even free. Given the relaxed audience attitudes, it is not unthinkable to roll up late if you get lost. Open-air concerts are usually in stunning settings, but prey to heavy traffic noise and terrible acoustics. No one seems to mind in Italy, so long as it looks good – the *spettacolo* is the important thing.

Important 20th-century musicians

- **Composers**
  Luciano Berio (*b* 1925).
  Sylvano Bussotti (*b* 1931).
  Luigi Dallapiccola (1904–75).
  Bruno Maderna (1920–73)
  Luigi Nono (*b* 1924).
  Goffredo Petrassi (*b* 1904).
  Nino Rota (1911–79) wrote scores for many Fellini films.
- **Conductors**
  Arturo Toscanini (1867–1957)
  Riccardo Muti (*b* 1941)
  Claudio Abbado (*b* 1933)
  Carlo Maria Giulini (*b* 1914)
  Giuseppe Patanè(*b* 1932)
  Giuseppe Sinopoli (*b* 1946)
- **Soloists**
  Salvatore Accardo (*b* 1941), Uto Ughi (*b* 1943): violinists.
  Maurizio Pollini (*b* 1942), Arturo Benedetto Michelangeli (*b* 1920): pianists.

There are few symphony orchestras in Italy; apart from the four RAI house orchestras, located in Turin, Milan, Rome and Naples, most of the orchestras are attached to opera houses. Of the latter, the best are La

Scala, Milan; San Carlo, Naples; and Santa Cecilia, Rome – in that order.

Rome has three orchestras – Santa Cecilia (good), the RAI (OK) and il Teatro dell'Opera (terrible), with a total of 1231 players. In 1987 they did a total of 323 performances, costing an average of 196 million lire each. Annually, ticket sales and sponsorship account for 9 billion lire, while the remaining 79 billion come from the State.

The opera season is very short – from December to May, with single rather than rotating productions on the programme. While Italy follows international trends – Mozart is very in vogue at present – there is obviously a strong bias towards its own opera composers, especially the big five: Rossini, Bellini, Donizetti, Verdi and Puccini. Thanks largely to the prestigious international festival dedicated to him at his birthplace, Pesaro, Rossini enjoys particular interest whilst the late *verismo* – realist – composers – Francesco Cilea and Umberto Giordano and co. are still out of favour, as they have been since the downfall of Fascism.

Despite the venerable tradition of Italian opera – San Carlo in Naples opened in 1737, although the present building dates back to 1816, and most of the operatic masterpieces had their premières in one or other of the great Italian opera houses – Italians show little compunction for the total chaos that reigns today. Behind the scenes, political fighting and complicated union demarcation disputes among both musicians and technicians cause many cancelled dates. Rome's Teatro dell'Opera (present building opened 1928) has gone for years at a time without a director, while around Italy, both orchestras and technicians will down tools at a moment's notice. The problem is exacerbated by the management never knowing when their government subsidies are going to arrive, and thus often being unable to pay salaries.

There are thirteen important opera houses in Italy, of which La Scala in Milan (opened 1778), San Carlo in Naples and La Fenice in Venice (opened 1792; rebuilt 1837) are the best, although many smaller provincial towns boast very reasonable ones. Emilia-Romagna is the most opera-mad region of Italy, where audiences are notoriously rowdy and give singers they don't like a very hard time.

Ballet is very much the Cinderella of the classical performing arts, even though ballet schools attached to the Naples and Milan opera houses were established in 1812. Typically, the greatest Italian *étoiles* go abroad. Contemporary dance has recently established itself very well, partly through constant exposure at *estate romana*-type events, but largely thanks to the persistent efforts of a few ballet critics, notable the RAI's Vittoria Ottolenghi.

(ii) Theatre

Looking at current productions, it is sometimes hard to imagine that Italy has an important theatrical tradition behind it. *La commedia dell'arte*, the works of the 17th-century Venetian comedy writer Carlo Goldoni, and those of the 19th/20th-century Nobel prizewinning Sicilian playwright Luigi Pirandello and of the more recent Neapolitan comedian Eduardo De Filippo, have all contributed substantially to world theatre.

Modern Italian theatre technique is based almost entirely on the declamatory style that was abandoned on the English-speaking stage in the last century. Although suitable for operatic delivery, it is equally ludicrous in Shakespeare and in modern productions. In Italy's burgeoning experimental theatre, it comes across as pure amateur dramatics. Fortunately, it is not much used in cinema. Italian theatre-lovers and professional critics usually profess much enthusiasm for the London and New York stage traditions, which is not surprising.

Part of the trouble is that there is no tradition of official drama schools, though some of Italy's best-known thespians – this seems a more suitable term for them than actor – like Vittorio Gassman and Gigi Proietti have set up their own, and the Accademia d'Arte Drammatica in Rome is shortly to be re-formed. The rather more original Dario Fo has even set up his own university – l'Università di Alcatraz.

It is surprising that theatres stay open at all, since so few people pay to go. (→ V, l:ii) The lack of personal involvement consequent to not paying makes theatre-going in Italy a fairly unattractive experience.

Italy contains far more fringe theatres and theatre groups than mainstream ones, on account of government funding, which works on the egalitarian criterion of 'something for everybody' rather than on a basis of merit or achievement. A new law in 1990 should alter this, by tightening qualifications for grants. Some 700 *spettacoli* – shows or plays – had some 134 billion lire showered on them in the 1987–8 season. There is to be a new non-political commission to decide on rents as part of the reformed ETI (Ente Teatrale Italiano).

There was an exciting period between the late 1970s and mid-1980s, when a series of Pina Bausch-inspired multi-media youth groups appeared, with names (Gaia Scienza, Falso Movimento, Magazzini Criminali) and presentation more reminiscent of those in rock-bands.

It appeared for a while that the impossible had happened – namely, that Italy had finally produced some genuine, original youth *and* theatre culture; unfortunately, the movement disappeared as rapidly as it had started. Present-day experimental Italian theatre is none too gripping.

Irrespective of talent, to work in theatre production requires political backing, just as to tread the boards usually means a bit of the casting couch. Italy does boast some directors and designers of international fame, particularly Giorgio Strehler, founder of Milan's Piccolo Teatro, and currently director of the EC's European Theatre in Paris. Unsurprisingly, he is also a Socialist MP. The strongly neo-classical set designer Pier Luigi Pizzi is also much in international demand.

Going to the cinema

Curiously, for the land of hyper-choice, Italy has no multi-screen cinemas; instead, it is full of splendidly unrestructured movie houses dating back to the 1930s, 1940s and 1950s. Sadly, so does much of their projection and sound equipment. Some Italian directors (Bertolucci is especially vehement) don't like showing their films in Italian theatres.

All newspapers have full-page cinema listings, with first and last showings (*primo/ultimo spettacolo*). Times given on the twenty-four-hour clock, and are invariably 16.30, 18.30, 20.30 and the highly civilized 22.30. All films have a five-minute *intervallo*, permitting you to have a smoke and a chat outside. In some cities, Rome and Naples in particular, there is a great popular tradition of making wise-cracks during the film, especially during slightly unbelievable American films. This is often very amusing. Less so, when people talk loudly through something more serious – they often won't stop even if you ask them. (→ V, 1:iii)

● Festivals: the Venice festival (first two weeks of September)

(iii) Cinema

Italian cinema is generally as good as Italian theatre is disappointing. Although box-office takings are gradually falling, in contrast to US/UK figures, almost yearly, cinema attendances are still higher than in any Western nation except France, whose cinema tradition is very similar to Italy's. It is a question not only of quantity, but of quality: Italian movie-goers are extremely discriminating and sophisticated. Important US movies appear in Italy faster than in any other European country, including Britain, despite the need for dubbing.

If there is a lacuna in the knowledge of Italian movie-goers, it is that they have never heard the original voices of any English-speaking or foreign stars – everything is dubbed, even Italian language films. They are extremely proud of their dubbing industry, since the lip synching is so expert that you'd think the film was shot in Italian. Consequently, many dubbers are stars in their own right.

Rome's Cinecittà may lack Pinewood's special FX talent and facilities, but it is the only place in Europe with the full cycle of production facilities. Built by Mussolini in the 1930s, it has its own subway stop, is currently undergoing something of a renaissance, and is even making a profit. Workers have expertise and show more job flexibility (safety regulations are horrific) than usual, even if the pace is maddeningly slow for most hyper-amphetaminic members of international moviebiz. Italians understand movies.

Everyone always says Italian cinema is *in crisi*: compared to what it was doing twenty years ago, maybe, but it still has lots to say, and has excellent technicians, like Oscar-winning cameramen Giuseppe Rotunno and Vittorio Storaro. Popular with American production teams in the 1950s (Hollywood on the Tiber) for making cheap costume blockbusters, it is again in demand with directors like Francis Coppola, Robert Altman, who has settled in Rome, Ridley Scott and Terry Gilliam. RAI TV is now Italy's largest film producer, accounting for almost 50% of total output.

Many famous Italian directors enjoy far more prestige abroad than at home, where most of the 1960s and 1970s figures are considered overrated. Federico Fellini has not been well considered since he made *8¹/₂*; Michelangelo Antonioni's recent work has been very patchy; while Franco Zeffirelli's films are often laughed off the screen. Most movie buffs lament the passing of the post-war *neo realista* generation – Vittorio de Sica, Luchino Visconti, Roberto Rossellini. The 1980s have been quietly successful for directors like Ettore Scola, Pupi Avati, Nanni Moretti and the Taviani brothers, of whom the first three have set up their own schools or production houses. As a result of legislation similar to that regarding the theatre, first-time directors can get some 400 million lire in State contributions towards making their first film; this is then topped up by private sponsorship. In this way, some thirty-five to forty 'first films' are now made annually, of which only seven or eight will be commercially released. Some 150 new directors have surfaced during the 1980s. Rossellini was instrumental in setting up the left-wing-inspired Gaumont film school, which until its mid-1980s demise produced many interesting young directors, with lessons given by hands-on film-makers like Bernardo Bertolucci and Martin Scorsese.

is almost on a par with Cannes and Berlin; the annual film season starts when it ends, on 15 September. There are lots of rather improvisatory regional ones.

- **Categories of cinema:**
  Prima visione – new releases, comfortable theatre;
  Seconda visione – catch what you missed first time round, in a flea pit;
  Cinema d'essai – poky little arthouse showing obscure, subtitled foreign films. A nominal membership fee is usually required for tax reasons;
  Cinema all'aperto – in summer, there are a few open-air cinemas; some others open their roofs (*aria condizionata* – air-conditioning – is still a novelty). *L'estate romana* pioneered theme-sites: seeing *Ben Hur* at Rome's Circus Maximus, where the film's action is actually set, was a memorable experience.

- Tickets: usually cost 7000–8000 lire, but an annual AIACE (Italian Cinema-goers Association) membership card (cost 12,000 lire), widely available, makes seats half-price on weekdays, except Friday.

Major Italian film-makers

- **Dead**

Roberto Rossellini (1906–77)
Vittorio de Sica (1902–74)
Luchino Visconti (1906–76)

- **Alive**

Lina Wertmuller
Taviani Brothers
Francesco Rosi
Ermanno Olmi
Liliana Cavani
Federico Fellini
Bernardo Bertolucci
Michelangelo Antonioni
Franco Zeffirelli
Mario Monicelli
Ettore Scola
Pupi Avati

(iv) Humour

Italy once had an exceptional music-hall tradition, which lasted right up until the television era. Rome and Naples were probably its finest *luoghi sacri* – 'sacred places'; Fellini's films often hark back to the *avanspettacolo* – the stand–up comic before the main show – tradition. The most sublime proponent was the Roman stand-up comedian Ettore Petrolini – the only man in Italy allowed to poke fun at Mussolini in front of him; Il Duce himself was an assiduous visitor to Rome's Teatro Ambra Jovanelli, now a porno cinema. The *avanspettacolo* was also the tough but useful starting point for generations of Italian comic actors and light entertainers, including Italy's answer to Chaplin, the sublime Neapolitan Totò. The light-hearted manner in which private television is used now reveals much of the *avanspettacolo* tradition. Modern Italian humour is altogether less remarkable. (→ II, 3:i)

(v) Pop music

Italian pop music is a real disappointment for those who might have imagined that all that street cool, design flair and good looks could have been forged into a workable musical tradition. Young Italians are just not raunchy or original enough, and, as passive consumers, are too easily influenced by US/UK models to desire any of their own. Being so emotionally and financially dependent on their parents makes any rock'n'roll/rebel rhetoric way off line. Italy's carefully groomed, raunchy rockers – Vasco Rossi, Zucchero and Gianna Nannini as well as Deejay TV's ex-DJ, the boyish white rapper Jovanotti – have all enjoyed sustained European success, but to Anglo-Saxon ears (and eyes) look uncomfortably like a parody of the real thing.

The consumer power of parents makes a clean-cut, boy/girl-next-door-look the dominant one. Italian music is thus far more pop than rock. There are very few groups, and many more single singers. There is an incredibly slow turnover of performers, who tend to stick around for twenty years or more without losing favour, not unlike Cliff Richard.

At a slightly more arty level, there is a tradition of adult *chanteurs/chanteuses* on the French model, some of whom are popular in Europe and South America. Genoa's Gino Paoli, Paolo Conte and suicide Luigi Tenco, and Milan's Enzo Jannacci are all worthy of note. Italy boasts one exceptional female vocalist, who is a legend in her lifetime: Mina, from a similar mould to Barbra Streisand, though her vocal talents far exceed Streisand's.

The only city that has an interesting, funky, rock scene

is Naples, which has produced eminently exportable rhythm 'n' blues acts, notably Pino Daniele, Enzo Avitabile and James Senese.

Italy's contribution to the ephemeral and overrated Eurodisco movement has been a few bimbos like Spagna and Sabrina, who have emerged with the help of massive TV exposure, including the non-stop televised open-air concerts that are used as programming fillers during the summer months.

Although Italian fans are perfectly trained to assimilate whatever is on world offer, there are two specific market niches that sell better in Italy than anywhere else, and that record and tour promoters exploit ruthlessly: these are off-beat, intellectual student angst, from early Genesis or Van der Graaf Generator to Japan and Eno; and pretty boys like Nick Kamen, Spandau Ballet, even Duran Duran, all of which have much greater, and more lasting, success than elsewhere, continuing, even now, to sell out concert dates and do well in the charts.

Only in one respect does Italy lead the rock world – in the number of rock stations on television. The twenty-four-hour, free channel Video Music has been broadcasting since 1984, showing videos, concerts and rock interviews, and has sparked off hordes of imitators. It is possible to see rock acts on up to six channels simultaneously in Italy, especially since RAI started collaborating with Video Music, and now constantly broadcast major international rock concerts. (→ 6: i, below)

The gradual globalization of record companies, with simultaneous release dates for important products, together with the fast turnover of new rock videos, has revolutionized the Italian rock market in a short time: once UK/US records hit the Italian charts months later, even after they'd peaked in places like the Philippines or Singapore; now they tend to come out simultaneously.

There has been a big change in rock concerts, too. From 1968 until the mid-1980s, they were regularly transformed into political riots, with the result that few international tours ever went near Italy. Most punters insisted on being let in free, despite tear gas and police charges. Most young Italians are now prepared to pay for their tickets, which means that, after twenty years' absence, the big foreign stars have returned. Politics apart, Italian rock audiences remain extremely fickle: groups that are *di moda* are slavishly applauded, especially if they try to say something in Italian. This is invariably 'Ciao Roma/Milano' etc., which foreign singers, if they go by the tumultuous audience response, must each think they've thought of first. This contrasts with the extremely uncivil treatment destined for support groups, who are rarely given more than ten minutes' grace before being howled off stage. This is ironic, since many of them return as headliners next time round, and to their share of audience rapture.

(vi) Jazz

Jazz may have experienced a big revival elsewhere over the last few years, but in Italy it never went away. Every large Italian city has a number of jazz clubs, where generally proficient bands play. All the big US stars play Italy constantly, some of them flattered and bemused to be invited at all. The wide-eyed enthusiasm of Tavernier's jazz film *Around Midnight*, although set in Paris, is typical of Italian fans. Most jazz clubs are listed in the newspapers. However, Italy has never produced any significant jazz players of international note. (→ above, 2:ACCESS: Nightlife)

5. The visual arts: *l'occhio deve avere la sua parte*

(i) Modern architecture: *razionalismo* and *monumentalismo*

Quite apart from what preceded them, it seems quite unnecessary to even mention the importance of Renaissance and Baroque, Palladian and neo-Classical architecture in Italy. Yet for at least a century (1820–1920), nothing original of any importance was built in Italy. France and Austria provided second-hand role models, from Napoleonic and Habsburg through to Art Nouveau and Sezessionstil – the latter distilled into the blandly provincial *stile novecento*–20th- century style.

Especially during the period from reunification (1860) onwards, Italian architects dedicated their energies to simply building larger cities – hence the generally uninspiring, Haussmann-esque *stile umbertino* – contemporary to King Umberto – which characterizes most late 19th-century/early 20th-century Italian buildings.

However, the enormous Viennese architectural boom at the end of World War I typified by *die Wagnerschule* and Erich Mendelssohn, followed up by the whole Modernist movement, from Le Corbusier to Bauhaus, were to trigger off a far more robust response among Italy's young architects. Italy's home-grown Futurist movement set things off, while the complex political situation created by Fascism's rise to power gave *razionalismo*, as Italy's Modernist movement became known, an enormous boost. What Mussolini saw in it was obviously pure propaganda value – something vulgar and authoritarian, know as *monumentalismo*. This was reasonable to expect, since in the confused political situation of the time, almost all progressive young architects were quite happy to embrace Fascism. Much of the output of the inter-war period in fact conforms to this stereotype, especially the official projects overseen by his architectural supremo Marcello Piacentini – but much of it didn't, coinciding largely with the best works of Giuseppe Terragni, Adalberto Libera and others. Despite its often considerable architectural merit, *l'architettura razionalista* has been something of a taboo subject since the downfall of Fascism. Only now is it beginning to be reassessed in a less ideologically loaded context, both in Italy and abroad. Italy is well worth visiting just for this period of architecture, and it is well worth your while to seek it out. (→also II, 1) Its low status is especially ironic in comparison with the relentless image bombardment now associated with the modern Italian design movement, which could not have existed without it.

The main names to look out for

- *Razionalismo*: Antonio Sant'Elia (1888–1916), Mario Chiattone (1891–1957): post-World War I Futurists. Nothing ever built, but their designs are classics of the Blade Runner genre.

Giovanni Muzio (1893–1982): established first Milanese condominium buildings, e.g. Ca' Brutta (1921–3)

Giuseppe Pagano (1896–1945), Gino Levi Montalcino (1902–74): mostly in Turin; e.g. Via Roma development (1931)

Marcello Piacentini (1881–1961): Mussolini's pet architect, responsible for the most imposing-looking Fascist architecture; e.g. Rome's EUR area. His public buildings are pompous but fun. He was also responsible for the policy of *decentramento* – ripping out historic city centres for Fascist ones. (→ II, l)

Pier Luigi Nervi (1891–1979): from Florence's Futurist football stadium (1930–32) to the Vatican's Pope Paul VI audience hall (1972), a consistently important figure. (→ also Ponti, below)

Giuseppe Terragni (1904–43): the greatest of them all; it is worth making a pilgrimage to Como, which is full of his work; e.g. la Casa del Popolo (once the Casa del Fascio; 1935–6) and l'Asilo Nido Sant'Elia (Kindergarten; 1937).

Luigi Figini (1903–83) and Gino Pollini (*b* 1903): La Casa Elettrica (1930), for the Monza Triennal with Terragni and others, part of the Gruppo Sette; responsible for Le Corbusier – influenced Milan housing blocks (1950s).

Adalberto Libera (1903–63): still working after the war, but his best work was before 1940 – Villa Malaparte, Capri (1938); several Rome post offices; EUR public buildings.

Angelo Mazzoni (1894–1979): responsible for the most important of the smaller railway stations; slightly top-heavy constructivist style.

Giuseppe Vaccaro (1886–1970): architect of the League of Nations building, Geneva, and Naples Central Post Office (1935), possibly Italy's most beautiful modern building.

BBPR: Gianluigi Banfi (1910-45), Ludovico Belgioioso, Enrico Peressutti (1908-76), Ernesto Rogers (*fl*:. 1900–76): worked together on a range of buildings, including the deliberately anti-establishment, non-monumental pre-war architecture, from nursery schools to the neo-medieval sky-scraper Torre Valesca, Milan (1956–8).

Giò Ponti (1891–1979): like Nervi, a constant figure, from the monumental Rome University Mathematics Faculty (1934) to (with Nervi) Milan's 127 metre Pirelli skyscraper (1955–9).

● Postwar architecture: building on the legacy of the international reputation of Nervi and Ponti through the 1950s and 1960s, a whole new school of architects have come to prominence in the last two decades. Many of these have also become equally important as furniture or object designers. The most important names currently working now include:

Aldo Rossi: Venice Biennale architectural director; housing and office blocks in Milan and Turin (GFT HQ, Turin, 1986).

Paolo Portoghese: Italian high priest of post-Modernism, whose friendship with Craxi has helped him dominate the whole field, becoming a latter-day Piacentini. He is currently the overall Director of the Venice Arts Festival; Rome Mosque, near Via Salaria (1986–90).

Marco Zanuso: important furniture designer; Piccolo Teatro, Milan (1987–9).

The *razionalista* movement was held together – or rent in two – by critics like Raffaello Giolli and Edoardo Persico (1900–36), who were as important as the actual architects. Apart from their monographs, they also wrote for the great architectural magazines of the day, several of which survive. The Italian capacity for intellectual controversy (→ IV, 3:ii; VIII, 6) and endless verbal abstraction has always given these publications real zest, and this tradition continues today, with polemical, pro-conservationist critics like Bruno Zevi alongside heavyweight scholars like Carlo Giulio Argan (Rome's first Communist mayor) and urbanologist Cesare De Seta. The red-hot atmosphere created by the various movements by and around architect/designers like Ettore Sottsass junior, of the design group Memphis, and Alessandro Mendini, of the Alchymia design group, has helped keep this spirit going.

It is interesting that Italy has room for both the rigidly intellectual style magazines and for a glossier, more American, comfort-based ethos. Generally, they have a very healthy circulation, selling an average of 60,000 copies.

Architecture / design magazines

L'Architettura (1921): trenchantly pro-Fascist view, directed by Piacentini; now defunct.

Casabella (1928): directed by Pagano and Persico from 1930 to 1936; later run by BBPR survivor Ernesto Rogers, uncle to Richard Rogers; still going under Vittorio Gregotti.

Domus (1928): founded by Giò Ponti, who directed it for a long period, except for the 1940–46) break; later Alessandro Mendini; latterly Mario Bellini. It is by far the most interesting currently on sale.

Casa Vogue: classic post-war Condé Nast interior design formula.

Abitare (1962): a high-brow version of the above.

Modo (1975): very avant-garde; founded by Alessandro Mendini; currently directed by Andrea Branzi.

Architectural Digest Italia (mid-1980s): smooth, international style.

(ii) The Italian design myth

Milan's post-war emergence as a major design capital has specific roots: in the tradition of design-orientated pre-war architects (→ 5:i above), who designed most of the objects for their own buildings; in the post-war concentration of Italian industry around Milan; and in the physical smallness of most production firms, and the fact that they were based around highly skilled artisans. Italian design, in fact, owes perhaps more to these firms than it does to the actual designers.

The Italians' famous skill of improvising had been stimulated by over a decade of Fascist-imposed *autarchia* – economic self-sufficiency. Design and architecture during the Mussolini years had managed brilliantly to overcome shortages, and the immediate post-war years often recycled the technology and discoveries of war-time. The development of the Piaggio Vespa from a small war-time aircraft engine is a good example.

The immense optimism created by the economic boom of the 1950s and 1960s, coupled with the need to create an industrial infrastructure from nothing – *autostrade*, automobiles, factories, consumer goods – more than compensated for the non-existence of anything resembling design schools.

The outside world was first really exposed to Italian design at the beginning of the 1970s, when the 1972 New York MOMA exhibition, *Italy: The New Domestic Landscape*, put Milan on the map. It has evolved considerably since then, both in style and in quality, but the basic message of the 'idea' of design has remained unaltered. The emergence of Alchymia and the neo-Modern movement around Alessandro Mendini in 1978, and then Ettore Sottsass junior's Memphis in 1981, added stimulating new elements to the Milan myth. The design world was entranced.

Whereas the Italian intellectual approach to most of the arts tends to leave most Anglo-Saxons quite cold – we don't need to be told all those theories – design was different. Until the Italians made it their big contribution to post-war culture, we saw design as a functional, not an aesthetic, matter. Since the 1970s, the world has allowed the Italians to persuade them that design is (a) a bona fide art form, and (b) a very marketable one. For once, all this theorizing has a concrete result: inventing a formal category for design helps to sell it.

The way that design as a commodity has filtered into our lives over the last decade is interesting: contrary to what many international design-conscious people must imagine, Italian homes are hardly full of it. ($\rightarrow$ I, 1:ACCESS – Inside Italian homes) Would-be 'designer homes' have been conscientiously assembled in London, New York or Sydney in the same way that immaculately groomed punks or hip-hoppers have taken to the streets of Stockholm, Munich or, indeed Milan. It is called investing in a myth.

Where Italy really had the edge was on 'designer-ish' goods which filtered down into ordinary shops and chain-stores some five years before anywhere else. Since the early 1980s, this marketing ploy has been so globalized that you can no longer tell the difference: foreign design shops look, if anything, more Italian than they do in Italy. The obsessive, 'designer everything', phenomenon is in many respects non-Italian. The matt black dream home, replete with accessories like clever lamps (cheaper than actually buying any furniture), looks identifiably Italian, but it's not especially how Italians live, even the smart ones.

However, if the image has now been successfully exported everywhere, it is the idea that Milan still keeps close to its chest. No foreign publication would dare print the 'philosophy of design' articles that *Domus*, *Modo* and *Abitare* turn out: they'd be laughed off the news-stand. Behind every Memphis boxing-ring sofa and Richard Sapper Tizio lamp, there are pages and pages on the concept of pastel shades, or the alchemical nature of texture, waiting to jump out. Rather than scoff, the design-hungry accept the gospel in good faith.

Important design names: know them by their fruits

Gae Aulenti: interiors: the Fiat gallery in the Palazzo Braschi, Venice; Musée d'Orsay, Paris.
Achille Castiglioni: chairs; lighting for Flos.
Vico Magistretti: chairs for Cassina.
Richard Sapper: Tizio lamp, Alessi kettle, Brionvega radios.
Mario Bellini: Olivetti cash registers, Cassina chairs.
Ettore Sottsass: Olivetti typewriter; most of Memphis.
Giorgio Giugiaro: cars: Fiat-Uno, Panda, Alfa-Sud, VW Golf; cameras for Nikon; *pasta* for Barilla.
Michele De Lucchi: Artemide lights; Milan designer shop interiors.
Marco Zanuso: Zanotta, Brionvega radios.
Sergio Pininfarina: cars for Ferrari, Alfa-Romeo.

The design world: fairs, awards, schools

● Milan Triennale, at Parco Sempione: this has been going since the late 1920s, as an architectural/design fair; found ingenious solutions to problems of *autarchia* shortages; was seriously compromised by post-1968 hostility from students, and came back into its own only at the end of the 1970s.
● Compasso d'Oro: important biannual award since 1954.
● Domus Academy: founded in 1983 as a postgraduate school. The teachers are all hands-on designers. Directed by Andrea Branzi, with staff including Marco Bellini and fashion designer/architect Gian Franco Ferré.

The firms

Whatever the design magazines may show, at a practical level it is more a question of *la ditta* – the firm – than *la firma* – the designer's name. Although many production firms are not Milanese, or even based in Lombardy, they have their main showrooms there, usually in the central area between Piazza San Babila and the Brera business district. You can wander around and browse without much trouble.
Alessi: stainless-steel kitchen ware.
Arflex: furniture.
Arteluce/Flos: lights.

Artemide: lamps, furniture.
Brionvega: radio/TVs.
Cassina: reproduction furniture, from classic modern (Le Corbusier, Mackintosh) to the latest modern furniture.
Fontana Arte: glass.
Kastell: plastic objects, furniture lamps.
Olivetti: office equipment.
Poltrona Frau: wonderful armchairs and sofas since 1912.
Zanotta: furniture.

(iii) Modern art and sculpture

20th-century Italian art has its high and low points; high points including the turn-of-the-century *novecento* movement; Marinetti, Giacomo Balla and the Futurists; and its best-known artist this century, Giorgio de Chirico (1888–1978), one of the few artists ever to fake his own work: he discovered that a certain period sold better, so he returned to that style, and added false 'early' dates. His brother Alberto Savino is equally worthy of attention.

Among post-war artists, the figurative Renato Guttuso (1912-88) predominates, thanks as much to his close relations with the Communist Party and society hostess Marta Marzotto as to his talent, which was slight. Lucio Fontana (1899–1968), Giò Pomodoro (*b* 1930) and Emilio Greco (*b* 1913) and sculptor Giacomo Manzù (*b* 1908) are the remaining grand old men of the Italian visual arts. The golden age of post-war Italian painting was the 1950s and 1960s, centred largely in Milan.

Italy's high profile over the last twenty years has more to do with its critics and gallery owners than with its actual painters. Magazines like *Flashart* and events like the Venice Biennale have proved to be important forums for influential critics like Maurizio Calvi, Renato Barilli, Federico Zeri and Achille Bonita Oliva. The post-war arts scene in general has been largely dominated by the Communist Party, nowhere more so than in painting. The PCI's grip is now loosening, as the arts are no longer perceived as left-wing, with the business-chic Socialists of the PSI muscling in on their ground. The directorship of the Venice Biennale is a significant barometer of political power and influence over the arts, and, however irrelevant it may seem to foreigners, Italian artists watch every development with great interest; their career may depend on their faction being in the saddle. (→ IV, 4:i)

Each of the critics plays godfather to a painting movement, with a series of painters filling his court. PCI-backed Calvesi directed the 1984 Venice Biennale, which he filled with his neo-Mannerist or Anachronist painters (slightly pompous post-modern Titian clones), while the tireless, PSI-backed, *presenzialista* Bonita Oliva had previously launched his *Transavanguardia* movement – including the three c's: Enzo Cucchi, Francesco Clemente and Sandro Chia from the same venue.

New York-based gallery-owners like Leo Castelli have guaranteed an important place for Italian artists in America, while Bonito Oliva devised a brilliant way of launching his own group of artists, by leap-frogging the galleries and, trading on a supposed 'huge European reputation', selling his *Transavanguardia* artists directly, and for huge prices, to museums, before returning to the New York galleries with them at even higher prices. In this way, Clemente, and to a lesser extent Cucchi and Chia, became for a while one of the most expensive living painters in America.

6. The electronic media

(i) TV

RAI – Radiotelevisione Italiana – the Italian State broad-casting monopoly, started transmissions in January 1954, eighteen years after Britain, fourteen after the USA, five after France and two after West Germany. For over twenty years it had a single channel, in black and white, and was strongly influenced by Church standards of morality. The first programme to win a mass audience was *Lascia o raddoppia* – double or quits – in 1956, presented by Mike Buongiorno, still the doyen of game-show hosts. Maria Luisa Garoppo, a woman contestant who won so many weeks running that she became a house– hold name throughout Italy, was obliged by the Vatican authorities to bind her gener-ous breasts, lest they over-excite the fledgling television audience.

In 1976, a rather obscure judgement of la Corte Costituzionale ruled that the RAI monopoly was uncon-stitutional, and that, in theory, anyone should have access to the air-waves, as to the printed media. In true Italian manner, no thought was given to the practical implications of this ruling, and the air-waves were thereby opened to all comers. Initially, it was thought that *la TV privata* would be local, and some provision was made in order to prevent nationwide rivals to RAI coming forward: live broadcasts, essential for news and sports coverage, were to remain a State monopoly. No ground rules were laid down governing the use of frequencies, advertising ratios, broadcasting standards or the siting of transmitters. This caused extraordinary problems – technical, ethical, environmental and moral. Within months of the decree, there were several hun-dred local TV stations on the air. Over the following years, this reached a peak of some 1300 stations, a figure which has remained more or less constant. With a population of 57 million, Italy now has more TV stations per head than does any other country in the world, including the USA.

Out of this media free-for-all, there emerged only one significant figure, the Milan real-estate moghul Silvio Berlusconi. ($\rightarrow$ VI, 2:iv) Starting in 1974 with a tiny private cable station, Telemilano, he entered the local broadcasting arena as late as 1979 with the station that in 1982 became Canale 5. In swift succession, he bought up two other Milan stations, both from publishing houses – Rusconi's Italia 1 (1982) and Mondadori's Rete 4 (1984). He found a wonderfully Italian loophole to the nationwide broadcasting veto, by programming

TV channels

RAI

● **1 Uno: Christian Democrat,** family audience, most popular station. Its news programmes, true to its political matrix, heavily feature the doings of the Pope.

● **2 Due: Socialist; slightly more** upmarket, with more documen-taries and middlebrow films. On RAI 2 News, Craxi plays the role the Pope does on RAI 1.

● **3 Tre: Communist; more intel-**lectual programmes, has more regional, experimental and edu-cational programmes. By far the best TV channel in Italy.

Although each channel is run by one party, the rules of *lottiz-zazione* mean *poltrone* have to be found for other parties' peo-ple too. ($\rightarrow$ IV, 4:i) Only the three RAI channels produce any sig-nificant amount of their own material. They are now increas-ingly producing movies, which end up on TV after a short time; their skill at mini-series is increasing, with some products like *La piovra* – *Octopus* ($\rightarrow$ V, 2:ii) – an international success.

They are now trying to reduce the number of long variety/game-shows, which have dominated prime time over the last decade, in favour of more drama series. The only home-grown Italian soaps so far have been unmitigated dis-asters; hence the reliance on American ones. All three channels screen more quality feature films than any other European network, as a means of challenging the Fininvest channels.

Their news programmes are weak, full of technical mistakes (news-readers never seem to know which camera to face, news film footage is regularly mixed up between stories) and saddled with heavy political intransigence. Many Italians watch all three to get a more balanced view. There is a new attempt to make more news documentaries and information-based programmes. News times: lunch-time (1.00, 1.30 p.m.); mid-evening (7.00, 7.45, 8.00 p.m.); late evening (10.30, 12.30 p.m.). RAI 2 and 3 have improved considerably since 1988.

There is excellent use of flexible programming: thus, if a major actor/director dies, two of their films will be shown the same evening, replacing the advertised programmes, although live shows often overrun by up to ten minutes, creating havoc with the scheduling.

Only RAI 3 has discovered specific target-group programming, with valid minority interest shows commanding critical acclaim. Despite its role as the Cinderella of the three (lowest funds, least political clout), it now produces many of the most original shows.

After the BBC, RAI has now become Europe's most important State network, although it is diametrically opposed to the British TV style. It excels in terms both of film production and of TV technology; it is spearheading Europe's High Definition TV research.

Fininvest

- Canale 5: modelled on classic US network format; no live TV, no news but quite good news comment/documentaries. *Dallas* and *Dynasty* on Tuesday evenings. Ever more quizgames; fewer variety shows.
- Rete 4: slightly more upmarket version of the same: higher-brow films, slightly less crass soaps.

each recorded segment a few seconds out of synch. from region to region.

Thanks to his exceptional business expertise, a canny intuition of the advertising potential of his three channels in a rapidly expanding national economy, a determined hunt for the most prestigious American soaps (*Dallas*, *Dynasty*, *Falcon Crest* are all his) and, above all, his close relationship with the immensely powerful Socialist Party leader Bettino Craxi, he soon built up a media network to rival RAI's in every respect.

The two groups emblematically represent the two main camps of modern Italy: RAI is State-owned and public-spirited, Rome-based, massively over-manned and under-paid, Vatican-influenced and Christian Democrat-controlled; Berlusconi's Fininvest corporation is private enterprise – Milan-based, ruthlessly run on a well-paid skeleton staff, and owes everything to an American-style, secular, Craxi-ite Socialist ethic.

Berlusconi declared war on RAI at all levels, by luring away its top stars with fabulous fees, buying up any new American film or TV film at premium prices, wrestling a vast chunk of commercial revenue from the State channels through his highly efficient Publitalia advertising company, and deliberately 'spoiling' RAI audiences by competitive programme-timing.

Although his three channels are much further downmarket than are RAI's (now also with three channels), his challenge made the State operation get its act together. RAI had many advantages – the live broadcasting monopoly, excellent facilities, a considerable licence fee income (though they have the greatest difficulty getting viewers to pay up), as well as advertising on all three channels. The losers were all the other private channels who had to face up to minimal audiences, while the winners were the viewers, who now had six national channels to choose between, ranging from highbrow culture (RAI 3) to non-stop game-shows and soaps (Canale 5).

While RAI has improved all round, the Christian Democrats have favoured the expansion of other powerful private channels to challenge Berlusconi's Socialist-orientated monopoly. TeleMonteCarlo, 80% owned by the Brazilian mega-communications corporation RedeGlobo, and Christian Democrat Callisto Tanzi's Odeon TV are being encouraged to form a strategic pro-DC alliance (although Fiat's pro-Republican Gianni Agnelli wants to buy into the former station), while Berlusconi has now extended his sphere of influence to a new nationwide network, Italia 7, as well as the kiddy-orientated Junior TV and the Yugoslavian-owned Capodistria, which has, like

TeleMonteCarlo, the all-important live broadcasting faculty.

In 1987, the two sides agreed to a common Neilsen-ratings system, Auditel, which finally showed that RAI had the all-round lead. The gap is now widening, with RAI's share at 48.6% to Fininvest's 37.4% (1988–9). Fininvest, however, continue to dominate daytime viewing, aiming at housewives (40% against RAI's 39.5% in 1989). Between them, they dominate nearly 90% of viewing. In 1988, the two sides, having bled each other so seriously, came to a gentleman's agreement dubbed *pax televisiva*, promising to tone down hostilities until Parliament decided what future broadcasting was to have in Italy. The debate as to what guidelines should be enforced upon the private sector has been going on since 1976; if there were no political complications, this would have been achieved years ago. By late 1989, nothing had been decided, but whatever happens, Berlusconi is unlikely to lose anything: Craxi would never let down a friend of the PSI.

For the time being, Italian television remains a remarkably accurate mirror of the society it serves: colourful, volatile, often amateurish, imaginative, acritically Americanized, frequently hysterical. In some respects, it leads the world, with highly imaginative, spontaneous, live programming that contrasts with the sober, often dull, TV of the British model. There may be well over 1000 channels in all, but there are only ten or eleven that are nationwide, and that matter. Even if the overall incidence of 'quality' programming is low, the punters are happy: Italy still has by far the lowest number of video recorders per home in Europe – there's plenty to see on TV without either recording shows or renting/buying tapes.

Apart from the merits of the national stations, it is really the local privates that make Italian television so interesting. They serve up a low-cost diet of B-grade movies, unwatchable Japanese cartoons, corny 1960s' TV series re-runs, but above all tele-shopping and phone-ins that radically alter the role of television. These programmes run for several hours at a time, with a salesman/woman offering consumer goods – hi-fi, cosmetics, kitchen equipment, oriental carpets, furniture. You are supposed to phone in and order. The majority are presented by anonymous off-screen voices, but of those with on-screen presence several are so odd they must be seen to be believed. Best is hysterical cosmetics empress Wanna Marchi (Rete A), who barks her home-spun philosophy down the phone at callers in between frenzied bouts of sales spiel for her wildly overpriced quack products. Despite being sued several

- **Italia 1: more youth-aimed version of both the above: has a rival to Video Music-Deejay TV; more youth-orientated soaps.**

Fininvest are now attempting to produce more home-grown films and drama series, after the expensive, disastrous, variety shows of 1987–8. Their main strategic weapon is now the quiz-game, and they produce up to 15 hours daily of them on a highly efficient, industrial-style conveyor belt. They make no bones about producing shows for advertising first, viewers second. They show the cream of the crop of American soaps, as well as Japanese cartoons and Brazilian *telenovelas* – ultra-sentimental soaps – and are hoping to have the faculty to broadcast live and thus introduce sorely missed news and sports shows. Rete 4 has very good news documentaries. Lots of high-cost recent US/European films; Italia 1 shows one un-dubbed English language film every Monday night.

Their aggressive advertising strategy (16 minutes an hour; breaks every 15 minutes – even in films; advertising volume far louder than programme volume) alienates the public and infuriates film-makers, but pleases advertisers. A noisy campaign was conducted by Fellini, Bertolucci and co. to reverse this tendency in 1988; Fininvest are now revising their advert. carpet-bombing ploy. Berlusconi also controls three minor channels.

- **Italia 7: further down-market than previous three channels. Sports Italy's most famous programme (among sanctimonious UK TV pundits), *Colpo Grosso* – nightly.**

Capodistria

- **Capodistria: live sports, other programmes in Serbo-Croat.**
- **Junior TV: non-stop Japa-**

nese and American cartoons; ads only for toys and sweets.
● Italia 7: Berlusconi-linked; only station still to feature blatant sex: a strip-poker chat-show game.

Video Music

● Video Music: free 24-hour youth music channel on the lines of MTV, which has been imitated by other private channels for part of their daily schedule. Often involved in live link-ups with RAI of international concert events. (→ 4:v, above)

TeleMonteCarlo

● TeleMonteCarlo films, telefilms, youth shows; only private channel with good live news, arts and sports coverage.

Two national privates

● Odeon TV: reasonable films, telefilms, chat-shows.
● Rete A: sales shows – Wanna Marchi; *telenovelas*.

times for fraud, and having her house burnt down by an enraged client, she has become very rich, and is a great favourite even among sophisticated Italian viewers. This is the stuff of electronic folklore.

Furniture salesman Ugo Rossetti has constructed a low-rent Disneyland in Rome, which features on his six-hour show. It is called *la Città del Mobile* – furniture city – and he styles himself mayor of it, escorted by curvaceous sheriffs; there he organizes semi-pornographic beauty contests and kiddy talent shows, shown in between shots of furniture.

The big names

Although the influence of the main *presentatori* is beginning to wane, there are a few names that, more than in most countries, dominate the Italian TV screen.
● **Mike Buongiorno: the doyen – very avuncular; Canale 5.**
● **Pippo Baudo: the most professional (→ III, 6); now RAI 3, after a long career on RAI 1, and then Canale 5.**
● **Corrado: the most popular – and the most low-brow; Canale 5.**
● **Raffaella Carrà: singer, dancer, housewives' friend; the size of her renewal fee almost caused a *crisi di governo*; now RAI 2, after RAI 1 and Canale 5.**
● **Renzo Arbore: the most sophisticated and original, with a rare irony, and an off-beat sense of humour; RAI 2.**
● **Enzo Biagi: the doyen of serious investigative interviewers (→ V, 2:ii); RAI 1.**

There is something Warholesque about the half-hour close-ups of a beringed hand that form the substance of the jewellery sales programmes, while the numerous phone-in shows with fortune-tellers and tarot card readers bring about a spookily medieval atmosphere.

None of these shows can be watched for more than a few moments, but they provide wonderful entertainment in rotation. Italians are extremely adept at using the *telecomando* – remote control device – to spin constantly between the forty-odd channels they receive. (Italians are still waiting for the 250-channel *telecomando*.) The principle of hyperchoice works with TV as it does with political parties: flicking through one's channel buttons by rote, one inevitably accords as much time to the tackiest private channel as to the major national ones – a triumph of the mediocre.

Italy has no taboos about TV violence, with TV news frequently featuring the goriest of scenes. TV nudity and sex is tolerated far more than in the USA, in adverts, feature and made-for-TV films. The same goes for swearing. Church influence until 1988 prevented anti-AIDS ads, on the grounds that they sanctioned the use of condoms. Nonetheless, many TV commercials sport the most explicit phallic imagery. (→ VIII, 3:i)

(ii) Radio

Like Italian TV, the Italian radio was deregulated in 1976; ever since then, a myriad of often unobtainable signals from fuzzy stations may be picked up.

RAI has five channels. Radio 1 and Radio 2 feature light music, comedy and talk-shows, and carry advertising; they appear to a mostly adult or family audience and peak at 3 million. Radio 3 is similar to the British Radio 3 – a serious discussion, arts and classical music station; it rarely exceeds 150,000, but is highly influential. Although technically part of RAI, Radio 1 and Radio 2 rock stations are on separate wavelengths.

All five channels link up from midnight to 5.45 a.m. for the all-rock format RAI Stereonotte, an arrangement now common to most State broadcasters in Europe.

Radio Vatican carries a mixture of good quadrilingual news programmes, with a mish-mash of music of all styles. It has fairly good rock coverage, which, however, reveals some intriguing moral censorship: the Eurythmics pass muster; Boy George, for example, does not.

The major private radio stations have a regular, and high, turnover. Most cities boasted 'underground', left-wing stations following the student riots; these either disappeared completely (Rome) or went yuppie (Milan).

Berlusconi (→ 6:i, above) is behind Network 105, the only private national network rock station. The accumulated audience for rock stations is immense – 12–15 million listeners – but there are so many stations that the audience is hopelessly fragmented. Some local stations are estimated to have just a few dozen listeners.

(iii) Advertising

Italian copy-writers are convinced that the Milan-based advertising industry is first-rate. Except for the odd campaign, however, it is actually extremely banal and unimaginative.

Adverts usually give some insight into a society's inner self; Italy's is too crass to be true, and seems more a simple projection of consumer desires. There was a good deal of hype when several famous film directors started doing television ads in Italy – Fellini for Barilla *pasta* and Campari; Zeffirelli for Annabella furs (with Jerry Hall); Martin Scorsese for Armani – but none was particularly successful.

Italian consumers, unlike the British, who are intrinsically suspicious of adverts, can easily be persuaded to buy, so long as the advert looks flashy. Hence campaigns are very elementary, and stereotyped. They represent naïve images of a presumed American lifestyle (culture cloning again), with insulting racial or sexual stereotypes: blacks are portrayed as friendly, but inferior; women are invariably shown as incompetent, hare-brained housewives, dominated by their own mothers; husbands are either cuddly and amenable, or obviously child-like. The voices are always extremely unnatural: older people sound exaggeratedly ancient; women sound syrupy and breathy; young men are hysterically enthusiastic; children are either squeaky or very goofy.

Comparative advertising is totally banned; the verbal and conceptual subtlety of the British or the classy construction of French advertising is only occasionally evident.

Many adverts, whether billboard or TV campaigns, have discovered a new pompousness, often using rhetorical, abstract or even meaningless terms, like '*l'ottimismo della volontà*' – 'the optimism of will' – to plug the Socialist Party, or *oltre lo yogurt* – 'beyond yoghurt'. . .

The major international houses – Ted Bates, Saatchi & Saatchi, McCann Erickson, Young & Rubicam (their Gavino Sanna is Italy's most talented adman) – dominate the Milan ad-world, while the top Italian firm is Armando Testa. The seriousness with which Italians take this 'new art form' means that there is now a plethora of advert critics who write in the papers about the semantics of Italy's essentially mediocre advertising industry.

7. The printed word

The printed word in its three major forms – newspapers, magazines and books – is traditionally, and to a much greater extent than in other countries, concentrated in the same hands in Italy.

There are over 200 publishing houses in Italy, of which more than 20% are situated in Milan, which can claim to be the book capital, since over 15% of all books in Italy are bought there. The Vatican has some six publishing houses alone. Unlike France or Spain, with their large, ready-made, overseas markets, or Germany and Switzerland, with their state-of-the-art printing techniques, Italian publishing cannot muster a particularly imposing international profile. Evidence of this can be gauged from its muted presence at the Frankfurt International Book Fair, where Italy fields some 240 publishers, no more than the much smaller Netherlands, and less than Switzerland, France (both 425), Spain (650) and Britain (700).

One feature of Italian publishing that doesn't help is the exorbitant cover price, which has risen far in excess of inflation. The average price for a book in 1975 was 4500 lire, while in 1987 this had reached 27,000. The hard/softback marketing policies common to English-speaking countries are radically different. Paperbacks have a rather unsatisfactory, and consequently much less important, role for several reasons: new editions remain in hardback for much longer, while attractive editions of paperback novels are extremely expensive (an Adelphi paperback costs 21,000 lire), with economy editions at around 8000 lire that are very cheap-looking indeed.

(i) Books

The Press always scolds the Italians for reading so little. Apart from the fact that papers are usually owned by publishing houses, there is a basic marketing problem around the middlebrow area, similar to that of newspapers and the arts in general: only the intellectual and the very down-market are catered for. 85% of Italians have never heard of any of the books in the best-selling lists.

The pragmatic, user-friendly publishing traditions of the English-speaking world can rely on people's practical interests to sell to the middlebrow market. The Italians do not have a sector, like the British, that buys books about gardening, or the Royals (they like the latter served up in lurid magazines); nor are they interested in American-style how-to psychology

The major publishing houses

It is usual for most big houses to have their own bookshops in the major cities: the following all do in Milan, and some in Rome, Turin, Naples etc. Most of the major (and, even more so, the minor) publishers are still closely connected with the philosophy of their founders.

● **Milan-based**

Mondadori – biggest and most dynamic, founded by Alberto Mondadori and housed in the notable Oscar Niemeyer building. Backlist of 4000 titles. They own a major part of the paperback market with their cheapo 'Oscar Mondadori' range. Major papers/magazines: *Panorama*, 50% of *La Repubblica*.

Rizzoli – formerly the most important publishing company, the owners of *Corriere della Sera*. No more: their empire is collapsing through mismanagement. Still have a backlist of over 3000 titles.

Garzanti – excellent for dictionaries, budget paperback encyclopedias, as well as better quality cheap paperbacks; founded by Livio Garzanti.

Fratelli Fabbri: now *Fabbri-Bompiani-Sonzogno-Etas* – Fabbri pioneered weekly instalment encyclopedias in Italy, to great effect; Bompiani's fortunes are sustained by their interest in Umberto Eco.

Feltrinelli – formerly owned by quixotic anarchist millionaire GianGiacomo Feltrinelli, who apparently blew himself up with a bomb during the post-1968 riot days. Still run by his highly capable wife, Inge; still with left-leaning sympathies.

Adelphi – expensive but classy paperbacks, often by obscure, decadent, mid-European novelists. They enjoy, and deserve, an excellent international reputation.

Electa – most important glossy art-book publishers, with an excellent catalogue.

Sterling & Kupfer – one of the most dynamic fiction/non-fiction houses, with interesting Italian/foreign titles.

● Outside Milan

Einaudi (Turin) – most important non-Milanese firm, until recently controlled by celebrated liberal/intellectual Einaudi family, currently *in crisi*.

ERI (Rome) – publishing arm of RAI, putting out books and magazines; currently and rapidly expanding.

Istituto Geografico de Agostini (Novara) – excellent glossy illustrated technical reference books.

Laterza (Bari, Rome) – interesting architectural, archaeological and art catalogue.

Tullio Pironti (Naples) – run by its founder; Italy's most interesting (and one of its most recent) small publishing house, with a courageous publishing policy similar to the 1950s Olympia press of Paris.

Edizioni Sellerio (Palermo) – smart, small-format paperbacks with unusual catalogue.

or business-achievement manuals. They have no real hobbies, and would never think of using books for access – they'd rather ask a relation or friend. Travel guides are the only 'practical' books that have a big market.

The Italian best-seller lists therefore reflect the refined intellectual tastes of the literary minority. There are plenty of American authors, but few airport books. Reflecting their cultural xenophilia, foreign authors often outsell national ones: Marguerite Yourcenar, Milan Kundera, Gabriel García Márquez, and Jorge Luis Borges often sell better even than prestigious Italians like Primo Levi or Leonardo Sciascia. The American brat-pack authors tend to sell better than their own.

A simple way of proving that the vast majority of Italians do not read books is to travel by train: on the *metropolitana*, you will find almost no one reading at all; on intercity trains, you will see a lot of people reading an easy crossword magazine like *Settimana Enigmistica*. Young adults as well as children read cartoon books and comics; a lot of Walt Disney stories are actually published first in Italy, where Paperino – Donald Duck – and Topolino – Mickey Mouse – are household names to a greater extent than they are in their homeland. *Topolino*, the magazine, enjoys heavy TV and billboard advertising.

There are also several best-selling genres of magazines for the uneducated which are almost unknown abroad: *fotoromanzi* – romance stories illustrated with photos as though they were cartoons; and *giornaletti* – part-cartoon, part-pop'n'football magazines for young adults. For housewives, there are *rotocalchi* – illustrated news and gossip magazines, some of which are the film-stars-in-drugs-orgy-shock-horror variety, while others are more 'serious'. The best-selling author in Italy is Liala, whose work is similar to that of her best-selling rival, Barbara Cartland.

Nonetheless, as well as lavishing attention on foreign writers, Italy also treats its own as real stars. Even the most obscure novelists are considered VIPs. This glamorization process reaches its apotheosis with Umberto Eco, whose *Il nome della rosa* – *The Name of the Rose* – has become an international phenomenon, as well as being the best-selling book in Italy this century. Awaiting news of his follow-up, *Il pendolo di Foucault* (Bompiani) – *Foucault's Pendulum* – the Italian media indulged in the hysterical enthusiasm the British Press lavishes on royal babies: bets were placed on both the title and the subject; *La Repubblica* published a double-page feature of cartoons and skits about it.

The grand old man of Italian letters, Alberto Moravia, despite his enormous and on-going literary reputation (he is still writing both novels and weekly film reviews), is almost better known as a social ligger and a Don Giovanni. His fame has a certain knock-on effect: the three main women in his life, Elsa Morante, Dacia Maraini and current wife Carmen Llera, have all become important novelists in their own right.

The main Italian literary prizes – Viareggio, Strega, Campiello and la Penna D'Oro – have all the resonance of the Academy awards: they are choreographed and televised as pure *spettacolo*. There are over a hundred other literary awards in Italy, most of which are controlled by political interests, guaranteeing that twice a week, somewhere in Italy, another team of authors is being lavishly crowned with laurels – although no one may have read a word they have written. It is the idea, not the content, of *la cultura* that matters.

Contemporary Italian writers like Andrea De Carlo, militant gay author Aldo Busi or Dario Bellezza are guaranteed lots of media attention, thanks to all the rhetoric about *i giovani* – being young. (→ I, 2)

Italian winners of the Nobel prize for literature
Giosuè Carducci (1906): poet and critic from Tuscany.
Grazia Deledda (1926): novelist from Sardinia.
Luigi Pirandello (1934): dramatist, poet, novelist from Sicily.
Salvatore Quasimodo (1959): poet and translator from Sicily.
Eugenio Montale (1976): poet and translator from Liguria.

So what books *do* Italians have on their bookshelves? If most English-speaking countries would choose the 1662 Bible and Shakespeare, the Germans Goethe and Schiller, the French Molière and Racine as their seminal 'Desert Island Books', Italians would certainly plump for Dante's *La divina commedia* and Alessandro Manzoni's *I promessi sposi – The Betrothed*. Once every Italian had to read Manzoni at school, and every Italian town has a street named after him, yet scarcely any non-Italian has ever even heard of him, let alone read him. *I promessi sposi* was virtually his only book, but it is sufficient to guarantee him the title of 'father of modern Italian'. Written between 1821 and 1827, at a time when Italy was politically divided, and possessed no national tongue, the Milanese Manzoni chose to write his *magnum opus* in the Tuscan dialect, the language of Dante, as a political and patriotic gesture – almost as though Umberto Eco were to write his next one in Esperanto, for world peace. As literature, the book makes very dull reading, even though as an exercise in language it was a considerable *tour de force*. As a historical novel, it is very similar to the Waverley novels – Sir Walter Scott and Manzoni were mutual admirers, Scott even claiming it as his own, telling Manzoni in jest that *I promessi sposi* was his best book. When the Ministero della Pubblica Istruzione decided in 1988 to remove *I promessi sposi* from the school curriculum, there were loud protests from the entire *mondo della cultura*.

Important post-war novelists

Giorgio Bassani: *Il giardino dei Finzi-Contini* (1962) – *The Garden of the Finzi-Continis*.
Italo Calvino: *Le città invisibili* (1972) – *Invisible Cities*.
Umberto Eco: *Il nome della rosa* (1980) – *The Name of the Rose*.
Ennio Flaiano: *Tempo da uccidere* (1947) *Time to Kill*.
Carlo Emilio Gadda: *Quel pasticciaccio brutto de via Merulana* (1957) – *That Awful Mess on Via Merulana*.
Natalia Ginzburg: *Lessico famigliare* (1963) Family Sayings.
Giuseppe Tomasi di Lampedusa: *Il gattopardo* (1958) – *The Leopard*.
Carlo Levi: *Cristo si è fermato ad Eboli* (1945) – *Christ Stopped at Eboli*.
Primo Levi: *Se non ora, quando?* (1982) – *If Not Now, When?*
Alberto Moravia: *La Romana* (1947) – *The Woman of Rome*.
Godfredo Parise: *Sillabario* (1972).
Pier Paolo Pasolini: *Una vita violenta* (1959) – *A Violent Life*.
Cesare Pavese: *La bella estate* (1950) – *The Beautiful Summer*.
Leonardo Sciascia: *Il giorno della civetta* (1964) – *The Day of the Owl*.

Important medieval writers include Boccaccio and Petrarch, while Ugo Foscolo and Giacomo Leopardi (considered by Arnold as 'greater than either Goethe or Wordsworth') were the leading poets of the late Classical/Romantic era. The late 19th century/early 20th century produced the eccentric Gabriele D'Annunzio (→ III, 1:i), as well as playwright Luigi Pirandello, poets Giuseppe Ungaretti and Giosuè Carducci, and novelists like the *verista* – realist – Giovanni Verga and Italo Svevo. Unlike the visual arts, literature was largely stifled during the Fascist era, when most authors were in exile, but then enjoyed a renaissance on their return in the post-war era. Post-war writers best known abroad are those like Moravia, Calvino, Primo Levi and Eco, whose work concentrates on universal, rather than localized, themes.

(ii) Newspapers

Italians are not great newspaper readers either, and for much the same reasons as with books: what they are offered is so uncompromisingly serious. All Italian dailies, whether national or local, correspond to the definition of 'quality papers'. There isn't a tabloid in sight: one that was launched eight years ago lasted only a few months. Not only that, but they are curiously old-fashioned in lay-out and style, rather like parts of the *New York Times* without the ads.

You can get easily lost in an Italian newspaper, partly because there is never any front-page list of contents telling you where to look for the TV, the sport or the stock-market pages. Even more annoying is the total absence of distinction between facts and comment: the two are indistinguishable. For this reason, many Italians read several papers of different political shades, in order to get a balanced view.

There are numerous leading articles, not just on the centre pages, but on the front page, too. This sometimes makes frustrating reading, as when Italian leader writers air their own pet theories at the expense of news content, but connoisseurs of 'good old-fashioned journalism' will find much that is impressive among leader writers and foreign correspondents – that scholarly, pioneering tone absent from English language correspondents since they discovered that it is easier to be wry and whimsical. Although Italian papers have less foreign news coverage than most serious British papers, there are certain areas, like Eastern Europe, that they cover much more thoroughly, and with greater insight. (→ III, 4) Italian journalism has traditionally produced great foreign correspondents, like Luigi Barzini, who covered the Boxer rebellion in China for *Il Corriere della Sera* in the 1900s, the only Western correspondent on the spot at the time.

Unlike the English-language Press tradition, there is no rule about the first paragraph of each story containing the 'who, how, where and when' details. It is usually necessary to read three or four paragraphs to find out what the story is about. Because of all the preamble, articles are much longer – an Italian Press

The regionally based papers

Il Messagero	(Rome)
Il Resto del Carlino	(Bologna)
La Nazione	(Florence)
Il Giorno	(Milan)
Il Mattino	(Naples)
Il Secolo XIX	(Genoa)
Il Tempo	(Rome)
L'Ora	(Palermo)
La Gazzetta del	
Mezzogiorno	(Bari)
La Nuova Sardegna	(Cagliari)
Paese Sera	(Rome)
Il Piccolo	(Trieste)
La Nuova Venezia	(Venice)

The political party papers

L'Unità: PCI
Il Popolo: DC
L'Avanti!: PSI
Il Secolo: MSI
(→ also IV, 2)

Business dailies

Il Sole/24 Ore	(Milan)
Italia Oggi	(Milan)

Sports dailies

(Monday editions have a much higher circulation than the other days, since Sundays is when football matches are played.)

Gazzetta dello Sport	(Milan)
Corriere dello Sport	(Milan)
Tuttosport	(Milan)

Association survey recently showed that Italian newspapers contain only a third the number of stories of British ones: they don't print many 'shorts'. Despite the serious tone, headlines are often very misleading, and unsubstantiated by the article underneath. This practice was introduced by Eugenio Scalfari's *La Repubblica*, and was soon copied by most of the others. If a headline says 'IL PAPA È FURIBONDO' – 'The Pope's furious' – you will find nothing in the article except that he wasn't very thrilled about something.

The most important event in Italian newspaper publishing is the circulation battle between Italy's traditional leading paper, the Milan-based *Il Corriere della Sera*, and the Rome-based *La Repubblica*, founded by Scalfari in 1976. During the mid-1980s, *La Repubblica* was decisively in the lead, in terms both of circulation, and of ideas. It was the first paper to be tabloid, and the first to adopt a non-party, but radical-chic, tone. It anticipated the hedonistic, post-ideological 1980s by pioneering a particularly irritating, gossipy, confidential tone in describing current affairs. In so doing, it struck an Italian chord: the obsession with the visual. Formerly, political articles juggled with abstract ideas and predictions; *La Repubblica* started talking about what politicians were wearing, and what dinner parties they were seen at. Now all the Italian papers have adopted this pop-semantics approach.

Since the mid-1980s, most Italian dailies have followed the lead of *The Times*' 'Portfolio' game, with dramatic success in terms of increased circulation. Since 1988, *Corriere della Sera*'s 'Replay', a brilliant idea for using unsuccessful national lottery tickets, has helped it regain a decisive lead over *La Repubblica*. Ironic that such a banal element should decide the ascendancy in such a deliberately intellectual field.

In keeping with the strong Italian regional tradition, most Italians read local, rather than national, papers. These have a basis of national news, but also contain several pages of local news and sport. Thus, there are almost no purely local papers, just as there are no purely national papers: each one has a few pages dedicated to the city where it is printed. *La Repubblica* has made great national headway by having a Milan, Bologna and Catania edition, as well as the main Rome one. Italians away from their home-town will endeavour to get their regional paper wherever they are. A Turinese in Bari will be able to find *La Stampa*, while a Barese in Turin will be able to get *La Gazzetta del Mezzogiorno*, with all the local news they want: very reassuring.

National news is divided between '*interno*' which is 'Home Affairs', and '*cronaca*', which is human interest stories. Only a few papers, like the slightly more down-market *Il Messagero* and *Il Giorno*, have horoscopes, cartoons and fun features.

There are no Sunday papers as such, though all the national dailies print on Sunday, with some of them (*La Repubblica, La Stampa*) not coming out on Monday. Colour sections are a very new innovation, and were launched as recently as autumn 1987, with *Corriere della Sera*'s Saturday supplement '7' and *La Repubblica*'s Friday supplement '*Venerdì*'; most of the others have since followed suit, since the supplements have boosted the circulation of the main two by 200,000 per issue.

Italian attitudes to the Press in 1988

54% believe what they read; 36% are sceptical. 56% think that Italian industrialists buy papers only to increase personal clout; 39% have no objection to their doing so.
(L'Europeo)

All the Italian papers share a certain number of pet clichés, some of which are rather speculative: another *Repubblica* innovation. The imminence of the EC Single Market Act means that '1992' articles are on every page, mostly ridiculously rhetorical; when someone launched a futuristic plan to link the business centres of Milan and Turin in the mid-1980s, there were constant articles about 'Mi-To' (Torino), until the project was dropped. The much-heralded but as yet unrealized currency reform guarantees a steady stream of triumphant articles about 'LA LIRA PESANTE' – 'the heavy-duty lira'.

Media intake of average Italian home

- **Every home contains/consumes:**

a television	98%
at least one daily newspaper	60%
at least one weekly news magazine	42.5%
a detective novel	13.5%
a personal computer/word-processor	6.3%
a video recorder	3.3%

- **increase 1985–6 in reading:**

newspapers up	12.8%
magazines up	17.7%

(CENSIS, 1988)

Papers sold per 1000 worldwide

● **The lowest:**

Portugal	50
Chile	87
Italy	93

● **The highest:**

Sweden	526
Japan	569

Anything about the future is always described breathlessly as '*sulla soglia del 2000*' – 'on the threshold of the 21st century'; Italian journalists cannot refer to the London *Times* without calling it '*l'autorevole quotidiano londinese, il Times*' – the authoritative London daily. Apparently, none of them has picked it up in years.

Ownership of the Press and monopolies is a major issue in Italy. (→ also VI, 2) Fiat's boss Gianni Agnelli owns both *La Stampa* from his home-town Turin, and part of *Il Corriere della Sera*, which has been through very rough waters over recent years. *La Repubblica* was independently owned until 1989, when it was bought by Carlo De Benedetti for Mondadori; the extreme left-wing, somewhat earnest, *Il Manifesto* is a co-operative; while Socialist-backed TV magnate Silvio Berlusconi owns a major share in *Il Giornale*, edited by the charismatic, self-described 'anarcho-conservative', Indro Montanelli. That Berlusconi could join forces with a political rival shows the importance of having a foot in both TV and newspapers in Italy. Agnelli's attempt to buy into TeleMonteCarlo and Odeon TV (→ 6: i, above) has been fiercely attacked by Berlusconi: no one wishes to give an inch.

The national papers: editors and circulation

La Repubblica (Eugenio Scalfari)	664,500
Il Corriere della Sera (Ugo Stille)	515,500
La Stampa (Gaetano Scardocchia)	433,400
Il Giornale (Indro Montanelli)	175,000
Il Manifesto (Co-operative)	45,000

(Accertamenti Diffusione Stampa, Milan, 1987–8)

News magazines

Panorama	(Mondadori)
Espresso	(Espresso Ed.)
Europeo	(Rizzoli)
Epoca	(Mondadori)

(iii) Magazines

Le edicole – Italian newspaper stands (you rarely go to a shop to buy papers) – are bursting at the seams with new titles, in a seriously overloaded market. The main three magazine publishing groups – Mondadori, Rizzoli and Rusconi – fight with their eyes closed, often all three launching a new title in the same field, when there is room on the market for one at most. In autumn 1987, there were three rival 'sophisticated new woman' glossies launched in as many weeks. Rusconi's *Eva* collapsed within weeks; Rizzoli's *Elle* had to be seriously re-vamped to stay afloat; while only Mondadori's *Marie Claire* has done well.

Italian magazines have their strong and weak points. The serious weekly news magazines mould themselves on *Time* and *Stern*, simply because they have no original ideas themselves. While Italian dailies have much in their favour, the weeklies are the nadir of Italian publishing – pretentious, provincial and unprofessional. They limit themselves largely to political navel contemplation, publishing endless accounts of minor political gossip disguised as analysis; dream up new cultural or social fashions – articles constantly begin with the words '*Adesso, è scoppiata la moda di. . .*' – 'Now, it's all the fashion to. . .' – and chart some hyped-up craze; the summer silly season lasts twelve months a year in Italy. In summer itself, quite often all four 'serious' weekly news magazines carry nude-girls-on-beach photos on some pseudo-sociological pretext: fear of skin cancer; can the monokini overtake the bikini; crisis in swimwear industry . . .

The paucity of good ideas, or substantial foreign journalism, is due to a lack of funds: none of them can afford foreign bureaux, so their news from abroad is second-hand. They pad out the issues with a stream of surveys – *inchieste*, or *indagini* – about equally trivial subjects. Despite their avowedly serious content, nude women feature on the cover almost every other week, tied in with the most serious topics.

For decades, the family-orientated *Famiglia cristiana* was Italy's best-selling publication, partly since it was the only major one to be sold in church, and was thus Vatican-endorsed – the ultimate sales pitch. It has now yielded to Berlusconi's sharply edited TV listings magazine, *TV Sorrisi e Canzoni* – TV smiles and songs – which prints the birth date and star sign of every single

Gossip/news magazines

Italy's more down-market gossip magazines are much more professionally produced. *Gente* and *Oggi* have a good deal of serious news and photos, and even arts coverage, mixed in with the bare breasts of Europe's lesser royalty. Well written and graphically pleasing, they resemble the old-style *Life* or *Picture Post*. *Novella 2000, Eva express* and the incredibly lurid *Stop* are pure gossip and scandal, and represent the world peak of the *paparazzo* school of journalism.

Gente	(Rusconi)
Oggi	(Rizzoli)
Novella 2000	(Rizzoli)
Eva Express	*(Rusconi)*

The big sellers in 1988

TV Sorrisi e Canzoni	2,458,200
Famiglia cristiana	1,109,400
Selezione/Reader's Digest	871,400
Quattro Ruote	568,100

person mentioned in it. *Selezione/Reader's Digest* has a steady position, while *Quattro Ruote* (four wheels) is one of Europe's best-selling motor magazines.

●**Fashion weeklies in 1988**

Grand Hotel (Universo)	518,600
Intimità (Ed del Duca)	424,000
Gioia (Rusconi)	378,300
Grazia (Mondadori)	342,000
Anna (Rizzoli)	218,000
Amica (Rizzoli)	203,200

●**Fashion monthlies in 1988**

Moda (ERI–RAI)	145,400
Marie Claire (Mondadori)	101,200
Max (Rizzoli)	114,200
King (ERI–RAI)	60,000
Vogue Italia (Condé Nast)	48,500
Uomo Vogue (Condé Nast)	41,700

Italy does have arguably the classiest selection of women and men's fashion, and homes and furnishing magazines in the world. Condé Nast have some ten *Vogue* titles in Italian, while Rizzoli's *Amica* and *Max*, and ERI's *Moda* and *King*, for women and men respectively, are all highly innovative in both graphics and contents.

● In 1986–7, circulation of newspapers went up from 1759 million copies to 1817 million – a 3.3% increase. Circulation of news magazines, however, dropped, from 104 million copies to 92 million.
● In 1987, 9194 periodicals (magazines, papers etc.) were published, with a total circulation of 3955 million copies.

Having opened with a chapter about the Italians as individuals, both in the home, and in their personal relations, this book also ends with a chapter about them as individuals, but in a more inward-looking context: how they view and treat themselves physically, mentally and spiritually. Obviously, in this frame of reference, *l'uomo* refers not to the male of the species, but to the human species itself.

More than any other nation, apart, perhaps, from the French, Italians seem to form a role model for every aspiring *buongustaio* – connoisseur of food and drink. Although *la dieta mediterranea* is now widely hailed as the ideal food-fitness régime, the Italians don't give a fig for healthy eating as such. Their attitude to their bodies is radically different to that of Anglo-Saxons. On the one hand, they are far more fastidious about physical comfort and personal hygiene; on the other, they seem impervious to the dangers of smoking or not using a seat-belt.

Italy has many excellent doctors, but a quite catastrophic public health system. Similarly, although the Italians may not have invented any major sports themselves, they behave as though they have, justifiably calling their football championship *il più bel campionato del mondo* – the best in the world. But if the professional clubs boast world-class stadiums and hyperbolic sign-up fees, facilities for amateur players of all sports are very limited. And while the education system can boast well-qualified teaching staff, operating a worthy, but rather old-fashioned approach to learning, they are up against a chronic shortage of facilities. Nonetheless, despite serious underfunding and appalling overcrowding, especially at university level, *la scuola* – Italian education – has an impressive academic success rate. As we have seen, the Italians take intellectual matters extremely seriously, although often in preference to, or to the exclusion of, any concrete action. Critics tend to overshadow the artists whose work they are commenting on.

The relationship between most Italians and the Catholic Church is much less spiritual than many foreigners, particularly fellow Catholics, imagine. Having the seat of the Church in their midst for centuries has accustomed Italians to seeing Catholicism as more of a political and social force than a spiritual one. The prevalence of atheism and anti-clericalism is essentially an emotional rather than a rational reaction, just as the religious devotion evident in southern Italy is often far more pagan than Christian in character. The Italians' deeply superstitious attitudes towards life, but above all death, can be seen as confirmation of this attitude.

---

1. Eating and Drinking

(i) Food

As with so many things Italian, there is really no such thing as Italian cuisine, but rather a series of generally distinct, but sometimes overlapping, regional cuisines. (→II, 3:i) Many dishes that are national now have quite distinct origins. *Pasta* may have been imported by the Venetian Marco Polo, but it is essentially a Neapolitan dish, as is *pizza*. Before the nationwide spread of *pasta*,

Meals

• *Colazione* – breakfast: many Italians don't eat anything, or just a *cornetto* – croissant – or *biscotti* – biscuits; breakfast cereals are now sold at some supermarkets, but at delicatessen prices.

- *Pranzo* – lunch – is still a main meal in central/southern Italy for those who can get home from work, although increasingly it means convenience foods.

- *Cena* – dinner – is comparatively late: people rarely eat before 8 p.m., and in the South this may become 10 p.m., especially in the hot summer months.

Northerners always started their meals with *polenta* – a semolina-like savoury dish – or rice. Now, both North and South use rice and *pasta*, although *polenta* has never dared go elsewhere: Southerners call Northerners by the derogatory term *polentoni*.

There are essentially two types of *pasta*: the regular kind, made with *grano duro* – durum wheat; and the fancier *pasta all'uovo* – with eggs added. It is strictly illegal in Italy to make it with *grano tenero* – soft wheat – not that anyone would, because it goes mushy when cooked; Italians want their *pasta al dente*, not *una colla* – a sticky mess. Most other countries produce the lower quality version, and under current EC rules, Holland, Belgium, Britain and West Germany, who between them produce 10% of Euro *pasta*, are now free to flood the Italian market, although it is unlikely any Italian would knowingly buy it. It is also unlikely that Voiello or De Cecco, the best of them, or Barilla and Buitoni, the two biggest sellers, will go to the wall: Italy has increased its *pasta* exports sixteen-fold over the last twenty years.

Despite the effective standardization of cuisine, you will still see *ristoranti regionali* in each Italian city, billed as though they were foreign cuisines. Although every region or province proclaims the excellence of its own *cucina*, the region of Emilia-Romagna and particularly the province of Modena are reputed to have the finest of all: it is certainly the richest. Tuscany produces by far the finest meat, Genoa has perhaps the subtlest herb-based dishes, and the South the most *piccante* – spicy. The theoretical variety, and quality, of Italian food is certainly magnificent, but in practice it has become homogenized and simplified to a great extent.

Although the Italians have resisted *la dieta all' americana* longer than practically anyone else in Europe, there are now strong signs that they are gradually betraying their culinary origins in favour of convenience foods. A parliamentary commission in 1981 had already foreseen that by 1995 85% of Italian food would be processed, packaged or frozen: anathema to such a labour-intensive cuisine. There continue to be more corner shops, and fewer supermarkets, per head than in any other industrialized country, but this ratio is beginning to alter as food advertising expenditure increases (from 28,000 lire per head in 1982 to 102,000 in 1989), encouraging brand loyalty where previously there was none, and improved nationwide distribution (some 33% of *comuni* are in mountainous areas). Other factors are the common social ones: many more women now work, and far more people live alone – Italian *alimentari* – food shops – are now beginning to stock single-portion frozen food packs, although grocers still find it odd if you buy less than six portions of anything. (→ I, 1:i)

A sure indicator of economic well-being is the ratio of protein:carbohydrate intake, with its resultant impact on physical stature. (→ I, 2) Meat consumption has shot up by 300% since the war, despite its exorbitant cost and generally low quality; and *pasta* consumption is decreasing: in 1974, Italians ate 3.5 kilos a month (100 grams in an average *porzione* – serving), or slightly more than one portion a day, while in 1984 it was only 2.9 kilos. Since the late 1980s, there has been a further swing of the pendulum, with international dietists now lauding the qualities of the Mediterranean diet (*pasta*, fish, olive oil, fresh fruit and lots of vegetables); it is now considered one of the healthiest in the world. Italians have always been extremely pernickety about fresh fish, refusing to eat fish in all but the best restaurants. Although frozen fish must by law be indicated on menus, they continue to suspect that anything labelled '*pesce fresco*' is in fact *surgelato* – frozen – or simply *cattivo* – off.

Italian food is largely sugar-free, since few meals end with a *dolce* – sweet; if anything, people have *frutta* – fruit – which is cheap and extremely plentiful. Fruit consumption in the period 1974–84 rose by some 20% per head – from 5.6 kilos to a massive 6.8 kilos a month.

Food facts and figures

• **Italians are now spending 10% less of their incomes on food than they did a decade ago. The current average expenditure is 167,500 lire a month corresponding to 20% of total expenditure of professional white-collar workers and 29% of that of manual workers.**
• **Surprisingly, although their ice-creams are the world's best, they consume less than many countries: a Dane eats eighty-three a year; an Italian is happy with only sixty-one.**
• **Carbohydrates represent 50% of food intake, protein 13.6%.**
• **Italians eat 24 kilos of meat a year, of which 62% is of local production (cf. USA, 35 kilos; Japan 4.6).**
(ISPES, 1988)

(ii) Drinks
As a result of flagging alcohol sales (→ 1:iv, below), the consumption of mineral water is experiencing a huge expansion. Italy now ranks only behind France, and

ahead of Germany and Belgium, in annual consumption, which is currently 60 litre bottles a head, reaching a total of 4.1 billion litres.

Foreign mineral waters – expensive to transport, and made unnecessary by the abundance of the local supply – are extremely rare. Italy has some 260 serviceable sources, run by government licence by some 250 different firms.

Surveys show that consumers start off wanting fizzy water, as if to remind themselves of the distinction from tap water, but then graduate to the subtler tastes of still mineral water. The connoisseur French drink 80% of still, while the Italians are catching up: 35% want still, as opposed to 65% who still want to taste bubbles. The terrible restaurant etiquette problem of *gassata* or *naturale* – fizzy or still – has been cleverly solved by Ferrarelle, whose adverts claim their mineral water to be an exact cross between the two: they have subsequently increased their tiny share of the market to become overall leaders. Some still waters, like Fiuggi and Levissima, are marketed as medicinal, and can cost three times the price of others like Fabia, Uliveto or San Paolo. Few Italian mineral waters have been successfully marketed abroad, with the sole exception of San Pellegrino, America's favourite.

Italian Coke consumption is increasing rapidly, but is still not in the big league: USA, 150 litres a year; Germany, 75; Italy, 25. Coca-Cola, rather than Pepsi, is definitely 'it' in Italy; other brands are very rare. The pre-Coke Italian dark brown sodas are called '*Spuma*' or '*Chinotto*', and make a pleasing variant.

Tea is still considered by many to be a beverage for the sick, rather like camomile tea, which is extremely popular as a nightcap, both at home and at the bar. In general, tea is poorly prepared: in a bar, you will be served a cup of tepid water with a tea-bag beside it. Italians who like to think of themselves as well travelled become curiously obsessive about tea, and will have dozens of fake Victorian canisters of obscure types of tea, often containing dried fruit, on display in their kitchens. Ironically, many Italians are equally amused by those British and American wine snobs who earnestly discuss rare vintages.

Italian coffee has enough variants to confuse the uninitiated. The basic drink is *caffè espresso* – a small quantity of black coffee in a small cup: variants on this include *doppio* – double quantity; *lungo* – slightly diluted; *corretto* – a drop of spirits added; *al vetro* – in a little glass; *macchiato* – with a drop of milk; and *amaro* – without sugar, since in the South they add it automatically. *Cappuccino*, the variety that so obsesses most foreigners, is something Italians drink for breakfast or at mid-morning, or possibly mid-afternoon. They never drink it after meals, and cannot contain their amusement when foreigners do. Watch your waiter smirk as you order it after dinner – as if an American were to order tea in an English pub. A glass of hot milk with coffee added is *latte macchiato*, while in summer iced coffee in a glass is *cappuccino freddo*.

Italians annually consume 4.37 kilos of coffee, to the UK's 2.43. Denmark somehow manages to get through 11 kilos.

(iii) Eating out

The rather patronizing stereotype image of southern Italians with extended families eating out in barn-like restaurants isn't accurate at all. Large-scale tribal happenings like that are usually occasioned only by a family celebration; few families could afford to eat out *en masse* that regularly. The standard of restaurant food and service is declining sharply, in inverse proportion to prices. Most restaurants continue to preserve their traditional appearance, but there has been a massive increase (15%) over the last decade in down-market, pseudo-American style *locali* catering to younger people, with less to spend, and lower expectations of quality. This includes ice-cream or *pizza* parlours – *gelaterie*, *pizzerie* – and fried chicken joints – *rosticcerie* – as well as the notorious fast-food outlets. Fast customer turnover, and a large passing trade, makes it easy to make a living: tourist-rich Tuscany boasts one fast-food outlet for every 195 locals, while the less visited, poorer South has only one public eating place of any kind for every 1000 inhabitants.

(iv) Alcohol

Italians annually drink an average of 90 litres of wine per head, but the figure is dropping all the time, to the extent that both beer and wine have to be advertised by their respective marketing boards in order to encourage flagging consumption. The so-called 'yuppie wines' most promoted in Italy are those low-alcohol-content, fizzy whites that resemble 7-Up, like Galestro and Canei, although some 'traditional' *frizzantini* – especially from the north-east region (Veneto, Friuli, Alto Adige) – are well worth investigating. In Rome, it is normal to mix table wine with mineral water, or even *gassosa* – lemonade soda. When they do drink wine,

Eating out

- Assuming that you wish to sample traditional Italian food, you must stick to places labelled '*ristorante trattoria*' or *pizzeria*. Theoretically, the first is smarter than the second, but this is not always the case. Don't be fooled by appearance: the kind of interior design intended to denote classy food in the English-speaking world has no equivalent in Italy; it is technically the food and the service that counts. Even places with paper tablecloths and napkins may be good.

- As a general rule, avoid places that display the legend '*menu turistico*' in four languages, although in some towns it is hard to find places that don't.

- Regular Italian restaurant meals have between three and five courses: waiters usually get shirty if you ask just for *pasta*; *pizzerie* are designed for one-course eating.

- The *antipasto* – hors-d'oeuvre – and the next course – *il primo*, consisting of *pasta* or soup – are usually more exciting than *il secondo* – the main meat or fish course – with the follow-up *il contorno* – the vegetable or salad course (always served and eaten on separate plates), which can often be disappointing. Many people skip *il dolce* or *la frutta* – dessert or fruit – altogether.

• The very unassuming quality of most Italian restaurants is evident from customers' drinking habits: restaurant-goers in Italy tend to go for the house carafe wine – *vino sciolto* – which is often disappointing – but then, so is the wine list in all but the best places: most *trattorie* all over Italy stock at least six out of a dozen of the same wines.

• Don't be afraid of making a fuss and sending your meal back: they'll take it without making a scene, although you may have to wait unduly for its replacement.

• Some cities, especially from Rome southwards, are full of wandering minstrels, who tend to play at your table and expect to be paid for it: they will want at least 1000 lire. Equally trying are the gypsy rose-sellers, who hone in on single couples dining out, especially foreign ones. They can be very insistent and their flowers are expensive. Unless you're trying to live out a Barbara Cartland fantasy role, just say no. A decisive 'tut' or nod of the head will do.

• If eating out with Italians, expect to split the bill *alla romana* – divide it by the number of those present. To go dutch, even if you have eaten much less than someone else, is considered unpardonably mean. If you have been invited out in southern Italy, old-fashioned manners may mean an embarrassing scene as they insist on paying the whole bill. Another unreconstructed habit is for the men to pay for the women, more common among older couples dining together.

• The question of tipping is complicated: until recently, service was added as a sepa-

it is almost exclusively at table, and then sparingly. Likewise, *aperitivi* and *digestivi* – aperitifs and digestifs – are drunk only by virtue of their relevance to the meal. Many *aperitivi* are *analcolici* – alcohol-free – to cater for all those Italians who are completely *astemio* – teetotal. At parties, it is the Coke and the fruit juice, not the alcoholic drinks, that run out first. The walls of Italian bars look impressive with all those bottles, but count how few people actually order from them. When Italians go out after a meal, it is almost never 'for a drink' but for *un caffè* or *un gelato*. (→ I, 4)

Since the Italians do not need alcohol in order to relax and be jolly, persuading them to drink away from the table has not been easy; despite retail prices about half those in the UK or USA, sales of spirits are relatively low. The Italians' taste for luxury has been pandered to by the skilful marketing of single malt whiskies, which outsell the more common blended ones by about two to one. On the other hand, purchasing an expensive bottle of some obscure Glen doesn't mean they actually drink it.

Getting drunk – *ubriaco* – in Italy carries the maximum social disapproval, and many Italians have never done such a thing in their lives. (There isn't even a word for 'hangover' in Italian.) There is consequently an extremely low level of alcoholism; the meetings of Alcolizzati Anonimi cater to a limited clientele. The only exception to this rule is in certain northern mountainous communities, where they drink a glass of hot wine, or even *grappa*, for breakfast.

Just as the distinction between *ristorante* and *trattoria* rarely holds good, so the one between *vino d.o.c.* and *vino da tavola* wavers. There are over 400 wines that qualify for the theoretically prestigious *denominazione di origine controllata* label, but in the past this qualification was merely bought for money by unscrupulous growers whose wine was often worse than the humbler *vino da tavola*. Following the decline in credibility, a new improved label has been brought in – d.o.c.g., the 'g' standing for *garantita* – guaranteed. After decades of using inefficient, unscientific production methods, many Italian growers have swallowed their pride and absorbed the technical advances pioneered in California, with immensely gratifying results. Many of these 'interesting' new wines are practically unknown in Italy, let alone abroad. In the wine trade, Italy's general reputation remains rather more down-market. The high gradation of Italian wine makes it a suitable mixer for lower octane foreign wines, so over 30% of national production crosses the Alps to beef up low-alcohol French wines.

Despite the massive variety of Italian wine production – they produce more different types than does any other country – many of the wines get no further than their region of origin. Even wine connoisseurship is new: it wasn't until Luigi.Veronelli wrote his first annual wine guide in 1959 that it occured to the Italians that they too could be *enologi* – wine bores. You may well find your knowledge outstrips that of waiters in all but the classiest restaurants. As a rule, Italians know quite a bit about wines from their *regione*, but not too much about those from elsewhere. Apart from the odd Portuguese *rosé*, you are unlikely to encounter French, Spanish, German or American wines in Italy. If this is surprising, so is the fact that so few non-Piedmontese Italians know much about wine from Piedmont – the finest wine-growing *regione* in Italy.

rate 10%; it is now in theory included in the total, though waiters like to make you think it isn't. Beyond the 10% (occasionally 15%) standard charge, Italians usually make up the total to a round sum, though this is by no means obligatory.

● By law, the waiter should give you something called *la ricevuta fiscale* rather than *il conto*, the bill. This is the bill with the restaurant owner's tax and VAT details printed at the top, and a serial number. In theory, you can be arrested for leaving the restaurant without it, since it makes you an accomplice to the restaurant's tax evasion (a serious problem in Italy). Of course, the police never stop anyone, but many Italians insist on getting it all the same, especially if they actually pay theirs.

● →also VI,1:ACCESS.

Terms for wine

Bianco: white.
Rosso: red.
Rosato: rosé.
Frizzante: fizzy.
Spumante: sparkling.
Secco: dry.
Dolce: sweet.
Vino locale: local.
Novello: young – usually local.
Vino sciolto: by the carafe.
d.o.c.g.: *denominazione d'origine controllata garantita.*

- Standards of nursing and ancillary help in Italian *ospedali* – hospitals – are such that, if you have to go in one, it's useful to have someone from outside on call to look after you. Italians have several family members on duty, less to provide little creature comforts than to guarantee basic things like meals. The constant presence of friendly faces obviously has its positive, reassuring side. In private clinics, it is normal for a family member to sleep in your room, in order to look after you and keep you company.

- The dismal quality of most hospital meals is in a way a blessing: you may actually get them; alternatively, you may be told, 'There's not enough to go round' – i.e. the kitchens have been hijacked and the raw ingredients resold.

- The erratic efficiency is evident from the bed occupancy rate. The classic vision of *la corsia* – the Italian hospital ward – is jammed with beds, which reach out into the corridor; only 25% of urgent cases get beds within a month of diagnosis, although other official statistics speak of a 67% bed occupancy rate, rising to 77% in the private sector. This paradox is even more pronounced in the South, where the occupancy rate is lower still, despite only 6.9 hospital beds per 1000, as opposed to 8.2 per 1000 in northern regions.

- EC citizens, as well as those of other countries with specific bilateral agreements, enjoy free treatment in Italian hospitals and surgeries. For those who become residents, officially or unofficially, it is necessary

2. Medicine

(i) Hospitals and the *Unità Sanitarie Locali*

> In Italian hospital wards, people die alone and abandoned: the Italian citizen is helpless in the face of the health service. Here, you have to take what you get and be grateful.
>
> Carlo Donat Cattin, Minister of Health, 1986–9.

It seems curious that a country that turns out more doctors per head than any other in the world except Cuba, among them a good handful of world-class specialists, should have such a catastrophic health system.

The professionalism of many Italian doctors is remarkable, in view of their dodgy training system. University medical faculties are packed to bursting, but provide a rather partial training: it is entirely theory-based. It is sometimes pointed out that in Italy you can become a fully fledged doctor without ever having seen a corpse.

There are few teaching hospitals. Rome's Policlinico Umberto I is the largest, but it is hopelessly overcrowded with trainee doctors and students. Since attendance is non-obligatory, many would-be doctors are put off. Most young doctors try to get in with the all-powerful *baroni* – 'barons' – or *primari* – departmental heads – in a regular hospital, and follow them around on an *ad hoc* basis. To become a *primario*'s favourite involves serious sycophancy – hence over-eager pupils' derisive label, *portaborsa* – bag-carrier.

Pin-up doctors and leading specialists

A distinguished career and an incisive or controversial media profile have turned some of these doctors into glamour figures; others quietly beaver away out of the limelight.

- **Ferdinando Aiuti (Rome): leading the fight against AIDS led him into a spectacular public battle against ex-Health Minister Donat Cattin; he has been rehabilitated by the more enlightened Francesco De Lorenzo.**

- **Gaetano Azzolina (Sicily): major international career as cardiovascular surgeon; currently directs Tuscany Chest and Heart Centre; has written two extremely vituperative pamphlets against the corrupt management of the Italian health service.**

- **Daniel Bovet (Rome): Swiss-born; 1957 Nobel prize for Medicine; his discoveries have been vital in the treatment of Parkinson's disease, allergies and infectious diseases; currently dedicated** to psychobiological and psychopharmacological research.

● **Ettore Cittadini (Palermo):** introduced controversial artificial insemination methods into Italy; over fifty *in vitro* births and a best-seller under his belt.

● **Antonio Del Monte (Rome):** Italy's leading sports doctor – a charismatic ex-pilot/speedboat champion, whose imaginative studies into athletics' problems have greatly helped Italian sportsmen and women.

● **Beniamino Guidetti (Naples):** Italy's leading brain surgeon; visiting professor at Edinburgh and New York universities.

● **Enzo Jannacci (Milan):** real-life Dr Kildare – good-looking, bespectacled heart surgeon who sings, with fifteen hit LPs (sophisticated satirical songs) to date.

● **Edward Luria Salvador (Turin):** taught biology and microbiology at the Massachusetts Institute of Technology; received joint Nobel prize for Medicine in 1969, for discoveries in viral and bacterial genetics.

● **Attilio Masari (Pisa):** highly skilled cardiologist responsible for several innovative techniques, equally well known for his work in London, at the Hammersmith.

● **Umberto Veronesi (Milan):** leading breast cancer expert; one-time President of the International Union against Cancer; has written a best-selling book on incurable diseases.

Iatrogeny

The theories of Mexican writer Ivan Illich receive some confirmation in Italy, where 700,000 patients contract further infections once in hospital (USA = 2 million), of which 80,000 prove fatal.

Hospital workers grumble about pay, and tend to vote with their feet; *assenteismo* is at its most common in the lower echelons of the health service, especially in central and southern Italy. (→ V, 1:vi) For this reason, many Southerners actually go up North just to be treated, to the considerable dismay of Northern health authorities.

Traditionally, medicine was in the hands of the Church in Italy, and it is certainly their hospitals that remain the best. When Pope John Paul II was shot in St Peter's Square in 1981, it wasn't to the State-run Santo Spirito, 300 yards away, that he was taken (despite the

to sign up with *un medico mutualistico* – a GP – and to get a medical health number. To do this, you must visit your local USL office (listed in *Tuttocittà*: → V, 4:ACCESS – Useful information) where they have a list of doctors to choose from.

● Treatment is normally free, although most medicines and analyses/tests are covered only in part by *il mutuo* – the free system. The remaining percentage must be paid for by you; a prescription charge is called *il ticket*; a surgery is a *studio medico* or an *ambulatorio*.

● Most foreign firms operating in Italy have a private health plan for their employees. *Le cliniche private* – private clinics – are often excellent.

Seeking medical help

● Free medical treatment is available to citizens of those countries that enjoy this reciprocal arrangement with Italy. EC citizens are furthermore automatically entitled to full treatment. Americans and citizens of other countries with limited public health provisions would be expected to foot a hospital bill the way an Italian would in the USA.

● Getting to hospital in an emergency may be difficult (as the Pope discovered). Waiting for an ambulance may be a serious waste of time: if you have a car, you can drive with a white handkerchief held out of the window, honking your horn – people will let you pass.

● All-night chemists: there is usually a list in the daily papers, or in the SIP *Tuttocittà* list for each city (→V,4: ACCESS – Useful information): note that the list is organized in sections of the city. Failing that, look for the nearest '*Farmacia*' sign; if it is closed, you will have to check the adjacent list for local pharmacies open out of hours.

● **If you are taking up employment for the first time in Italy, you should get your USL number.** (→ACCESS – You and Italian hospitals, above) **Don't forget to write your number somewhere else: you need it on every prescription. It is usually eleven digits long.**

aptness of the name), but to the Catholic-run Gemelli, five miles away. The Pope nearly died struggling through the traffic, but the Vatican weren't taking any chances.

The first private insurance schemes were set up for workers in the 1920s, and gradually became widespread, following the classic trade union model. Then the post-war Republican government attempted to set up a form of centrally controlled welfare system. In the meantime, most Italians who could afford it took out private medical insurance. At the beginning of the 1970s, the regional reforms (→ II, 3:ii) provided for the setting up of the now notorious USL system, which became operational in 1980. Each of the Unità Sanitarie Locali has a theoretical catchment area of around 150,000 people, and is run by a nine-man committee answerable to a fifty-man assembly. Democratic as this may sound on paper, in practice it constitutes one of the least edifying aspects of life in Italy, as the lives and good health of millions of patients are at the mercy of these sinister cabals, made up almost exclusively of the non-medical appointees of the political parties. The party that dominated the most USLs in the early 1980s was actually the PCI, whose self-proclaimed 'squeaky clean' political image thus revealed itself as less than lifelike. Since then, the PSI have conducted an infiltration campaign on a massive scale of the USL *consigli di amministrazione* – boards – where they now challenge PCI supremacy. Both hospitals and surgeries are controlled by the USLs.

Who pays what

● ISIS **findings (1988) show that it costs the State more to keep a patient in a public hospital (284,000 lire a day) than it does in a private clinic (221,000 lire a day), although the figures are reversed over the duration of the patient's stay: the average Italian patient spends eleven days in a public hospital, but eighteen in a private clinic.**

● **In 1988, 61,320 billion lire were spent on the Italian health service, eating up two-thirds of the funds of the *regioni*. Most of this money comes out of employees' and employers' pockets: *i contributi sociali* – effectively, taxes for health insurance – add a good 40% on to the cost of each wage packet. Self-employed workers are theoretically charged *la tassa della salute*, a health tax of between 4% and 6% on their certified income, though this new measure has met with bitter opposition, especially since most have had private health insurance for years.**

A 1988 CENSIS survey showed that the majority of Italians get their friends to suggest medicine and treatment for them, and apparently find compliant or indifferent doctors ready to satisfy their whims. 56% of Italian doctors admit to 'sometimes', and 13.5% to 'often', allowing their patients to tell them what medicines they want. The most common reason cited was that patients 'don't trust doctors'. An almost equally large proportion of patients admitted to not taking the prescribed medicines, since they didn't 'like' medicine. Overall, however, 90% of Italians said they 'trust their doctors', and evidently visit them: in an average month, 25 million Italians – almost half the population – visit the doctor, 20% getting a home call; 70% see their G.P., while 30% are seen by a specialist.

• **Italians love to hoard old medicines – they have whole cupboards full of them; this may be linked to why their average annual expenditure on drugs is lower than in most other countries:**
overall annual expenditure (in lire) per person for pharmaceuticals*

UK	**198,000**
Italy	**218,000**
France	**274,000**
Germany	**341,000**
USA	**336,000**
Japan	**369,000**

***In real terms – i.e. not just prescription charges.**

Another factor may be the low number of pharmaceutical products on sale: 1987 figures showed only 5455 products, two-thirds of which were on the national health. West Germany had 70,000, the UK 35,000, France 8000.
• **Medicine confections sold per annum: 1533 million – almost thirty a head.**
• **18% of pills prescribed are for pain-killers, 7% are vitamin reconstituents and tranquillizers.**

In country areas, especially in the South, the figure of the doctor resembles that of an old-fashioned feudal patriarch. On feast-days or name-days, they are liable to receive a non-stop line of patients, each one weighed down with farmyard presents, many of which are still alive and struggling.

The Italian health system divides drugs into three categories, with the most essential group heavily subsidized – by up to 90%. Furthermore, low-income citizens – 28% of the population in the south (Sicily,

Calabria and Basilicata consume by far the most medicines in the whole country), 17% in the North – pay nothing at all. But if the patient thus pays very little for medicine, unfortunately for chemists, so does the State: it is relatively common to find a total strike of all *farmacie* – pharmacies – especially when they haven't been reimbursed for over six months.

(ii) Dentistry

Dental treatment is in theory free, on the USL. However, it is such an inconvenient system – you have to see your doctor, who will refer you to a dentist of his/her choice – that most Italians go, for serious treatment at least, to a private practitioner. This is extremely expensive, even though the best Italian dentists are among the most advanced in the world. As a compromise solution, many Italians fly to London for dental care on the cheap. To be a USL dentist in Italy, you must also qualify as a doctor before specializing.

Health spending as % of GDP

West Germany	5.9%
Denmark	5.3%
UK	4.8%
Italy	3.1%
France	0.5%
Belgium	0.5%
Japan	0.4%

(iii) Alternative medicine

Homoeopathy is virtually unheard of in Italy, while acupuncture enjoys immense and widespread success. As old peasant herbal remedies are gradually forgotten, countless private TV channels offer the services of witches, healers and quacks, whose merchandise ranges from unguents to patent machines. Just one such branch, *la pranoterapia* – involving a laying on of hands – gives work to 50,000 *pranoterapisti*, who collectively do 250 billion lire worth of business per year.

(iv) AIDS

Italy has an anomalous position in the international struggle against AIDS: it has the world record (followed by Spain) for drug users as its main group, to the tune of some 70% of them, thus leading to worries of spreading through heterosexual contact without condoms. By contrast, it has one of the smallest percentages of HIV positive homosexuals:

the figure has gradually declined, to just over 16%.
($\rightarrow$ I, 3:xi)

Italy also stands out on account of its extremely tardy
information campaign: although the gay movement
FUORI started lobbying the Health Minister as early as
1983, the first TV adverts didn't appear until July 1988,
with leaflets provided by non-governmental bodies. The
information movement has been bitterly opposed by the
Catholic Church (they objected to the words *profilattico*
and *preservativo* being used on TV), and by the eccentric
Carlo Donat Cattin, Health Minister from 1986 to 1989.

Many in the Italian medical profession felt less than
happy about Cattin's refusal to attend the 1988 World
AIDS summit in London, since he was 'too busy with
more important things to attend', despite the fact that
the epidemic was rising faster in Italy than in any other
European country. Since 1987, 100 billion lire has been
allocated for AIDS research, although in 1988 the Corte
dei Conti complained that only 37 billion had reached
the clinics concerned.

3. Taking care and running risks

(i) Hygiene and feeling beautiful

There can be no cleaner race in the world than the Italians, although this may be surprising to tourists who blanch at the state of the streets in some of their cities. The apparent paradox is easily resolvable, in that Italians make a clear-cut distinction between the despised public domain and the private one, which is sacred: the inside of their homes, their clothes and their bodies.

There is almost Orwellian fanaticism about domestic cleaning and tidiness: one TV advert for a cleaning product shows a woman on trial before a jury of house-wives, guilty of not keeping her house spotless enough: paranoia in the broom cupboard. This collective Lady Macbeth complex is also visible in most other adverts, which show frenzied Italian housewives scrubbing and polishing kitchens, bathrooms and sitting rooms under the watchful surveillance of neighbours or mothers-in-law. (→ I, 1:i)

The same raccoon-like vigilance naturally extends to clothes and dishes: it is no coincidence that Italian homes (13%) have over four times as many dishwash-ers as British ones (4%); even the humblest of homes has a washing machine. Those that don't rarely resort to laundromats (which hardly exist), but do it by hand; or at least, *la nonna* does. However, dry cleaning – *il lavaggio a secco* – is a major item on the family budget; at each season's end, even the poorest of people seem to be able to afford to take their entire wardrobe in.

The national devotion to spotless clothes is evident from simply surveying Italians of all ages and back-grounds in the street. It is not so much that they are so well dressed (many Italians, like British or Americans, have zero dress taste) as that they are immaculately turned out. They are most fastidious about changing their underclothes daily, and shocked when they hear from media surveys that some nations don't. You will never, ever see a pair of white trousers or jeans in Italy that are less than spotless: as soon as the wearer gets home, they are ripped from their legs and shoved in the hot cycle with lots of bleach. The ecologically inspired move to reduce the use of phosphates and bleaches in washing powders meets a solid wall of resistance among Italian housewives. Detergents, more even than cars, dominate TV commercials, which is hardly surprising, since Italians buy more of them than does any other country in the world. (→ II, 2:i)

The same statistics apply to soaps and perfume:

the Italians beat even the French (whom the Italians consider almost as dirty as the British) in their massive consumption of toiletry articles, which in 1988 reached a total of 6000 billion lire. Their appetite for new lines and products seems bottomless: in 1987, seventy new scents alone were launched. One of the most booming areas in the services sector is *istituti di bellezza* – beauty salons – which are now doubling in number every few years: there are already a massive 20,000, where Italian women, and, increasingly, men can be made to feel even more beautiful.

In fact, the fastest growth area of all is in male cosmetics, which has now progressed way beyond posh-sounding colognes and scientific-looking skin treatments to offering *la deodorante intima*. The commercial assault on the Italians' crutch has involved careful, long-term planning. Ever since the 1950s' mass migration to the towns, Italians have been used to, and psychologically dependent on, their bidet. It is arguable whether this obsession with *l'igiene intima* is inherent, or, like their massive meat consumption, a question of compensating for centuries-old folk memories of doing without – in this case, Life Without Plumbing. They even have withdrawal symptoms, complaining about foreign homes or hotels having 'incomplete bathrooms', and, indeed, about foreigners themselves, who, they suspect, are not 'completely clean'. Against this backdrop, it was easy for marketing men to override doctors' objections to the first vaginal deodorants in the early 1980s, especially with a clever TV campaign. It was thus easy to persuade men that they needed one too.

By the same token, there has been a process of complete sanitization of lavatorial functions in Italy, which is also detectable in certain TV commercials for food and drink. In most countries, seeing advertisements of fruit juice or whisky being poured in a way that resembles someone having a pee or, worse still, close-ups of thick chocolate oozing out of cakes, might fascinate a few diehard Freud devotees, but would repel the average consumer. The location of the lavatory in the Italian home has much to do with this: it is never on its own, hidden in 'the smallest room', but sits alongside the bath, bidet and wash basin, firmly linked to the key concept – 'hygiene'. Lavatory paper is *carta igienica*, while the grim-sounding 'sanitary ware' becomes the more optimistic *servizi igienici*. This concept is reinforced by the expression *andare al bagno* (cf. the American expression 'To go to the bathroom'), with no words like 'toilet' or 'loo'. Even in a public place, you ask *'Dov'è il bagno?'*, rather than specify *il gabinetto*.

Since the war, Italy has also adopted the American

devotion to the shower – *la doccia* – rather than to the bath – *la vasca* – although most bathrooms have the one attached to the other. Italians shower at least once daily; in summer, this may stretch to three or four times.

It is tempting to give the modern Italians' *abitudini igieniche* a historical perspective, *vis-à-vis* the ancient Roman practice of the leisurely bath-house, where one performed one's toilet in the fullest sense, in the pleasant company of others.

(ii) Health and safety

Italian attitudes to health and safety are curiously contradictory. As in the case of hygiene, there is a fanatical attention towards health, closely connected to the mother's all-intrusive role, whereby from birth children are mollycoddled so they don't get ill: that is why Italians often seem to be wearing too many clothes, even when it is warm. Spot the Italian in a summer tourist crowd: he's the one still wearing *la maglietta della salute* – a woolly vest – because his mother warned him about chills. Just as Florence Nightingale discovered, to her cost, with the Indians, the Italians always sleep with the window closed, in both summer and winter, on what they see as health grounds. This is evidently a North–South argument, and it is doubtful the twain shall ever meet.

Italians find it very funny when foreigners stick thermometers in their mouths and shudder at the idea of suppositories or injections. Italian temperatures are measured from the armpit or bottom, the general area in which both suppositories and injections are administered. Every Italian home has a ready supply of syringes (frequently advertised on TV) for any kind of prescription.

Italians display an almost kamikaze indifference to risk, enough to make most English-speaking peoples blanch. This derives partly from considerations of *bella figura* (not wanting to wear a seat-belt or motorcycle helmet since it spoils your appearance), partly from arrogance towards statistics ('It'll never happen to me'), partly from primitive superstition about bad luck. (→ 10, below)

The lack of life assurance policies is perhaps due more to an ignorance of their existence than to anything else: to discuss even the prospect of an accident or death seems to Italians to be in extraordinarily bad taste, causing them to touch their balls or *fanno le corna.* (→ 3:iv, below; VI, 4:iii) Even in the face of major disasters, like earthquakes and landslides, which raise predictable outrage, the Italians simply can't be bothered with safety regulations. Electric wiring is suicidal; the flea-markets are full of electrical goods guaranteed to electrocute you. The annual hunting season regularly sees people killed in droves; buildings routinely collapse with numerous victims, especially in the South, and are usually shrugged off as *'una disgrazia'* – a mishap. The ecology issue triggers an almost schizophrenic response: the hygiene/aesthetic aspect causes much distress (Italians were horrified by Chernobyl), but the infrastructure damage aspect seems to worry them not at all. (→ II, 2:i)

Until 1986, it was quite legal to ride a motorbike without a helmet: it still is if you are over 18 and on a moped. Only since May 1989 has it finally become obligatory for Italians to wear seat-belts; the rest of the Western world, save only Greece, has been doing so for over a decade. Reports of rapidly reduced accident rates in other countries produced no effect. Significantly, Fiat, for all their boasts of advanced manufacturing techniques, have been mindful enough of the Italian taboo about mentioning things that bring bad luck never to so much as suggest their customers should wear one. Following EC directives, Italy is also due to introduce drink/drive legislation. This has not yet been done, although in October 1989, a breath test was brought in; the problem is, the authorities cannot agree what the limit should be.

Italian drivers are on the whole very proficient, which is fortunate, considering the enormous risks they take. (→ II, 7:ii) The generally lenient attitude of the police doesn't help, but although they turn a blind eye to many offences, there are still 2.5 million tickets issued each year, with 180,000 cases serious enough to warrant licence withdrawal. There are over 7000 deaths, with almost 250,000 injured (parliamentary estimates), in road accidents a year: twenty deaths a day, which ISPES calculate could be halved by introducing sterner measures, in line with the EC. Their findings show that 14% of Italy's 30 million vehicles are involved in a crash at some time. Industrial safety statistics tell the same story: a 1988 government survey showed that Italy's record is one of the worst in the EC.

(iii) Smoking

The anti-smoking message has definitely not caught on – possibly unsurprising in a country where most doctors not only smoke, but do so in their surgery. Lung cancer is for the next person. It is normal for a non-smoker to find they are the only one without a lit cigarette round a dinner table, in a car or at work. Fortunately, there are anti-smoking regulations in most public places. Italians start young, with a particularly high incidence of girls smoking; some 32% of 15-year-old Turinese smoke regularly. However, there seems to be a slight decrease in the overall number of smokers, above all in the 25–44 age group.

In 1987, 29% (down from 35%) were regular smokers; 9.2% (up from 5%) had given up; 61% (up from 59%) had never smoked.
(ISPES, 1988)

Talking drugs

Because of the prevalence of regional dialect, there is little nationwide youth slang. The drug culture has provided much of what there is.

Bucarsi, farsi una pera – to jack up.

Spada – literally sword – syringe.

Spinello, canna – joint (also used).

A rota – cold turkey.

Fatto – stoned.

Roba – drugs, usually heroin.

Fumo – smoke – i.e. dope.

(iv) Drugs

In a country where drinking, even among the young, poses no social problems at all, it is ironic that another field of self-abuse should. In fact, with 300,000 registered junkies on its hands, Italy has the most serious drug problem of any European country. As in so many other fields, it is a case of catching up fast. Until the mid-1970s, while other Western countries were experiencing the wide-scale use of soft drugs, it was relatively unusual in Italy to see people smoking joints, and the police were extremely harsh on offenders. In the intervening period, other countries have seen the genesis of a heroin problem, coinciding roughly with the decline of joint-smoking. In Italy, however, serious heroin use spiralled violently in the late 1970s, hand in hand with the whole radical post-1968 movement. Suddenly, people who had never so much as seen a joint were shooting up. It is hard to explain how young Italians suddenly became so susceptible to the charms of heroin, though there are some indicators. One was the sense of acute social alienation felt by many young Italians in the 1970s, which, fanned by the emotive political rhetoric of the day, gave heroin use a certain right-on legitimacy. *Farsi una pera* – jacking up – was a smart way to *épater la bourgeoisie*. But if heroin use first took off as something of a political statement, the reason for its subsequent diffusion among the less intellectually minded seems above all to be linked to the curious double-bind of the *famiglia italiana*. (→ I, 1:i) If young Italians share with their other Western counterparts a generalized desire for 'freedom' and independence from their family, they tend to be frustrated by their own acute lack of self-sufficiency; however much they despise their parents' values, they know which side their bread is buttered on, and it is a far richer butter than that offered in other countries. Hence, heroin offered the radical form of rebellion they desired, without actually necessitating their leaving home to find it: real ideological laziness. The all-accepting Catholic indulgence of the Italian family has managed to embrace *la piaga della droga* – the drug curse – and to cope with it surprisingly well. Mothers band together on marches, like the Argentinian *madres della Plaza di Mayo*, demanding adequate treatment and jobs for their *figli emarginati* – socially alienated children.

A well-organized, plentiful supply is of cardinal importance to a country's habit, and it is no coincidence that the Mafia in Sicily, the Calabrian 'Ndrangheta and the Neapolitan Camorra have finely tuned their drug distribution in Italy, from the overlords downwards. (→ V, 2:iii)

Economic background seems to matter little among the addicts: there are as many *tossicodipendenti* among the bored rich kids of prosperous northern cities like Verona and Bergamo as there are in the desperately poor southern ones like Reggio Calabria and Naples. The average age is 27, and seems to be decreasing; parts of Rome, like the sinister shanty town La Magliana, immortalized in the books of Pasolini, have a staggering 75% heroin dependency record in 18–25-year-olds, with a 35% rate among the under-18s. In the South, it is frequently much younger. Primary school children are increasingly used as carriers: Italian 'Just say no' TV adverts tend to feature early adolescents.

The police have been until now much more lenient, as was the law, permitting the carrying of small amounts of hashish, or a single dose of heroin. Only pushers are ever arrested, and in 1987 11,000 of them were; on the other hand, in 1988 the PSI were talking about recriminalizing simple possession as well, and in September 1989, the government decided to jump on the bandwagon of President Bush's anti-drugs crusade. The credit for this about-turn must go to Craxi, who is anxious to gain mass support for the PSI from their handling of this emotive issue.

Quite apart from AIDS as a killer of heroin users (→ 2:iv, above), deaths from overdose continue to rise. Ministry of the Interior figures for 1987 listed 516 such casualties (90% of which were male), but, as usual, the State does little to help. A mere 20 billion lire a year is devoted to combating heroin addiction, compared to 4500 billion donated to the Third World. The USL's aptly-named NOT clinics – Nuclei Operativi Tossicodipendenza – have some 473 centres at their disposal, and dispense large quantities of methadone, but little else. They are run by what private aid groups describe as the dregs of the Italian medical profession – doctors sacked from other posts. Apart from users' families themselves, most help comes from the 342 private clinics, most of which are run by religious groups. While some of these are small day centres, others are large, self-supporting communes in the country, often run by controversial, charismatic, patriarchal figures. The most celebrated is Vincenzo Muccioli, whose heavy-duty lose-the-habit techniques have won the applause of desperate parents, but sparked off police investigations. Catholic priest Don Ciotti's Gruppo Abele has had considerable rehabilitation success, but it is as weary as Muccioli over the sinister political battles taking place over the 30,000 supine bodies (5000 of them women) in drug clinics: the parties have discovered yet another area to carve up between them.

(v) Longevity and fitness

A sure indicator of economic growth is life expectancy. In 1920, a male in southern Italy could have expected to live to 48, now he may live to 71. However, women have shot even further ahead: in 1952, they outlived men by an average of three years six months; in 1985, the figure was seven years three months.

Although Italy is currently undergoing a collective obsession with *lo stress*, they are generally a healthy lot: 66% declared recently that they'd felt continuously in good health 'for at least a month'. A 1986 ISTAT survey shows this subjective judgement to be objectively true: in comparison with figures for the previous six years, there has been a significant decrease in many illnesses, ranging from heart and lung problems to ulcers, arthritis and nervous disorders.

If the inordinately high amount of Italians who smoke makes for a bad start, their basically sound eating habits and high degree of physical activity add up to an overall clean bill of health.

4. Sport

Italy's international sporting profile shadows its industrial and economic development – sport in Italy was a late starter, which has recently made up for lost time.

If the rapid spread of all forms of sporting activity in English-speaking countries in the mid- and late–19th century owed much to both religious and industrial support, Italy was at a disadvantage during that period. It lack the muscular Christianity espoused by the Victorian Protestant churches, which were so keen to keep the young and the working classes off the streets but out of the pubs; and it had no industrial cities to spawn working men's sporting associations, and no rich benefactors eager to make lavish endowments to nascent *circoli sportivi* – sports clubs.

In fact, the first football teams in Italy, founded at the turn of the century, were not set up by Italians at all but by English factory firms in northern proto-industrial cities like Genoa, Turin and Milan, where they were initially known as 'Football and Cricket Clubs'. It wasn't until the Catholic Church decided that sport wasn't sinful that it really became widespread. Italian football quickly assumed a national character as the second imported British sport was dropped, and as the *parroco* – parish priest – in *sottana* – cassock – and *berretta* – priest's hat – kicking a ball with the local *ragazzi* became a familiar national stereotype.

Sport in general, but athletics in particular, received a further boost during the 1920s and 1930s from a Mussolini keen to wed Hitler's *Kraft durch Freude* ethos with his own patent pseudo-Classical aspirations. Since there were few existing municipal facilities for sport at an active or spectator level, he embarked on an ambitious programme in many large cities to build sports complexes that would act as showcases for Fascist sporting prowess. Nervi's neo-Futurist Florence football stadium (1930–32) is a remarkable achievement, while Rome's Foro Italico sports complex (Del Nebbio, 1933) is to this day a triumph of Fascist kitsch, with its remarkable marble statues surrounding the athletics track, and, more surprisingly, a huge gilded obelisk bearing the legend 'Dux' and 'Mussolini', which still guards the stadium. The 1960 Olympics, staged in Rome, provided further encouragement to popular sporting enthusiasm, partly thanks to the construction of more sports premises (i.e. Nervi's Palazzo and Palazzetto dello Sport, Rome, 1958–60).

Thanks to the efforts of the Comitato Olimpionico

Sports facilities

Finding out about where to play sport is not easy in Italy; the best places to look are in the local paper (not guaranteed to be there) or in *Tuttocittà*, the street-finding guide that comes with the phone-book. (→ V, 4:ACCESS – Useful information) Apart from the swimming pool – *piscina* – and *calcio* – football – most Italian sports names are either English, or sufficiently like English not to require a glossary. Public swimming pools are disappointingly few and far between in Italy, but in summer are to be recommended in preference to most beaches near big cities, with their alarming pollution levels. (→ II, 2:iii)

Nazionale Italiano (CONI) – the Italian Olympic committee – Italy's Olympic performance has been fairly consistent since 1960, usually winning roughly the same number of medals as Britain, with its almost identical population (57 million in 1989). Among traditional strengths are team events like fencing, riding, rowing and the Pentathlon.

However, there is still a lack of satisfactory facilities, and this holds back Italian sport. Olympic hopefuls and amateurs alike are seriously hampered by not having subsidized municipal sporting premises, such as are common to most European countries. The familiar old cry, '*Qui mancano le strutture*' – 'There's no organization round here' – is as prevalent in sport as it is in education or health care (→ IV, 3:iii): in 1988, dozens of Palermo athletes who turned up for their daily training session were disconcerted to find that the city athletics stadium had been locked up without notice because the single caretaker had gone on holiday. Only a direct appeal to the mayor saw that fresh personnel was drafted in to keep the stadium open to athletes.

This disregard by the authorities starts early: even the national school curriculum has never made any allowance for sports practice. Neither, despite all the chat, did the vigorous left-wing *giunte*, which governed most large cities during the 1970s and early 1980s, do much to increase municipal sports expenditure.

However, the 1980s' leisure and fitness boom has revolutionized Italian attitudes towards sport, especially since it has been skilfully packaged as another way of demonstrating economic well-being, in a country where no opportunity to demonstrate *bella figura* ever gets overlooked. In order to swim, play tennis or work out, even the least wealthy Italians are now prepared to pay the inordinately steep fees of the 'exclusive' pseudo-American sports and health clubs that have mushroomed everywhere. Sport-as-lifestyle-choice has mobilized some 16 million Italians – well over 25% – to practise some sport, spending a massive 2.8 billion lire to do so.

It is easy to suspect that what really got the Italians interested in participatory sport was not so much the resultant fitness as looking good while doing it. With typical expertise, the Italians promptly turned an imported habit (sport) into a serious export – designer sportswear. It was not difficult to persuade the Italians to invest vast sums in the most expensive and most fashionable sports clothes and equipment; but it was a stroke of genius to get foreigners – particularly Americans – to follow suit. It was the Italians who first turned gyms, tennis courts and athletics fields into fashion catwalks. The shiny nylon tracksuit in those dodgy pastel shades, typical of the early 1980s, was launched by Italian labels like Sergio Tacchini and Fila, which quickly found themselves on a prestige footing equal to much longer-established names like Lacoste and Adidas.

Italy's enviable climate and geography has also aided the luxury sports boom. Only the meanest Italian parents can deny their children *la settimana bianca* – a skiing, or 'white', week – at a resort a coach-ride away; it is not just the high level of income tax fraud that permits every other executive to buy a power speed-boat. Milan can look deserted at weekends, in both summer and winter, as 'everyone' skis and sails.

Nevertheless, the spread of prestige sports is patchy: unlike another race they so resemble when it comes to slavishly copying Anglo-Saxon leisure habits, they lack the Japanese passion for golf. There are still only eighty-seven golf courses in all of Italy, and a mere 250 squash courts. Neither do polo or horse-racing have much of a chic following, although both the latter (usually American-style, with a buggy) and greyhound racing have a certain traditional currency among urban punters. (→ VII, 2:iii)

Italy is now second only to France in continental Europe as a rugby nation, but it is basketball that has made the most remarkable progress, since being imported from the USA after the war. Now Italy's second most popular ball-game, it has the best teams and players outside the USA. Teams are known by the names of the companies that sponsor them, and thus may change from season to season. At a spectator level, all American ball-games have a greater following in Italy than in any other European country. This is largely thanks to Berlusconi's Italia Uno TV channel, which broadcasts them all, with commentaries in heavily accented Italian by former basketball coach Dan Peterson. (→ VII, 6:i) The spin-off of all this exposure is their rapid development as active sports, particularly American football, so rich in butch appeal.

Italy has few indigenous sports. *Bocce* is a form of bowls played mostly by the old in the country; *calcio fiorentino* is a medieval form of football allegedly played in Florence, now revived as neo-folklore. (→ II, 4)

(i) Motor racing and cycling
As early as the 1920s, the proverbial Italian love for reckless speed ensured massive popularity for racing, with motor racing for rich aristocrats and cycling for everyone else. The Mille Miglia and Sicily's Targa Florio fast became classic international motor races,

as the Giro d'Italia ranked second only to the Tour de France on competitive cyclists' race cards. Racing drivers like Tadzio Nuvolari and Argentine-born Emiliano Fangio, and *ciclisti* like Gino Bartoli and Fausto Coppi, enjoyed an unusual degree of hero status. The news of Bartoli''s victory in the 1948 Tour de France was of such importance that historians consider it prevented the imminent armed uprising by Communist workers.

Cycling is an extremely popular active sport, especially in the flat regions of the Po valley, the roads of which are crowded at weekends with enthusiastic punters on their Bianchi or Campagnolo sports bicycles, all blissfully unaware that their standard attire has become high fashion in the bars and clubs of northern metropoli. *Il ciclismo* is so much part of the national fabric that some of its terms – more than those of any other sport – have entered into common parlance: *la maglia rosa* or *la maglia nera* – the pink jersey for the gold cup, the black jersey for the wooden spoon.

Although Italy has had – with the possible exception of Michele Alboreto – no motor racing champion of distinction in recent years, its continued importance in the field is guaranteed by the existence of a construction company like Ferrari, even in spite of a noticeable lack of Grand Prix victories in recent seasons and the death of its charismatic founder, *commendatore* Enzo Ferrari.

(ii) Football: *il campionato più bello del mondo*

Although its football is officially *in crisi* through declining crowds, Italy continues to be the ultimate paradise for football fans. Brazil could certainly compete in terms of supporter enthusiasm, but no other country offers such a total degree of public and media obsession.

Three national daily sports papers, numerous magazines, but above all tireless TV coverage remind even the most recalcitrant Italian football-haters of its existence. RAI's Sunday TV programming is dominated by *il calcio* – whatever the programme, each time a first division goal is scored an electronic scorecard scuds across the bottom of the screen to tell you about it. On the local private channels, there are constant soccer chat-shows, rebroadcasts of the local team's match, and highlights of all the others, even foreign games.

Ever since winning the World Cup in Madrid in 1982 (→ III, 6:iii), Italians have been obsessed by how exciting their brand of *calcio* is. Not just the disgruntled Ian Rush after a season with Juventus, but many foreign observers as well, insist that it is slow, overly rough

Going to football matches

● The fans: although there has been an alarming increase in violence both inside and outside the stadiums in recent seasons, *i tifosi* – the fans – are certainly far less violent than UK fans. They may make as much noise, but they are better natured. For one thing, they are sober – Italians don't need alcohol to get excited – so you are unlikely to come across the squalor of mass drunkenness, or flying bottles. As yet, the cages that adorn Italian courtrooms have not reached the stadiums. Italian football's British origins are still evident from less worrying things: in homage to football's homeland, fans' home-made banners often display the and far too defensive. There is, however, a unique and undeniable excitement about Italian football matches. This undoubtedly has something to do with the high expectations raised by the self-proclaimed *campionato più bello del mondo* – the world's hottest league championship – and the enormous sums paid for foreign players. Some may call it hype, but the effect of international players like Napoli's Diego Maradona and AC Milan's Ruud Gullitt, as well as a host of assorted Europeans, South Americans and now East Europeans (Russians are currently flavour of the season), makes Italian football into a remarkable experience.

Colour coding in Italian football

Teams are usually known by their team colours: the national team is called *gli azzurri* on account of their royal blue shirts.
Juventus: black/white striped livery (nicknamed *i bianconeri*), symbol, a zebra; stadium – Municipale, Turin.
Torino: dark red, white trim (*i biancorossi*), a bull; Municipale, Turin.*
Sampdoria: light blue with circle (*i blucerchati*) Ferraris, Genoa.
Inter: blue/black stripes (*i neroazzurri*); San Siro, Milan.
Milan: red/black stripes (*i rossoneri*), a dragon; San Siro, Milan.
Fiorentina: purple (*i viola*), a *fleur de lis*; Communale, Florence.
Roma: dark red, yellow trim (*i giallorossi*), a wolf cub; Olimpico, Rome.
Napoli: light blue, white trim (*i biancocelesti*), a donkey; San Paolo, Naples.
*As of the 1989 season, ignominiously relegated to Serie B.

The Italian football league is divided into series that resemble marketing research groups: Serie A, B, C1, C2. As of the 1988 season, Serie A has gone up from sixteen to eighteen teams, but continues to be as dominated by the North as is industrial development. The three large cities that form the northern industrial triangle have two teams each: Turin has Juventus and Torino; Milan has Inter and Milan (known abroad as Internazionale and AC Milan), Genoa has Sampdoria and Genova: all but the last are in Serie A. Rome is the other city to have two teams – Roma, and the less fortunate Lazio (traditionally supported by neo-Fascists and country folk). Florence

pattern of the Union Jack, but in their team's colours. Football slogans, both as street graffiti or *striscioni* – immense banners hung inside the stadiums – often read English-sounding things, like '*Boys Inter*' or '*Eagles Lazio*', as well as a slightly more sinister copy-cat vein ('*Gli hooligans*', '*English Violence*'); '*Boys*' (*ragazzi* would really make more sense), '*Ultràs*', '*Fedayn*' (sic) refer to the semi-organized supporters' gangs, complete with drummers, fireworks (illegal, but still used) and battle cries (Roma's '*alé-oo-oo, alé-oo-oo*' is particularly memorable).

● Getting tickets: how far in advance you need to get them obviously depends on the importance of the match. Expect the World Cup matches to have well-organized computerized sales; however, for regular league matches, the best place is the stadium itself, or the team HQ well before the game. Otherwise, expect to pay vastly over the odds from touts – *bagarini* – irrespective of whether you get *un biglietto numerato*, *non numerato* or *in tribuna* – standing room only, seated or in the Press section.

● The season: late August to early June.

Reading a sports paper

Being seen about town with a copy of *La Gazzetta dello Sport* or *Corriere dello Sport* seems to confer one with a certain Euro-street cred., though it undoubtedly helps if you can actually read it. The bare essentials are as follows:
L'allenamento – training.
L'arbitro – the referee.
Il calciatore, giocatore – the play er.
Calcio d'angolo – corner kick.
Calcio di punizione – free kick.
Calcio di rigore – penalty.

Il centroavanti – centre forward.
La classifica – the league table.
Il difensore – defence player.
Dribblare – to dribble.
Un fallo – a foul.
Giocare – to play – *in casa/fuori casa* – at home/away.
Pareggio – a draw.
La partita – the match.
Il portiere – the goalkeeper.
La schedina – the pools coupon.
Una sconfitta – a defeat.
Lo scudetto – the championship shield.
Segnare un gol – to score a goal.
La squadra – the team.
I tifosi – the fans.
Vincita – a win.
zero a zero – a draw.

(Fiorentina) and Naples (Napoli) have one team each. The South is very poorly represented: Palermo no longer has a Serie A team at all.

(iii) The 1990 World Cup

Italy knew about getting the 1990 World Cup games by 1984, and had indeed done everything possible to be awarded them. The COL (Comitato Organizzativo Locale) – local organizing committee – was formed under the excellent leadership of Luca di Montezemolo, who masterminded the Ferrari racing team for several seasons in the 1970s, as well as the (from the Italian point of view) highly successful Italian entry – *Azzurra* – into the 1983 America's Cup. (→ VII, 6:i) Surrounding himself with some of the most competent figures from Italian business management, seconded from their respective firms for the duration of the preparations for the games, he also managed to wrangle an important deal from FIFA (Fédération Internationale du Football Associations), allowing him to supplement the traditional all-powerful eight 'official sponsors' (multinationals like Coca-Cola, Philips, JVC, Fuji etc.) with another eight all-Italian firms designated 'official suppliers'. The purpose for this was not so much economic as logistical. Knowing that it would be difficult in a country like Italy to rely on strictly governmental resources for organization, he involved these eight companies, mostly *parastatali* – partly state-owned (→ VI, 1:iv) – to ensure smooth running operations. They included RAI, Alitalia, FS (Ferrovie dello Stato), BNL (Banca Nazionale del Lavoro) as well as the ubiquitous Fiat (Gianni Agnelli is, after all, Montezemolo's uncle). Another reason was that if Italy should be knocked out at an early stage of the games, these eight firms would still keep *il tricolore* flying by way of efficient organizational support.

The government itself pledged vast sums of money, mindful that such a prestigious event, due to be watched by the largest TV audience of all time (beating the finals of the Mexico 1986 games), would offer an excellent occasion for national PR. Unfortunately, the political parties have not shared this stirring patriotic vision: in the race to renovate – or in some cases (Turin, Bari) to build from scratch – the twelve stadiums necessary for the games, opposition parties, or internal *correnti* (→ IV, 2:i) hostile to the local *giunte*, have spent most of the time squabbling, with the express intention of putting a spanner in the works. Not until the last minute did it seem that Turin would get its stadium; Milan's planned stretch of underground to the San Siro stadium had to be scrapped as a result of *ostruzionismo*; most of the ambitious projects for improving Rome's rather limited public facilities (enlarged ring roads, parking, new bus routes) had to be abandoned. Due to a chain of industrial accidents, the causes of which are not yet clear, renovation work at the Palermo stadium had to be interrupted.

5. Education

(i) Schools

As in most other Western countries, the crisis in the Italian education system – decline in teaching standards, discipline problems, reduced funding – is a cause for much parental concern. By and large, Italian schools compare favourably to those abroad, despite some fairly dire areas. Like those in France, Italian schools tend to be intellectually more demanding, but less orientated towards practical skills than those in English-speaking countries. Italy is the only country in the world where philosophy is taught as a main syllabus subject, and one of the remaining few where Latin and ancient Greek are mandatory even for students majoring in science. Foreign languages are now being taught from primary level, with more and more Italian school-leavers being reasonably fluent in English or French (although private English-language schools tend to supplement the State school diet for the extra-motivated).

The legal school requirement is still only 8 years, with many pupils from poorer families leaving to find work at 14 but a change in the law is expected soon to bring Italy into line with other EC countries. Although free State schooling was introduced in the mid-19th century, it didn't become completely obligatory until 1962, when there was an overnight five-fold increase in student numbers, and a three-fold one in numbers of schools. Old habits die hard in some places: streetwise Naples has a 7.5% regular truancy problem.

Although teaching methods and overall educational objectives have changed immeasurably since the pre-1968 days (antiquated academic attitudes had much to do with student discontent), Italian teacher-training levels are far below those acceptable elsewhere. *La scuola magistrale* does exist for trainee teachers, but it is still possible for a class to be presented with an untrained graduate teaching a subject about which he or she knows nothing. *Nozionismo* – learning by rote – was officially abolished several years ago, but most schools still opt for the parrot technique to guarantee good exam results.

All through the education system, exams are oral, with students facing an *interrogazione* – oral exam – rather than a written paper. This system works both for in-class tests and for end-of-year exams, at university as well as at school. School exams are marked out of ten and the end of the summer sees the student being either *promosso* – 'promoted' (to the next year up) – *rimandato a settembre* – made to try again in September – or *bocciato* – failed. The hapless *bocciati* are then obliged to resit the whole year with the incoming batch. After being *bocciato* several years running, it is possible to find oneself in a class with other pupils radically younger than oneself. While quite a few students fail their school year, when it comes to *la maturità* – high-school graduation – the percentage of failures is ridiculously small, and is getting smaller each year. This is generally admitted to be more a question of teacher indulgence than of student rigour; in some schools the pass rate reaches 99.5%, as in Communist country elections. It does occasionally reflect academic prowess, however. One school class in the Tuscan town of Lucca produced five (out of sixteen) pupils who all scored 100% – sixty out of sixty – in their *maturità*.

What we did on our holidays

	Sat. a.m.	school-days	sum-mer	Easter	Xmas	other
West Germany:	varies	240	6 wks	2–3 wks		3 wks
UK/England/Wales Scotland	free	190	6 wks 33 days	2 wks	2 wks	3 wks
Italy	school	200	8-10 wks	1 wk	2 wks	none
Holland	free	190	7 wks	10 days	2 wks	4 wks

(Editori Riuniti Riviste), 1988

Something of this excellent school record may be due to ever smaller classes, like the one in Lucca; the rapidly shrinking school age population has lopped almost a million off the total numbers for the last five years, with numbers dropping by 4.5% in 1987–8 alone, while staff numbers have remained unchanged. It is estimated that the teacher/pupil ratio is now 1:10, though this does not prevent overcrowding and double-shift classes in some areas. (→ also I, 2) Regular school hours are 8/8.30 a.m. to 1.30/2 p.m, meaning that most children have lunch at home.

Poor labour relations, uncertainty over teaching policy and execrable ministerial management make *la pubblica istruzione* – State education – a political hot potato. As with every other government-controlled field, there is always talk of *la riforma*: major reforms seem to be tabled every few years, and then vanish; be enacted, and then repealed. Educational spending increased by 10% in 1987–8 to reach 35,000 billion lire, including huge pay increases for the disgruntled teaching unions, accustomed to being at the bottom of the pay claim heap.

The school system

- **Numbers: in the school year 1983–4, there were 10.5 million students at all levels: 4 million at elementary school; 2.8 million at *la scuola media*; 2.5 million at *la scuola superiore*; and 1 million at university.**
- **3–5 years: nursery school – *asilo nido* – now offering surprisingly good service in most areas.**
- **6–11: *la scuola elementare*; most pupils, of both sexes, wear a *grembiulle* – a Victorian-looking smock – over their clothes.**
- **11–14: *la scuola media*; obligatory; there is one in every *comune* with over 3000 inhabitants.**
- **At this point, secondary education – *la scuola secondaria superiore* – is voluntary, and splits into separate disciplines, lasting a further five years, until nineteen and the *maturità* high-school certificate, made up out of all subjects studied.**
- **There are four different kinds of *liceo* – *lycée* (humanities-based high school): *liceo classico*, *liceo scientifico*, *liceo artistico*, *liceo linguistico*.**
- **There are also four kinds of technical school – *istituto tecnico*: *istituto commerciale*, *istituto industriale*, *istituto agrario*, *istituto nautico*.**
- **As well as teacher-training school – *istituto magistrale* – there is *la scuola parificata* – a privately (usually Church) run school, whose syllabus has been brought into line with the State schools.**
- **Private education, which in Italy almost exclusively means Church-run (particularly by the Jesuits), has been enjoying a return to favour since State school chaos made tight-lipped religious instruction seem an attractive alternative. These are usually day-schools; *il collegio* – boarding school – is a bleak, correctional or charity, institute, quite distinct from *il college*, as Italians call British public schools and American residential high schools and military academies.**

(ii) Universities

There is much controversy as to which is the oldest university in the world, but it is certainly in Italy. Salerno, Bologna, Padua and Pavia all date back to the early Middle Ages. Despite the growth of Paris, Oxford and Cambridge over the following centuries,

Italy retained overall supremacy among European universities throughout the Renaissance period. Since then, they haven't fared too well, and are at present far from distinguished. It is not that they lack eminent scholars among their staff, but that their lack of organization and proper funding makes them an unenviable choice for the foreign exchange student.

Italian universities are not residential, and do not even organize accommodation for students from elsewhere. In such a family-orientated society, it makes more sense to live at home and frequent one's local university. Students from areas outside commuting distance have considerable difficulty in finding affordable accommodation, as there is no grant or loan system. (→ also I, 1:i) On the other hand, university education is free, and has the added advantage that anyone can attend. Since the reform of 1977, when the *numero chiuso* – ceiling number – principle was abolished, anyone who has the *maturità* can attend. As a result, enrolments have gone up enormously, making Italy the country with the highest proportion of university students in the world. They currently number over a million, almost 2% of the population.

The system is free and easy in other respects. Although courses are designed to last a regular four or five years, there is no obligation to complete one's course in that time: as a result, most *studenti* get a job, or get involved in other projects, while they are technically studying for exams. Many students are so in name alone, but numbers are so high that getting into a lecture hall for popular subjects such as *economia e commercio* – economics and business studies – or *legge* – law – is like trying to break the record number of people in a phonebox during rag week. Science subjects are studied without the benefit of practical experiments. Most students simply read the set books at home and go in for the exam when it comes up. Over the period of a standard graduate course, one takes some thirty oral exams, as well as writing the final thesis. If you fail an exam, you merely repeat it when it is posted next, which may be in a matter of months. In this way, one gradually builds up the necessary total.

As with school exams, the marking system for university ones seems very generous: individual exams are marked out of thirty, while your degree is out of 110, with the vast majority of students invariably arriving within a few points of the full score. There seem to be more students around with 110 *con lode* (*cum laude*) – a triple 1st – than any other mark. Whatever your *voto* – final marks – as a graduate, you get to be called Dottore or Dottoressa rather than plain old Signore or Signora. (→ I, 6:ACCESS)

6. Intellectuals and critics

Whether they have received higher education or not,
Italians always have enormous respect for the realm
of ideas. (→IV, 3:ii) The tradition in English-language
countries is rather the reverse, where brainy people
are considered more or less suspect. Italians, like the
French, are proud to be considered *un intellettuale*, and
will describe themselves or others as such in a positive
way. If we tend to see ideas as useful only if they lead
to positive concrete results, the Italian attitude is to
appreciate them as an end in themselves: to discuss
philosophy, politics or the arts in purely abstract terms
is as pleasurable to them as it seems 'pseud' to the
average English speaker.

There are certain areas of human endeavour where
the Italians' obsessive attempt to intellectualize everything comes unstuck – mostly in the field of popular
culture, like rock – but in general, cultural life is
enriched by their approach. The success of Italian
cinema, architecture and design owe everything to their
inbuilt intellectual mystique.

However, the corollary to this essentially positive
reflex resides in the role of the critic. Italy's Catholic
tradition has familiarized people with the role of
the priest as mediator to the extent that they are
instinctively willing to delegate intellectual authority
as easily as spiritual. The recipients for their trust are
the critics: the whole cultural system is dominated by
their presence. In Italy, they are nearly all so closely
connected to the political parties that their real power
is immense – even Mafia-like: they are entrusted with
the job of enrolling potentially fashionable or influential
arts figures to their, and hence their party's, standard.
It is not an official position; it is 'influence'. This is
exercised largely through the Press, but also in their
involvement in administering, in an official or unofficial
capacity, party funds for some cultural event. Thus the
critic has the power to make a movement live or die, or
to make or break an artist's career, in a way that would
be unthinkable in most countries.

What makes the Italian critical system so unattractive
is that often it is so obviously dominated by people who
have a limited grasp of their field, and who owe their
position of dominance to political patronage, not to an
original, incisive mind.

Even where politics has less direct impact, the arrogant, unprofessional tendency of trying to talk over
everyone else's heads is still all too present. Many
Italians will reason that, since intellectual ideas are

evanescent and impalpable by definition, it is fine for critics or intellectuals to waffle, and be incomprehensible: if the reader or listener doesn't understand, that must be their fault. But careful study of the speeches at a writer's presentation, or the notes in an exhibition catalogue, or the speaker presenting classical music on RAI Radio 3, and you realize that it is so much *pippe mentali* – intellectual masturbation.

7. Mental health

Until 1976, according to authoritative, eye witness, reports, Italian mental hospitals were among the most cruel and backward in the Western world. Then, almost at a stroke, there was a radical motion put through Parliament with the support of the Communist Party which effectively abolished the concept of mental illness. Such are the grand gestures of Italian public life. Influenced by the R. D. Laing/David Cooper school of thought, that mental illness is merely a condition imposed by the system, Trieste psychiatrist Franco Basaglia finally managed to have his dream come true, and see Parliament close down all mental hospitals with *Legge 180* – Law 180.

The patients were simply put out on the streets, or sent back to their often extremely reluctant families; only violent patients were not invited to leave: they were merely transferred to regular hospitals and put under heavier sedation than usual.

Legge 180 is being hotly debated to this day: although it was undoubtedly an interesting social experiment, it obviously doesn't work that well. Italians are essentially very tolerant of the deranged (though, interestingly, not of minor departures from social convention – *bella figura*, again), and have little objection to often almost naked old men or women in rags standing raging and frothing at statues, parked cars or passers-by. Gratifying as this novel form of 'reinsertion into the community' may be, however, there remains a sizeable proportion of patients who can't cope. Psychiatrist Umberto Dinelli recently complained, 'This law has cost us ten years of suicides, and yet there are still 40,000 poor creatures who are still dying of hunger and cold in hospitals and clinics.'

8. Science and research

The Italian scientific mind has in the past made significant contributions towards international progress, although research is currently so poorly funded that Italy is being left behind. An easy way to offend someone's national pride is to belittle the importance of their inventors: Italians are no exception. Although no one disputes the importance of Galileo for gravity, Alessandro Volta for the volt, or Guglielmo Marconi for the radio, many non-Italians tend to question Italian assertions that it was Meucci, not Bell, who really invented the phone, and that Enrico Fermi and Ettore Majorana were those really responsible for the atom bomb.

Scientific research is largely co-ordinated by the CNR (Consiglio Nazionale per la Ricerca) – the National Research Council – set up in 1923 and directly answerable to the Prime Minister's office. It oversees some 291 smaller bodies and employs a total of 4000 technicians and 2000 researchers, operating on a meagre 1000 billion lire annual budget. ENEA (Ente Nazionale per le Energie Alternative) – the National Commission for Nuclear and Alternative Energy Sources – works on an annual 1.2 billion lire budget, and employs 4500 people, with the universities fielding a smaller workforce and budget.

These three wings of the public sector, when added to the private sector, reach a total of about 100,000 people between researchers, technicians and helpers: the lowest ratio among the major industrialized powers.

Researchers per 10,000 industry workers

USA	42
Japan	31
West Germany	28
UK	22
Holland	15
France	14
Italy	6

(Ufficio del Presidenza del Consiglio, 1986)

European Patents Office

Italy's low level of scientific research (shown as % of GDP) is reflected in its bottom of the table position in lodging industrial patents:

West Germany	2.7%

USA	**2.8%**
Japan	**2.8%**
France	**2.3%**
UK	**2.2%**
Italy	**1.4%**

(World Economic Forum, 1988)

Nobel prize winners

● Considering the largely political reasons that characterize Russia's relatively poor showing, Italy comes the lowest (up to 1987) of all major European countries, and lower than many smaller ones too.

	Chemistry	Physics	Medicine	Literature	Peace	Economics
USA	31	50	58	8	16	14
GB	21	20	19	7	7	4
West Germany	24	17	12	7	4	0
France	6	8	7	11	9	0
Sweden	4	4	7	6	5	2
Holland	2	6	3	0	1	1
USSR	1	7	2	4	1	1
Austria	1	3	6	0	2	1
Switzerland	4	1	5	2	3	0
Italy	1	3	3	5	1	0

● **Italian Nobel prize winners**
● **Physics**

1909	Guglielmo Marconi
1938	Enrico Fermi
1959	Emilio Segré
1984	Carlo Rubbia

● **Medicine and Physiology**

1906	Camillo Golgi
1957	Daniele Bovet
1975	Renato Dulbecco
1986	Rita Levi Montalcini

● **Economics**

1985	Franco Modigliani

9. Religion

Ten favourite saints

• For all its aggressively secular exterior, Italian society is still deeply permeated by the saints. The language is full of it: to know *la vita*, *morte e miracoli* – life, death and miracles – of someone means knowing all about them. But then, Italy has always been called *il paese dei santi, navigatori ed eroi* – the land of saints, naval explorers and heroes; its output for saints has been unrivalled by other countries. Many of its most important names date back to Roman times, from the apocryphal S Sebastiano (saint's day 20 January) and S Lucia (13 December) to S Ambrogio/Ambrose (7 December) and S Benedetto/ Benedict (11 July). Since medieval times, Italy has produced a steady stream of sanctity, and has provided a haven for other countries' saints. In the full flow of the Counter-Reformation, three important Spanish saints were canonized in 1622 alone: Teresa d'Avila (15 October) – the subject of one of Bernini's greatest erotic-religious masterpieces; St Ignazio Loyola – founder of the Jesuit movement (31 July) – and his follower S Francesco Saverio/Xavier (3 December).

The secular or superstitious importance of saints continues undiminished, S Rosalia (4 September) of Palermo and S Gennaro (19 September) of Naples continuing to be the subject of pilgrimage and superstitious adoration.

• Canonization dates and saints days

1228: S Francesco di Assisi (4 October).

1232: S Antonio di Padova (13 June).

1234: S Domenico (8 August).

(i) Attitudes to Catholicism

Despite being the world centre of Catholicism, Italy is also deeply hostile to religion. This apparent paradox appears quite normal to Italians, and has a perfectly simple explanation. Western countries with a predominantly Protestant culture gradually, from the Reformation onwards, removed Church influence from secular society; the United States from its outset constitutionally forbade it. In this way, alongside committed believers, there is a huge mass of people who are largely indifferent to religion, or who possibly classify themselves as agnostic. In Catholic countries, where the Church has never accepted anything less than the starring role, the choice is much more black and white. Hence Italians class themselves as *cattolico* or *laico* – 'lay', secular – or *ateo* – atheist: in the traditional battling Catholic world view of the Church Militant versus Evil Godlessness, there can be no neutral position.

Interestingly, Italian non-Catholics have always accepted the Church's rather Manichaean ground rules. This is because Catholicism as a cultural reflex (as opposed to its religious practice) has totally permeated the soul of every Italian. Significantly, the key-word is *cattolico*, not *cristiano*; an Italian may reject the latter label, but never the former. Even the most priest-hating atheist will admit to being an *ateo cattolico*. It is no accident that the Catholic Democrazia Cristiana's main political rival is the equally ideological Partito Comunista, which admits to having a rigid, ecclesiastical structure to match the Vatican's – so much so, that it is not even classed as a *partito laico*. (→ IV, 3:iii) Although the PCI, unlike the Vatican, has now shed nearly all its ideological militancy, the struggle between the two has been one of the most characteristic features of Italian post-war life. While Pius XII threatened excommunication for all Communist voters, and the PCI publicly declared the Church *anathema*, they were constantly doing behind-the-scenes deals, because they instinctively understood each other so well. The Giovanni Guareschi 'Don Camillo and the Devil' books underscore this basic irony.

The Vatican doesn't just have it in for Communism: prior to the 1929 Lateran Pact between the Church and the State, the former went so far as to refuse Communion to the Royal family, members of the government or even anyone who took part in the public life of the reunited country. Even voting in elections of the blasphemous *laico* State go the papal thumbs down. The Lateran Pact was redefined in 1985 after negotiations between PM Craxi and Cardinal Casaroli, with the Church receiving a number of guarantees in exchange for backing down over certain former claims: Catholicism ceased to be the official *religione di stato*, for example.

Certain areas of the country are traditionally in one of the two camps. Most of the South is still pretty much in the grip of the Church/Christian Democrat partnership, as is the Veneto, the region around Venice. Other areas, like the overwhelmingly left-wing regions Emilia- Romagna, Umbria and Tuscany, are famous for their anticlericalism. Several different *regioni* vie as to who first invented *strangolapreti* – 'priest-stranglers' – a kind of home-made *pasta*. The fact that *atei* in Italy are almost more obsessed by religion than are *cattolici* is evident from their gratuitous use of blasphemy, for which the Tuscans are particularly notorious: everything is *porca Madonna* – the Madonna's a pig – *Dio cane* – God's a dog! – or even *Ostia!* – Communion wafer!

There are visual signs of the almost peaceful coexistence of the two camps in most public buildings, which still have a crucifix up in every room; when the *laico* lobby attempted to have this changed, the Corte Costituzionale ruled that they were permissible since 'Italy was still overwhelmingly *cattolica* in character'. Quite so. But what of the constant cartoons of a crucified Christ in the mainstream daily *La Repubblica*, or the fact that *laico* heads of State or government never go near a place of worship? Both extremes would be unimaginable in any English-speaking country.

For decades there has been a gradual erosion of numbers in the Italian priesthood: in the six-year period between 1982 and 1988 alone there was a 10% drop, from 39,620 to 36,575, with 8.3% of *preti* over 75 years old. Signs since 1988 show that there may now be a reversal of this trend.

In Rome, the city where St Peter decided to build the church for Christ, there are more religious buildings than in any other place in Christendom: a total of 610 consecrated edifices, of which 315 are parish churches (165 run by diocesan priests, 150 run by religious orders). 5000 priests and 20,000 nuns live there. Most of the 11 million tourists who came to Rome in 1987 visited at least one of its places of worship, many of them as devoted pilgrims. Little did they realize how irreligious the actual inhabitants of the Eternal City

1255: S Chiara di Assisi (11 August).

1323: S Tomaso Aquino/Thomas Aquinas (28 January).

1461: S Caterina di Siena (29 April).

1500: S Francesca Romana (9 March).

1610: S Carlo Borromeo (4 November).

1622: S Filippo Neri (26 May).

1934: S Giovanni Bosco (31 January).

1950: S Maria Goretti (6 July).

are, and how concerned the Church authorities feel about it.

In fact since ancient Roman times, the local populace has traditionally been cynical and worldly, rather than pious. Romans are proud of their city's unique religious heritage, on condition that they need take as little part in it all as possible. In 1985, some 20% of the 25,000 babies born in Rome were not baptized; for *la cresima* – confirmation – that figure doubles; only *la prima comunione* – first communion – still remains popular, but only because it has been transformed into a totally non-religious, sickly sweet photo-opportunity for pre-teens in white dresses. Almost 4000 out of 14,000 weddings were register office only. (→ I, 3:iii) The attendance at Mass is about level with the national average, at 25%, but that figure also includes the professionally pious. In the northern industrial cities, the figure slides to 14%.

Going to Mass has declined sharply over the last twenty years. Pope Paul VI was already horrified when the survey he commissioned from the Jesuits' Università Gregoriana in 1968 showed that only 42% of Romans communicated regularly, while 20% did so only occasionally and 38% never at all. Now the statistics are 25%, 25% and 50% respectively.

'*Quando muore il Papa, se ne fanno un altro, no?*' – 'When the Pope dies, they just elect another one, don't they?' – is a time-honoured Roman expression for saying, 'Life goes on – big deal.' Their relationship with *oltre il tevere* – the other side of the Tiber – is bitter-sweet. While many Romans curse the Pope every Wednesday, when it is almost impossible to drive in the city (the weekly papal audience attracts hundreds of coach-loads of pilgrims), or snarl at nuns for driving too slowly at any other time, they are conveniently forgetting that the Vatican provides direct and indirect employment for thousands. Quite apart from the enormous Vatican staff (who are allowed to enjoy the duty-free shopping and petrol the Vatican's extra-territorial status permits: (→ III, 2:ii), there are countless more self-employed ones, who hawk 3D blinking Christ postcards and plaster statuettes of the *Pietà* in the streets.

For all the dynamism of Pope John Paul II and the stridency of his statements, the Catholic Church has lost so much moral authority over the last two decades that the old *cattolico* versus *laico* dispute seems positively out-dated. The Pope has evidently reached this opinion too. Addressing a group of Rome parish priests in 1988, he said, 'We have now to face the problem of secularism – no longer a militant, hostile atheism, but something close to indifference, whereby baptized Christians live as though God just didn't exist.'

Since Pope Paul's *Concilio Vaticano II* in the 1960s, which had the intention of stripping a great deal of pomp from the Church and 'bringing it nearer the people', a significant percentage of Italian priests have dedicated themselves to hands-on, no-questions-asked, social work. The almost total collapse of the State-provided services has made their contribution essential in combating problems like drug abuse, homelessness and *emarginazione* – social alienation. Part of the Church has recently turned its enormous facilities to aiding the plight of the million-strong immigrant community in a way even the trade unions have often been unable to do. (→ V, 1:vii)

(ii) The Vatican organization and the Italian Church

'How many divisions has the Pope got?' Stalin is supposed to have asked, but few non-Italians, irrespective of their religious convictions, have any idea just what a political institution the Vatican is. This naïvety is commonest in believing that the election of popes, with its characteristic *fumata bianca o nera* – white or black smoke – is anything different from the tough lobbying that goes on in any of the world's parliaments – or boardrooms. The fact that Italians have been running this universal organization for centuries almost single-handed inevitably means the Catholic Church is as faction-ridden as any other body in the country.

After the death of the extremely conservative Pius XII ('Papa Pacelli' – popes in Italy are generally known by their surname) in 1958, the Vatican underwent two decades of rapid liberalization at the hands of the charismatic Pope John XXIII ('Papa Roncalli'), followed by the Hamlet-like Pope Paul VI ('Papa Montini'). Most of their work was consolidated into the reforms proclaimed by the Second Vatican Council, which Paul VI called in 1965. During this period, important positions in the Italian Church and its lay organizations were filled by their liberal-minded followers: men of the moral and intellectual stature of Alberto Monticone, president of the 0.5 million-strong lay group Azione Cattolica: Domenico Rosati, leader of the Catholic workers' association Associazioni Cristiane dei Lavoratori Italiani (ACLI); Padre Bartolomeo Sorge, editor of the influential Jesuit paper *Civiltà Cattolica*; and the cosmopolitan Don Virgilio Levi, deputy editor of the Vatican daily *L'Osservatore Romano*.

Within a few years of the election of 'Papa Wojtyla' in 1978, all these, and many other 'Montiniani', fell from grace, in the same way that a new government routinely replaces senior diplomats and civil servants to suit its new political complexion. Wojtyla has naturally surrounded himself with men more congenial to his outlook on life: his right-hand man is the German Cardinal Joseph Ratzinger, whose pessimistic philosophy concerning the future of mankind makes one recall Pope John XXIII's famous dictum: 'Beware the harbingers of doom.' *L'Osservatore Romano* is now less incisive, but more *Wojtyliano*. The Jesuits (Sorge should never have printed phrases like 'neo-medievalist revival' and 'listening before speaking'), Azione Cattolica and ACLI are now all more or less formally in disgrace; while the Pope has recently bestowed full recognition on the sinister, slightly kinky Opus Dei movement, which previous pontiffs kept at arm's length.

However, the most important grace-and-favour innovation Papa Wojtyla has made was that towards the Comunione e Liberazione (CL) movement. Founded over thirty years ago by prelate Don Giussani, it was run until 1987 by the ambitious Roberto Formigoni, now in his 40s, and Rocco Buttiglione. Under them, the movement has become an interesting fusion between two quite disparate elements: a Counter-Reformation fundamentalist doctrine, dressed with the trappings of the *generazione post-sessantotto*. Its members are familiarly known as *ciellini* – taken from the Italian pronunciation of its initials, CL – and make a point of looking very 'street': trainers worn with blue jeans and Lacostes, a few acoustic guitars and annual week-long mass conference-happenings in shameless imitation of the 1970s Communist-style ones. (→ IV, 3:ii) CL also indulge in some vintage Jimmy Swaggart-style razzmatazz – majorettes and mass releasing of doves, along with the *de rigueur* nod towards hi-tech. – walls of video screens, and digital dot display boards. CL also has a political wing, il Movimento Popolare, who see themselves as the shock troops of a morally-reformed DC (an idea the latter are understandably reluctant to accept). Formigoni, who is now deputy speaker in the European Parliament for the DC (he was elected a second time in 1989, with a massive *voto preferenziale*), enjoys needling the leadership by flaunting his political contacts with Claudio Martelli of the PSI. The hyperorganized CL also has its mouthpieces: *Il Sabato* is a well-written but extremely vituperative weekly; *30 Giorni*, as the name implies, is a monthly, specializing in hysterical denunciations of 'rival' Catholic sects.

The resemblance between the current pontiff's own style and that of Formigoni is remarkable: they both combine dynamism with asceticism, and are both as adept in manipulating the media technology of the late 20th century as they are devoted to the religious philosophy of the late 19th century. As Pope Wojtyla himself put it in 1988, in a public declaration to the head *ciellino*, 'Your way of relating to the problems of mankind is close to mine: in fact, it's the same.' Relations have since cooled somewhat: in 1989, the Pope rebuffed CL on various occasions.

Cardinal virtues: major figures in the Italian Church
- **Cardinal Giacomo Ballestrero (Turin), President of CEI: noted for smooth handling of 'Turin Shroud' controversy. Supportive of Fiat workers in his archdiocese. Retired in 1989.**
- **Cardinal Carlo Maria Martini (Milan): hot tip for being *papabile* – i.e. he stands a good chance of being elevated as John Paul's successor: makes trenchant denouncements of capitalist excesses. Charismatic: left-wing guerrillas laid down their arms to him. ($\rightarrow$ V, 2:v)**
- **Cardinal Salvatore Pappalardo (Palermo): equally *papabile*; has been conducting, at times almost single-handed, a crusade against the Mafia in Sicily.**
- **Cardinal Ugo Poletti (Rome): technically, the Pope's deputy in the Rome diocese. Convenient location for one so close to so many DC politicians. Very conservative; close to CL.**
- **Cardinal Giacomo Siri (Genoa): remained until his death in 1989, even after retirement, a towering influence on the Church; last survivor of pre-John XXIII liberalism; unreconstructed 19th-century views, though much respected. Was invited to solve troublesome local labour disputes.**

If the Pope's impact on the Church's lay organizations has been traumatic, no fewer shock-waves have been sent through its ecclesiastical structures. Wojtyla has shaken up the universal Catholic Church enormously, although many of his cabinet members were inherited from the previous administration – notably Cardinal Agostino Casaroli, the brilliant diplomat who has been the Vatican's Foreign Minister for over two decades.

However, it is mostly the Italian Church that concerns us here. Only since the Second Vatican Council has Italy actually had its own internal structure, la Conferenza Episcopale Italiano (CEI) – the Conference of Bishops. Having been set up under the Roncalli–Montini pontificates, it retained a strong liberal identity when Wojtyla acceded to the triple tiara. Needless to say, that is changing fast, as all retiring cardinal bishops (seventy-five is statutory) are replaced by ecclesiastical conservatives. The still liberal majority of the CEI are quite candid in expressing their concern at the Pope's hostility towards them during their annual conference at Loreto.

The Pope has even revived the defunct College of Cardinals as an advisory body, in order to pass over the younger, less conservative, College of Bishops.

His influence on the lives of ordinary Italian priests has been less dramatic, since Vatican insider politics generally affects them much less. One order Wojtyla did give was to tell the Rome diocese priests to stop wearing a suit and dog-collar – the outfit the Italians call '*il clergyman*' – as being too Protestant-looking, ordering them instead to wear *la sottana* – their cassock – or, better still, *l'abito talare* – the bespoke version thereof, now seen only in Rome and Sicily – at all times.

Ordinary Italian Catholics are mostly quite proud of the Pope's newly won superstar status, and full of admiration for his high international profile, although many have serious misgivings about both the high expenditure and the low spirituality count of his obsessive overseas ministering. The people who complain most about that are those working in the Vatican bureaucracy, bitter at the pontiff's reluctance to bother himself with the banalities of day-to-day administration when he could be working the crowds in some ecstatic South American football stadium.

Over-achieving ... In his first ten years as Pope, Wojtyla created some 252 new saints and 400 *beati* – blesseds, far more than his predecessors.

Italians are generally less impressed than people abroad at the Pope's abilities as a great communicator, largely because they are more used to having him around – also, because over half the Italian Press is anti-clerical: the papal tour coverage by the veteran *Vaticanista* – church affairs correspondent – Ugo D'Assia on the *laico* RAI 2 channel is an amusing exercise in witty, cynical disenchantment. The most accurate assessment of the Italian Catholics' level of faith was recently made by another foreigner, the French ex-student leader Dany Cohn-Bendit, who recently told a shocked interviewer on the Catholic RAI 1 channel that the nature of Catholic support has changed in Italy over the last couple of decades. No longer is there an attitude of blind, if reluctant, obedience to all papal decrees;

Italian Catholics have adopted a consumer attitude to their religion, buying the bits they like (papal glamour, concern for the Third World, the sense of history) and putting what they don't like back on the shelf. Even among practising Catholics, observance of strictures like birth control and divorce are minimal, ever since the epic civil liberties battles of the mid-1970s, from which official Catholic morality has never recovered. (→ I, 3:iii and I, 3:vii)

(iii) Non-Catholic religions/sects

Italy's 40,000-strong Jewish community is the oldest in Europe, and is one of the most successfully integrated, never having experienced consistent anti-Semitism. Having lived in Rome in the *ghetto* continuously for over 2000 years, *gli ebrei* are considered, even by their fellow inhabitants, as the 'real' Romans.

The *valdesi* – Waldensians – are Lutheran Baptists who constitute Italy's only indigenous Protestant community, and are mainly based in small communities in the mountainous areas of Piedmont. Despite their diminutive size, the socially progressive *valdesi* have no compunction about taking their Catholic rivals to task, and, in view of his pronounced fundamentalism, are particularly polemical with the present Pope.

The second largest religious community in Italy is now the Jehovah's Witnesses, who expanded from 120 members in 1946 to 140,000 in 1988. Their proselytizing activities are no less tireless than in other countries, though they are often aided by phalanxes of eager young Americans. It is amusing to see the Italians' reaction as they are confronted in the street by some gigantic, fresh-faced Mid-Westerner in a white polyester shirt, grey sta-prest slacks and a name badge, pressing his fleshy hand into theirs as he begins his spiel: '*Ciao, io mi chiamo Chuck...*'

Oriental religions and sects are also very well represented throughout Italy, with a particularly high presence of the Sanyassin Orange People – *gli arancioni* – who run several vast *communes* in Sicily. Also well represented are Buddhists, particularly among the better educated in northern cities.

10. Death and superstition

Taboos and superstitions

Italians are still very superstitious, a left-over from their recent peasant past. Talking of death or accident is always awkward, even when it is being discussed at a preventative level. (→ 3:ii, above) Italians usually make a special gesture to ward off misfortune: *le corna* – the index and little fingers raised in the shape of horns. This is considered a very rude insult if aimed at someone else, but if aimed downwards, touching a hard object like the table (men often touch their balls, even in front of women), it is thought to be an effective guarantee against imminent disaster. However primitive this may seem, Italians of all walks of life *fanno le corna*. A recent Italian PM, Giovanni Goria, was photographed doing it in the Senate, to ward off bad luck, while former President Giovanni Leone, a Neapolitan, caused uproar by making *le corna* at groups of protesting students in the 1960s.

Southerners, especially Neapolitans, are very superstitious, and invariably have bright red plastic horns, which they hang in the car or at home as protection. Any propitious gesture to ward off *il malocchio* – the evil eye – is called *scaramanzia*, and is taken very seriously. Some classic superstitious beliefs are the opposite of ours: Italians touch metal, not wood, for luck; a black cat brings *la sfortuna* – bad luck – not *la fortuna* – good.

Never wish anyone *buona fortuna* – good luck; the correct expression is *in bocca al lupo* – in the wolf's mouth.

Never give someone a handkerchief, a knife or anything sharp or dangerous; such a gift

One area in which Italy has remained firmly rooted in its past is in that of death. The sanitized distancing process common to most other Western countries has not yet seriously affected the Italian way of dying, where the presence of the corpse remains the main event.

There is still, in most families, usually a *veglia* – wake, – with a *camera ardente* – a room at home prepared as an impromptu chapel of rest. This tradition is extremely strong in the South, where elaborate, peasant-derived rituals are also enacted. The Neapolitans go to considerable lengths on these occasions: there was a recent scam, uncovered and suppressed by the police, whereby doctors and hospital orderlies were being bribed several thousand pounds a head to resuscitate recently deceased patients by putting respiratory apparatus on them, pinning a note on the covers reading, 'This patient is discharging himself against doctor's advice' and then rushing them home, where the bereaved could mourn them at leisure, avoiding the dull anonymity of the morgue. Naturally, all this would take place after some very tough bargaining between the interested parties. (→ V, 1: Naples, a special case)

Funerals tend to be big affairs, with even quite distant relations, friends and neighbours making a big effort to turn up for the day. Needless to say, huge expensive floral tributes – *corone* – are the order of the day. In the South, and in rural communities elsewhere, Victorian-looking black-edged funeral notices are still pasted in the streets to inform the public of the proceedings, while many older people, and particularly Southerners, still adhere to the tradition of wearing a black mourning button for a statutory period.

Better off, or 'older', families tend to have a family burial chapel, which has a tiny altar and votive lamp, with the coffins installed in layers underneath, but for most people burial now means something rather more modernistic: after a year in a temporary, generic, grave, there is normally a ceremony in which the coffin is placed in a slot in a skyscraper-like construction, like a drawer in an enormous filing cabinet. Cremation is still very unusual, until recently being forbidden by the Church. The *comune* of Turin, worried by the lack of burial space, is now offering free *cremazioni*.

If the person was important, or died in particularly moving or heroic circumstances, like a Carabinieri gunned down by terrorists, *la bara* – the coffin – is likely to be applauded as it enters or exits from the church.

While any flower may be used, chrysanthemums are considered to be the flower for funerals and graves, and are used exclusively for this purpose. To give them to anyone for any other reason would seem appallingly macabre, and hence a terrific gaffe, to Italians.

Among Catholics, Tutti i Santi – All Saints' Day (1 November) – and the Day of the Dead – la Commemorazione dei Defunti or Tutti i Morti (2 November) – are the days when black-clad widows and relations all trundle off to the graveyard with their bunches of chrysanths.

Naples has a quite extraordinary relationship with its dead. Tutti i Morti sees festive picnics in graveyards, where the *defunti* are kept company: any clearly untended graves will have flowers laid on them by strangers, so that the inmates won't feel 'left out'. This imaginative interfacing with the *al di là* – the beyond – reaches extraordinary lengths: when il Napoli won the football league cup in 1986, jubilant fans adorned one large municipal cemetery with a banner for the benefit of the *defunti*, reading, 'You don't know what you've just missed!' – underneath which, the next day, someone added a second banner with the 'reply': 'Who says we missed it?'

Necrologi – newspaper obituary notices – are placed not just by the family, but by any mourners. Hence, the death of one single popular, distinguished person may warrant several columns of individual tributes from relations, colleagues and friends.

The way Italian TV deals with death is interesting: TV news cameras will show lingering close-ups of embalmed corpses in open-lidded coffins at funerals, just as they will lovingly zoom in on entrails or blood splattered in any kind of violent death. People don't want just to know about it; they expect to see it, in all its gory detail. This fits in with the Baroque tradition of funerary sculpture, which was clearly calculated to horrify, with its lurid portrayals of skeletons and corpses.

If the Italian attitude to death is explicit once it's happened, alluding to death as a hypothesis excites quite different emotions. To talk about one's own, or dear ones', death in a matter-of-fact way causes people to feel extremely ill at ease. Parents, for example, would not begin a sentence to their children, 'Well, when I'm gone . . .' or, 'One day, when I'm no longer around . . .' It just isn't mentioned.

is a serious error, suggesting you are willing the person's demise.

Never pour wine from a bottle with the palm of your hand upwards – this indicates treachery.

Sources

The research findings of the following organizations provided the basis for much of my observations and analysis:

AIED – Associazione Italiana per l'Educazione Demografica.

CENSIS – Centro Nazionale di Statistica Italiana.

CNR – Consiglio Nazionale per le Richerche.

DOXA

ISPES – Istituto di Studi Politici, Economici e Sociali.

ISTAT – Istituto Centrale di Statistica.

Vita Italiana, Documenti e Informazioni (Presidenza del Consiglio di Ministri) – bi-monthly reports.

For economic statistics and analysis, I also found very useful 'The Italian Economy', *The Economist*, 27 February 1988, a survey by Pam Woodall; and the 1988 and 1989 quarterly reports of the Economist Intelligence Unit.

Selected reading

(This list excludes books written in Italian; it would otherwise be much longer.)

●Visitors' access:

P.T.J. Glendening: *Cassell's Colloquial Italian* (Cassell, 1980) – extremely helpful and comprehensive book for those with some grasp of Italian; arranged in alphabetical entries, which can be read straight through or consulted.

Y.M. Menzies: *Living in Italy* (Robert Hale, 1987) – very thorough on practical topics like house-buying, though expresses somewhat dated views on life in Italy.

E.T. Roberts, ed.: *Rome Yellow Pages in English* (Fipiel, Milan, 1986) – found in English-language bookshops in Rome; aimed at those who can't or won't speak Italian; comprehensive details on dealing with bureaucracy.

Key to Milan, RDM Associati (Arcadia, Milan, 1986) – excellent all-round guide to living in Milan; lists everything you could possibly need to know.

Italy – Travellers' Handbook, ENIT – Italian State Tourist Office; ;annual; an invaluable free guide with details on transport, distance, ticket costs, cultural and other events, specialized holidays.

●Business access:

Guida Monaci – 3 vols; annual; detailed lists of all businesses in Italy; found in large post offices and public libraries.

Guida alle regioni – 3 vols; annual; lists all State organizations, private associations and their respective functionaries.

Who's Who in Italy – annual; similar to the above two, but in English.

L'annuario italiano (Mondadori annual) – thorough survey on the previous year's events in all sectors, with valuable profiles on key individuals and organizations.

●Chapter access: most of the books listed are limited to single subjects, but there are also quite a few whose contents span several chapter headings. They have been listed under the chapter heading where their contents are particularly relevant.

Chapter I

Luigi Barzini: *The Italians* (Hamish Hamilton, 1964)

Italy Today: Patterns of Life and Politics (Exeter University Press, 1985)

R. King: *Italy: Economic and Social Studies* (Harper & Row, 1987)

D. Sassoon: *Contemporary Italy: Politics, Economy and Society since 1945* (Longman, 1986)

D. Willey: *Italians* (BBC, 1986)

Chapter II

J. Haycraft: *Italian Labyrinth* (Penguin, 1985)

G. Procacci: *History of the Italian People* (Pelican, 1988)

I. de Wolfe: *The Italian Landscape* (Architectural Press, 1963)

Chapter III

M. Clark: *Modern Italy 1871-1982* (Longman, 1986)

D. Forgacs, ed.: *Rethinking Italian Fascism: Capitalism, Populism and Culture* (Lawrence and Wishart, 1986)

M. Grendel, ed.: *An Illustrated History of Italy* (Weidenfeld & Nicolson, 1966)

H. Hearder and D.P. Waley: *A Short History of Italy from Classical Times to the Present Day* (Cambridge University Press, 1963)

C. Hibbert: *Benito Mussolini: the Rise and Fall of Il Duce* (Longman, 1962)

D. Mack Smith: *Cavour* (Michigan University Press, 1985)
Italy: A Modern History 1860-1969 (Michigan University Press, 1969)
:*Mussolini's Roman Empire* (Penguin, 1977)
Chapter IV

J.C. Adams and P. Barile: *The Government of Republican Italy* (3rd ed: Houghton Mifflin, Boston, 1972)

J. LaPalombara *Democracy Italian Style* (Yale University Press, 1987)

P. Nichols: *Italia, Italia* (Macmillan, 1973)
Chapter V

P. Arlacchi: *Mafia Business: the Mafia Ethic and the Spirit of Capitalism* (Oxford University Press, 1986)

R. Blumenthal: *Last Days of the Sicilians* (Bloomsbury, 1988)

C. Duggan: *Fascism and the Mafia* (Yale University Press, 1989)

L. Gurwin: *The Calvi Affair: the Death of a Banker* (Macmillan, 1983)

N. Lewis: *The Honoured Society: the Sicilian Mafia Observed* (Eland, 1984)

C. Sterling: *The Mafia* (Hamish Hamilton, 1990)
Chapter VI

A. Friedman: *Gianni Agnelli and the Network of Italian Power* (Harrap, 1988)

F. Spotts and T. Wieser *Italy: a Difficult Democracy* (Cambridge University Press, 1986)
Chapter VII

R. Bergan and R. Karney: *Foreign Film Guide* (Bloomsbury, 1988)

A. Blunt: *Baroque and Rococo* (Thames & Hudson, 1982)

R. Buss: *Italian Films* (Batsford, 1989)

M. Caesar and P. Hainsworth: *Writers and Society in Contemporary Italy* (Berg, 1984)

J. Hale, ed.: *A Concise Encyclopaedia of the Italian Renaissance* (Thames & Hudson, 1981)

G.E. Kidder Smith: *Italy Builds* (Architectural Press, 1955)

J.H. Whitfield: *A Short History of Italian Literature* (Manchester University Press, 1980)

E.H. Wilkins: *A History of Italian Literature* (Harvard University Press, 1974)

D. Yarwood: *The Architecture of Italy* (Chatto & Windus, 1982)
Chapter VIII

P. Hebblethwaite: *In the Vatican* (Sidgwick & Jackson, 1986)

J. Julius Norwich: *The Italian World* (Thames & Hudson, 1983)

M. Walsh: *The Secret World of Opus Dei* (Grafton, 1989)

Index

(Figures in *italics* refer to ACCESS)

A note on the author

William Ward is a writer and broadcaster who has lived in Italy since 1979. He divides his time almost equally between devising radio and television programmes for RAI, and writing for a wide variety of English and American publications.